BAT MAN

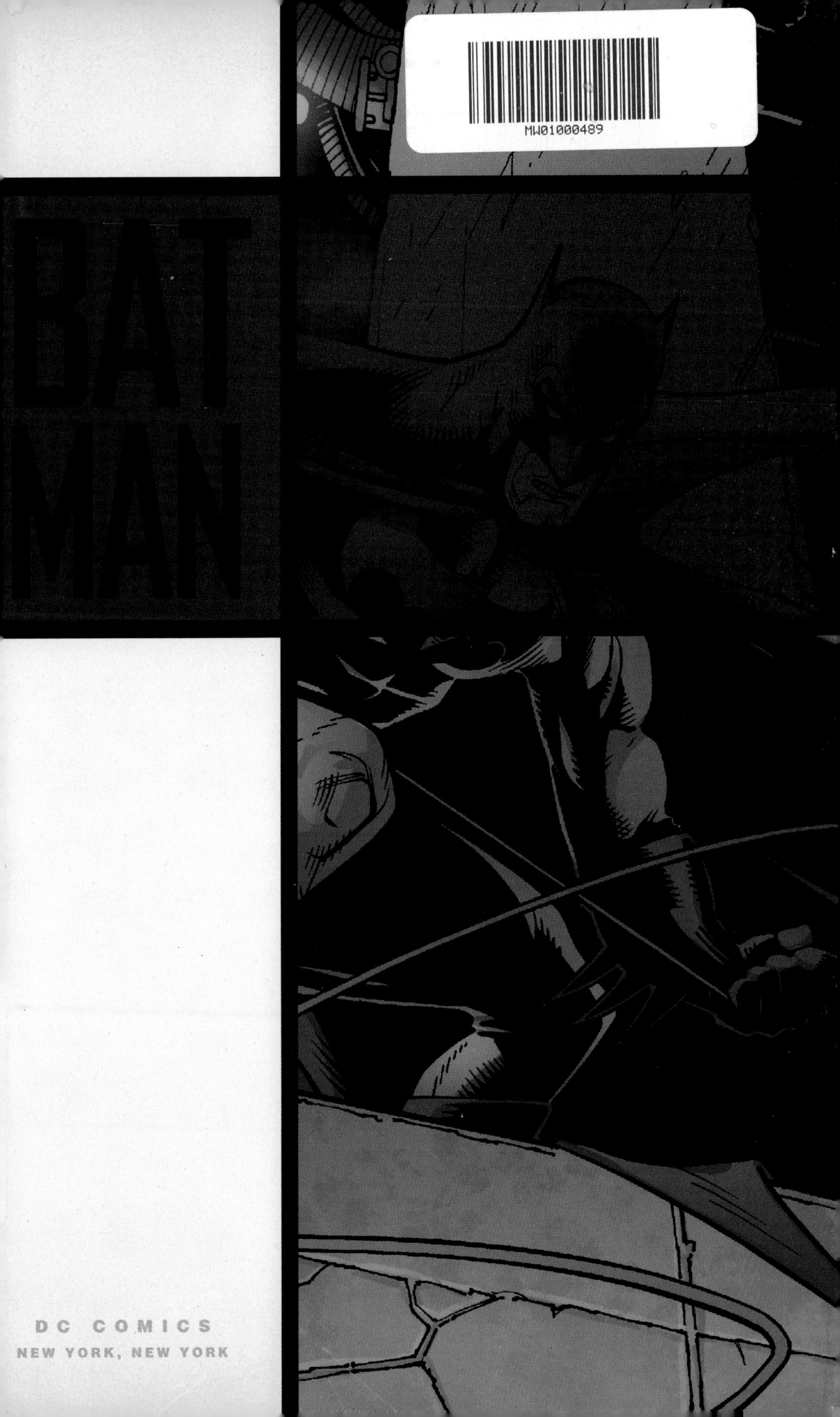

DC COMICS
NEW YORK, NEW YORK

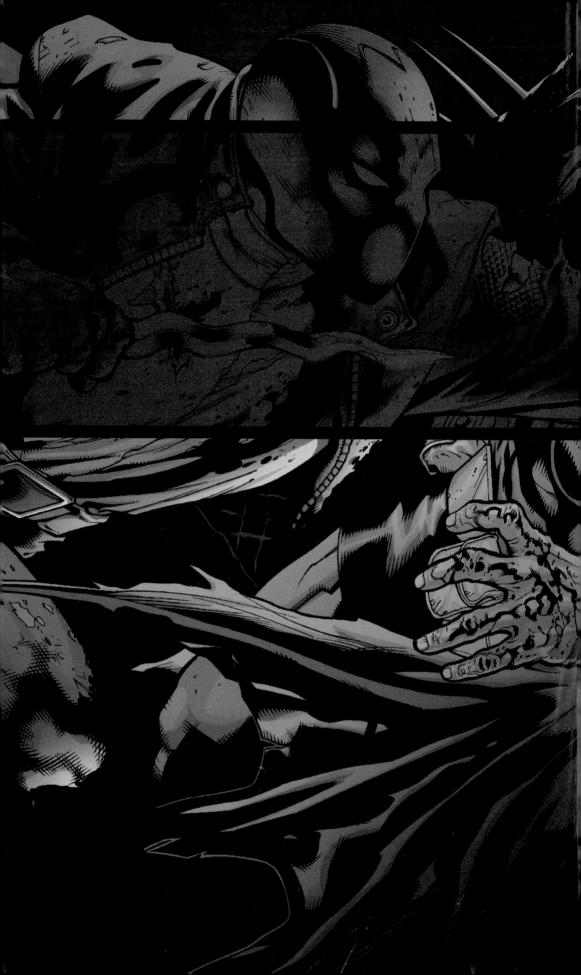

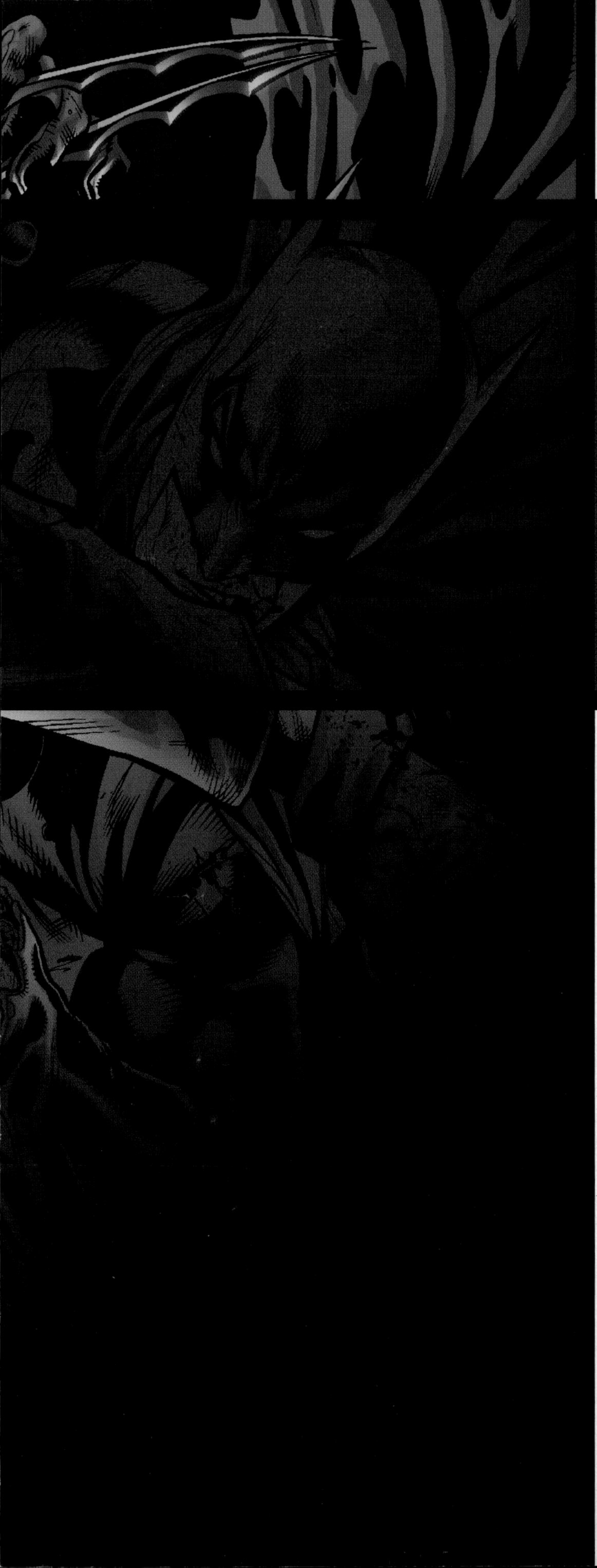

BATMAN

UNDER THE HOOD

JUDD WINICK
WRITER

DOUG MAHNKE
PAUL LEE
PENCILLERS

TOM NGUYEN
CAM SMITH
INKERS

ALEX SINCLAIR
COLORIST

PAT BROSSEAU
ROB LEIGH
PHIL BALSMAN
KEN LOPEZ
NICK J. NAPOLITANO
LETTERERS

MATT WAGNER
ORIGINAL COVERS

BATMAN CREATED BY
BOB KANE

DC COMICS

BATMAN: UNDER THE HOOD

PUBLISHED BY DC COMICS.
COVER AND COMPILATION COPYRIGHT © 2005
DC COMICS. ALL RIGHTS RESERVED.

ORIGINALLY PUBLISHED IN SINGLE MAGAZINE
FORM IN BATMAN #635-641.
COPYRIGHT © 2005 DC COMICS.
ALL RIGHTS RESERVED.
ALL CHARACTERS, THEIR DISTINCTIVE
LIKENESSES AND RELATED ELEMENTS
FEATURED IN THIS PUBLICATION ARE
TRADEMARKS OF DC COMICS.

THE STORIES, CHARACTERS AND
INCIDENTS FEATURED IN THIS
PUBLICATION ARE ENTIRELY FICTIONAL.

DC COMICS DOES NOT READ OR ACCEPT
UNSOLICITED SUBMISSIONS OF IDEAS,
STORIES OR ARTWORK.

DC COMICS,
1700 BROADWAY, NEW YORK, NY 10019
A WARNER BROS. ENTERTAINMENT COMPANY
PRINTED IN CANADA. FIRST PRINTING.
ISBN: 1-4012-0756-1

COVER ART BY MATT WAGNER

PUBLICATION DESIGN BY
AMIE BROCKWAY-METCALF.

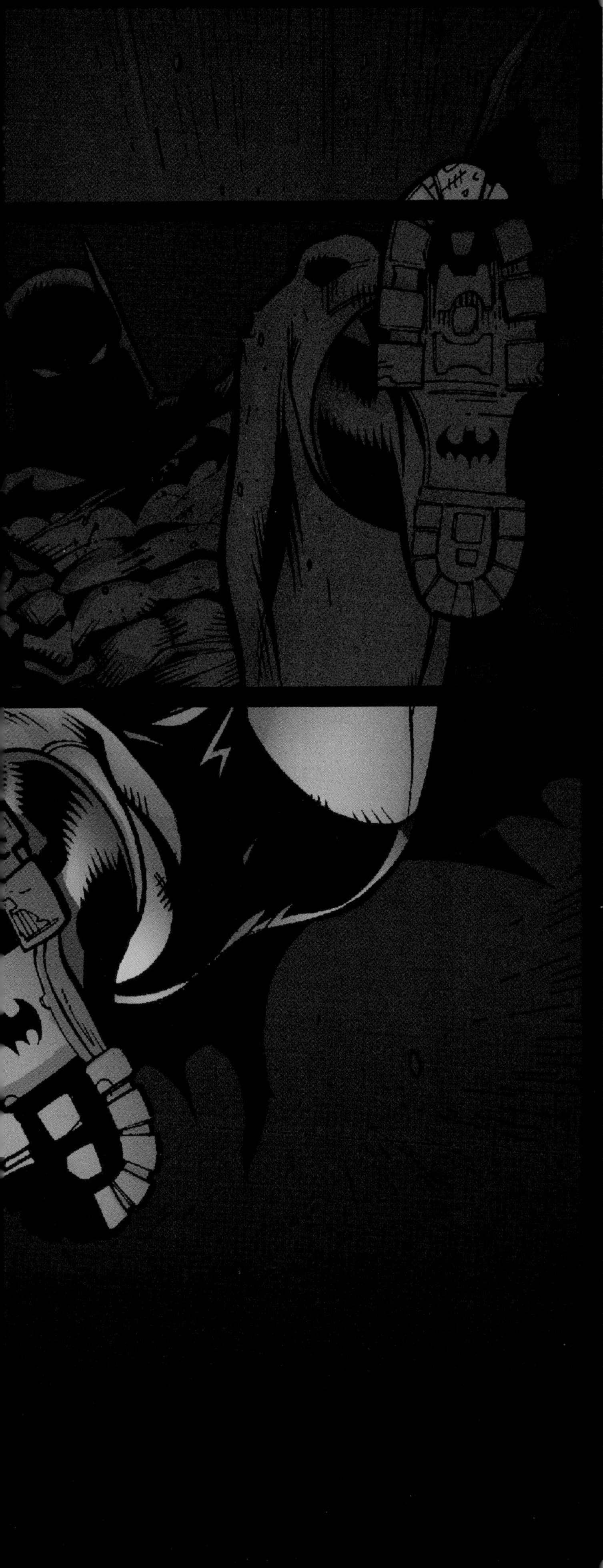

CAST OF CHARACTERS

B A T M A N

Dedicated to ridding the world of crime since the callous murder of his parents, billionaire Bruce Wayne dons the cape and cowl of the Dark Knight to battle evil from the shadows of Gotham City. Over the years, Batman has suffered the loss of two crime-fighting partners: Jason Todd, the second person to take on the mantle of Robin; and Stephanie Brown, formerly the Spoiler and for a brief period of time the fourth Robin, who died due to injuries inflicted by the Black Mask.

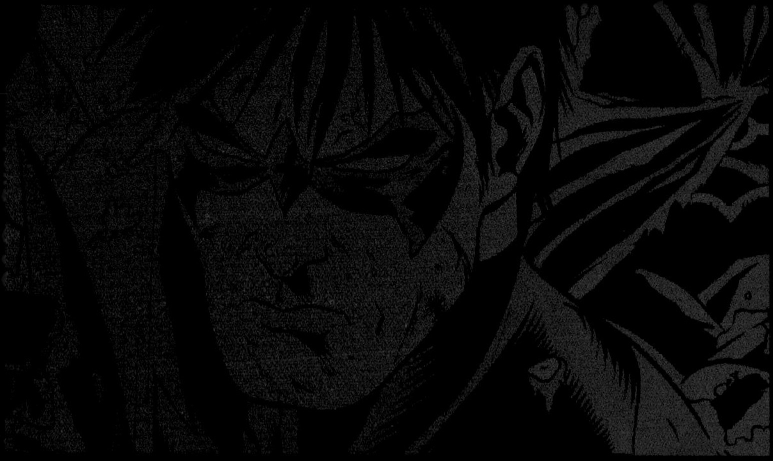

NIGHTWING

Dick Grayson's life changed forever when he witnessed his aerialist parents fall to their deaths, the victims of an extortion scheme. Knowing the pain of such a loss, the wealthy Bruce Wayne took in the youth, and in a short time Dick was being trained to work alongside Gotham City's famed crimefighter, Batman. Befitting his circus heritage, Dick chose a more colorful outfit than that of his new partner, and became Robin, the Boy Wonder. Batman and Robin proved to be a perfect crime-fighting team, but, as he grew to manhood, Dick began to separate himself from his mentor, unwilling to become a doppelgänger of the obsessed Bruce Wayne. Asserting his independence, he changed his persona from Robin to Nightwing.

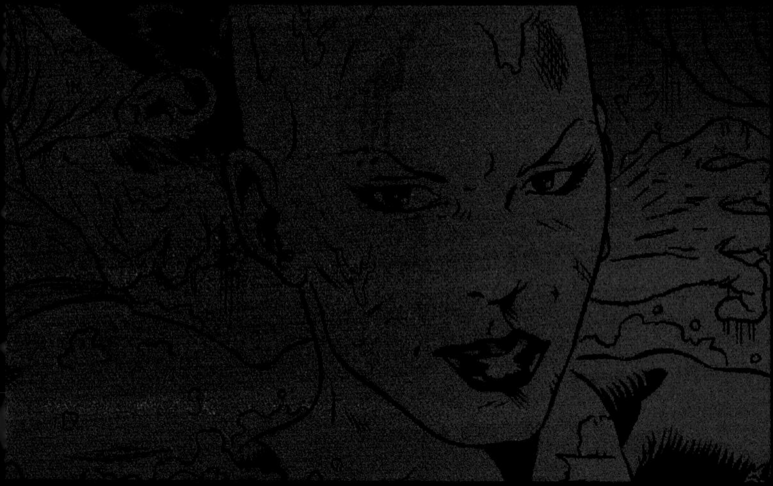

ONYX

Onyx was schooled in the Sanctuary, a monastery outside Star City. Pursued by an unknown agent who wanted to kill her, Onyx was admitted to the all-male Sanctuary by the Master, who trained her in martial arts and gave her a new identity. Upon the Master's death, Onyx sought out Green Arrow, another student of the Sanctuary, to protect the monastery from a takeover by one of the Master's more ambitious protégés, a man named Lars. Onyx stayed at the Sanctuary, guarding the key to the Master's mysterious Book of Ages. She has yet to discover the identity of the man, or woman, who pursued her to the doors of the Sanctuary.

BLACK MASK

Roman Sionis's face was horribly burned in a fire during a fight with the Batman. As the Black Mask, Roman has become one of the most feared and psychotic crime bosses in Gotham's underworld. His preferred form of execution is slow, methodical torture, usually focusing on the face. During Gotham's recent Gang War, Black Mask has managed to take control over all crime in the city. All criminals must pledge their allegiance to him, or die.

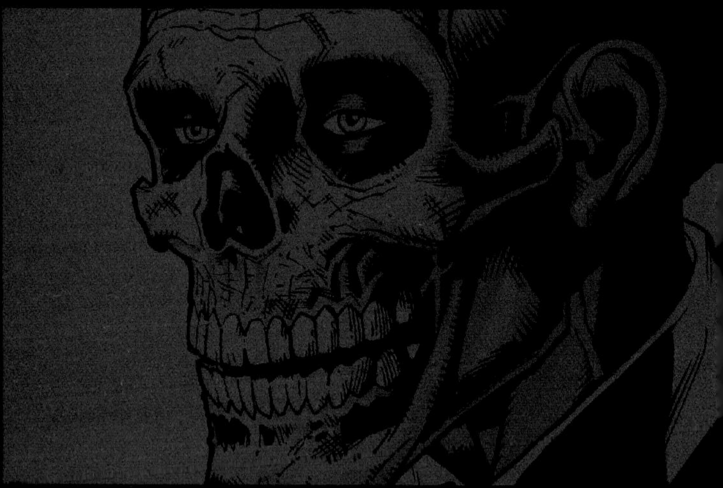

MR. FREEZE

In an effort to make himself a more formidable criminal in Gotham City, the man who would become Mr. Freeze experimented with a cold-generating gun that would help him with his crimes. But his lab work resulted in a dangerous accident that bathed his body in a super-coolant solution. As a result, he must now wear a refrigerated containment suit at all times in order to continue living. His fractured psyche has made him into one of Batman's most ruthless foes.

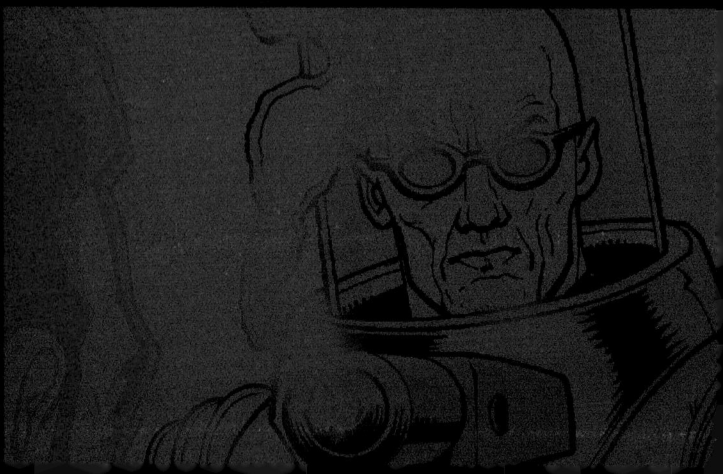

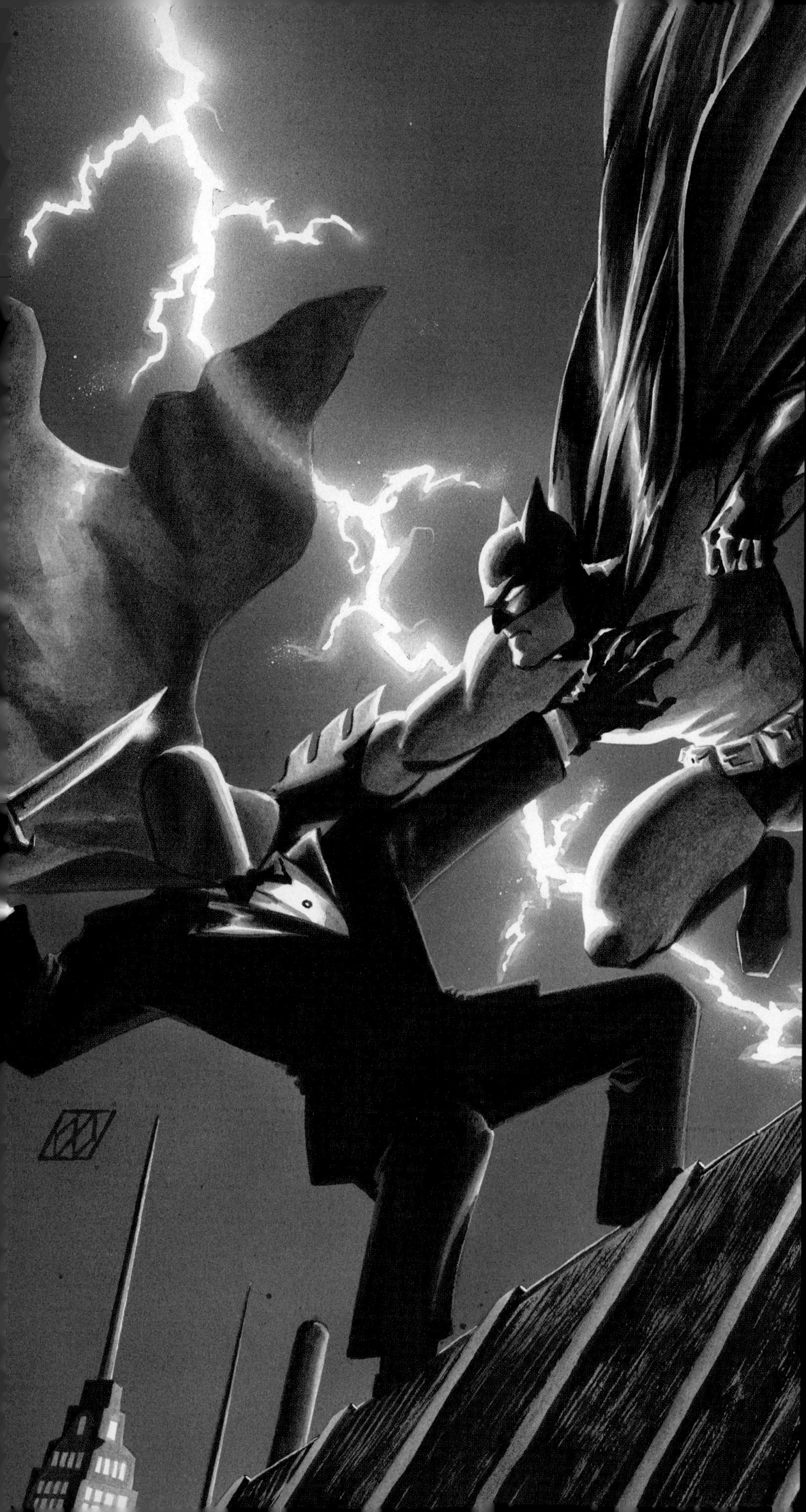

BATMAN #635 • ART BY MATT WAGNER

PART 1

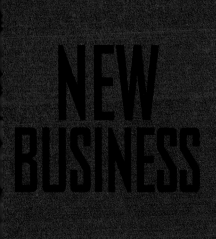

NEW BUSINESS

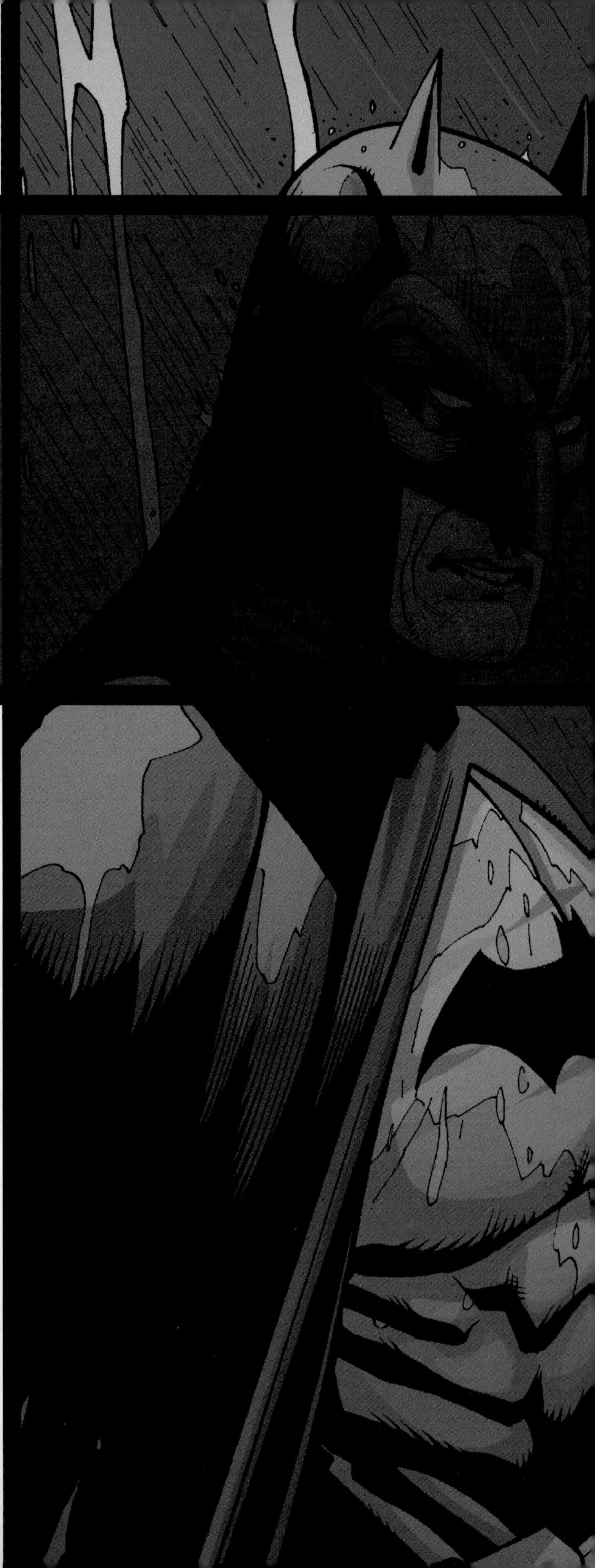

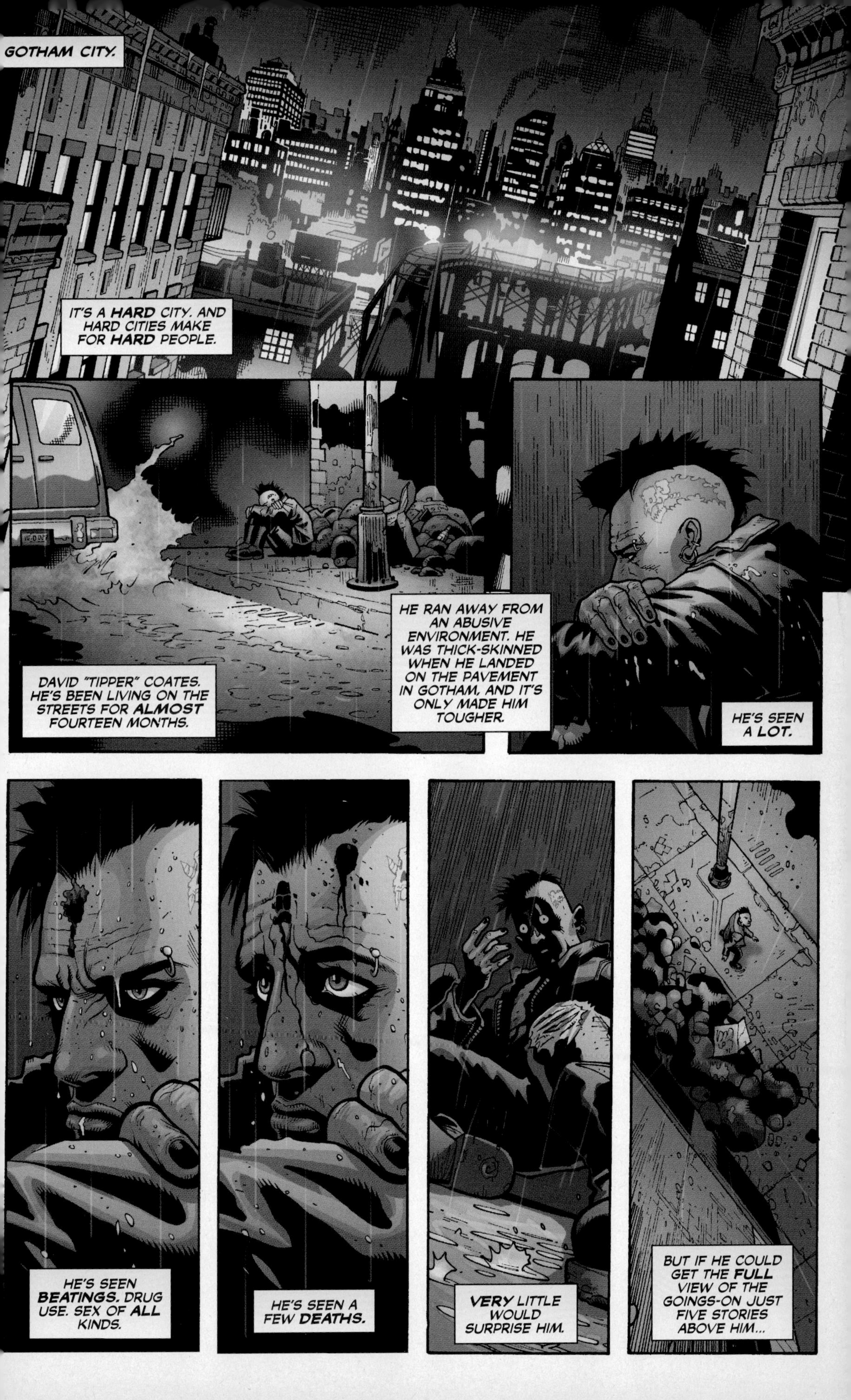
GOTHAM CITY.
IT'S A HARD CITY. AND HARD CITIES MAKE FOR HARD PEOPLE.
DAVID "TIPPER" COATES. HE'S BEEN LIVING ON THE STREETS FOR ALMOST FOURTEEN MONTHS.
HE RAN AWAY FROM AN ABUSIVE ENVIRONMENT. HE WAS THICK-SKINNED WHEN HE LANDED ON THE PAVEMENT IN GOTHAM, AND IT'S ONLY MADE HIM TOUGHER.
HE'S SEEN A LOT.
HE'S SEEN BEATINGS. DRUG USE. SEX OF ALL KINDS.
HE'S SEEN A FEW DEATHS.
VERY LITTLE WOULD SURPRISE HIM.
BUT IF HE COULD GET THE FULL VIEW OF THE GOINGS-ON JUST FIVE STORIES ABOVE HIM...

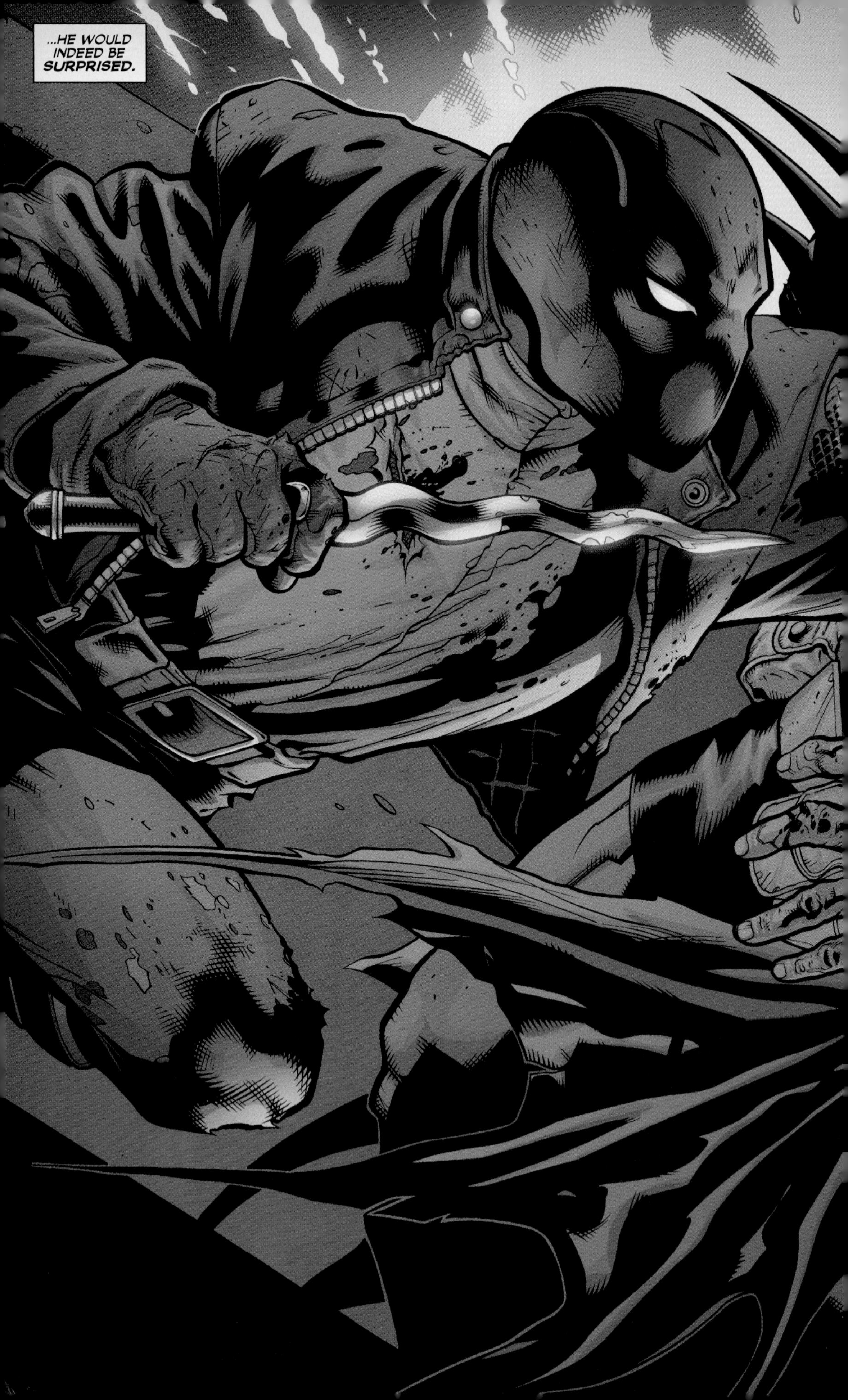
...HE WOULD INDEED BE SURPRISED.

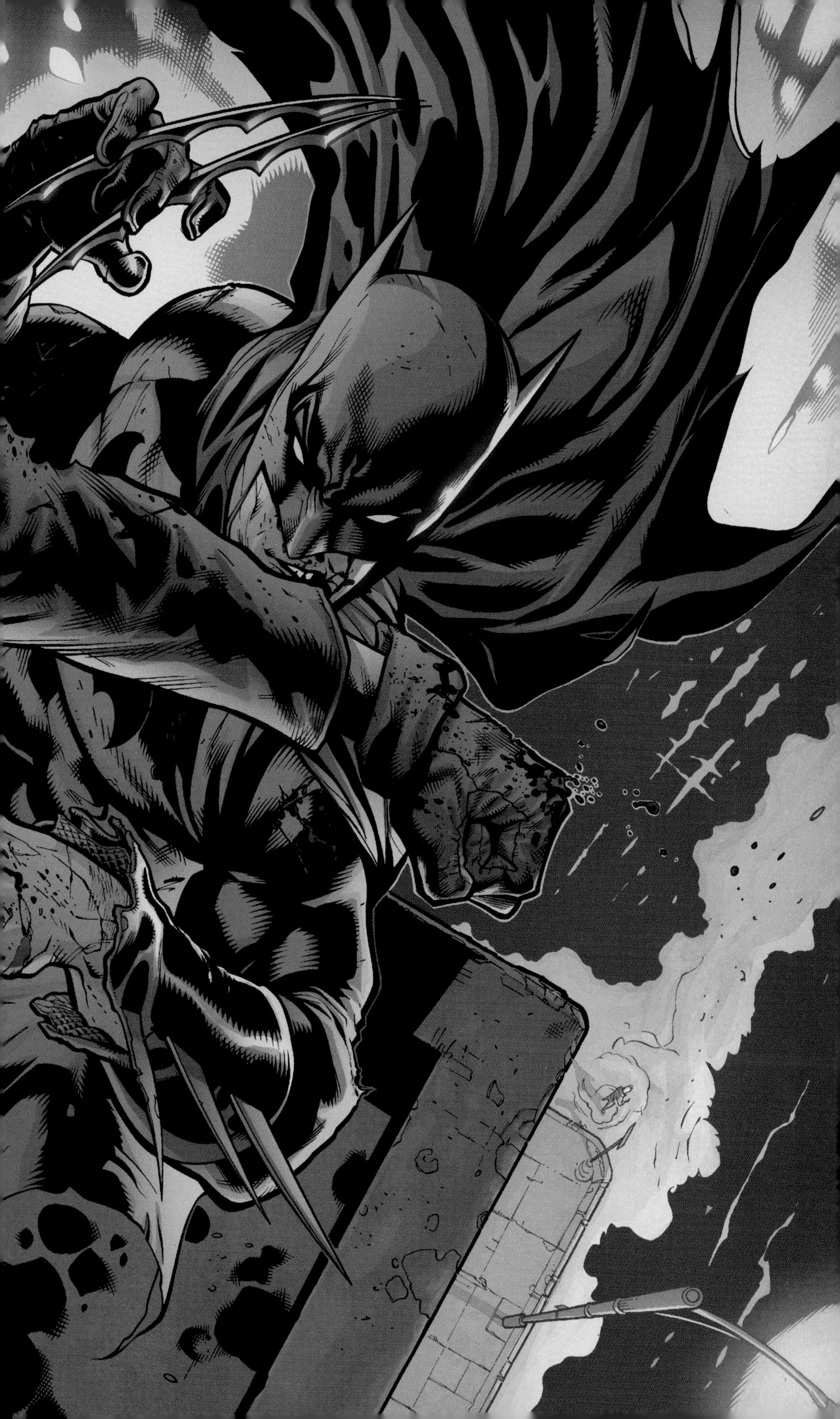

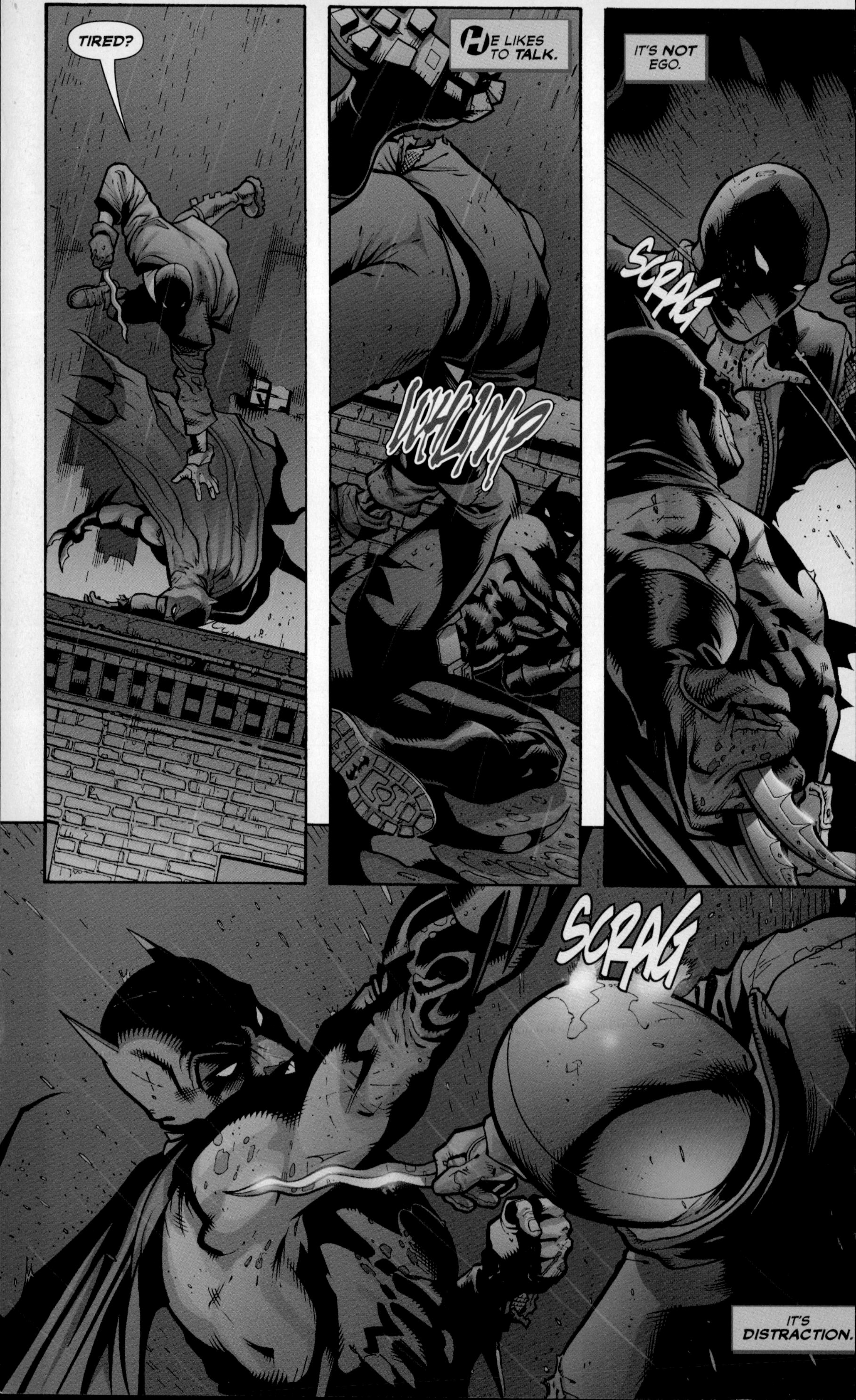

TIRED?
HE LIKES TO TALK.
WHUMP
IT'S NOT EGO.
SCRAG
SCRAG
IT'S DISTRACTION.

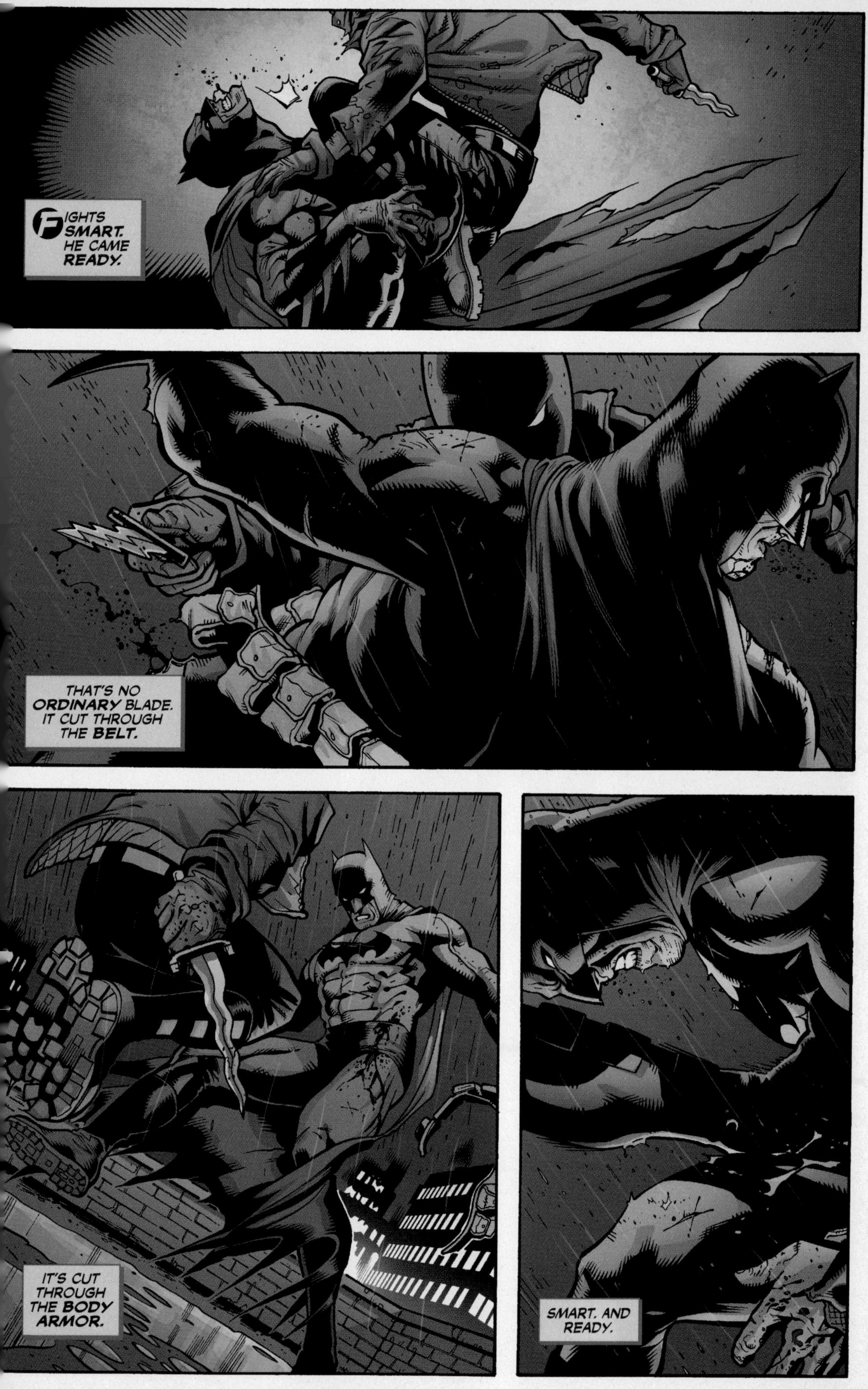
FIGHTS SMART. HE CAME READY.
THAT'S NO ORDINARY BLADE. IT CUT THROUGH THE BELT.
IT'S CUT THROUGH THE BODY ARMOR.
SMART. AND READY.

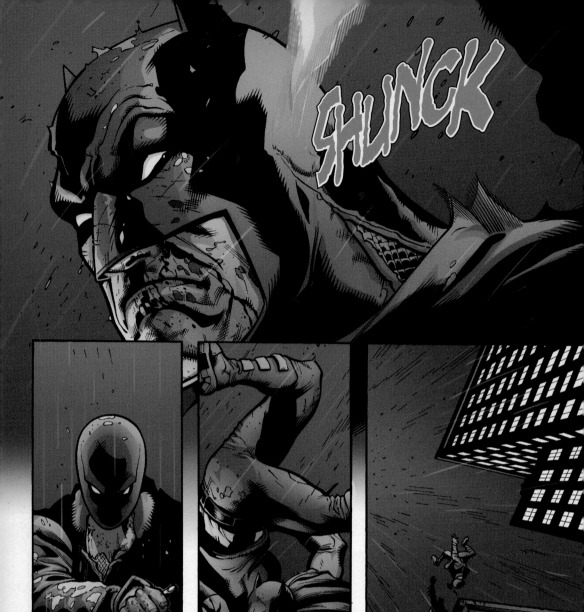

SHUNCK

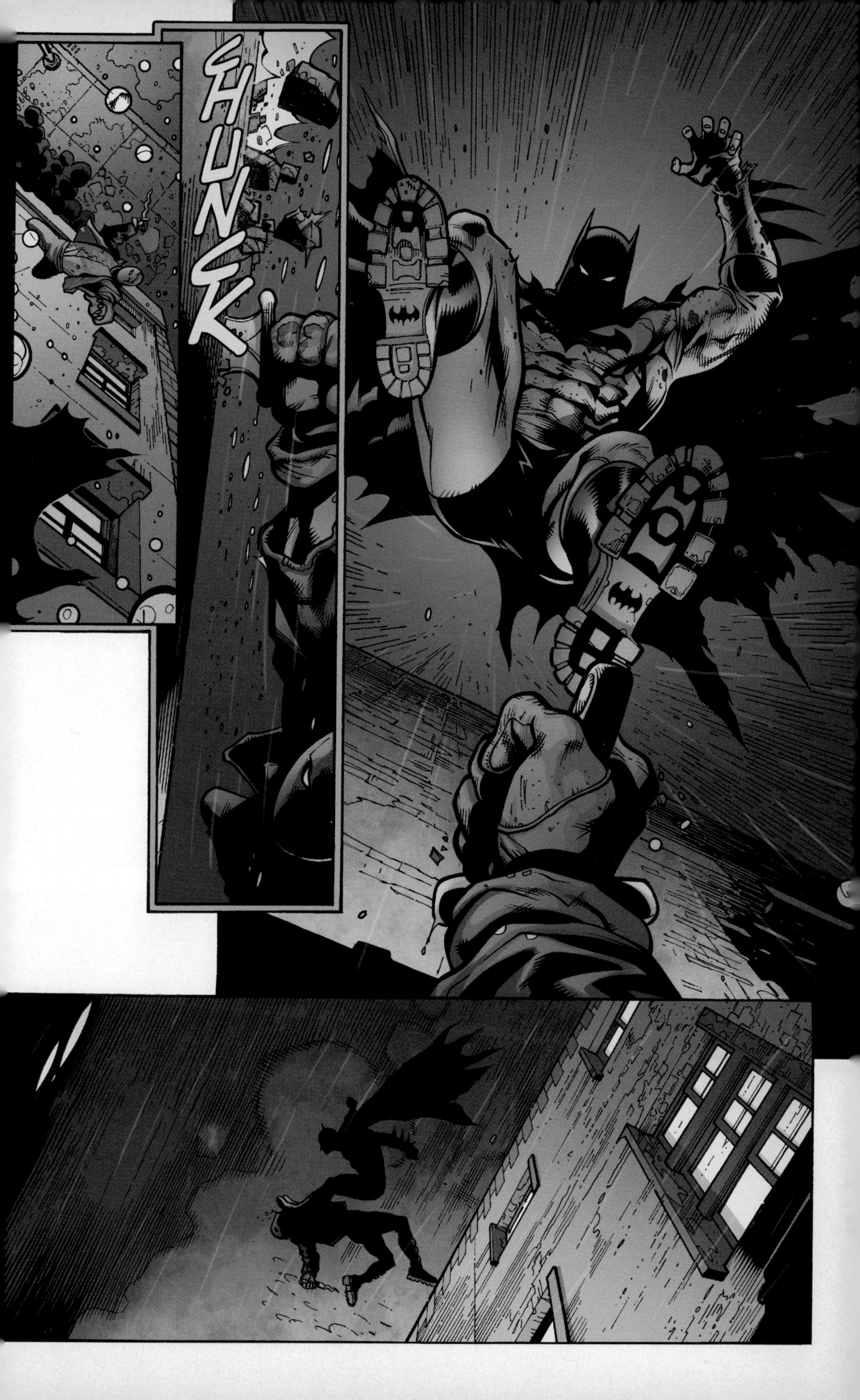
CHUNK

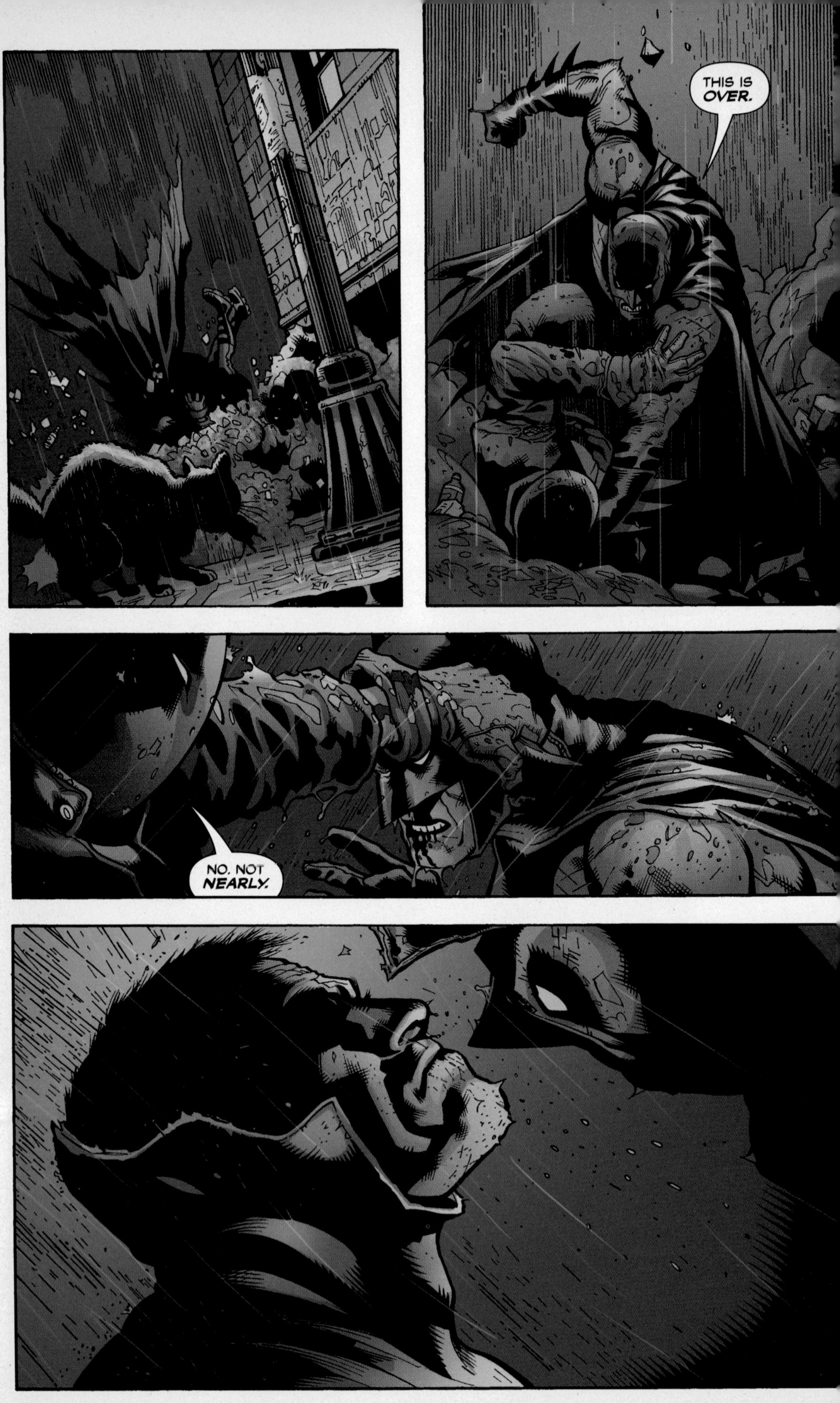
THIS IS OVER.
NO. NOT NEARLY.

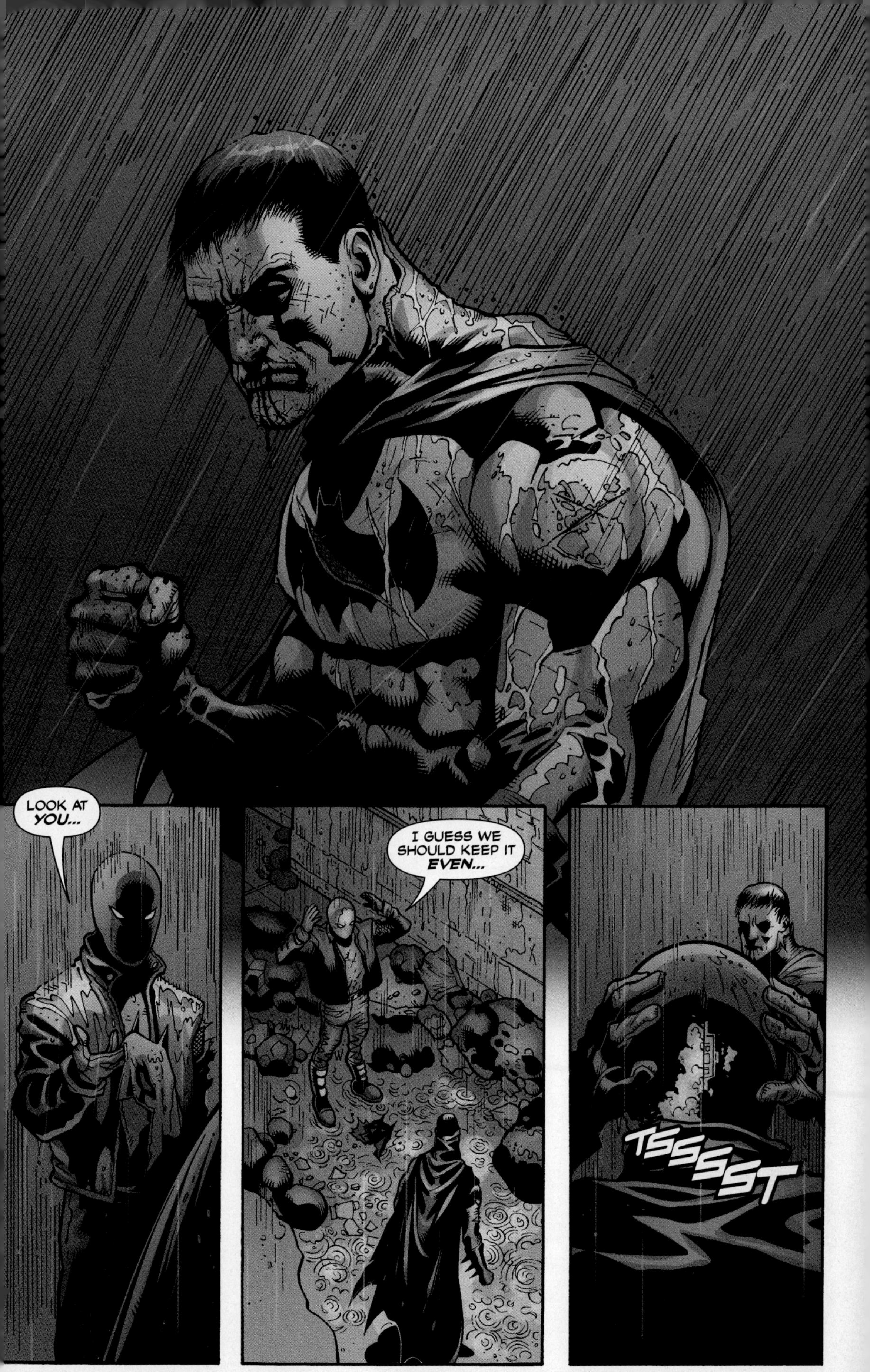
LOOK AT YOU...
I GUESS WE SHOULD KEEP IT EVEN...
TSSSST

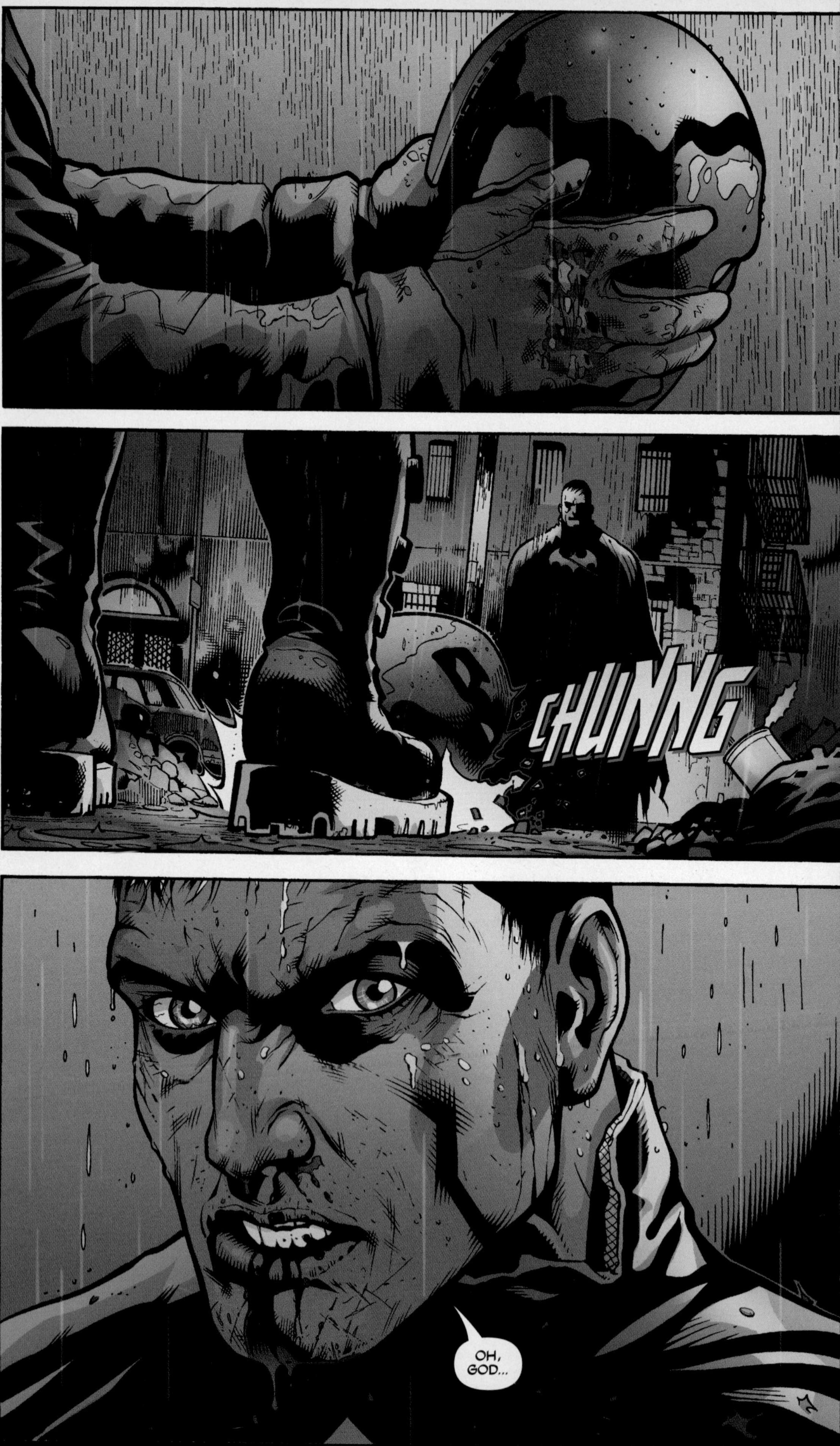
CHUNNG
OH, GOD...

FIVE WEEKS EARLIER.

WAYNE MANOR.

This is a house that has long sat in shadow.

It is a place of near constant mourning, proverbial mirrors draped in pitch black cloth.

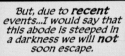

But, due to recent events...I would say that this abode is steeped in a darkness we will not soon escape.

Ties have been severed. Familial ties.

The myth seems more like a man.

And death has visited this house...again.

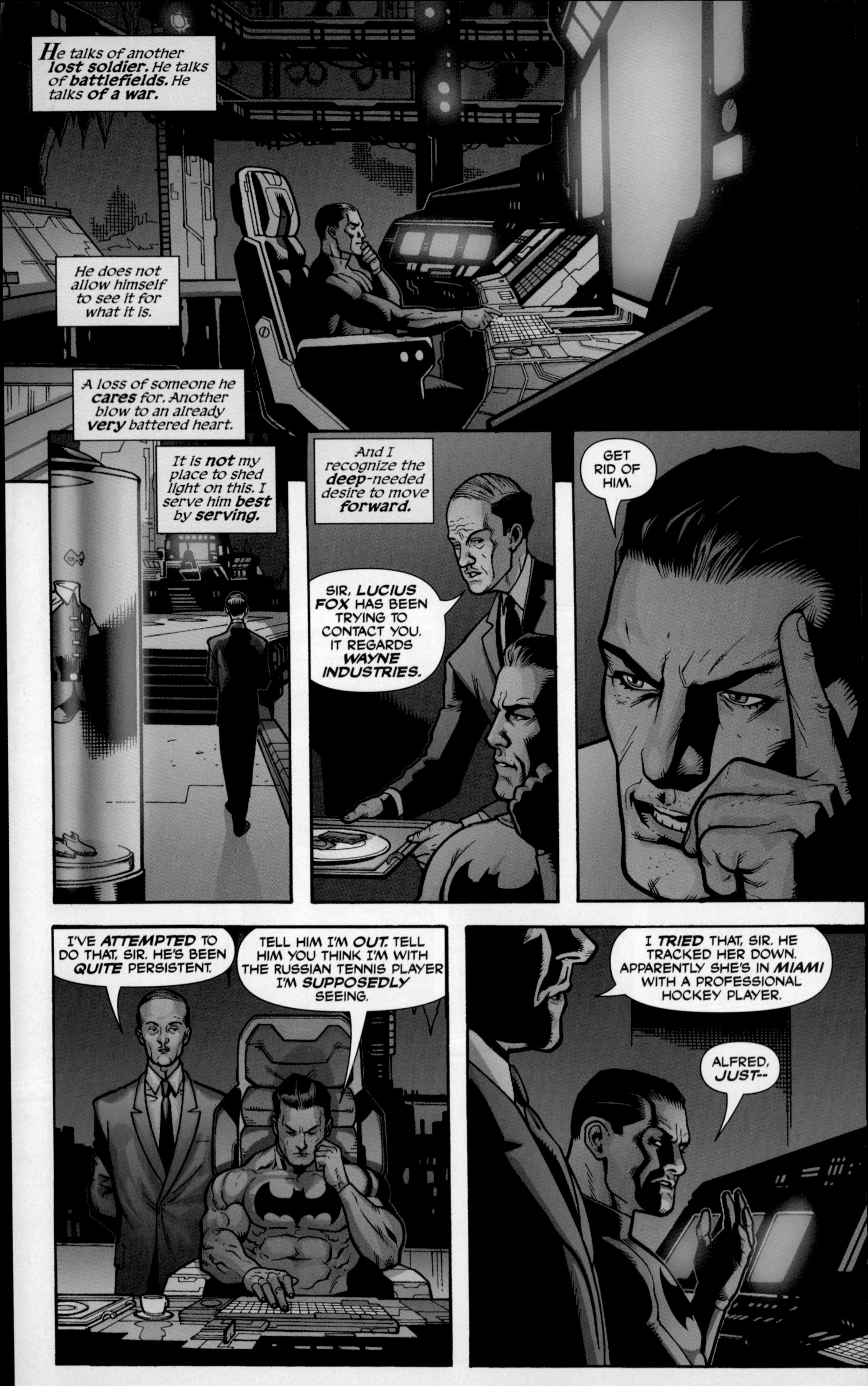
He talks of another lost soldier. He talks of battlefields. He talks of a war.
He does not allow himself to see it for what it is.
A loss of someone he cares for. Another blow to an already very battered heart.
It is not my place to shed light on this. I serve him best by serving.
And I recognize the deep-needed desire to move forward.
SIR, LUCIUS FOX HAS BEEN TRYING TO CONTACT YOU. IT REGARDS WAYNE INDUSTRIES.
GET RID OF HIM.
I'VE ATTEMPTED TO DO THAT, SIR. HE'S BEEN QUITE PERSISTENT.
TELL HIM I'M OUT. TELL HIM YOU THINK I'M WITH THE RUSSIAN TENNIS PLAYER I'M SUPPOSEDLY SEEING.
I TRIED THAT, SIR. HE TRACKED HER DOWN. APPARENTLY SHE'S IN MIAMI WITH A PROFESSIONAL HOCKEY PLAYER.
ALFRED, JUST--

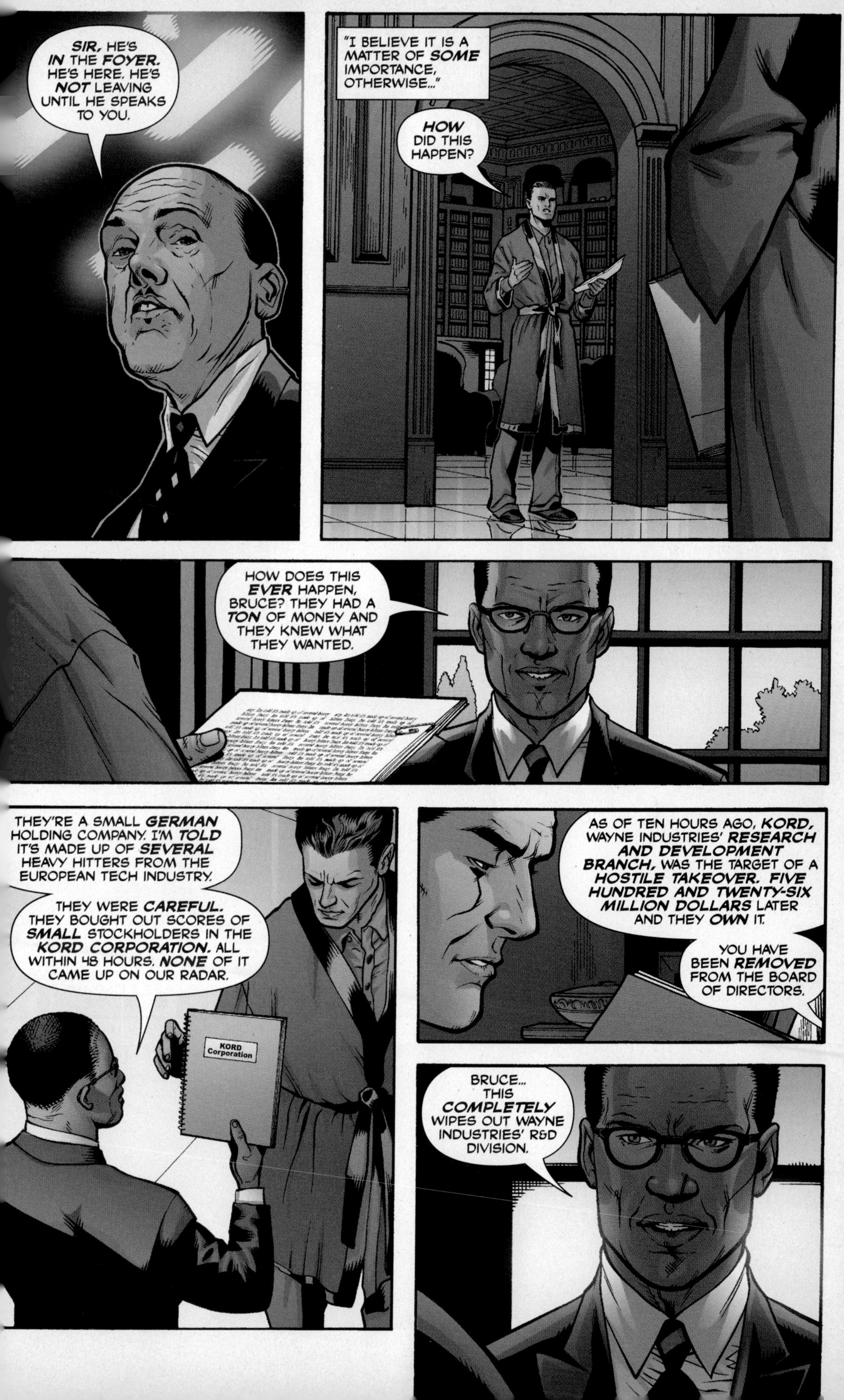
SIR, HE'S IN THE FOYER. HE'S HERE. HE'S NOT LEAVING UNTIL HE SPEAKS TO YOU.
"I BELIEVE IT IS A MATTER OF SOME IMPORTANCE, OTHERWISE..."
HOW DID THIS HAPPEN?
HOW DOES THIS EVER HAPPEN, BRUCE? THEY HAD A TON OF MONEY AND THEY KNEW WHAT THEY WANTED.
THEY'RE A SMALL GERMAN HOLDING COMPANY. I'M TOLD IT'S MADE UP OF SEVERAL HEAVY HITTERS FROM THE EUROPEAN TECH INDUSTRY.
THEY WERE CAREFUL. THEY BOUGHT OUT SCORES OF SMALL STOCKHOLDERS IN THE KORD CORPORATION. ALL WITHIN 48 HOURS. NONE OF IT CAME UP ON OUR RADAR.
KORD Corporation
AS OF TEN HOURS AGO, KORD, WAYNE INDUSTRIES' RESEARCH AND DEVELOPMENT BRANCH, WAS THE TARGET OF A HOSTILE TAKEOVER. FIVE HUNDRED AND TWENTY-SIX MILLION DOLLARS LATER AND THEY OWN IT.
YOU HAVE BEEN REMOVED FROM THE BOARD OF DIRECTORS.
BRUCE... THIS COMPLETELY WIPES OUT WAYNE INDUSTRIES' R&D DIVISION.

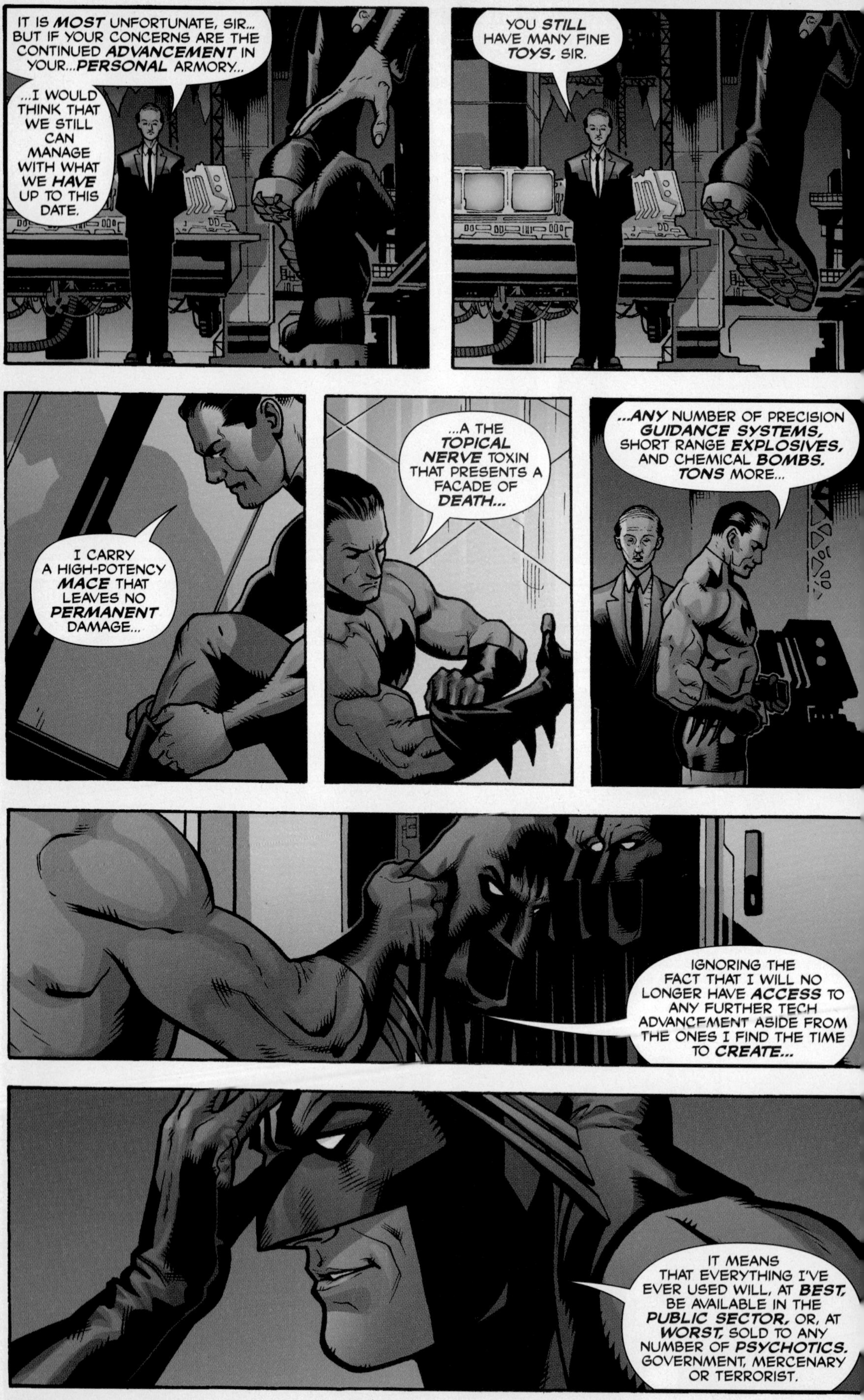
IT IS MOST UNFORTUNATE, SIR... BUT IF YOUR CONCERNS ARE THE CONTINUED ADVANCEMENT IN YOUR...PERSONAL ARMORY...
...I WOULD THINK THAT WE STILL CAN MANAGE WITH WHAT WE HAVE UP TO THIS DATE.
YOU STILL HAVE MANY FINE TOYS, SIR.
I CARRY A HIGH-POTENCY MACE THAT LEAVES NO PERMANENT DAMAGE...
...A THE TOPICAL NERVE TOXIN THAT PRESENTS A FACADE OF DEATH...
...ANY NUMBER OF PRECISION GUIDANCE SYSTEMS, SHORT RANGE EXPLOSIVES, AND CHEMICAL BOMBS. TONS MORE...
IGNORING THE FACT THAT I WILL NO LONGER HAVE ACCESS TO ANY FURTHER TECH ADVANCEMENT ASIDE FROM THE ONES I FIND THE TIME TO CREATE...
IT MEANS THAT EVERYTHING I'VE EVER USED WILL, AT BEST, BE AVAILABLE IN THE PUBLIC SECTOR, OR, AT WORST, SOLD TO ANY NUMBER OF PSYCHOTICS. GOVERNMENT, MERCENARY OR TERRORIST.

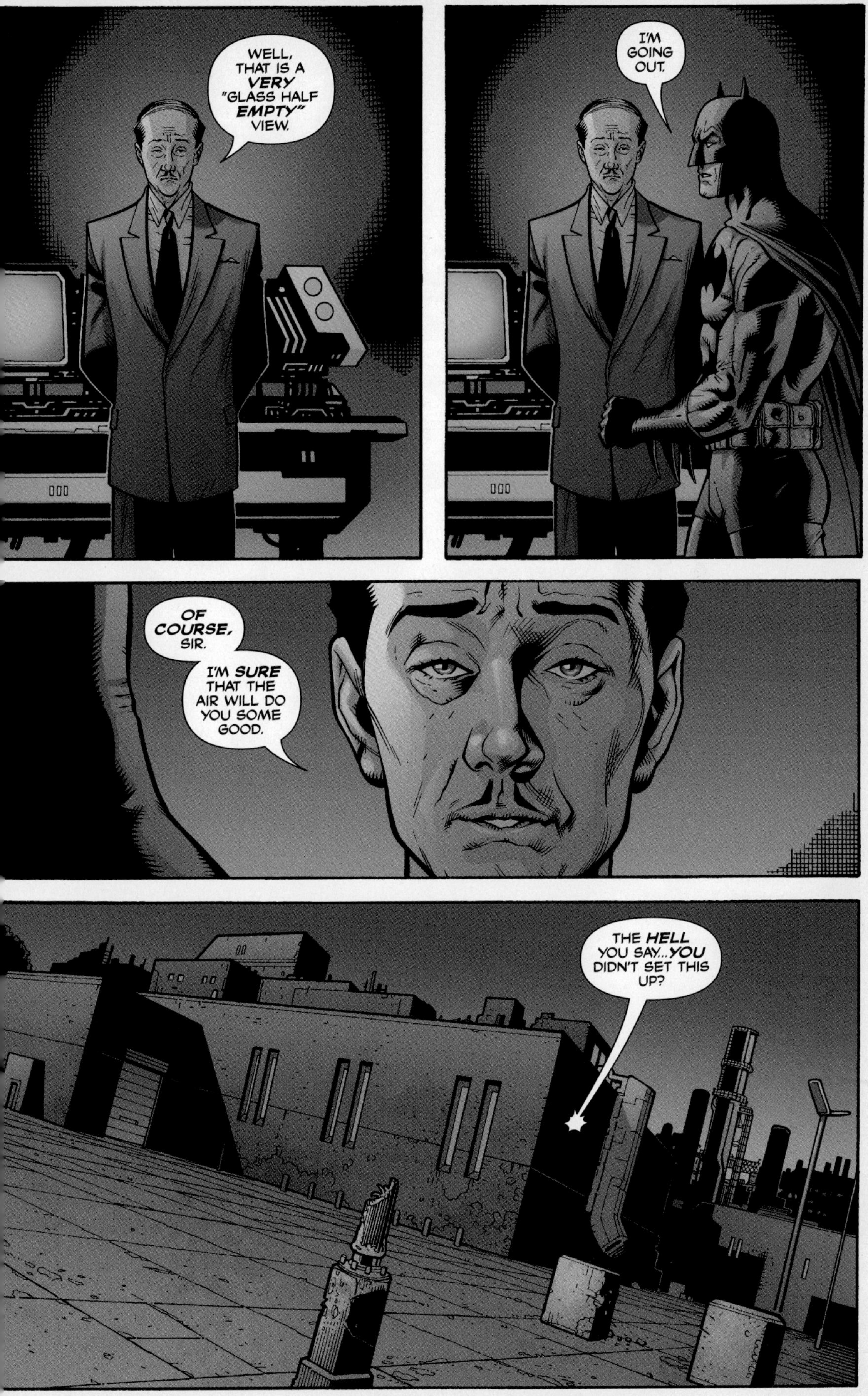
WELL, THAT IS A VERY "GLASS HALF EMPTY" VIEW.
I'M GOING OUT.
OF COURSE, SIR.
I'M SURE THAT THE AIR WILL DO YOU SOME GOOD.
THE HELL YOU SAY...YOU DIDN'T SET THIS UP?

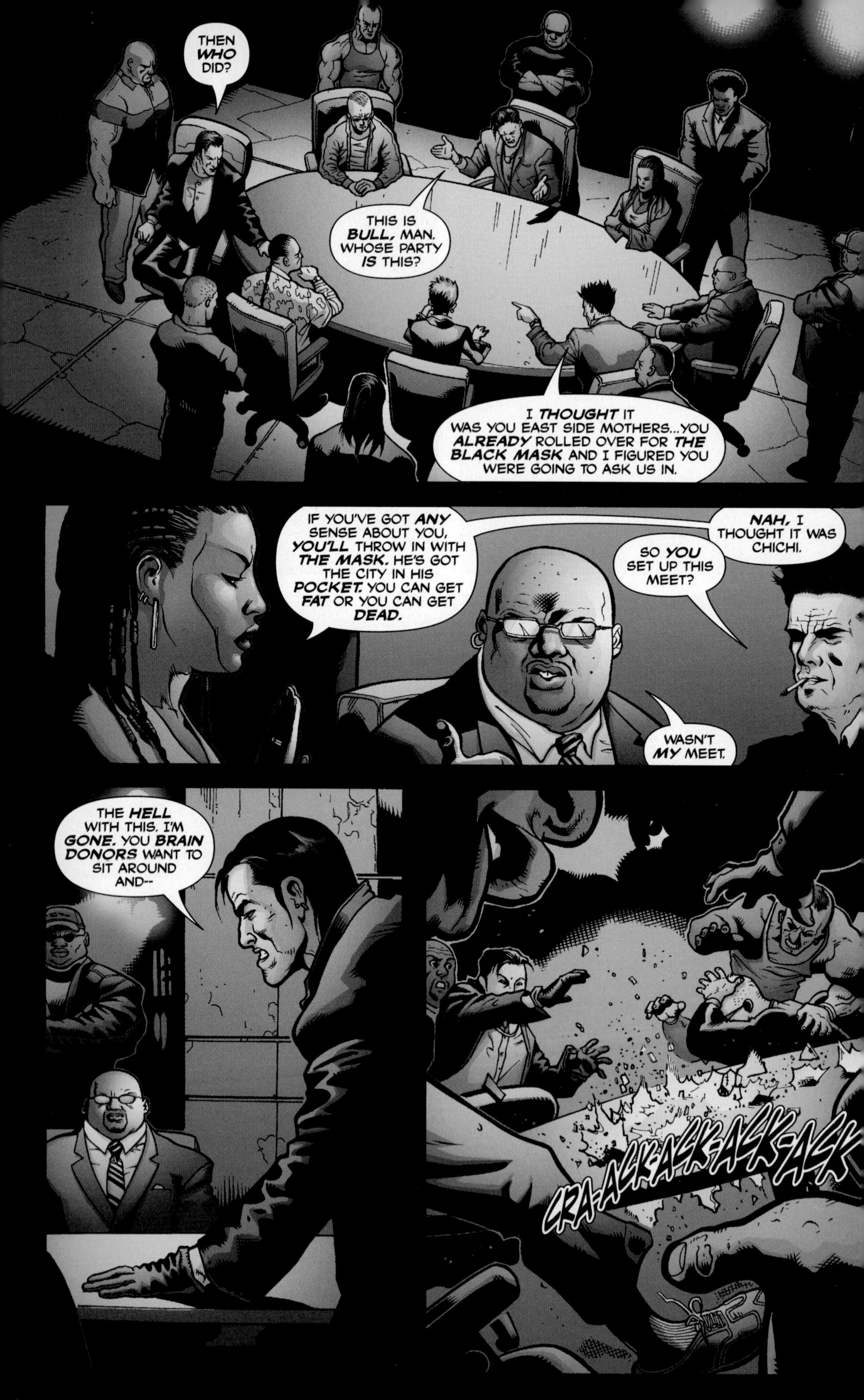
THEN WHO DID?
THIS IS BULL, MAN. WHOSE PARTY IS THIS?
I THOUGHT IT WAS YOU EAST SIDE MOTHERS...YOU ALREADY ROLLED OVER FOR THE BLACK MASK AND I FIGURED YOU WERE GOING TO ASK US IN.
IF YOU'VE GOT ANY SENSE ABOUT YOU, YOU'LL THROW IN WITH THE MASK. HE'S GOT THE CITY IN HIS POCKET. YOU CAN GET FAT OR YOU CAN GET DEAD.
SO YOU SET UP THIS MEET?
WASN'T MY MEET.
NAH, I THOUGHT IT WAS CHICHI.
THE HELL WITH THIS. I'M GONE. YOU BRAIN DONORS WANT TO SIT AROUND AND--
CRA-ACK-ACK-ACK-ACK

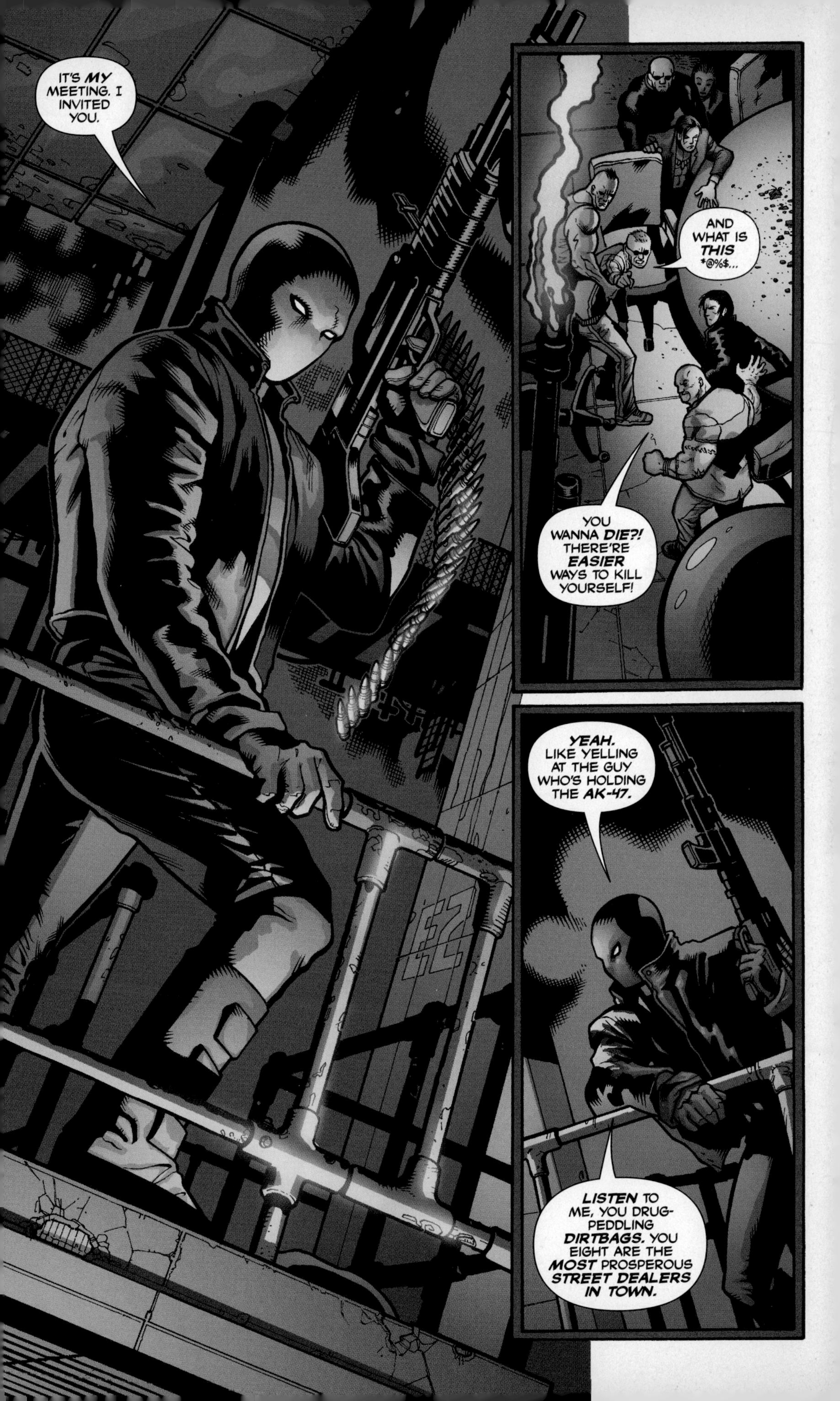
IT'S MY MEETING. I INVITED YOU.
AND WHAT IS THIS *@%$...
YOU WANNA DIE?! THERE'RE EASIER WAYS TO KILL YOURSELF!
YEAH. LIKE YELLING AT THE GUY WHO'S HOLDING THE AK-47.
LISTEN TO ME, YOU DRUG-PEDDLING DIRTBAGS. YOU EIGHT ARE THE MOST PROSPEROUS STREET DEALERS IN TOWN.

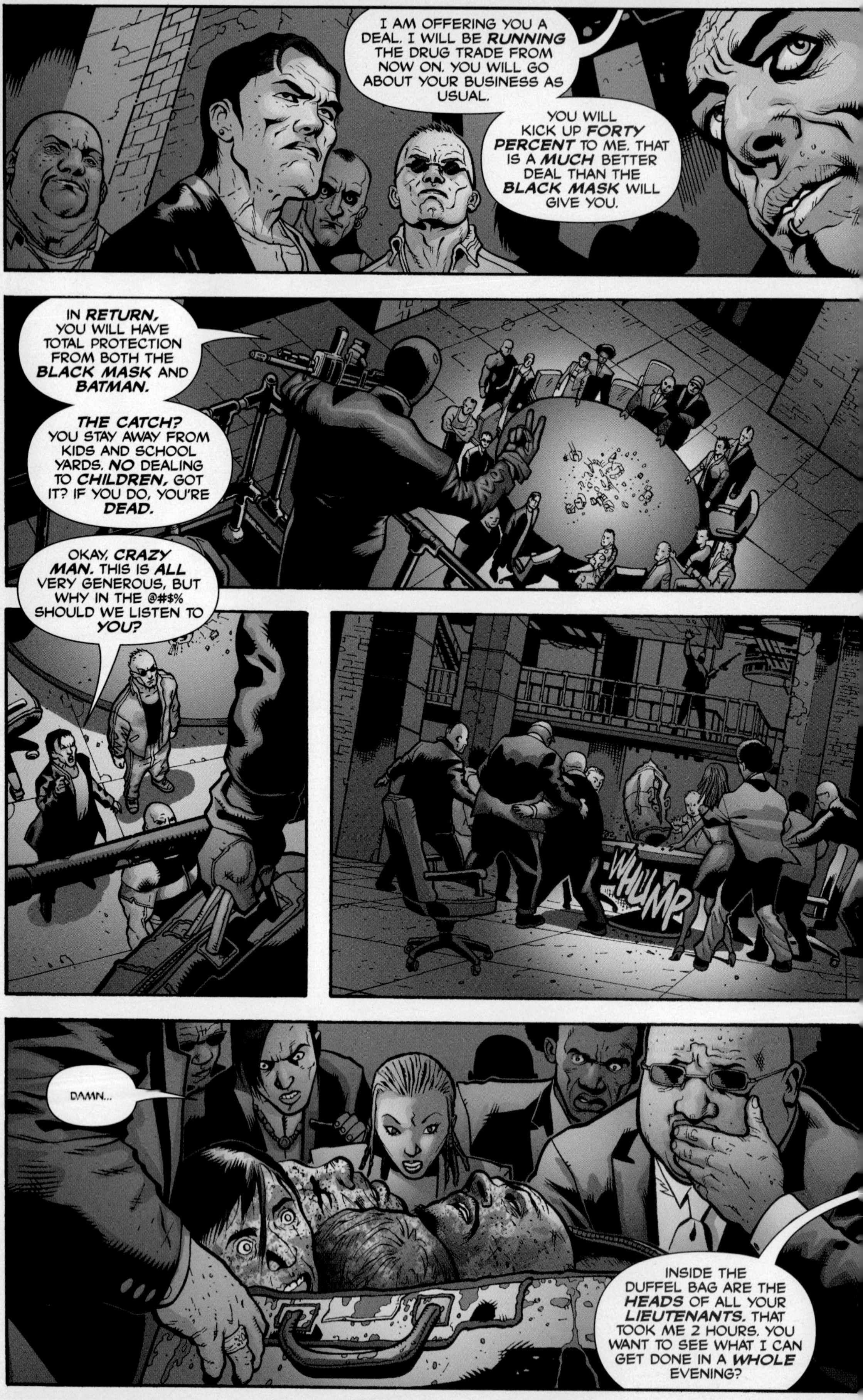
I AM OFFERING YOU A DEAL. I WILL BE RUNNING THE DRUG TRADE FROM NOW ON. YOU WILL GO ABOUT YOUR BUSINESS AS USUAL.
YOU WILL KICK UP FORTY PERCENT TO ME. THAT IS A MUCH BETTER DEAL THAN THE BLACK MASK WILL GIVE YOU.
IN RETURN, YOU WILL HAVE TOTAL PROTECTION FROM BOTH THE BLACK MASK AND BATMAN.
THE CATCH? YOU STAY AWAY FROM KIDS AND SCHOOL YARDS. NO DEALING TO CHILDREN, GOT IT? IF YOU DO, YOU'RE DEAD.
OKAY, CRAZY MAN. THIS IS ALL VERY GENEROUS, BUT WHY IN THE @#$% SHOULD WE LISTEN TO YOU?
WHUMP
DAMN...
INSIDE THE DUFFEL BAG ARE THE HEADS OF ALL YOUR LIEUTENANTS. THAT TOOK ME 2 HOURS. YOU WANT TO SEE WHAT I CAN GET DONE IN A WHOLE EVENING?

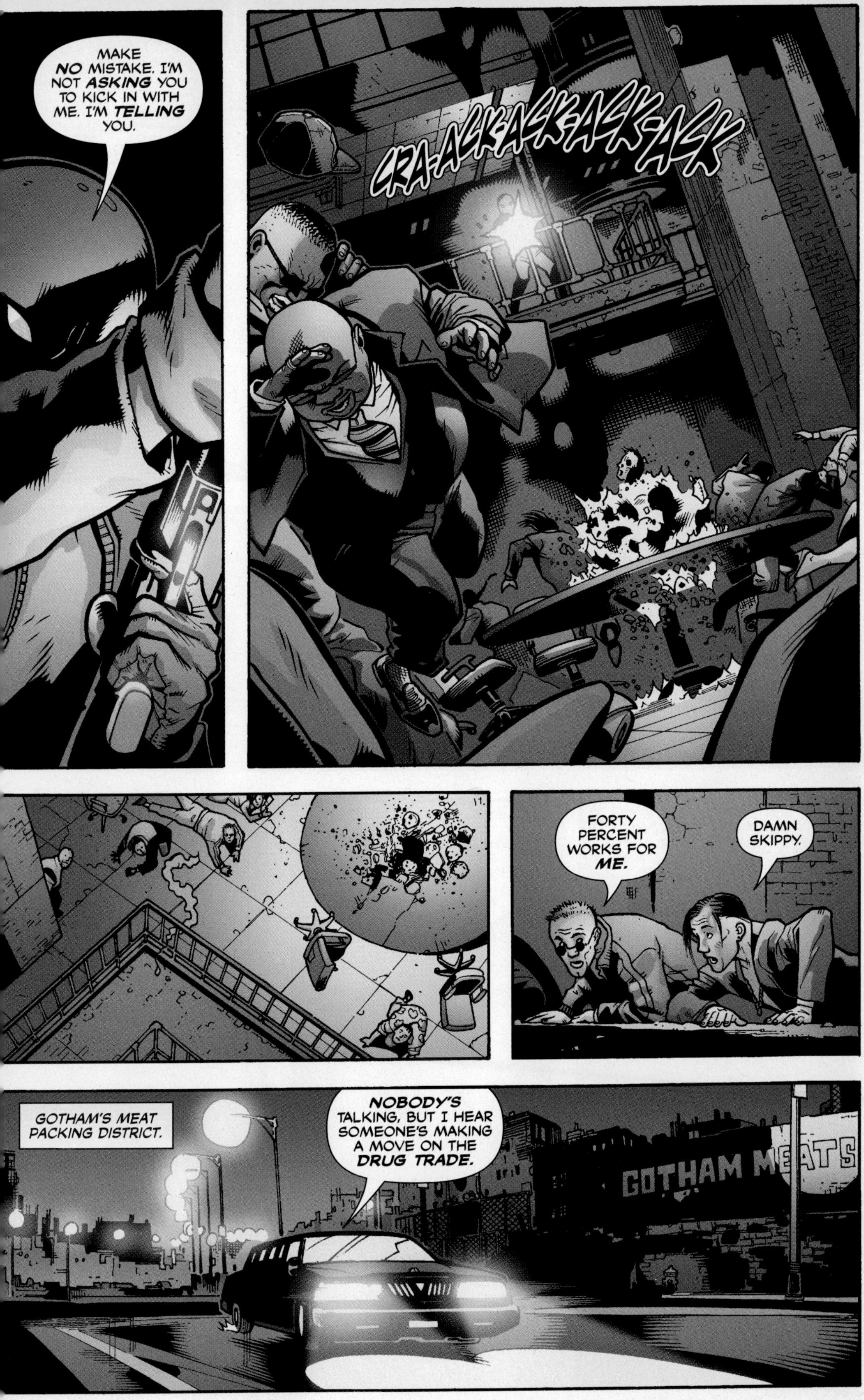

MAKE NO MISTAKE. I'M NOT ASKING YOU TO KICK IN WITH ME. I'M TELLING YOU.
CRA-ACK-ACK-ACK-ACK
FORTY PERCENT WORKS FOR ME.
DAMN SKIPPY.
GOTHAM'S MEAT PACKING DISTRICT.
NOBODY'S TALKING, BUT I HEAR SOMEONE'S MAKING A MOVE ON THE DRUG TRADE.
GOTHAM MEATS

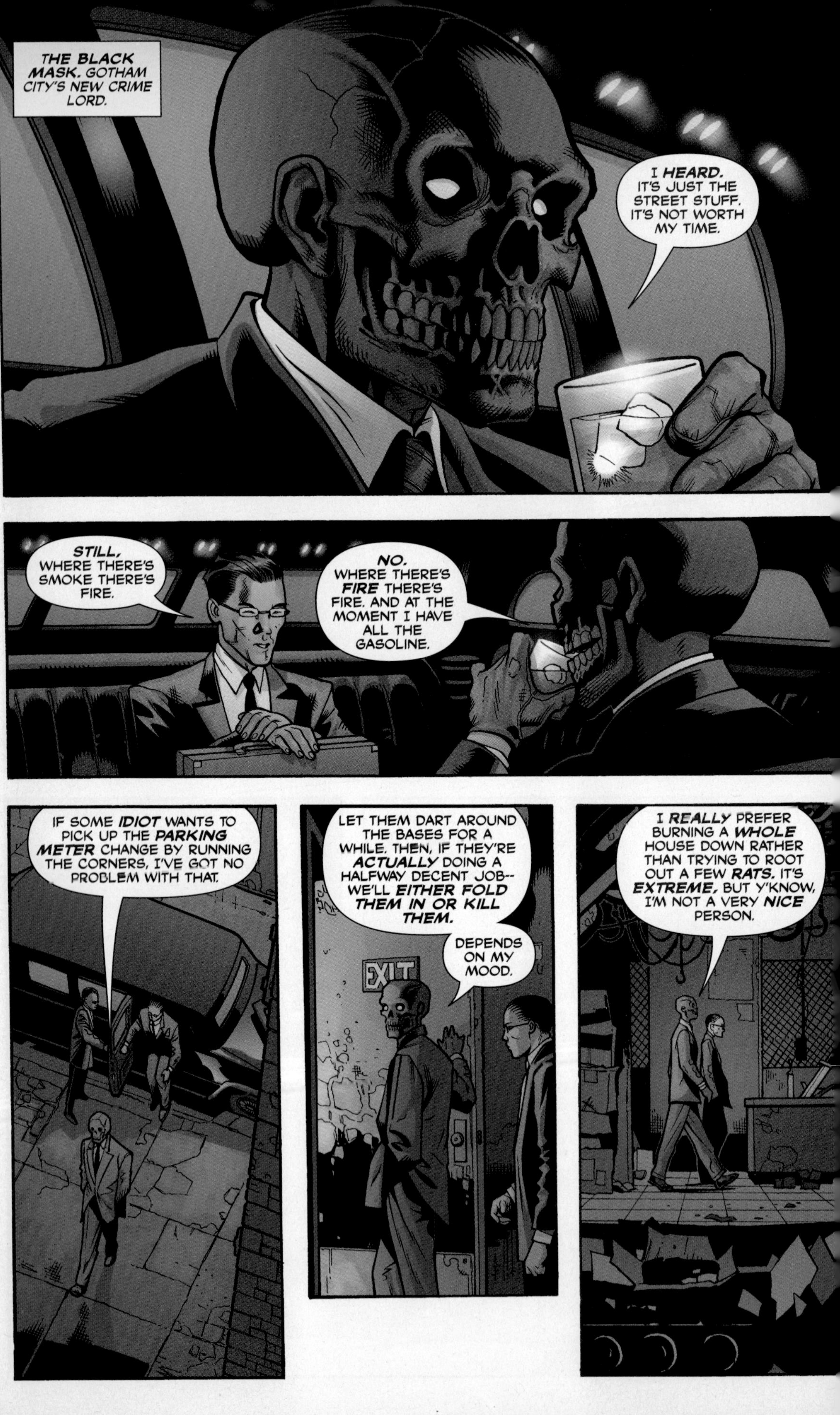
THE BLACK MASK. GOTHAM CITY'S NEW CRIME LORD.
I HEARD. IT'S JUST THE STREET STUFF. IT'S NOT WORTH MY TIME.
STILL, WHERE THERE'S SMOKE THERE'S FIRE.
NO. WHERE THERE'S FIRE THERE'S FIRE. AND AT THE MOMENT I HAVE ALL THE GASOLINE.
IF SOME IDIOT WANTS TO PICK UP THE PARKING METER CHANGE BY RUNNING THE CORNERS, I'VE GOT NO PROBLEM WITH THAT.
LET THEM DART AROUND THE BASES FOR A WHILE. THEN, IF THEY'RE ACTUALLY DOING A HALFWAY DECENT JOB-- WE'LL EITHER FOLD THEM IN OR KILL THEM.
DEPENDS ON MY MOOD.
EXIT
I REALLY PREFER BURNING A WHOLE HOUSE DOWN RATHER THAN TRYING TO ROOT OUT A FEW RATS. IT'S EXTREME, BUT Y'KNOW, I'M NOT A VERY NICE PERSON.

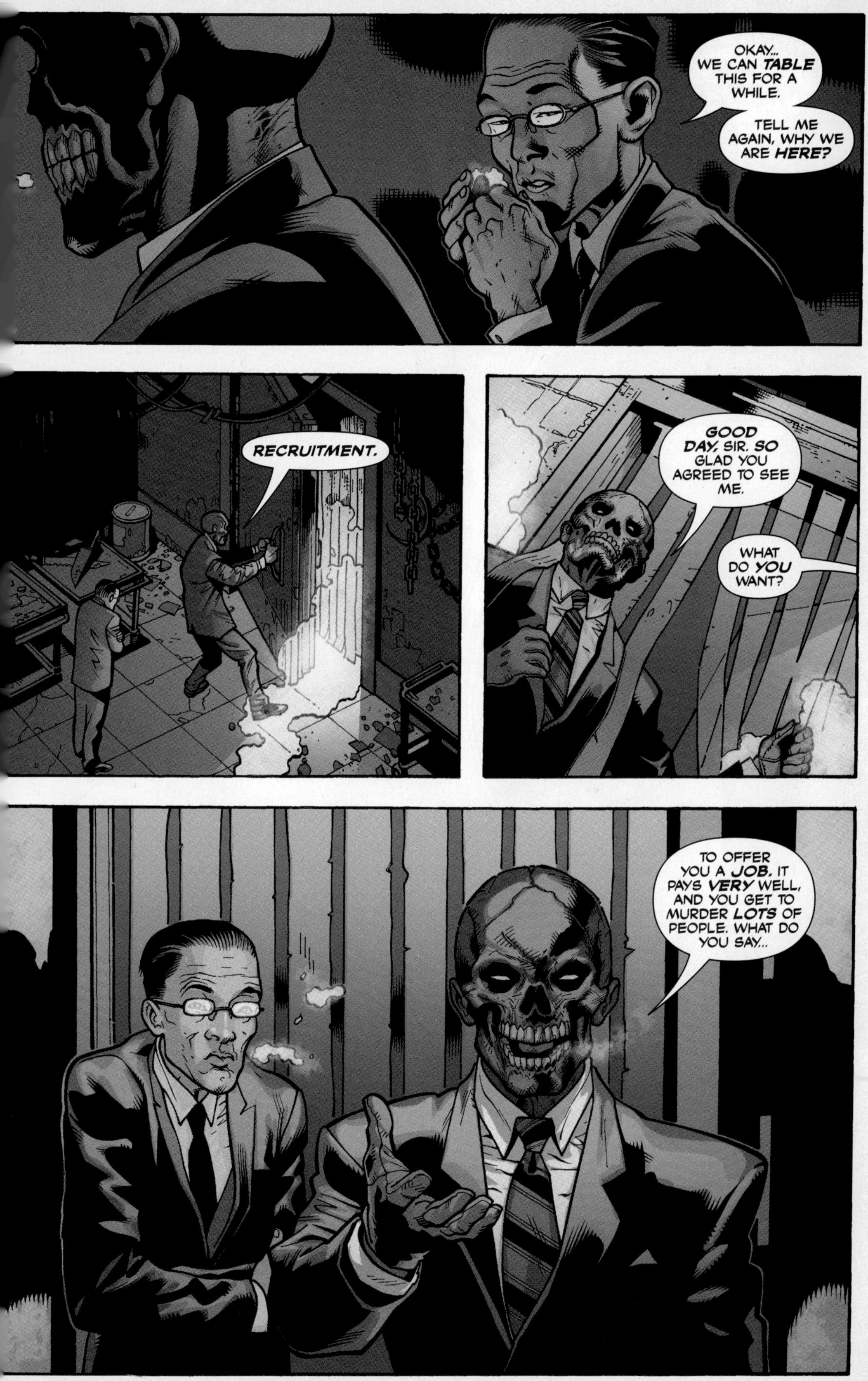
OKAY... WE CAN TABLE THIS FOR A WHILE.
TELL ME AGAIN, WHY WE ARE HERE?
RECRUITMENT.
GOOD DAY, SIR. SO GLAD YOU AGREED TO SEE ME.
WHAT DO YOU WANT?
TO OFFER YOU A JOB. IT PAYS VERY WELL, AND YOU GET TO MURDER LOTS OF PEOPLE. WHAT DO YOU SAY...

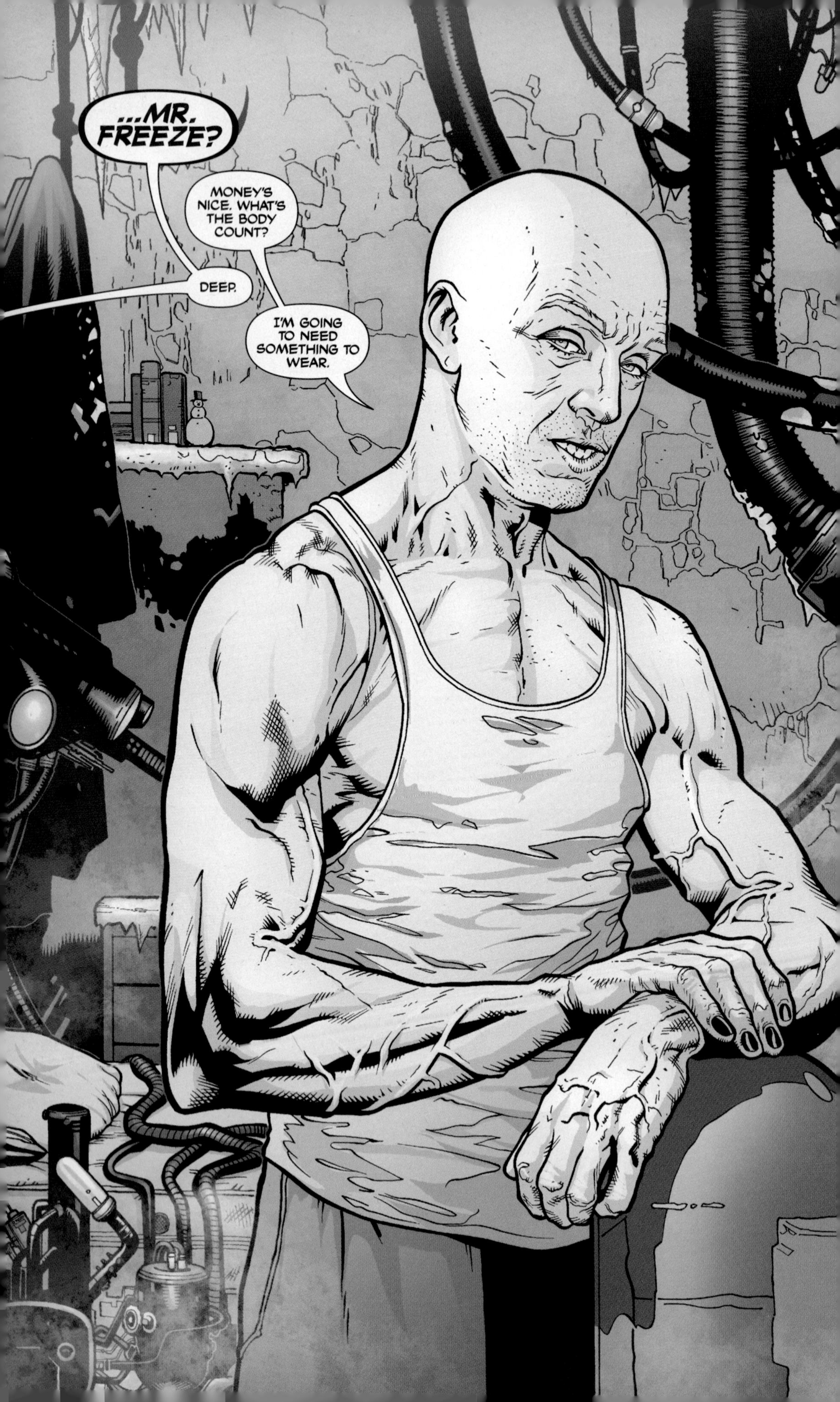
...MR. FREEZE?
MONEY'S NICE. WHAT'S THE BODY COUNT?
DEEP.
I'M GOING TO NEED SOMETHING TO WEAR.

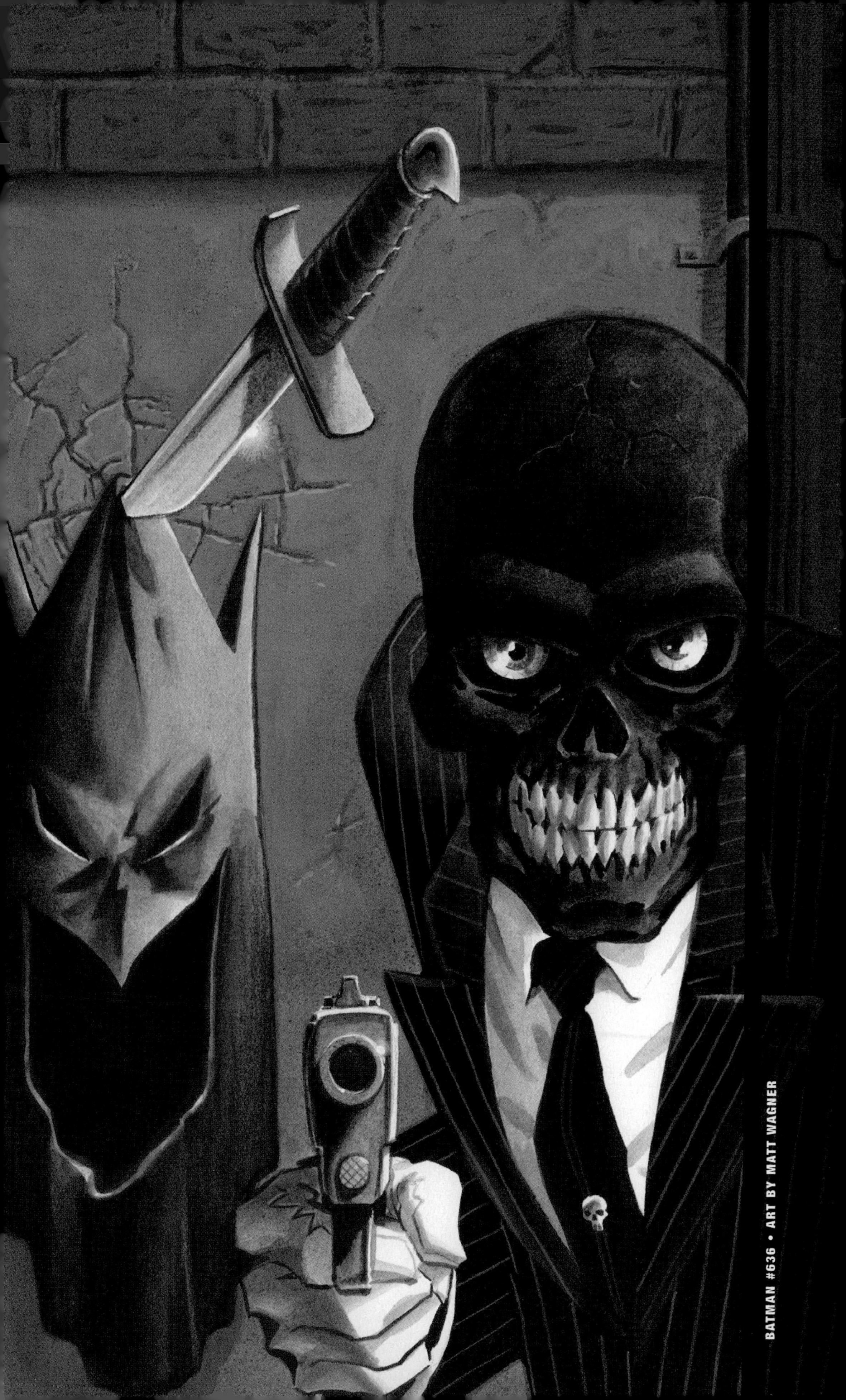

BATMAN #636 • ART BY MATT WAGNER

PART 2

FIRST STRIKE

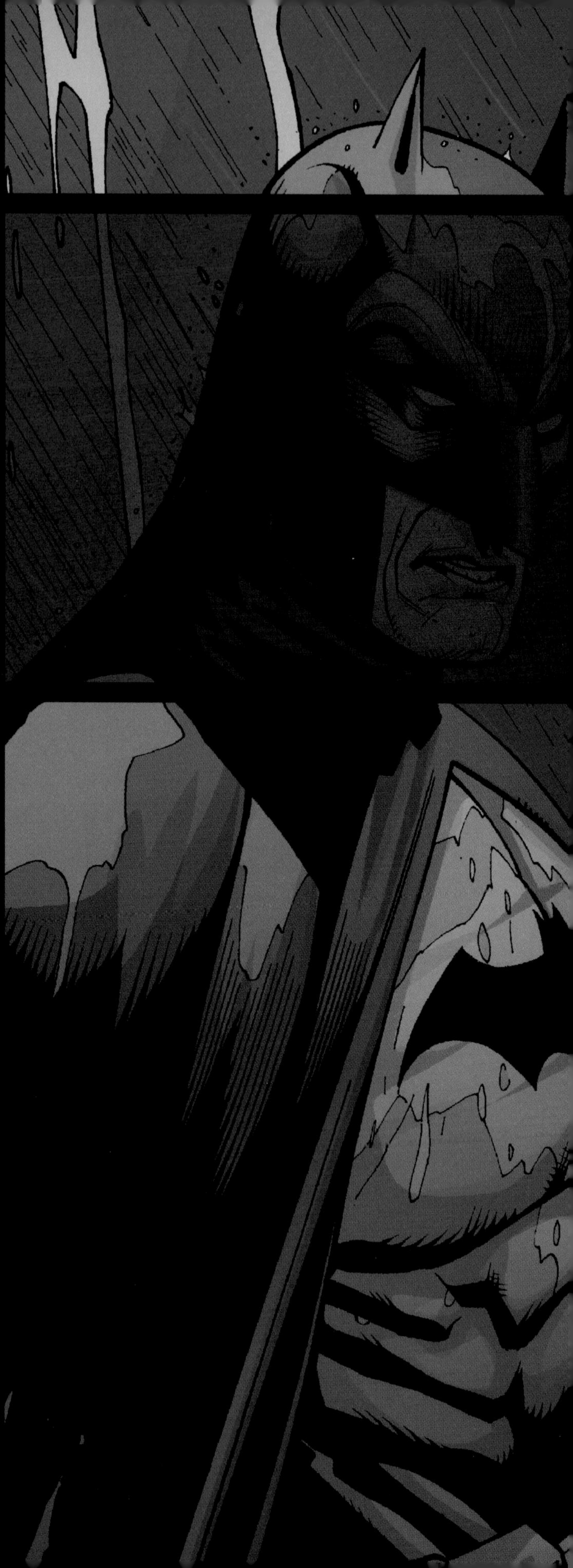

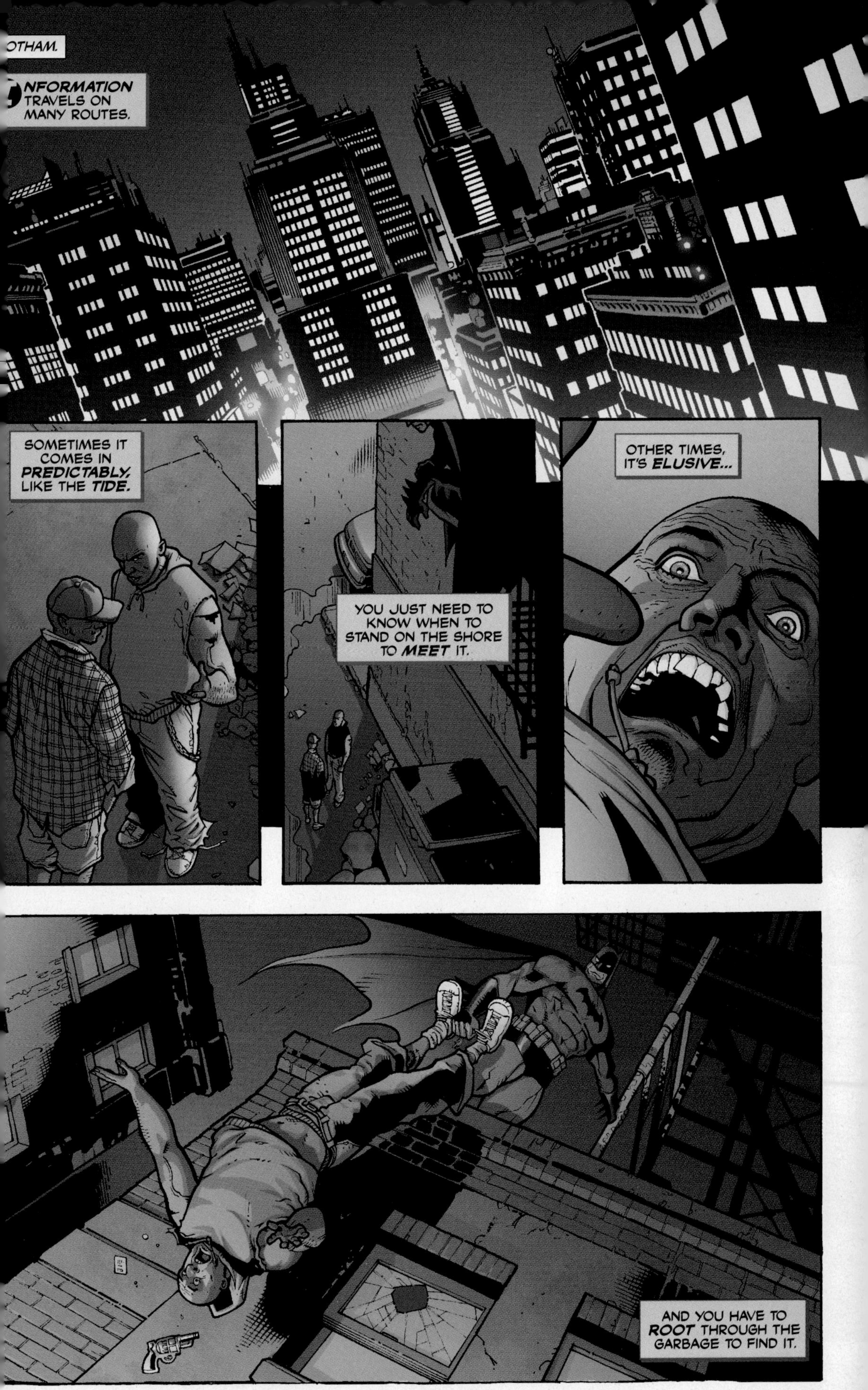

OTHAM.
NFORMATION TRAVELS ON MANY ROUTES.
SOMETIMES IT COMES IN PREDICTABLY, LIKE THE TIDE.
YOU JUST NEED TO KNOW WHEN TO STAND ON THE SHORE TO MEET IT.
OTHER TIMES, IT'S ELUSIVE...
AND YOU HAVE TO ROOT THROUGH THE GARBAGE TO FIND IT.

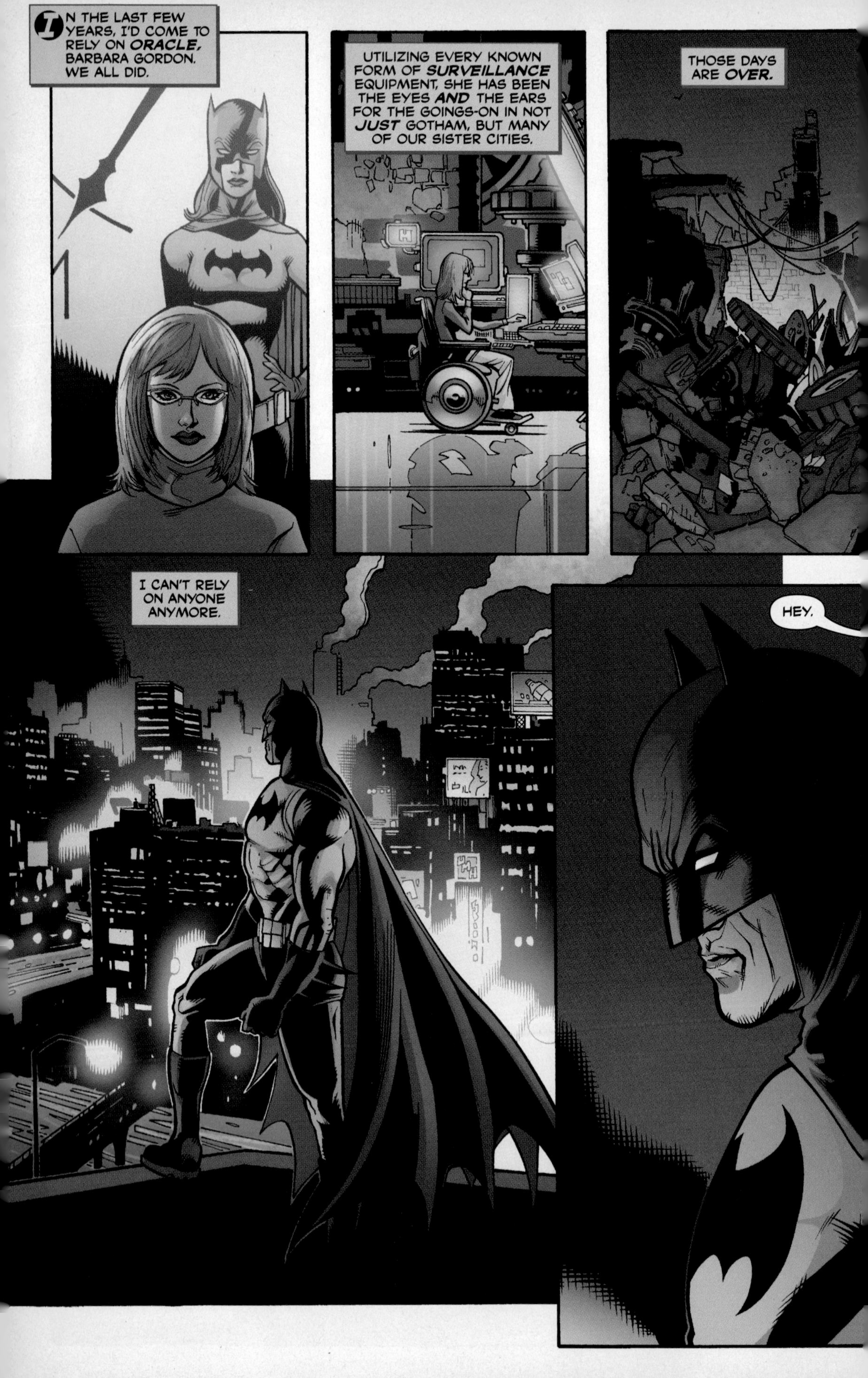
IN THE LAST FEW YEARS, I'D COME TO RELY ON ORACLE, BARBARA GORDON. WE ALL DID.
UTILIZING EVERY KNOWN FORM OF SURVEILLANCE EQUIPMENT, SHE HAS BEEN THE EYES AND THE EARS FOR THE GOINGS-ON IN NOT JUST GOTHAM, BUT MANY OF OUR SISTER CITIES.
THOSE DAYS ARE OVER.
I CAN'T RELY ON ANYONE ANYMORE.
HEY.

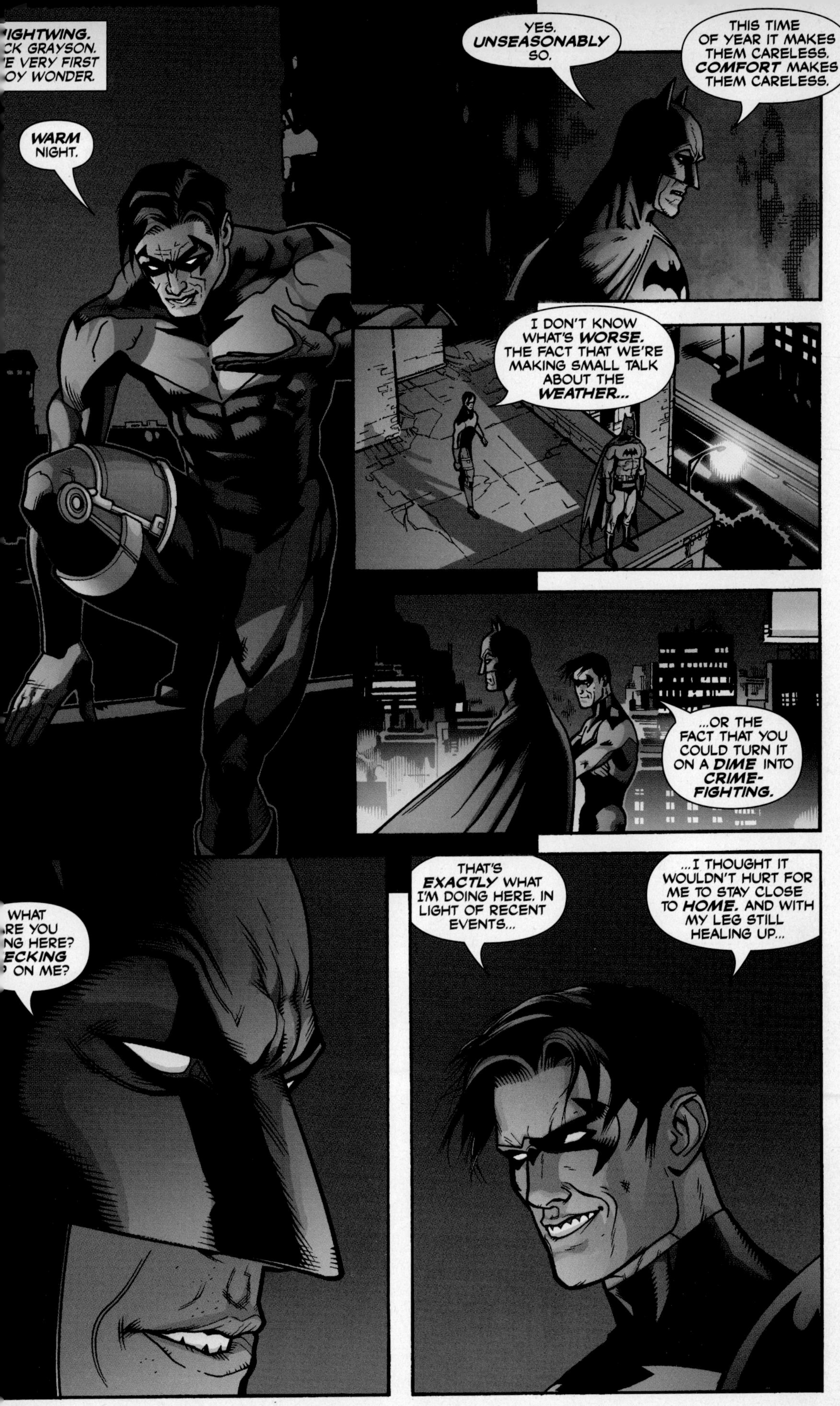
IGHTWING. CK GRAYSON. E VERY FIRST OY WONDER.
WARM NIGHT.
YES. UNSEASONABLY SO.
THIS TIME OF YEAR IT MAKES THEM CARELESS. COMFORT MAKES THEM CARELESS.
I DON'T KNOW WHAT'S WORSE. THE FACT THAT WE'RE MAKING SMALL TALK ABOUT THE WEATHER...
...OR THE FACT THAT YOU COULD TURN IT ON A DIME INTO CRIME-FIGHTING.
WHAT RE YOU NG HERE? ECKING ON ME?
THAT'S EXACTLY WHAT I'M DOING HERE. IN LIGHT OF RECENT EVENTS...
...I THOUGHT IT WOULDN'T HURT FOR ME TO STAY CLOSE TO HOME. AND WITH MY LEG STILL HEALING UP...

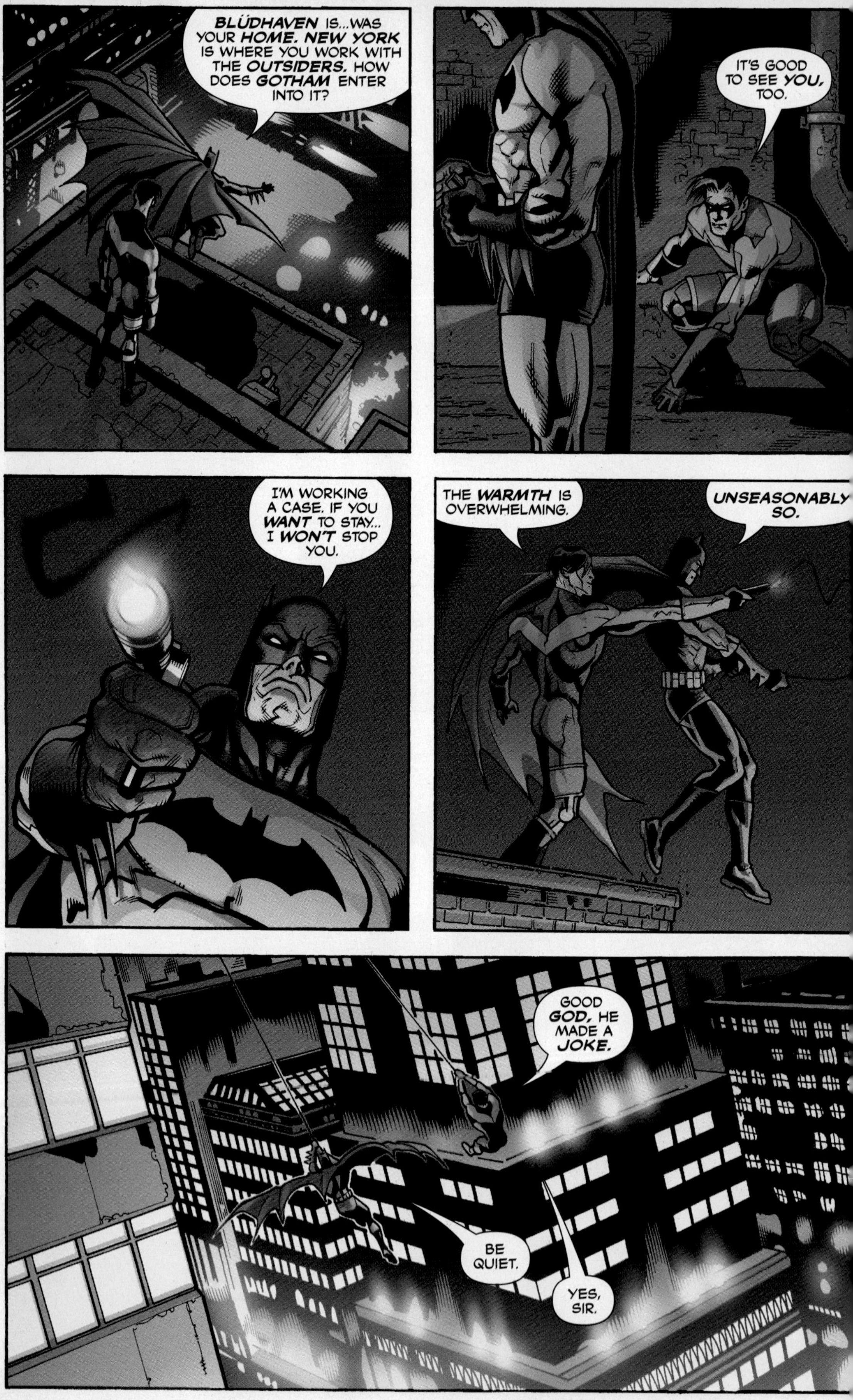
BLÜDHAVEN IS...WAS YOUR HOME. NEW YORK IS WHERE YOU WORK WITH THE OUTSIDERS. HOW DOES GOTHAM ENTER INTO IT?
IT'S GOOD TO SEE YOU, TOO.
I'M WORKING A CASE. IF YOU WANT TO STAY... I WON'T STOP YOU.
THE WARMTH IS OVERWHELMING.
UNSEASONABLY SO.
GOOD GOD, HE MADE A JOKE.
BE QUIET.
YES, SIR.

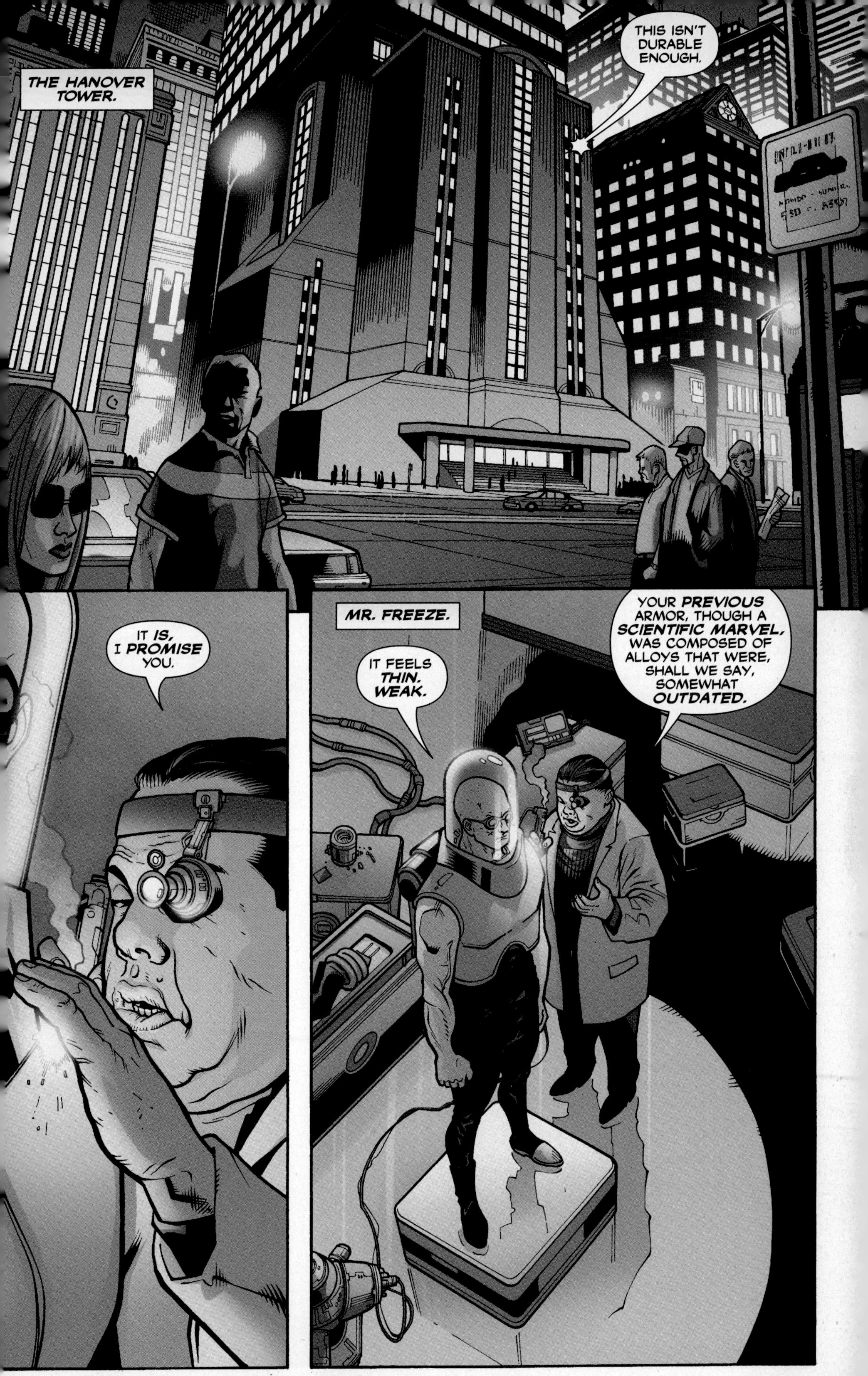
THE HANOVER TOWER.
THIS ISN'T DURABLE ENOUGH.
IT IS, I PROMISE YOU.
MR. FREEZE.
IT FEELS THIN. WEAK.
YOUR PREVIOUS ARMOR, THOUGH A SCIENTIFIC MARVEL, WAS COMPOSED OF ALLOYS THAT WERE, SHALL WE SAY, SOMEWHAT OUTDATED.

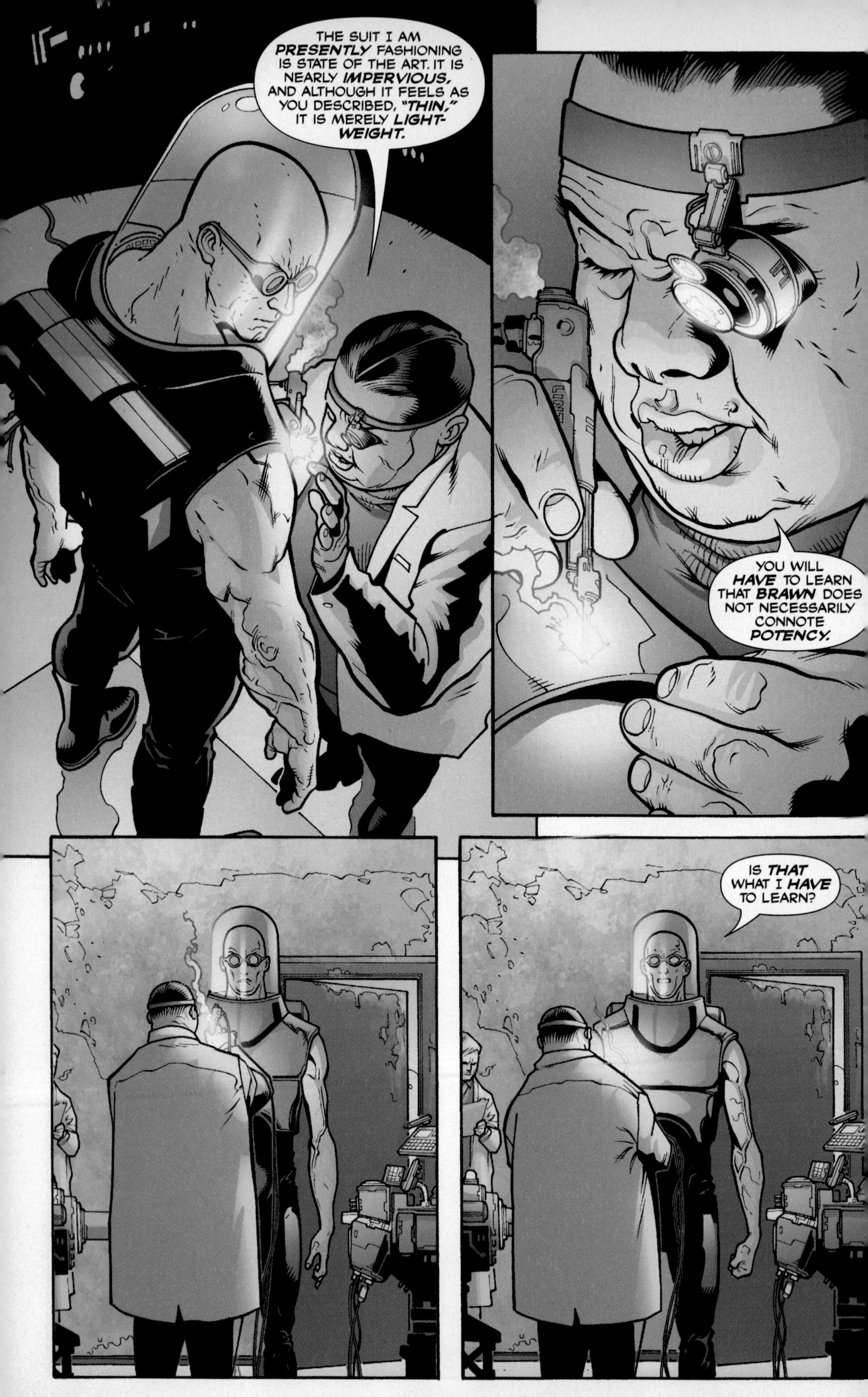
THE SUIT I AM PRESENTLY FASHIONING IS STATE OF THE ART. IT IS NEARLY IMPERVIOUS, AND ALTHOUGH IT FEELS AS YOU DESCRIBED, "THIN," IT IS MERELY LIGHT-WEIGHT.
YOU WILL HAVE TO LEARN THAT BRAWN DOES NOT NECESSARILY CONNOTE POTENCY.
IS THAT WHAT I HAVE TO LEARN?

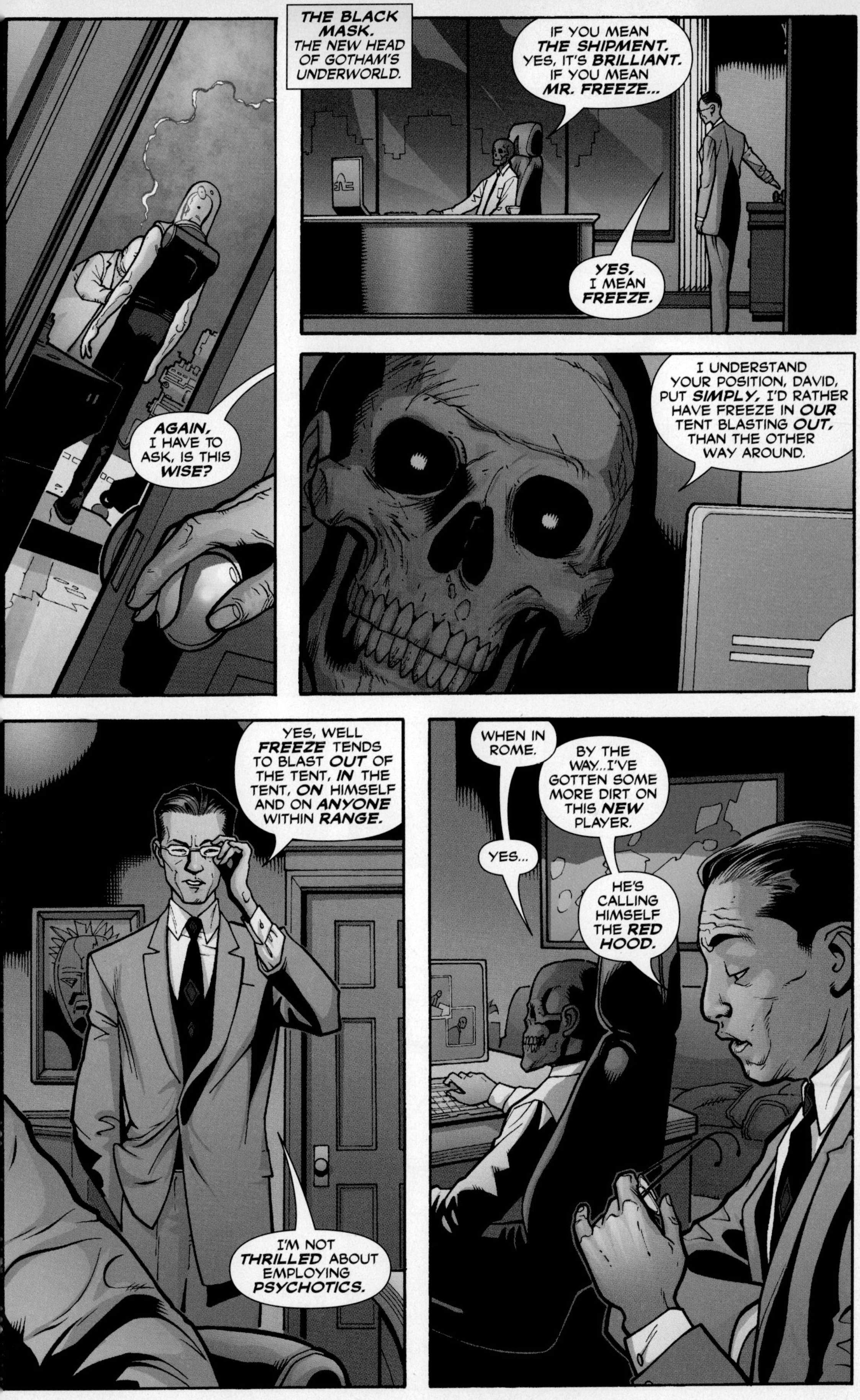
THE BLACK MASK. THE NEW HEAD OF GOTHAM'S UNDERWORLD.
IF YOU MEAN THE SHIPMENT. YES, IT'S BRILLIANT. IF YOU MEAN MR. FREEZE...
YES, I MEAN FREEZE.
AGAIN, I HAVE TO ASK, IS THIS WISE?
I UNDERSTAND YOUR POSITION, DAVID, PUT SIMPLY, I'D RATHER HAVE FREEZE IN OUR TENT BLASTING OUT, THAN THE OTHER WAY AROUND.
YES, WELL FREEZE TENDS TO BLAST OUT OF THE TENT, IN THE TENT, ON HIMSELF AND ON ANYONE WITHIN RANGE.
I'M NOT THRILLED ABOUT EMPLOYING PSYCHOTICS.
WHEN IN ROME.
BY THE WAY...I'VE GOTTEN SOME MORE DIRT ON THIS NEW PLAYER.
YES...
HE'S CALLING HIMSELF THE RED HOOD.

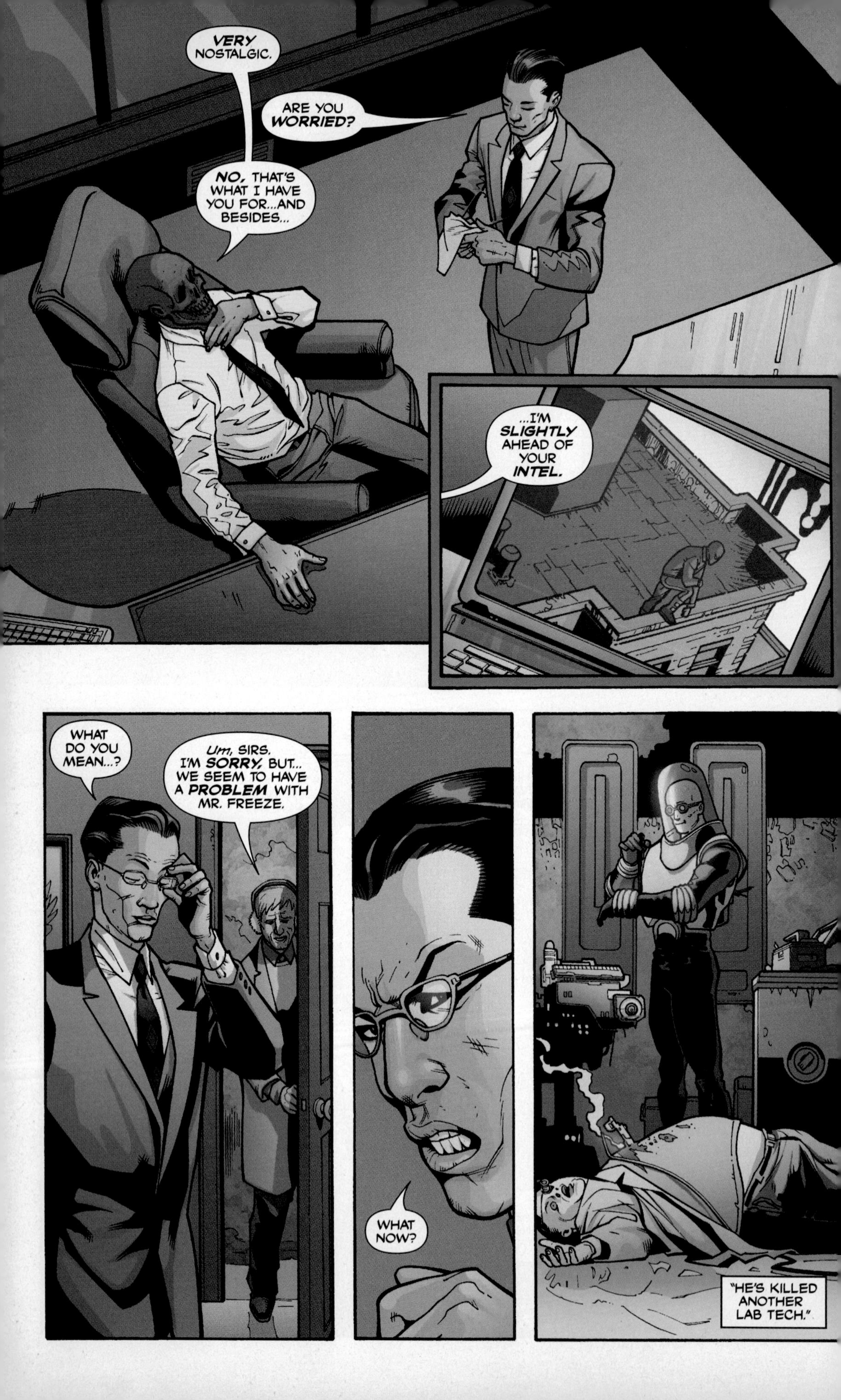
VERY NOSTALGIC.
ARE YOU WORRIED?
NO, THAT'S WHAT I HAVE YOU FOR...AND BESIDES...
...I'M SLIGHTLY AHEAD OF YOUR INTEL.
WHAT DO YOU MEAN...?
Um, SIRS, I'M SORRY, BUT... WE SEEM TO HAVE A PROBLEM WITH MR. FREEZE.
WHAT NOW?
"HE'S KILLED ANOTHER LAB TECH."

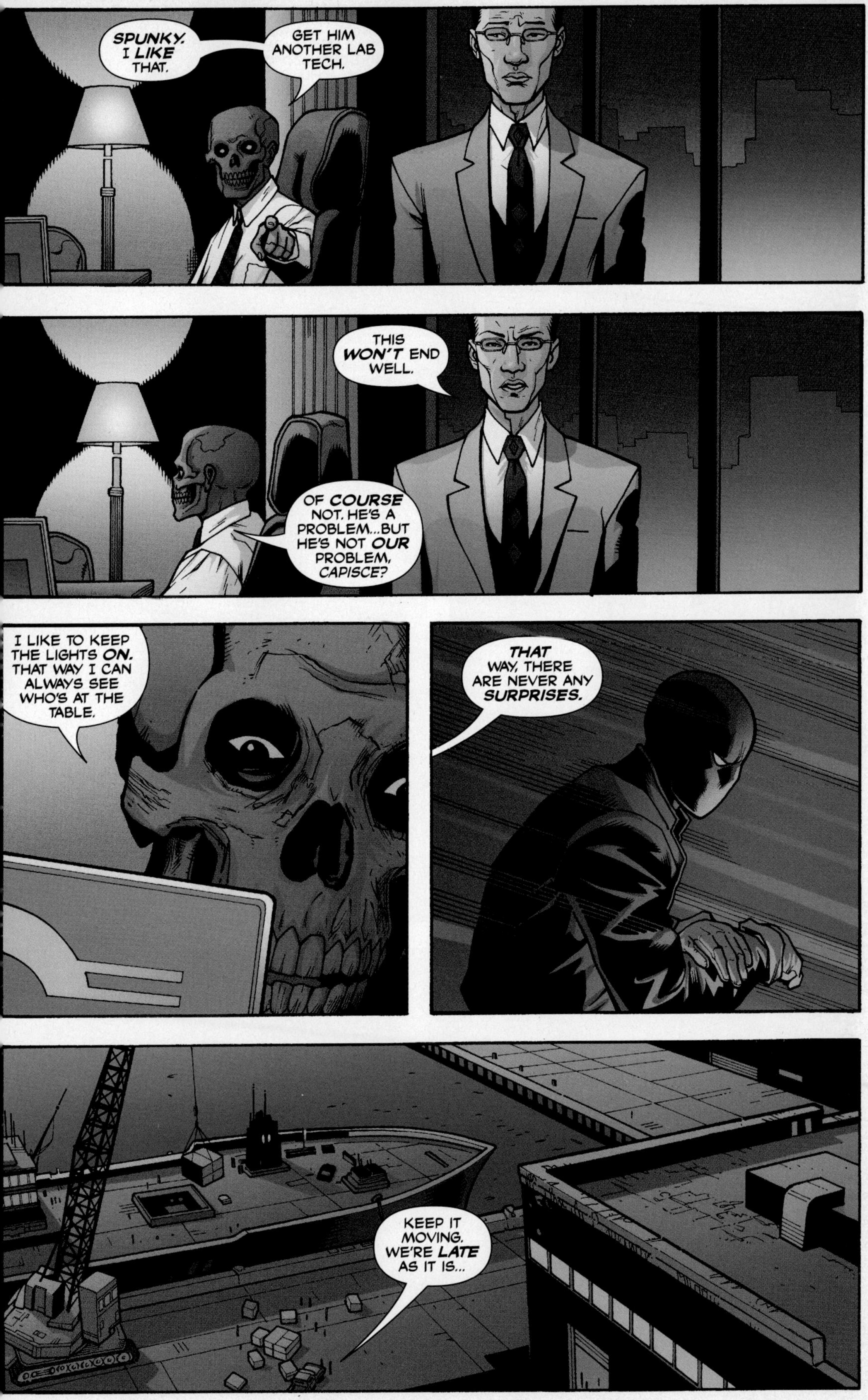
SPUNKY. I LIKE THAT.
GET HIM ANOTHER LAB TECH.
THIS WON'T END WELL.
OF COURSE NOT. HE'S A PROBLEM...BUT HE'S NOT OUR PROBLEM, CAPISCE?
I LIKE TO KEEP THE LIGHTS ON. THAT WAY I CAN ALWAYS SEE WHO'S AT THE TABLE.
THAT WAY, THERE ARE NEVER ANY SURPRISES.
KEEP IT MOVING. WE'RE LATE AS IT IS...

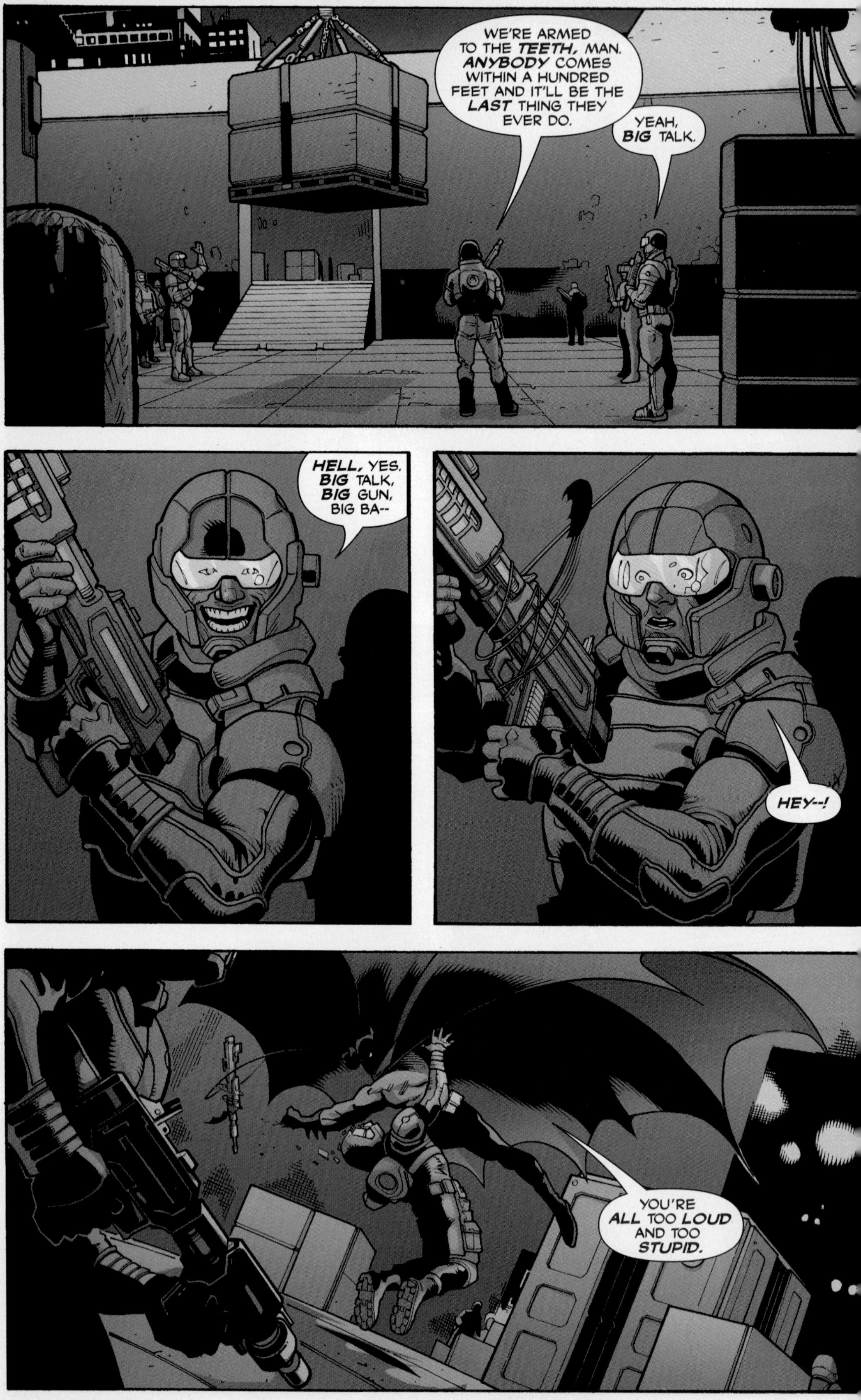
WE'RE ARMED TO THE TEETH, MAN. ANYBODY COMES WITHIN A HUNDRED FEET AND IT'LL BE THE LAST THING THEY EVER DO.
YEAH, BIG TALK.
HELL, YES. BIG TALK, BIG GUN, BIG BA--
HEY--!
YOU'RE ALL TOO LOUD AND TOO STUPID.

THE WORD WAS SOMETHING *BIG* WAS COMING IN.

THAT'S *ALL* WE COULD GET. IT WAS *BIG*.

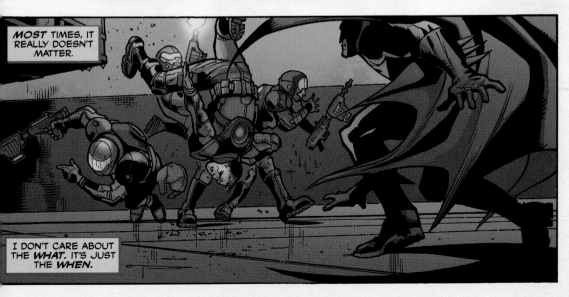

MOST TIMES, IT REALLY DOESN'T MATTER.

I DON'T CARE ABOUT THE *WHAT*. IT'S JUST THE *WHEN*.

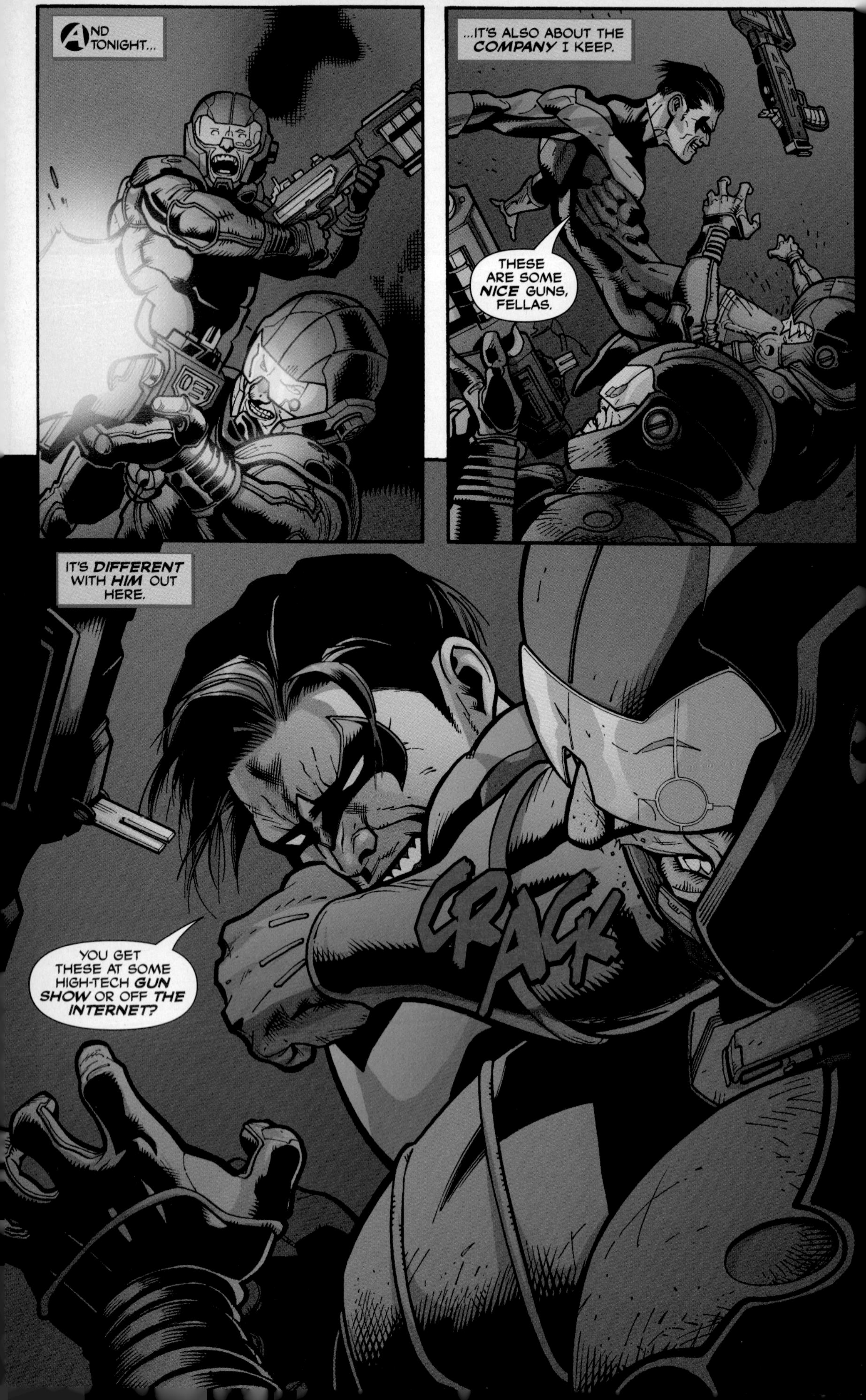
AND TONIGHT...
...IT'S ALSO ABOUT THE COMPANY I KEEP.
THESE ARE SOME NICE GUNS, FELLAS.
IT'S DIFFERENT WITH HIM OUT HERE.
CRACK
YOU GET THESE AT SOME HIGH-TECH GUN SHOW OR OFF THE INTERNET?

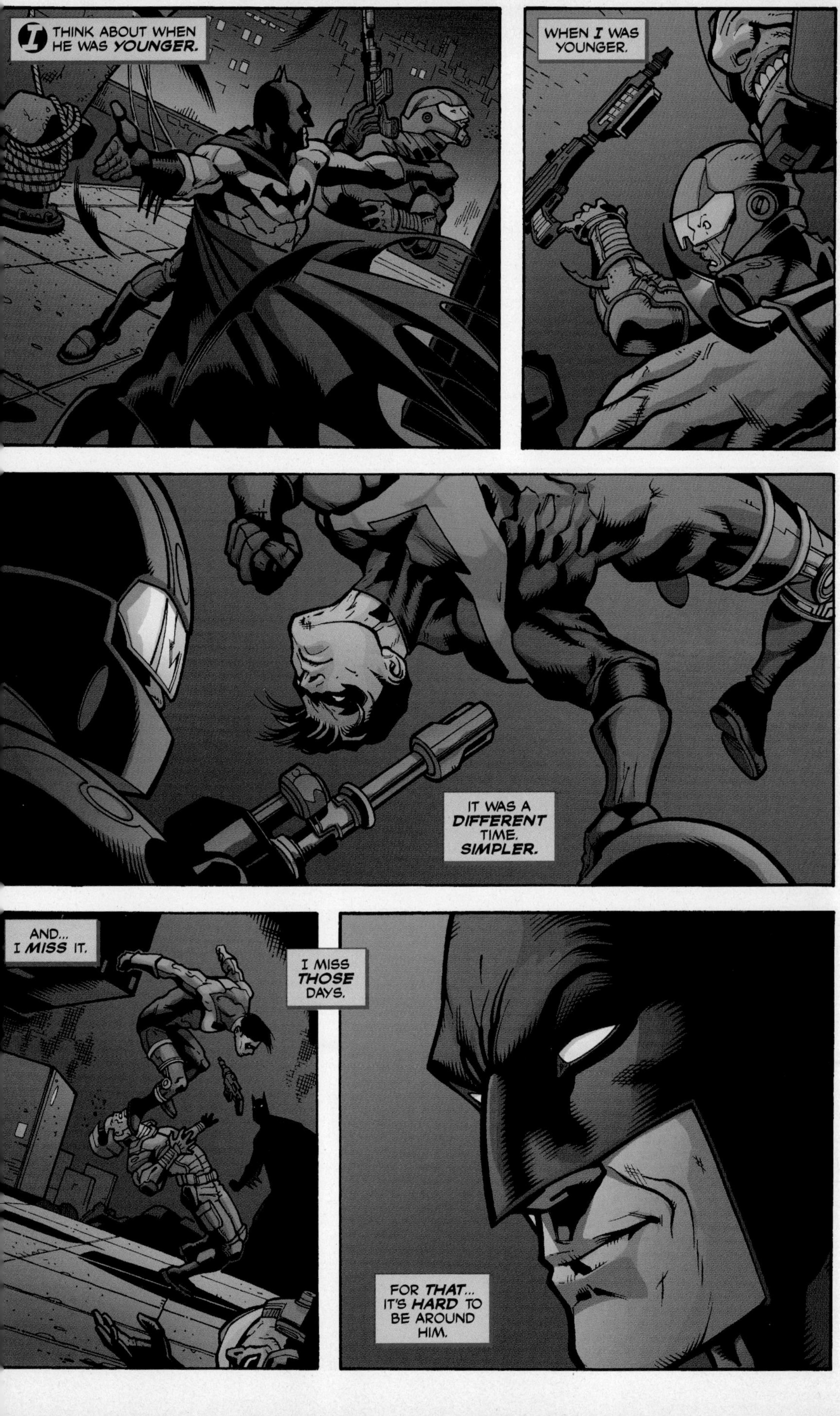
I THINK ABOUT WHEN HE WAS YOUNGER.
WHEN I WAS YOUNGER.
IT WAS A DIFFERENT TIME. SIMPLER.
AND... I MISS IT.
I MISS THOSE DAYS.
FOR THAT... IT'S HARD TO BE AROUND HIM.

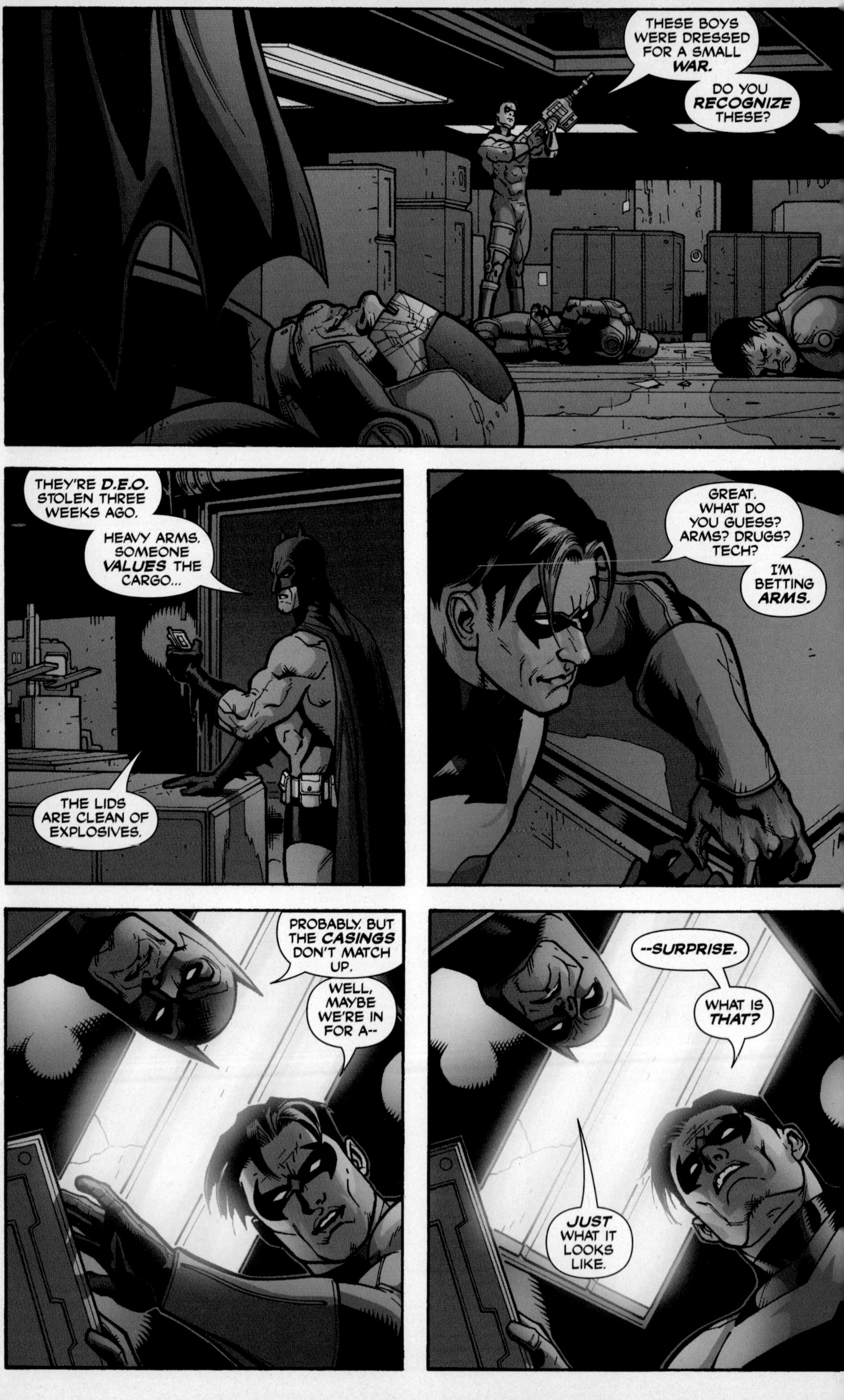

THESE BOYS WERE DRESSED FOR A SMALL WAR.
DO YOU RECOGNIZE THESE?
THEY'RE D.E.O. STOLEN THREE WEEKS AGO.
HEAVY ARMS. SOMEONE VALUES THE CARGO...
THE LIDS ARE CLEAN OF EXPLOSIVES.
GREAT. WHAT DO YOU GUESS? ARMS? DRUGS? TECH?
I'M BETTING ARMS.
PROBABLY. BUT THE CASINGS DON'T MATCH UP.
WELL, MAYBE WE'RE IN FOR A--
--SURPRISE.
WHAT IS THAT?
JUST WHAT IT LOOKS LIKE.

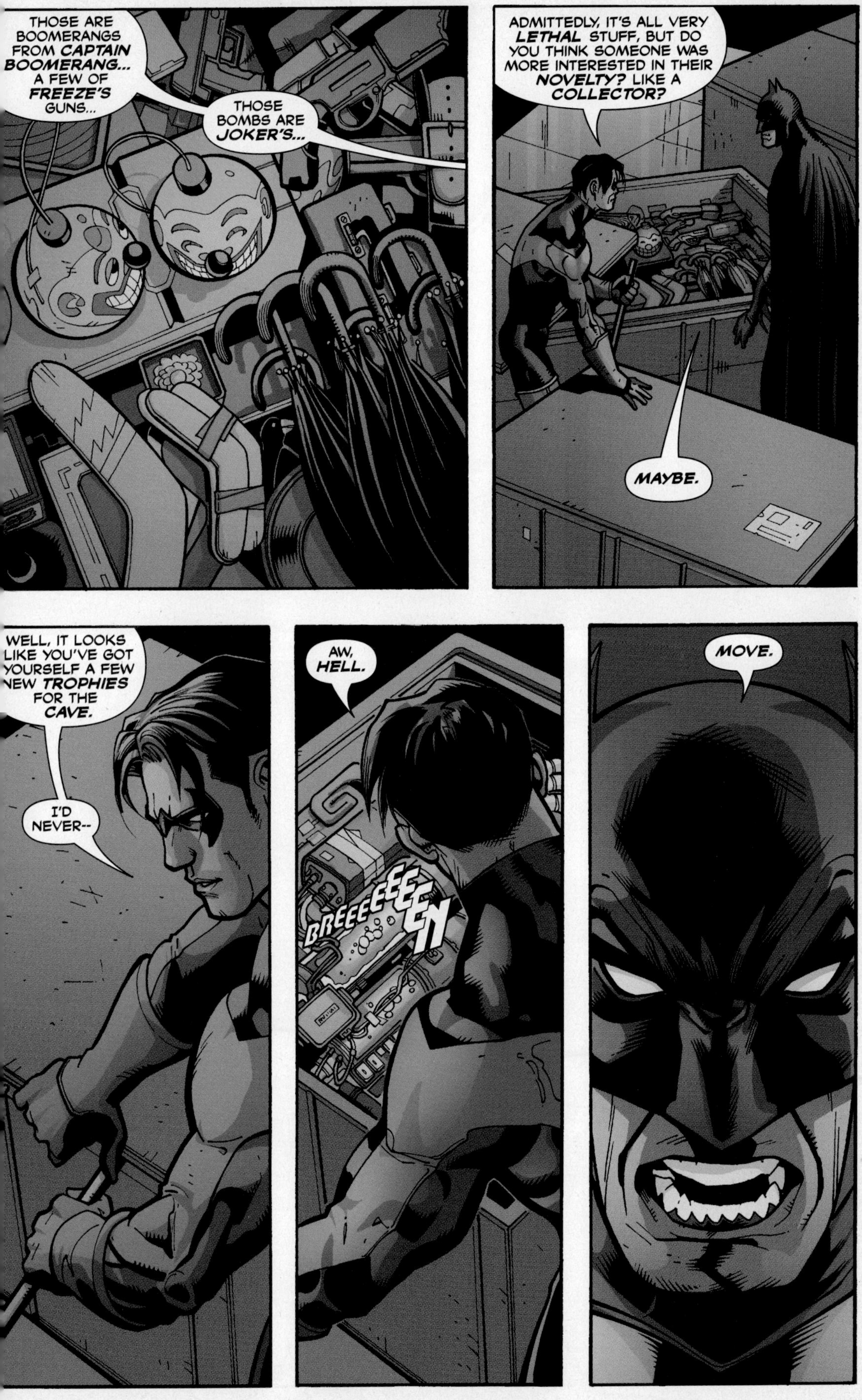

THOSE ARE BOOMERANGS FROM CAPTAIN BOOMERANG... A FEW OF FREEZE'S GUNS...
THOSE BOMBS ARE JOKER'S...
ADMITTEDLY, IT'S ALL VERY LETHAL STUFF, BUT DO YOU THINK SOMEONE WAS MORE INTERESTED IN THEIR NOVELTY? LIKE A COLLECTOR?
MAYBE.
WELL, IT LOOKS LIKE YOU'VE GOT YOURSELF A FEW NEW TROPHIES FOR THE CAVE.
I'D NEVER--
AW, HELL.
BREEEEEEEEN
MOVE.

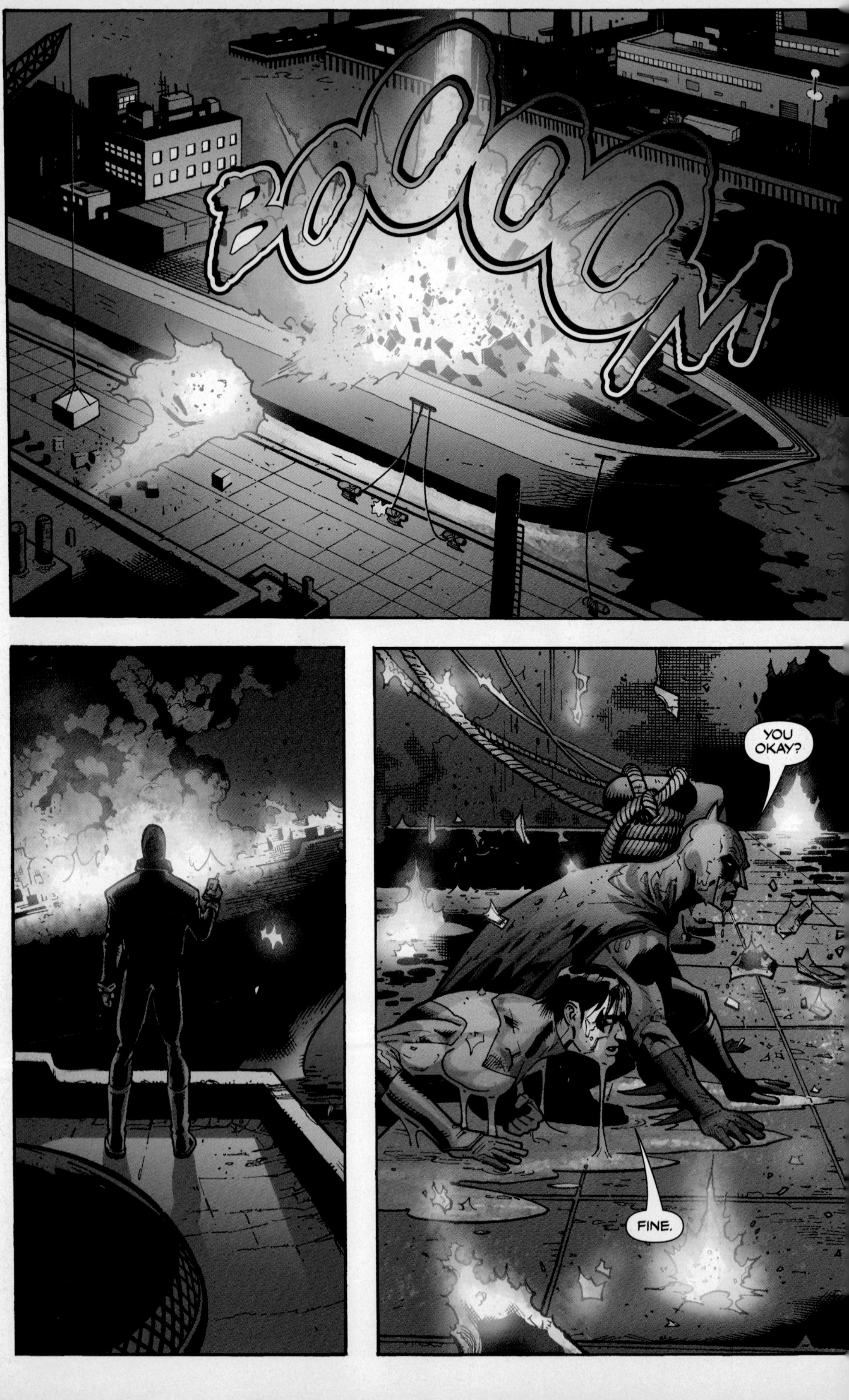
BOOOOOM
YOU OKAY?
FINE.

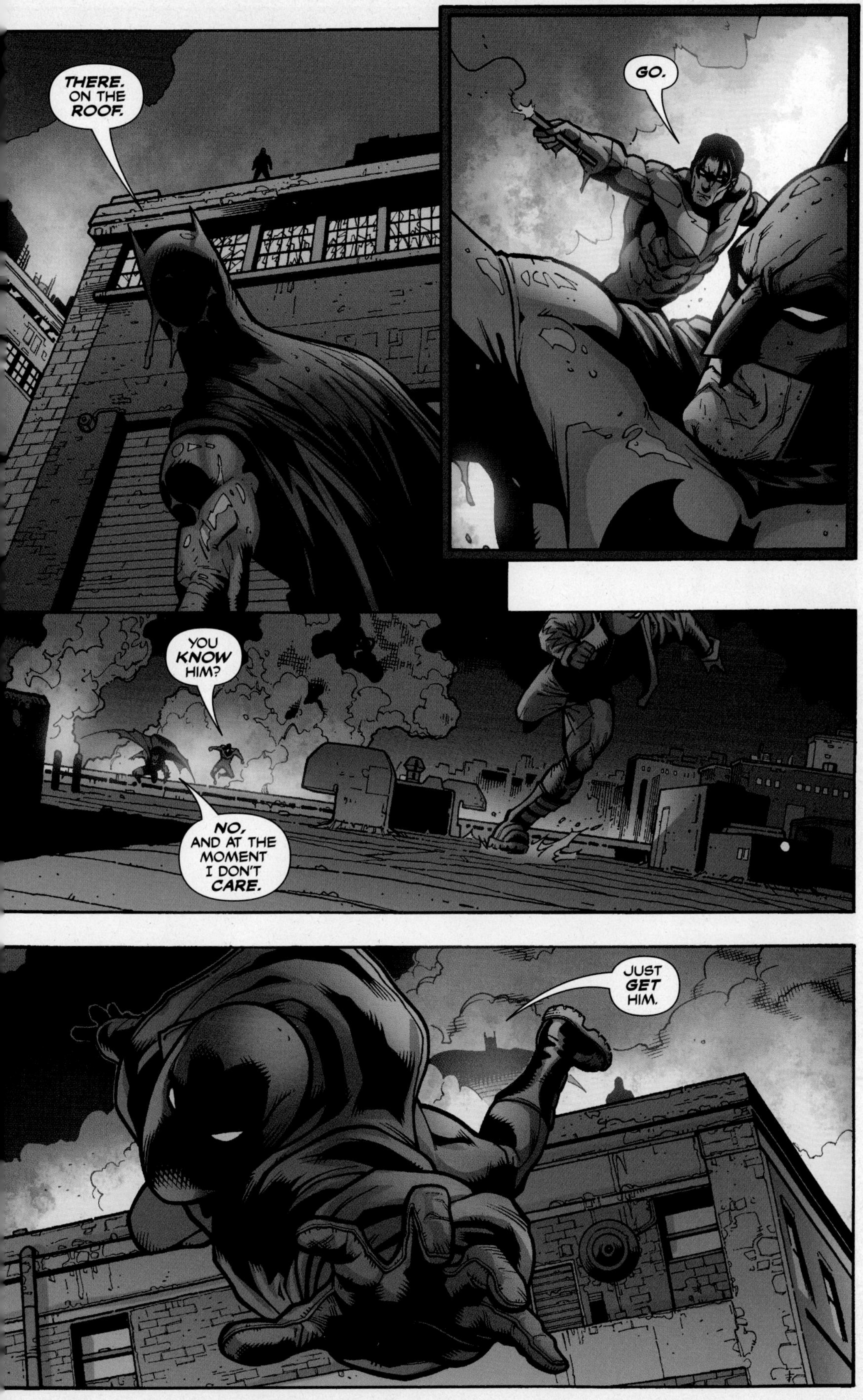
THERE. ON THE ROOF.
GO.
YOU KNOW HIM?
NO, AND AT THE MOMENT I DON'T CARE.
JUST GET HIM.

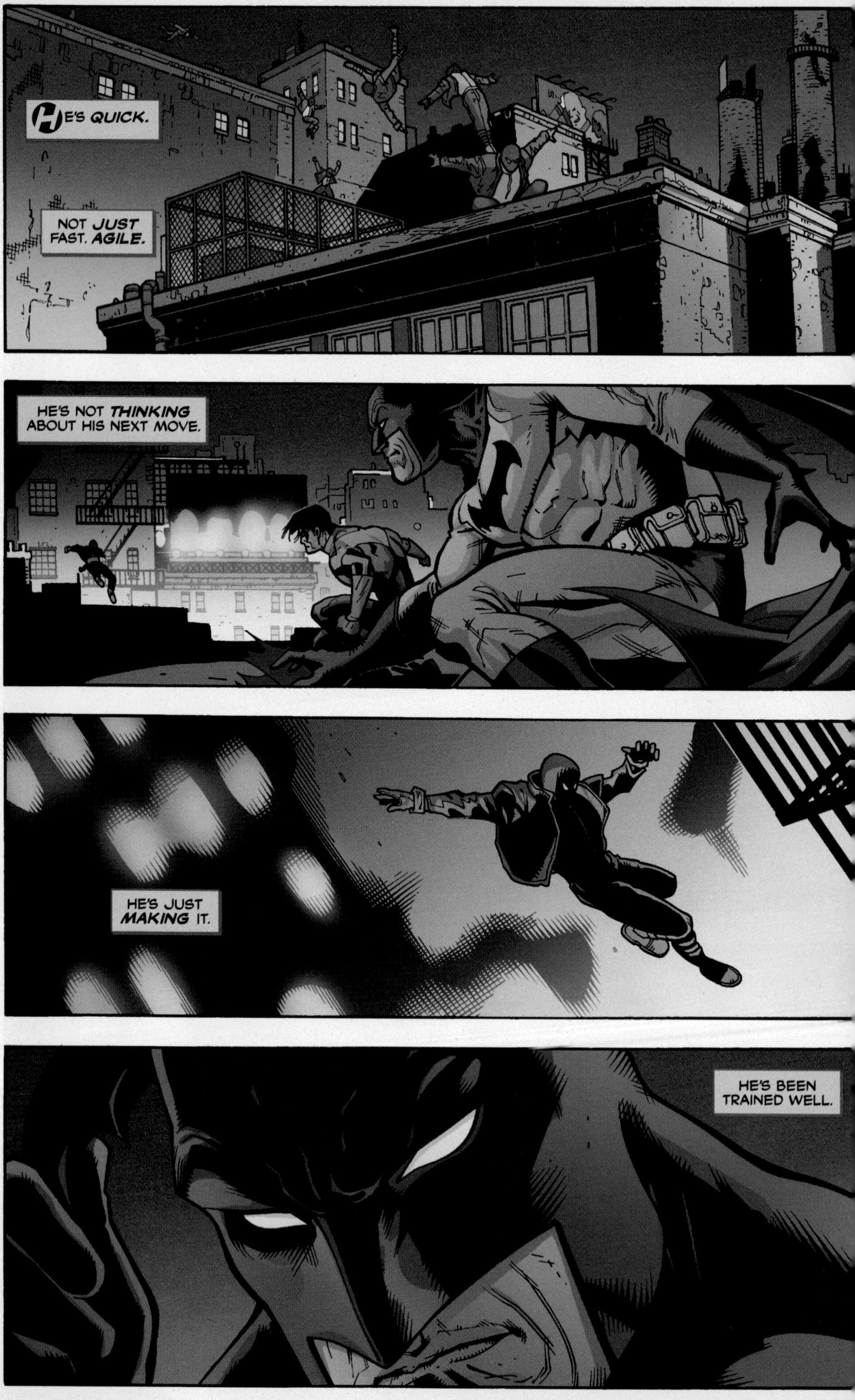
HE'S QUICK.
NOT JUST FAST. AGILE.
HE'S NOT THINKING ABOUT HIS NEXT MOVE.
HE'S JUST MAKING IT.
HE'S BEEN TRAINED WELL.

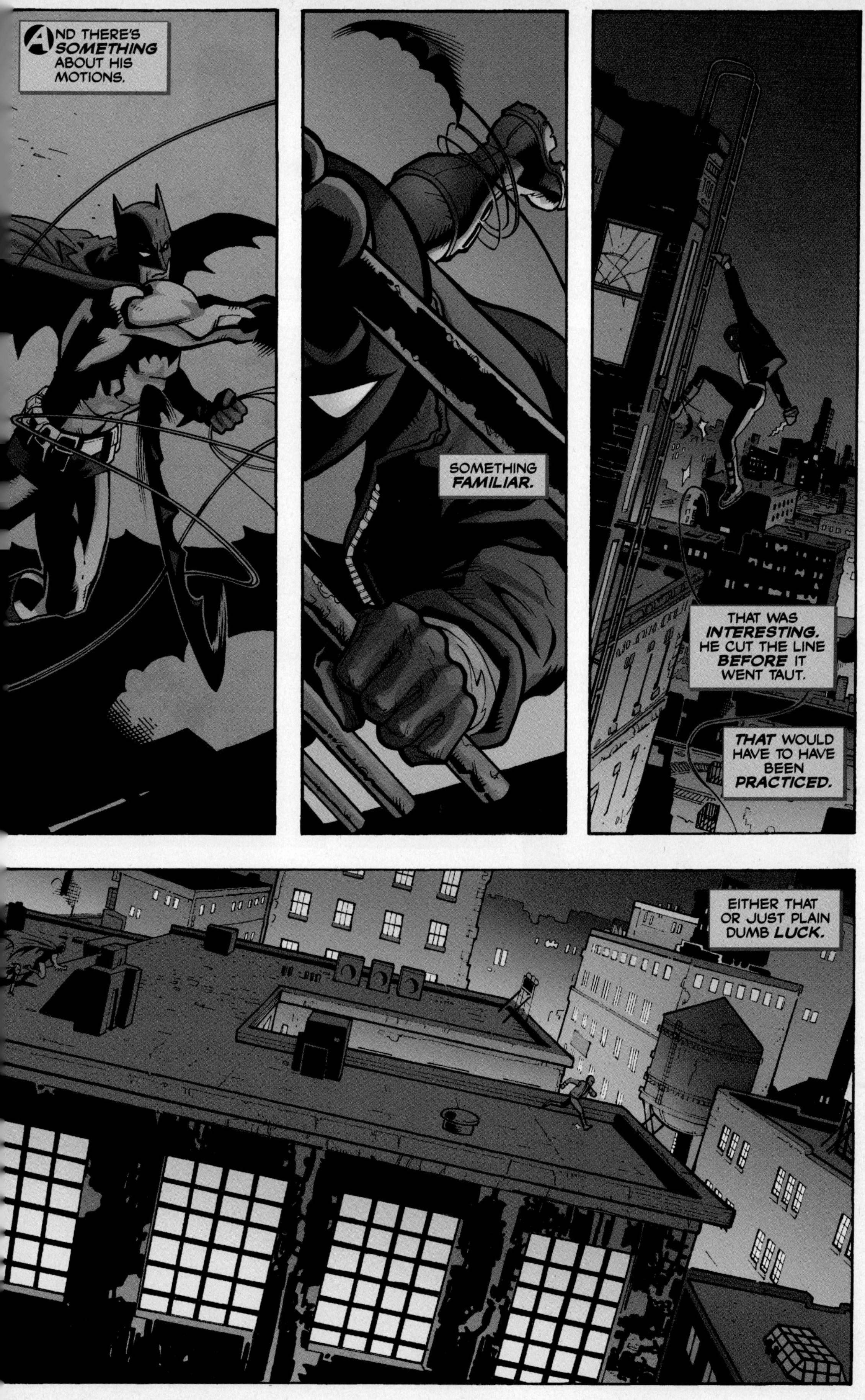
AND THERE'S SOMETHING ABOUT HIS MOTIONS.
SOMETHING FAMILIAR.
THAT WAS INTERESTING. HE CUT THE LINE BEFORE IT WENT TAUT.
THAT WOULD HAVE TO HAVE BEEN PRACTICED.
EITHER THAT OR JUST PLAIN DUMB LUCK.

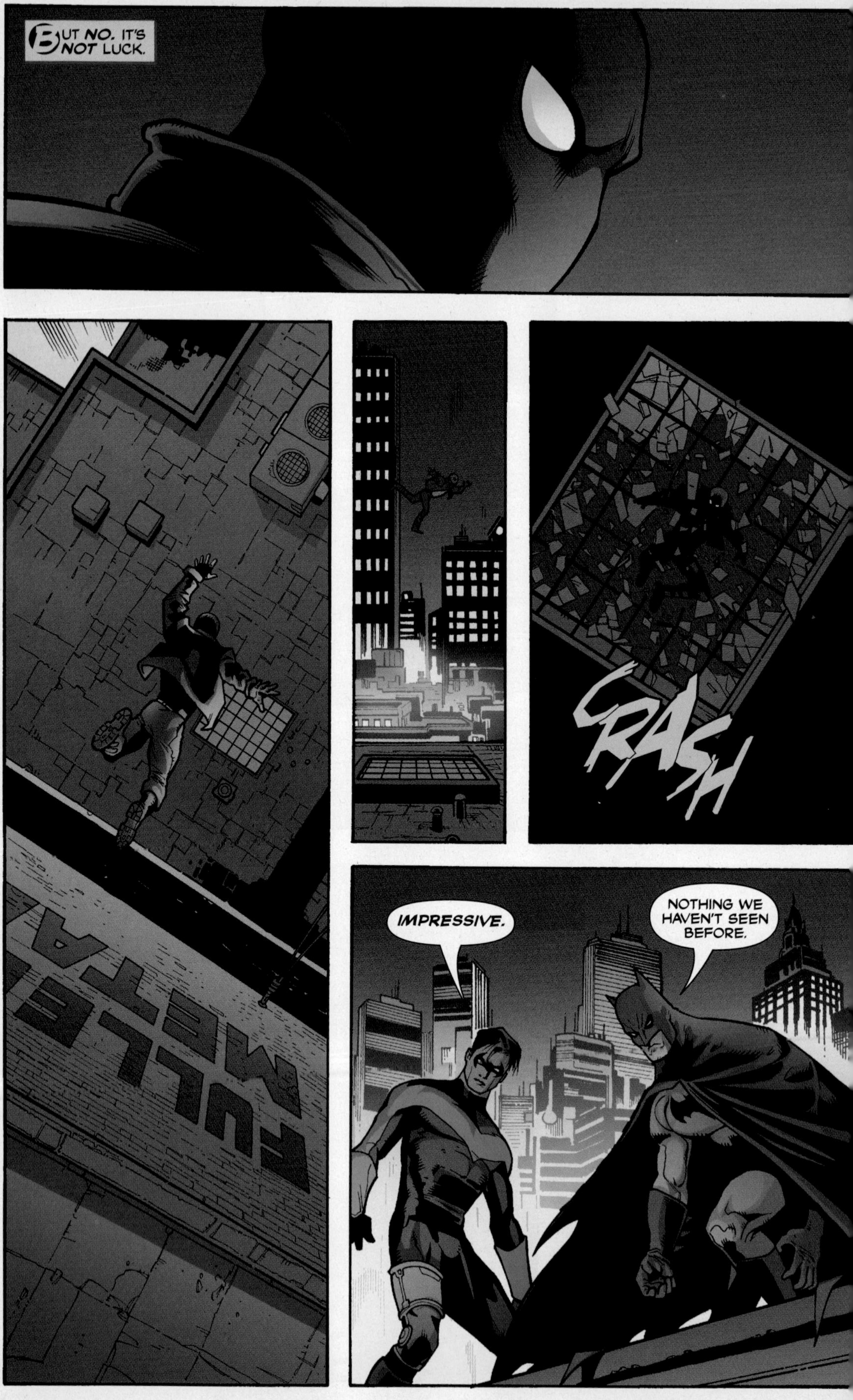
BUT NO. IT'S NOT LUCK.
CRASH
IMPRESSIVE.
NOTHING WE HAVEN'T SEEN BEFORE.

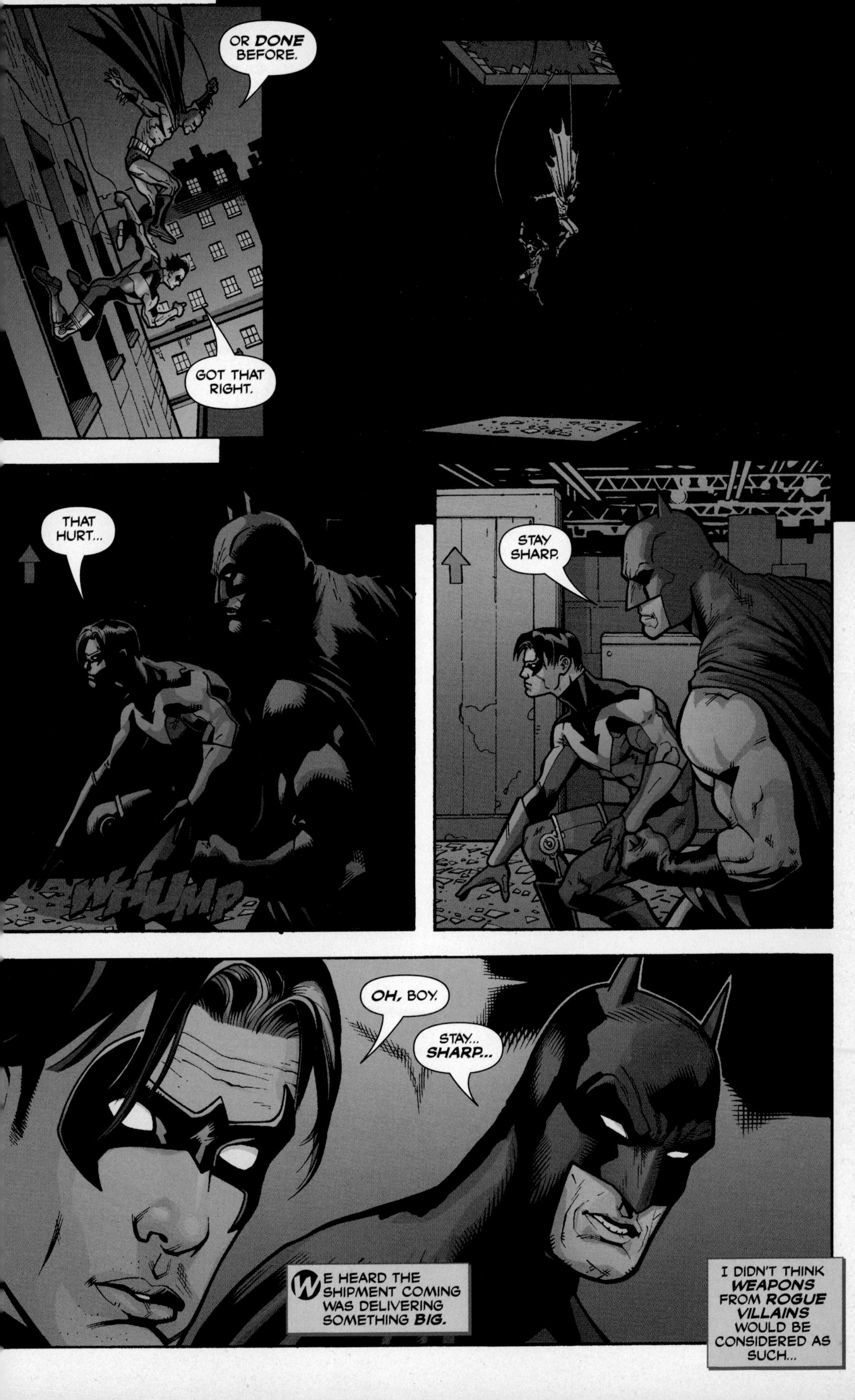

OR *DONE* BEFORE.
GOT THAT RIGHT.
THAT HURT...
WHUMP
STAY SHARP.
OH, BOY.
STAY... *SHARP...*
WE HEARD THE SHIPMENT COMING WAS DELIVERING SOMETHING *BIG.*
I DIDN'T THINK *WEAPONS* FROM *ROGUE VILLAINS* WOULD BE CONSIDERED AS SUCH...

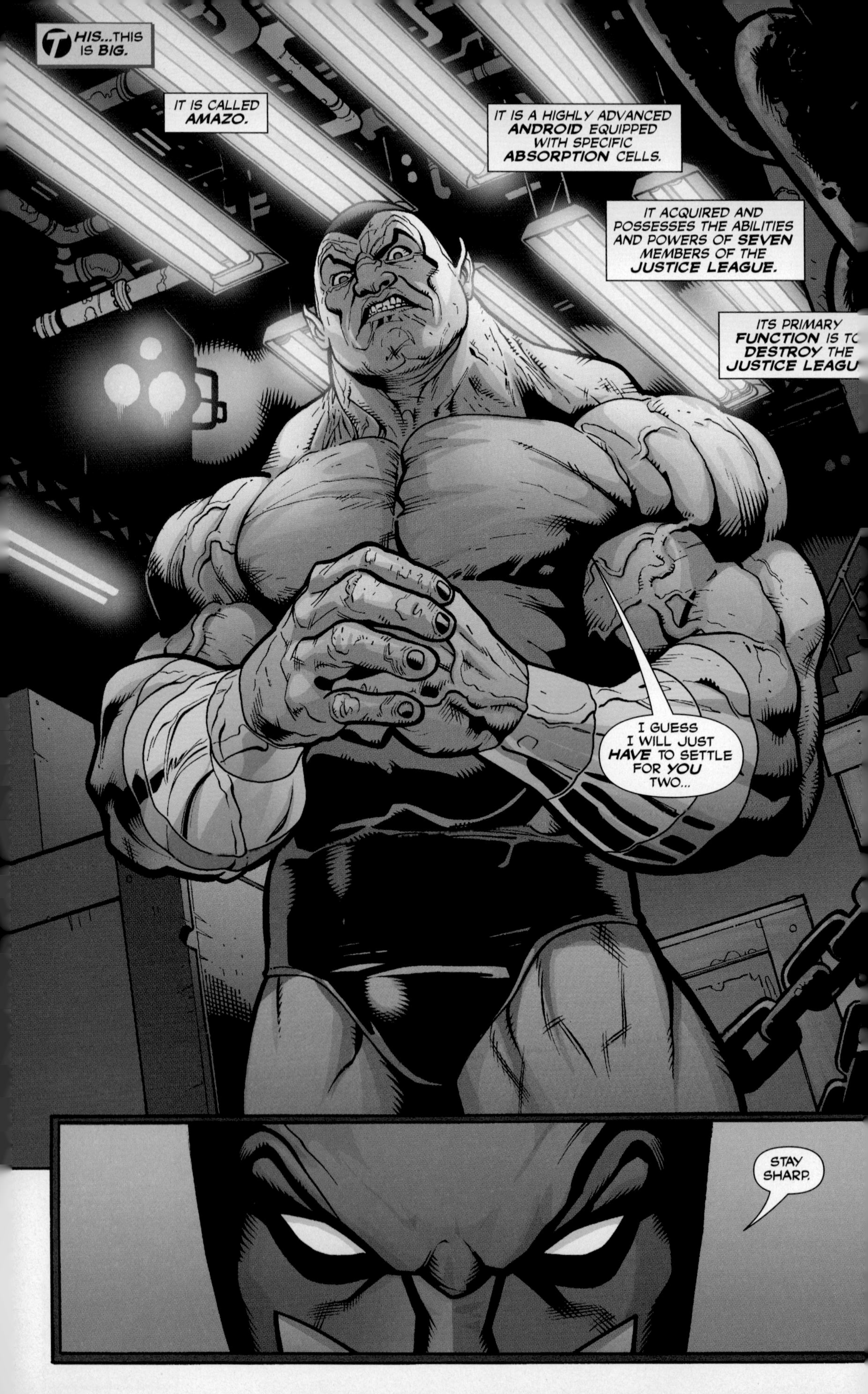
THIS...THIS IS BIG.
IT IS CALLED AMAZO.
IT IS A HIGHLY ADVANCED ANDROID EQUIPPED WITH SPECIFIC ABSORPTION CELLS.
IT ACQUIRED AND POSSESSES THE ABILITIES AND POWERS OF SEVEN MEMBERS OF THE JUSTICE LEAGUE.
ITS PRIMARY FUNCTION IS T DESTROY THE JUSTICE LEAGU
I GUESS I WILL JUST HAVE TO SETTLE FOR YOU TWO...
STAY SHARP.

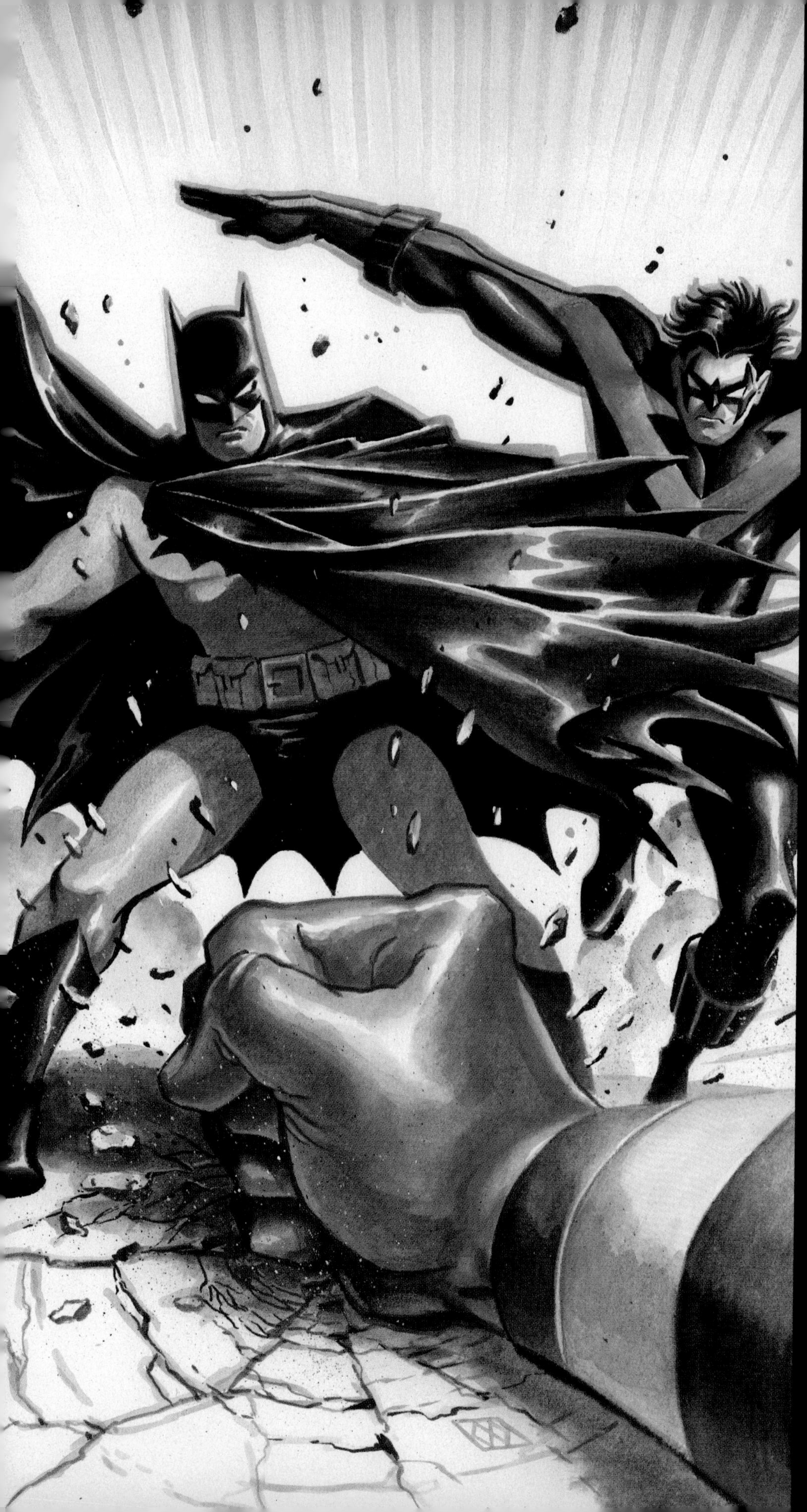

BATMAN #637 • ART BY MATT WAGNER

PART 3

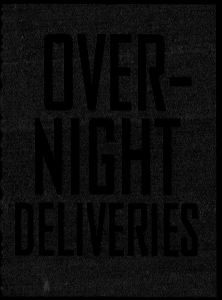

OVER-NIGHT DELIVERIES

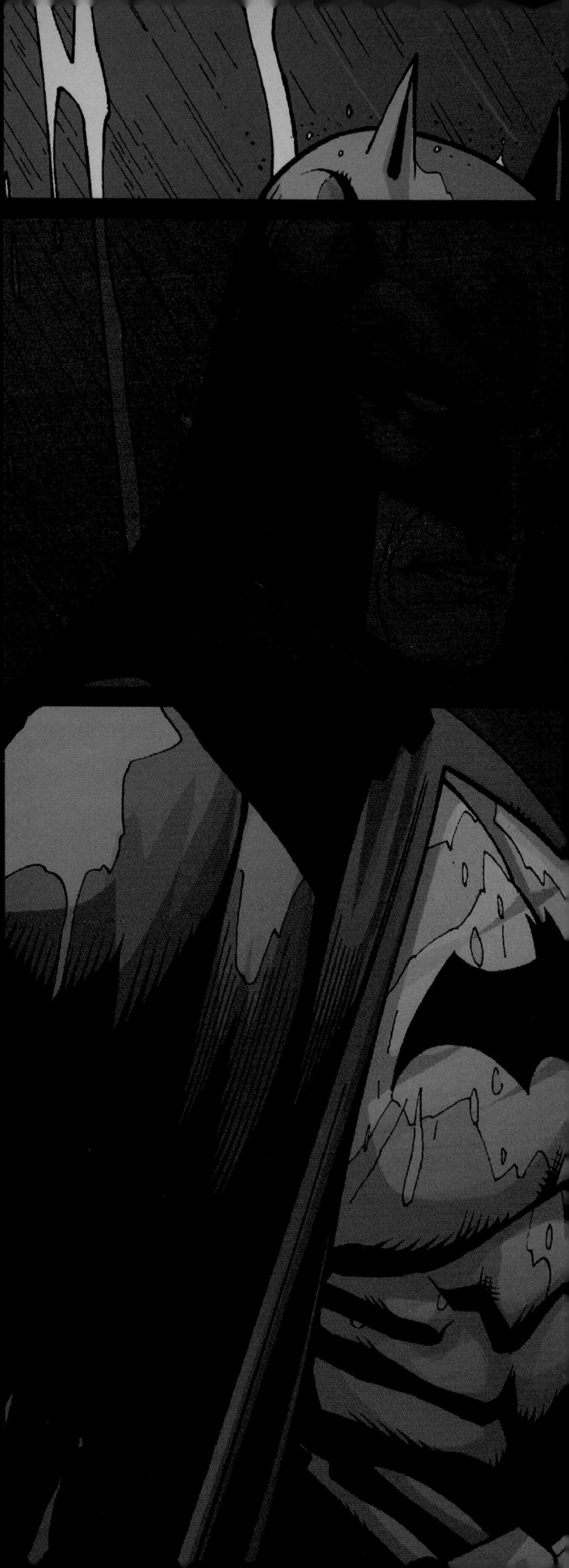

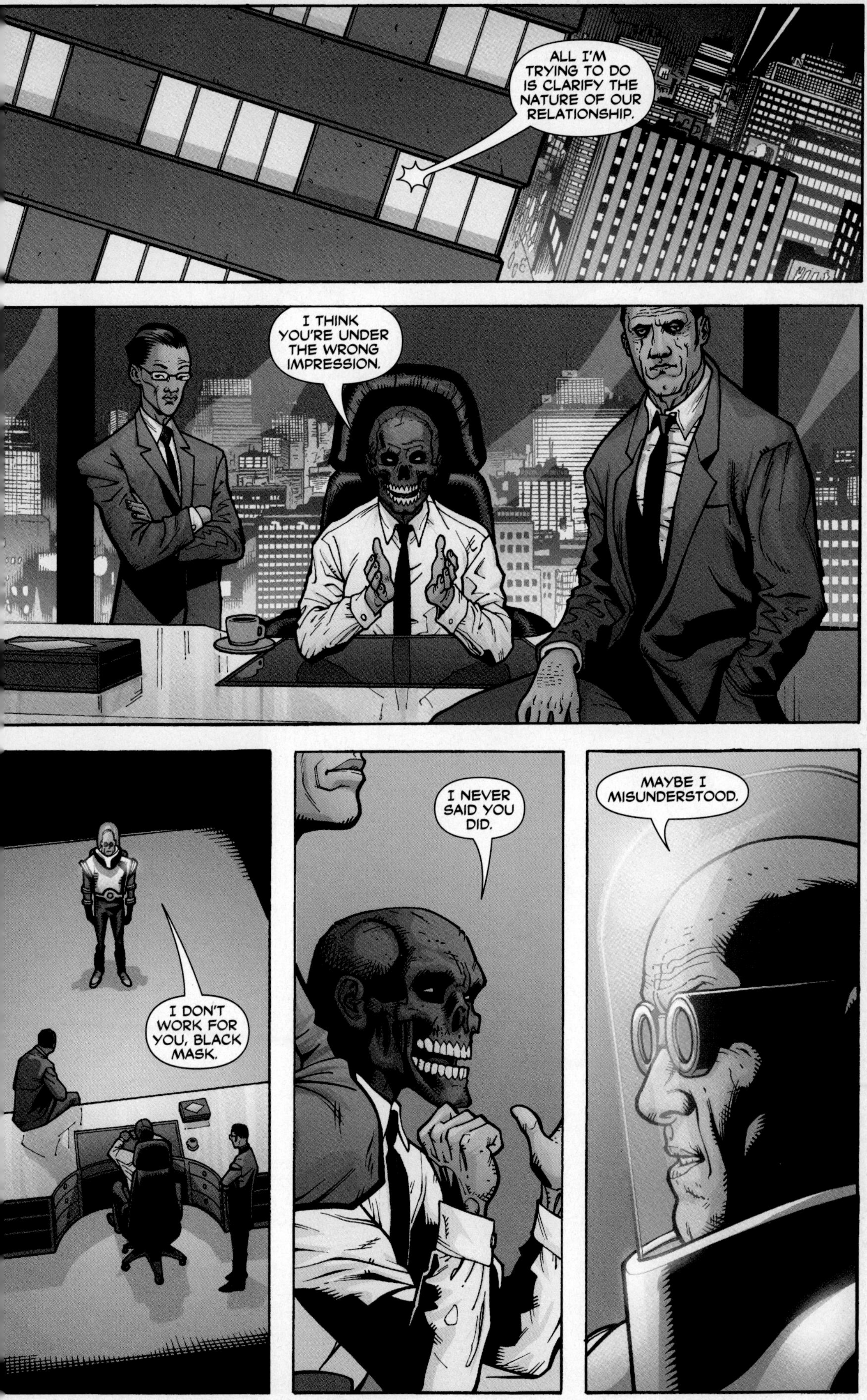
ALL I'M TRYING TO DO IS CLARIFY THE NATURE OF OUR RELATIONSHIP.
I THINK YOU'RE UNDER THE WRONG IMPRESSION.
I DON'T WORK FOR YOU, BLACK MASK.
I NEVER SAID YOU DID.
MAYBE I MISUNDERSTOOD.

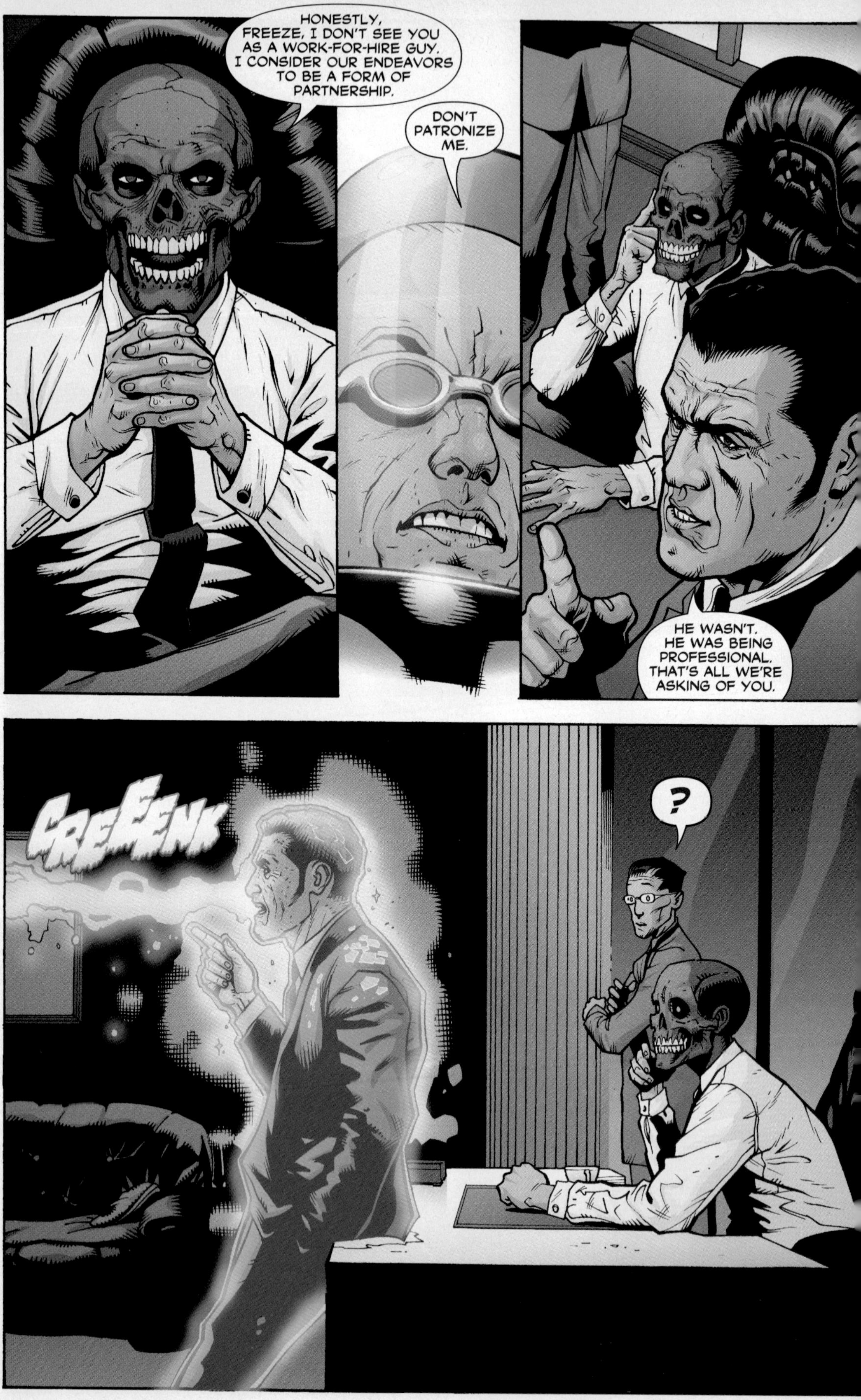
HONESTLY, FREEZE, I DON'T SEE YOU AS A WORK-FOR-HIRE GUY. I CONSIDER OUR ENDEAVORS TO BE A FORM OF PARTNERSHIP.
DON'T PATRONIZE ME.
HE WASN'T. HE WAS BEING PROFESSIONAL. THAT'S ALL WE'RE ASKING OF YOU.
CREEENK
?

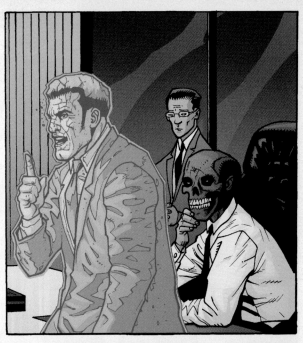

CRACK

I GET IT. YOU'RE UNPREDICTABLE. I CAN WORK WITH THAT.

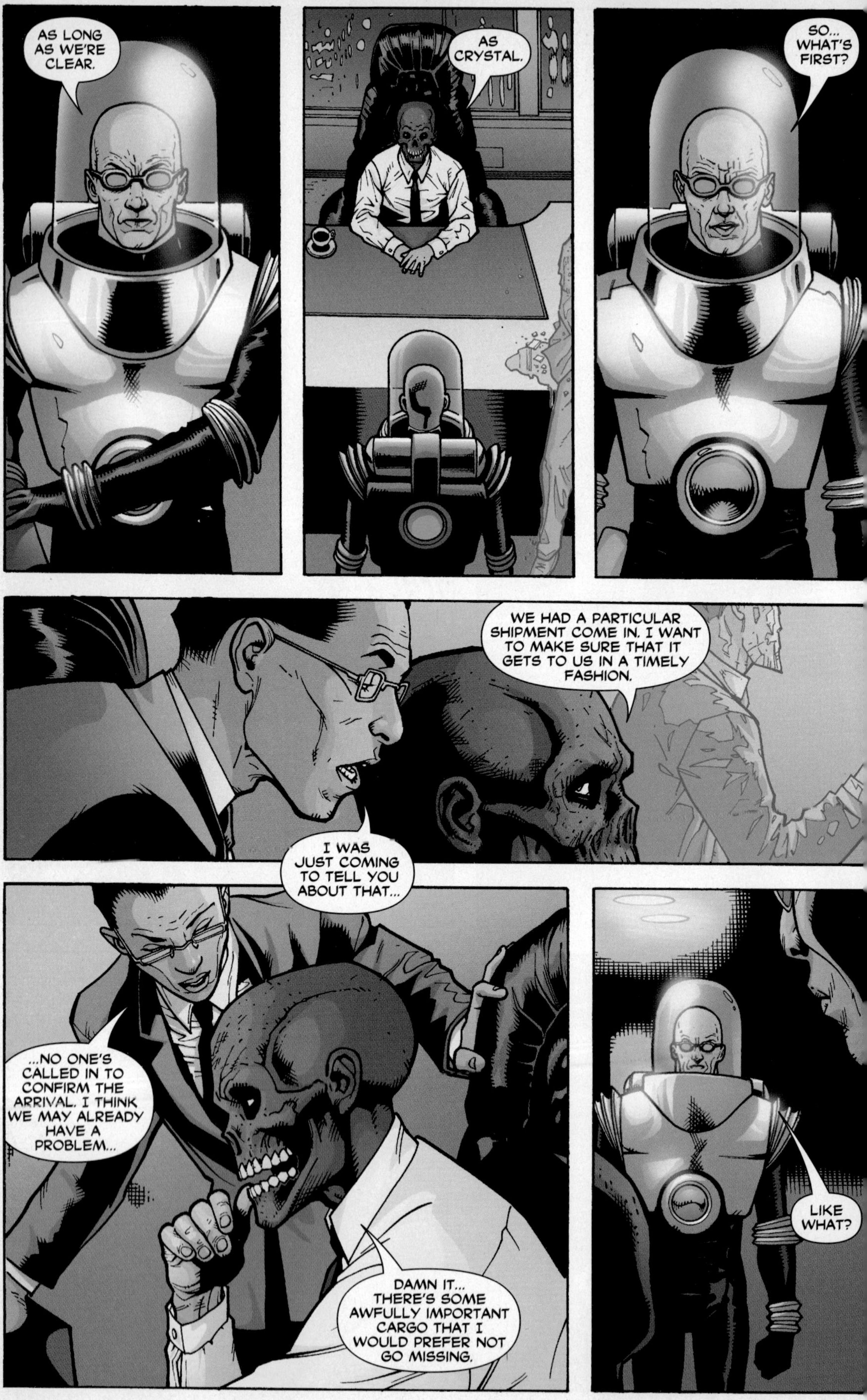

AS LONG AS WE'RE CLEAR.
AS CRYSTAL.
SO... WHAT'S FIRST?
WE HAD A PARTICULAR SHIPMENT COME IN. I WANT TO MAKE SURE THAT IT GETS TO US IN A TIMELY FASHION.
I WAS JUST COMING TO TELL YOU ABOUT THAT...
...NO ONE'S CALLED IN TO CONFIRM THE ARRIVAL. I THINK WE MAY ALREADY HAVE A PROBLEM...
DAMN IT... THERE'S SOME AWFULLY IMPORTANT CARGO THAT I WOULD PREFER NOT GO MISSING.
LIKE WHAT?

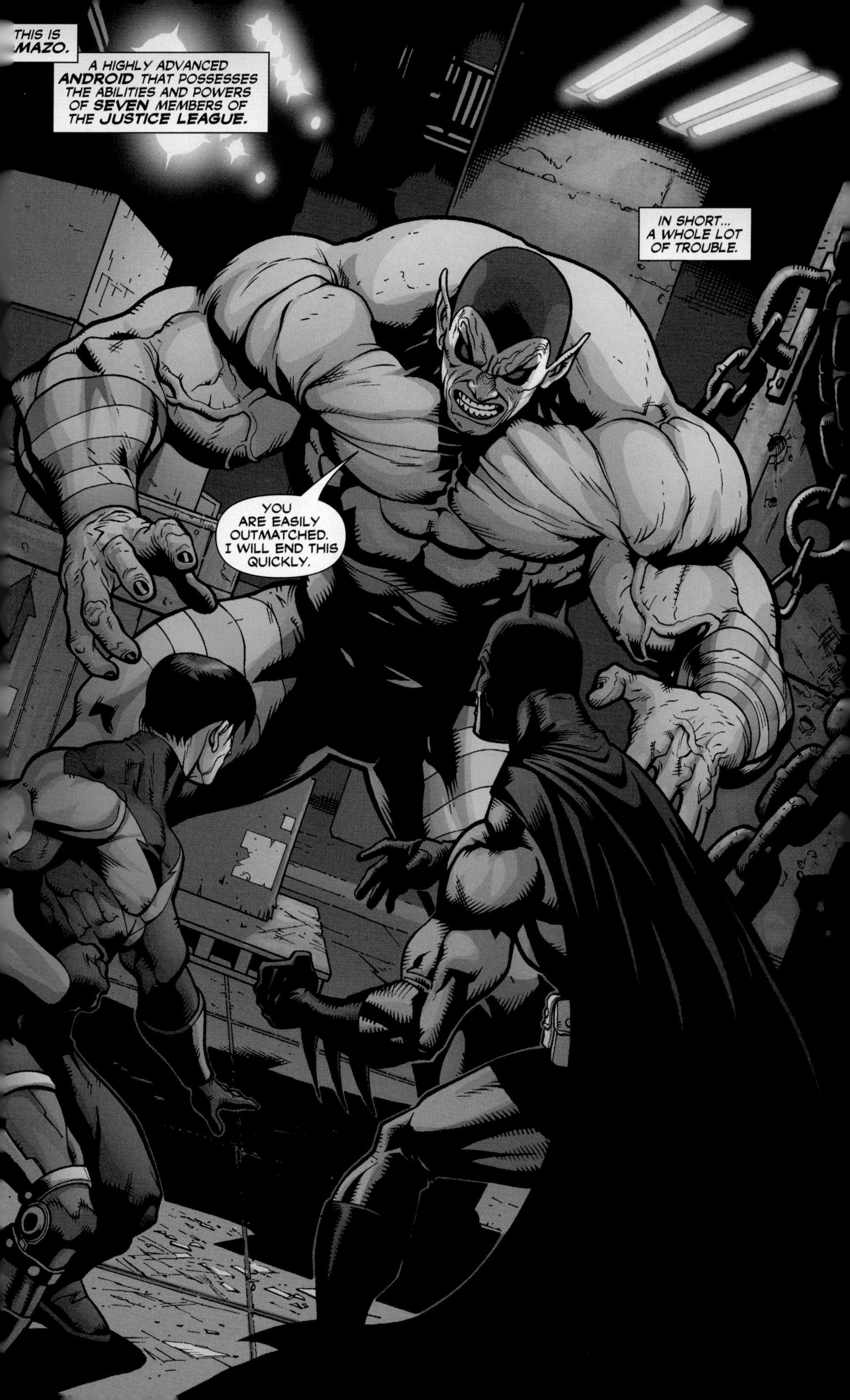
THIS IS AMAZO.
A HIGHLY ADVANCED ANDROID THAT POSSESSES THE ABILITIES AND POWERS OF SEVEN MEMBERS OF THE JUSTICE LEAGUE.
IN SHORT... A WHOLE LOT OF TROUBLE.
YOU ARE EASILY OUTMATCHED. I WILL END THIS QUICKLY.

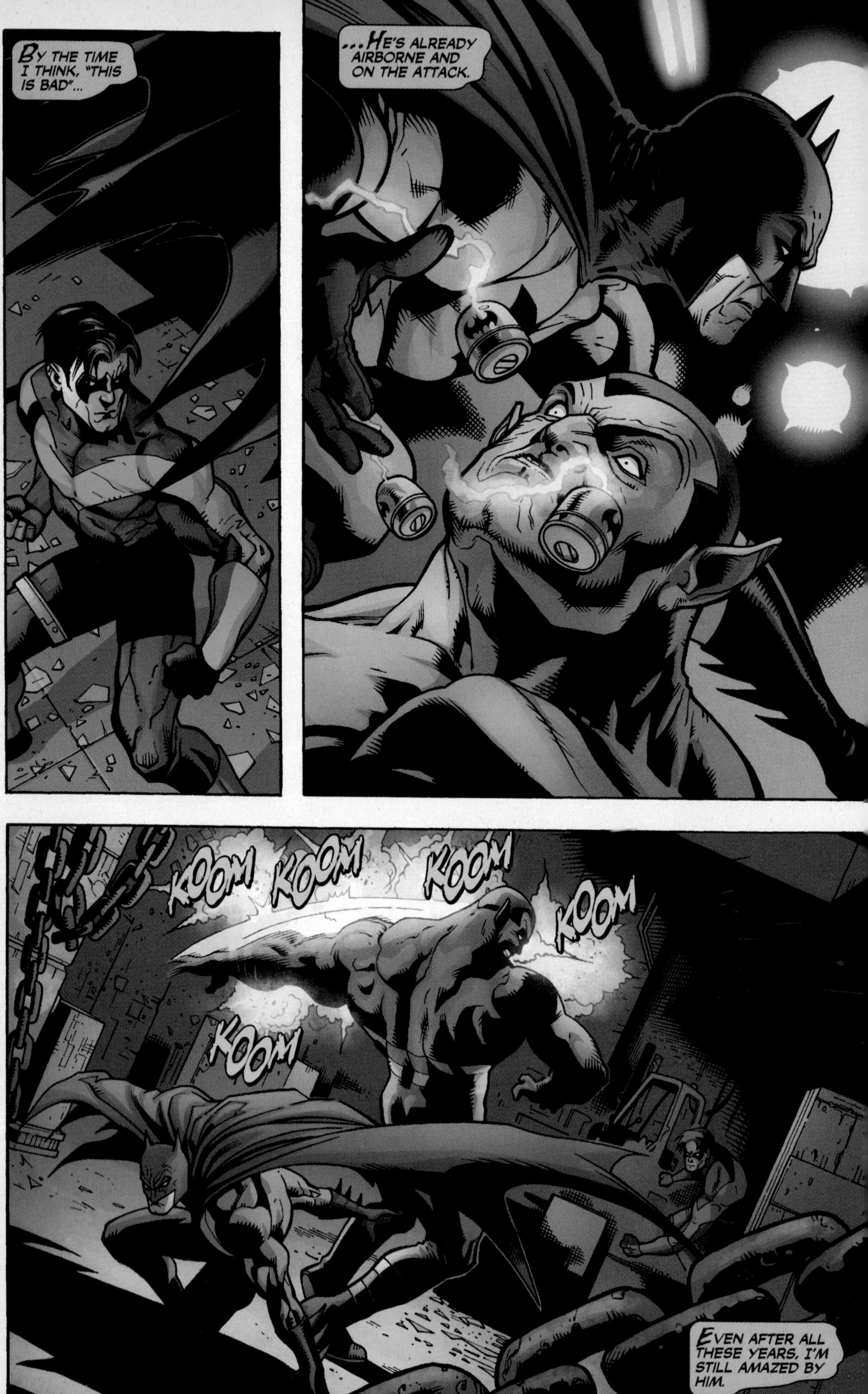
BY THE TIME I THINK, "THIS IS BAD"...
...HE'S ALREADY AIRBORNE AND ON THE ATTACK.
KOOM KOOM KOOM KOOM KOOM
EVEN AFTER ALL THESE YEARS, I'M STILL AMAZED BY HIM.

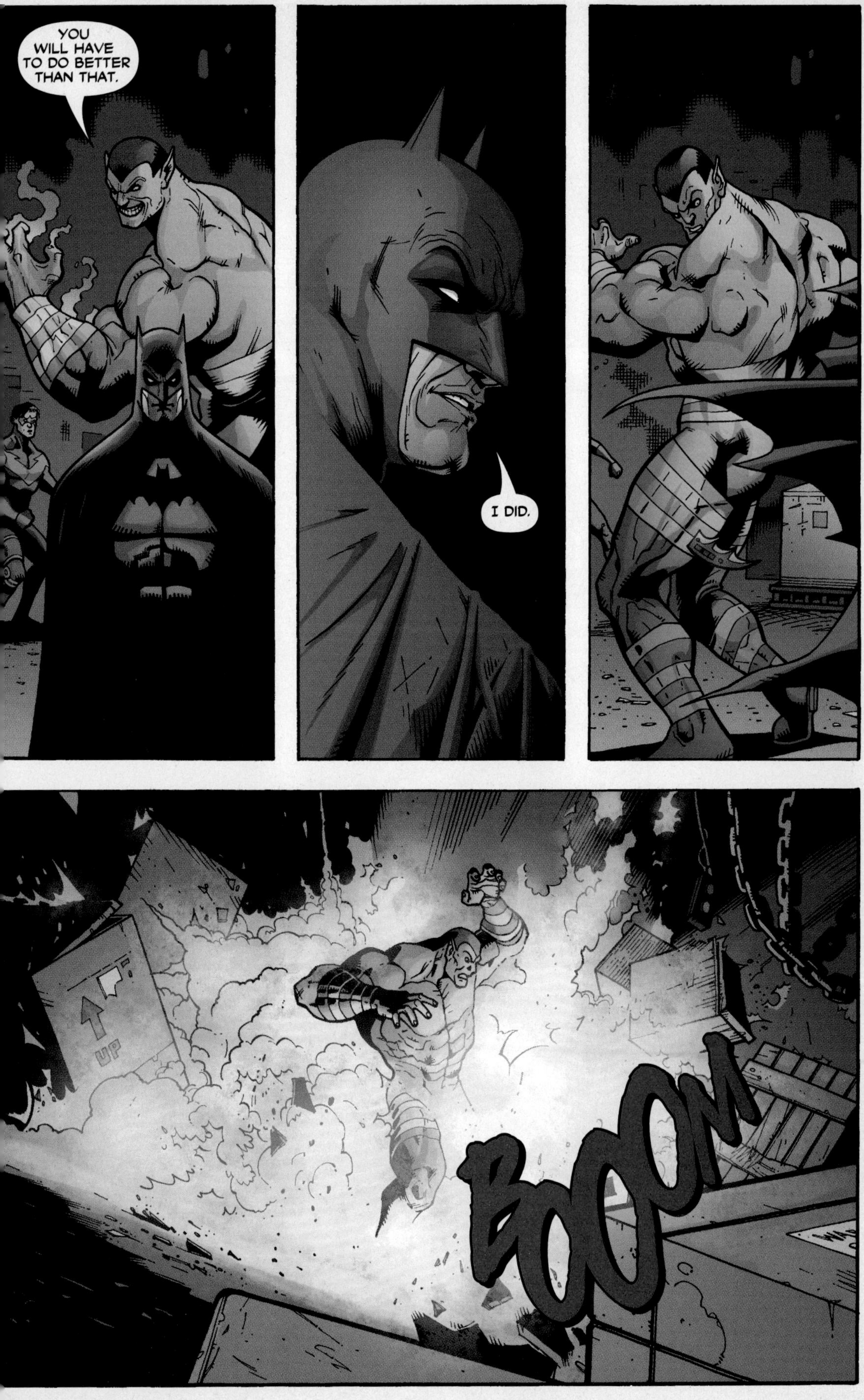
YOU WILL HAVE TO DO BETTER THAN THAT.
I DID.
UP
BOOOM

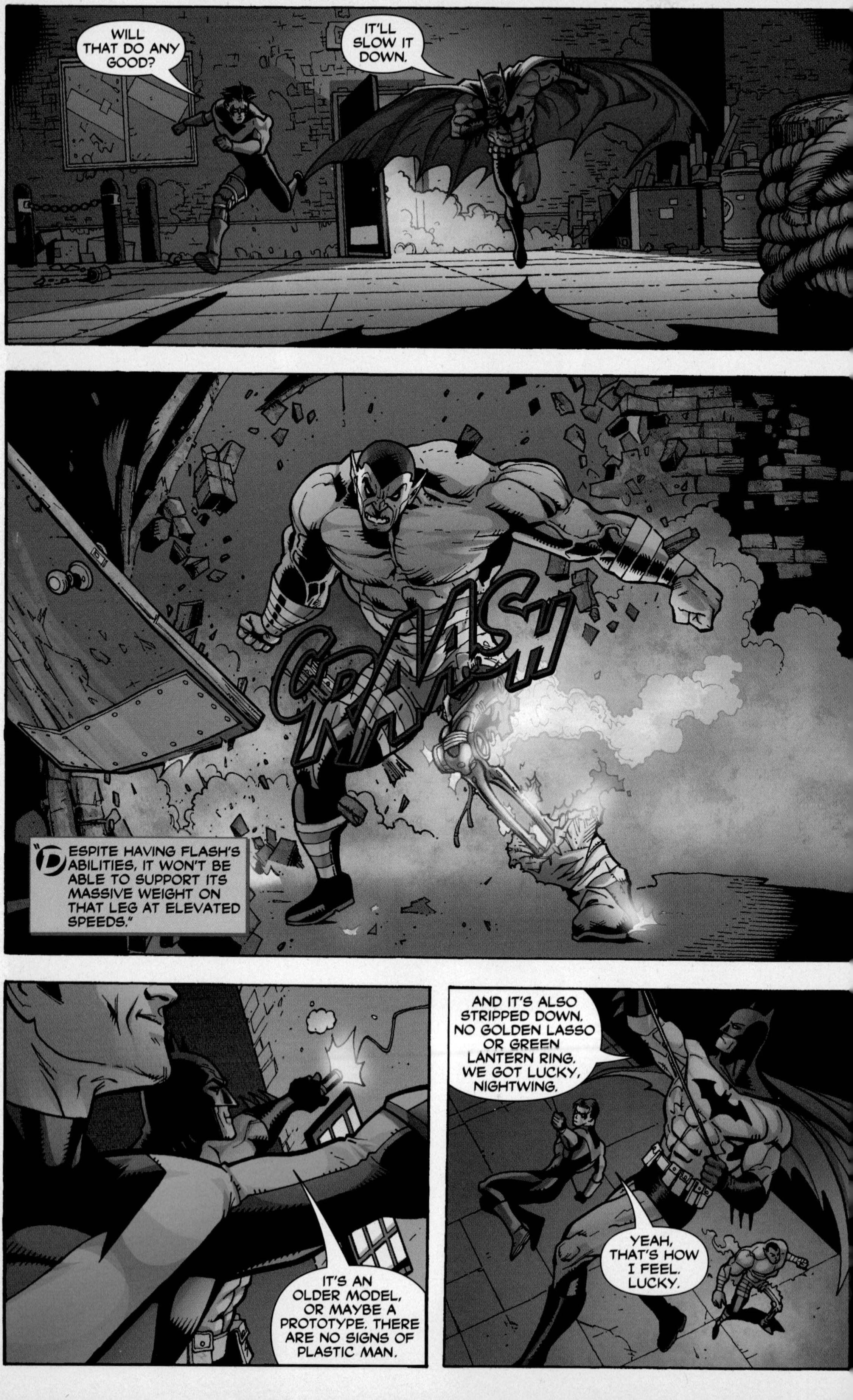
WILL THAT DO ANY GOOD?
IT'LL SLOW IT DOWN.
CRASH
"DESPITE HAVING FLASH'S ABILITIES, IT WON'T BE ABLE TO SUPPORT ITS MASSIVE WEIGHT ON THAT LEG AT ELEVATED SPEEDS."
IT'S AN OLDER MODEL, OR MAYBE A PROTOTYPE. THERE ARE NO SIGNS OF PLASTIC MAN.
AND IT'S ALSO STRIPPED DOWN. NO GOLDEN LASSO OR GREEN LANTERN RING. WE GOT LUCKY, NIGHTWING.
YEAH, THAT'S HOW I FEEL. LUCKY.

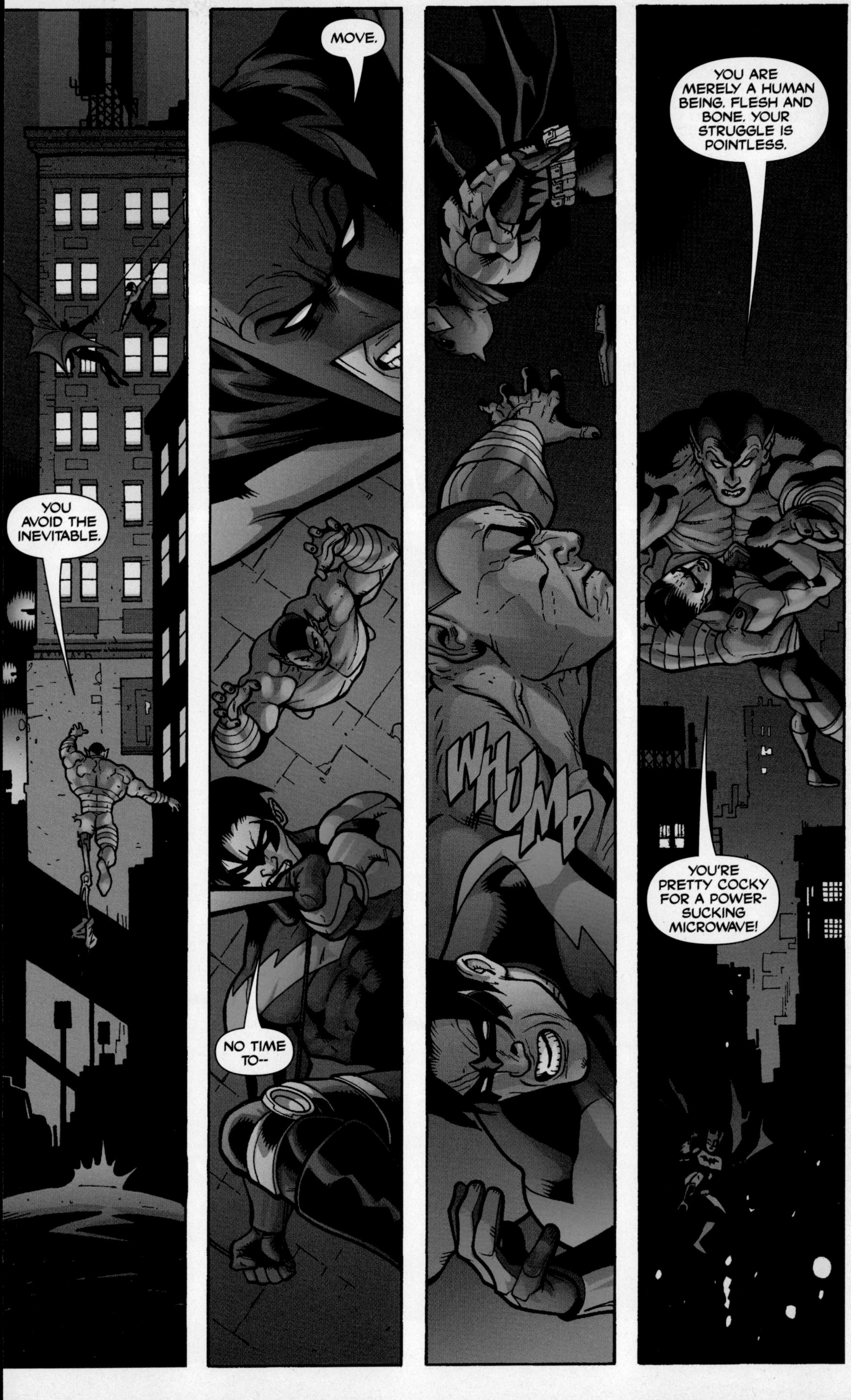
YOU AVOID THE INEVITABLE.
MOVE.
NO TIME TO--
WHUMP
YOU ARE MERELY A HUMAN BEING. FLESH AND BONE. YOUR STRUGGLE IS POINTLESS.
YOU'RE PRETTY COCKY FOR A POWER-SUCKING MICROWAVE!

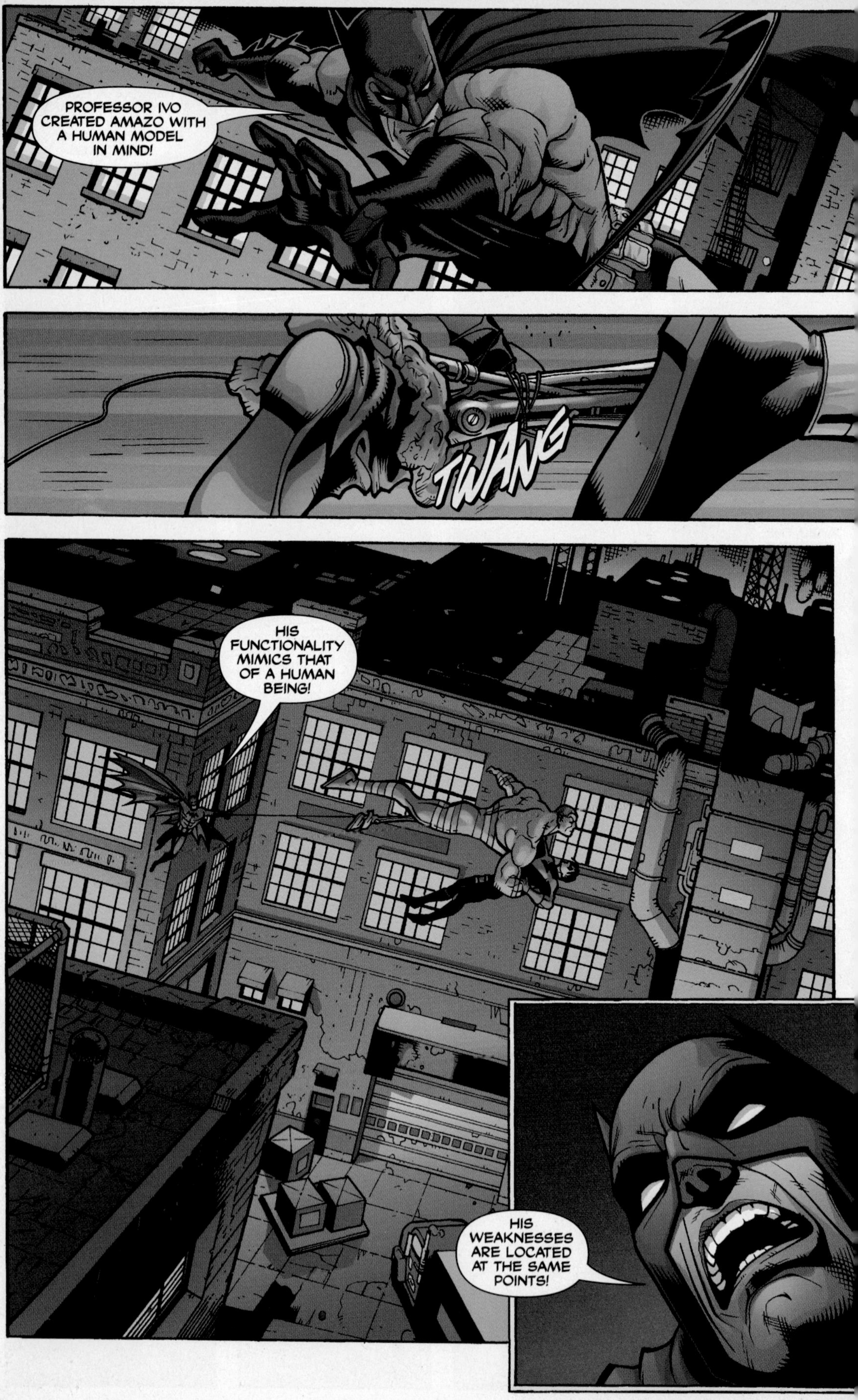
PROFESSOR IVO CREATED AMAZO WITH A HUMAN MODEL IN MIND!
TWANG
HIS FUNCTIONALITY MIMICS THAT OF A HUMAN BEING!
HIS WEAKNESSES ARE LOCATED AT THE SAME POINTS!

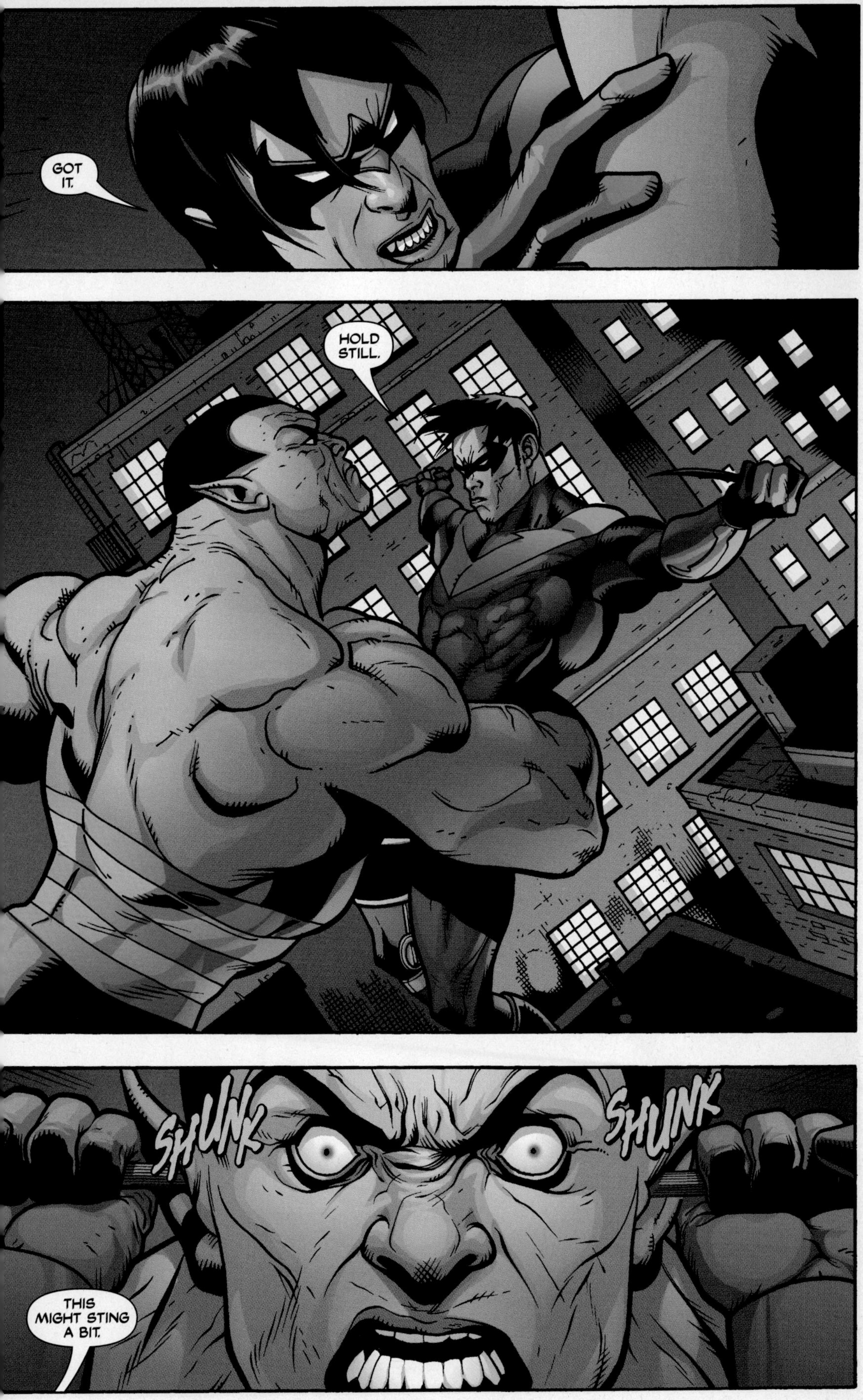

GOT IT.
HOLD STILL.
SHUNK
SHUNK
THIS MIGHT STING A BIT.

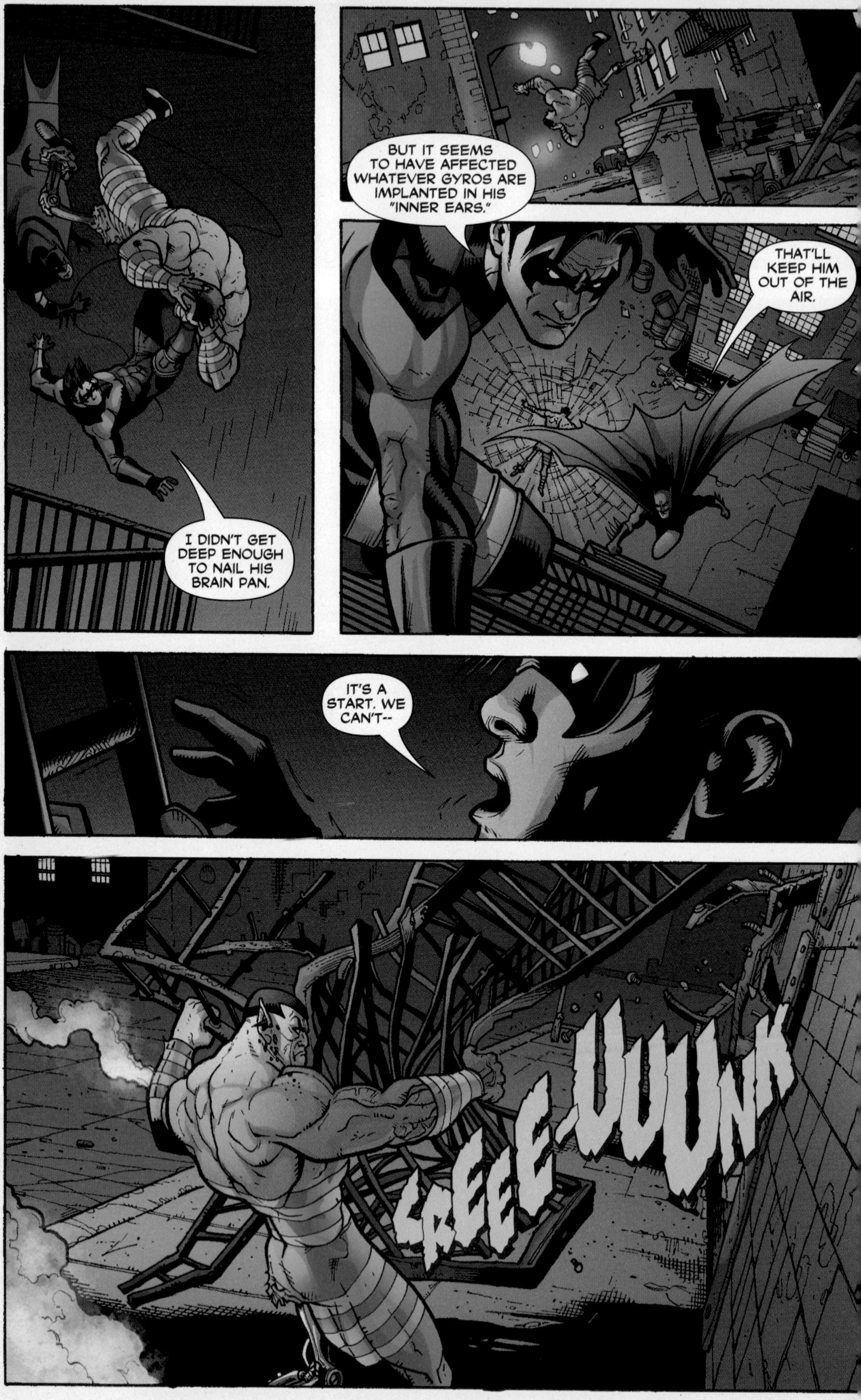
I DIDN'T GET DEEP ENOUGH TO NAIL HIS BRAIN PAN.
BUT IT SEEMS TO HAVE AFFECTED WHATEVER GYROS ARE IMPLANTED IN HIS "INNER EARS."
THAT'LL KEEP HIM OUT OF THE AIR.
IT'S A START. WE CAN'T--
CREEE-UUUNK

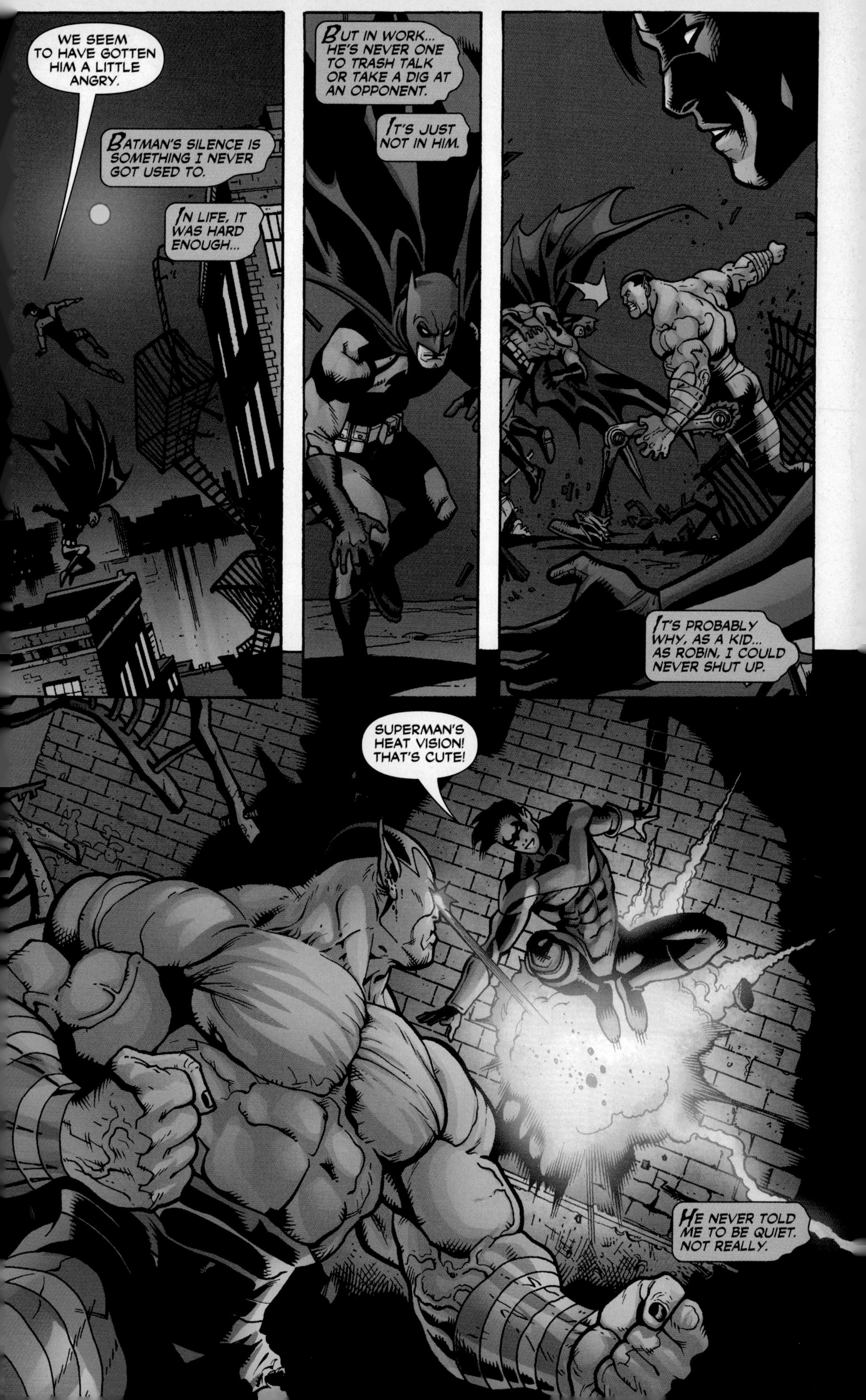
WE SEEM TO HAVE GOTTEN HIM A LITTLE ANGRY.
BATMAN'S SILENCE IS SOMETHING I NEVER GOT USED TO.
IN LIFE, IT WAS HARD ENOUGH...
BUT IN WORK... HE'S NEVER ONE TO TRASH TALK OR TAKE A DIG AT AN OPPONENT.
IT'S JUST NOT IN HIM.
IT'S PROBABLY WHY, AS A KID... AS ROBIN, I COULD NEVER SHUT UP.
SUPERMAN'S HEAT VISION! THAT'S CUTE!
HE NEVER TOLD ME TO BE QUIET. NOT REALLY.

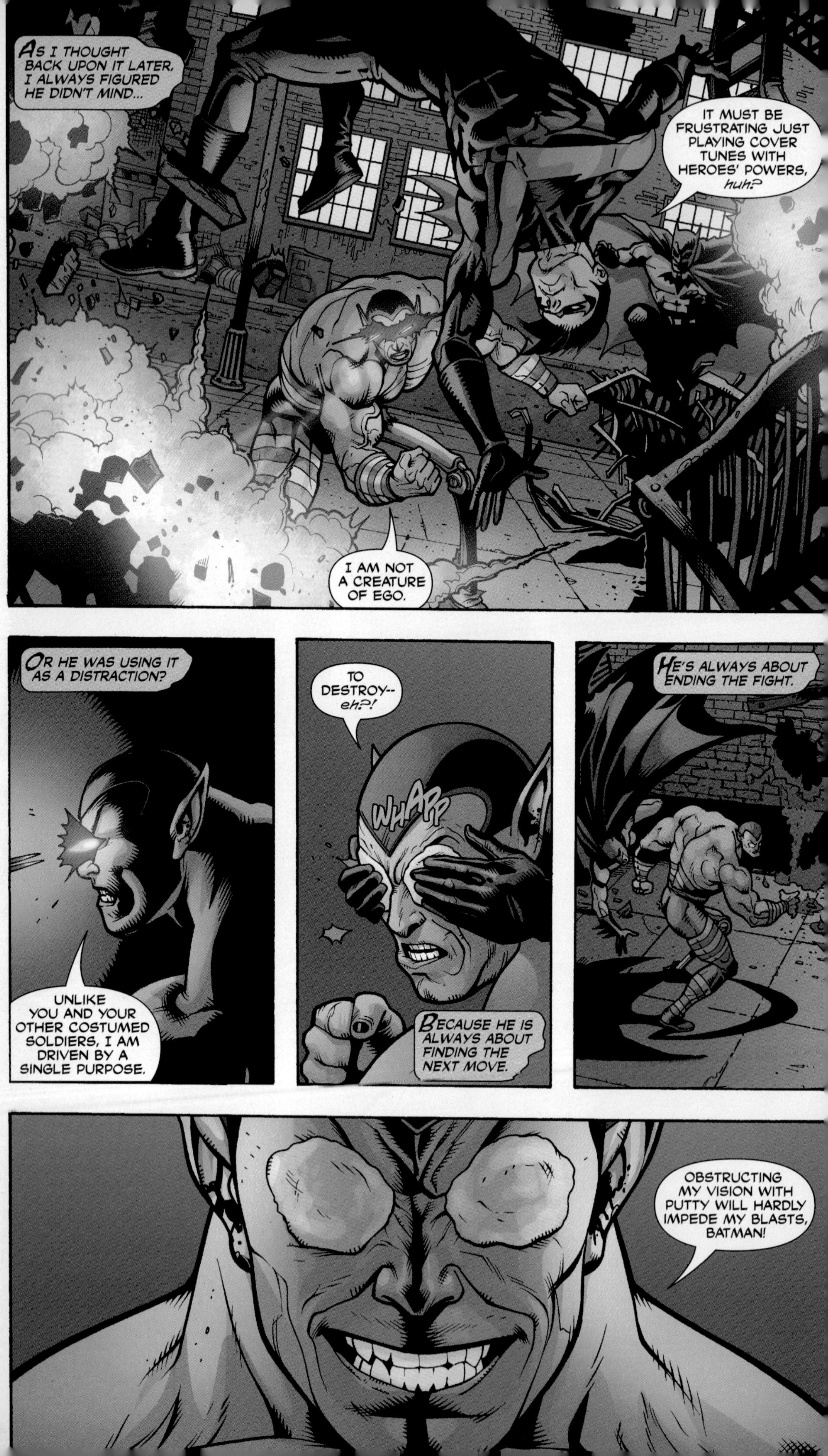
AS I THOUGHT BACK UPON IT LATER, I ALWAYS FIGURED HE DIDN'T MIND...
IT MUST BE FRUSTRATING JUST PLAYING COVER TUNES WITH HEROES' POWERS, *huh?*
I AM NOT A CREATURE OF EGO.
OR HE WAS USING IT AS A DISTRACTION?
UNLIKE YOU AND YOUR OTHER COSTUMED SOLDIERS, I AM DRIVEN BY A SINGLE PURPOSE.
TO DESTROY-- *eh?!*
WHAPP
BECAUSE HE IS ALWAYS ABOUT FINDING THE NEXT MOVE.
HE'S ALWAYS ABOUT ENDING THE FIGHT.
OBSTRUCTING MY VISION WITH PUTTY WILL HARDLY IMPEDE MY BLASTS, BATMAN!

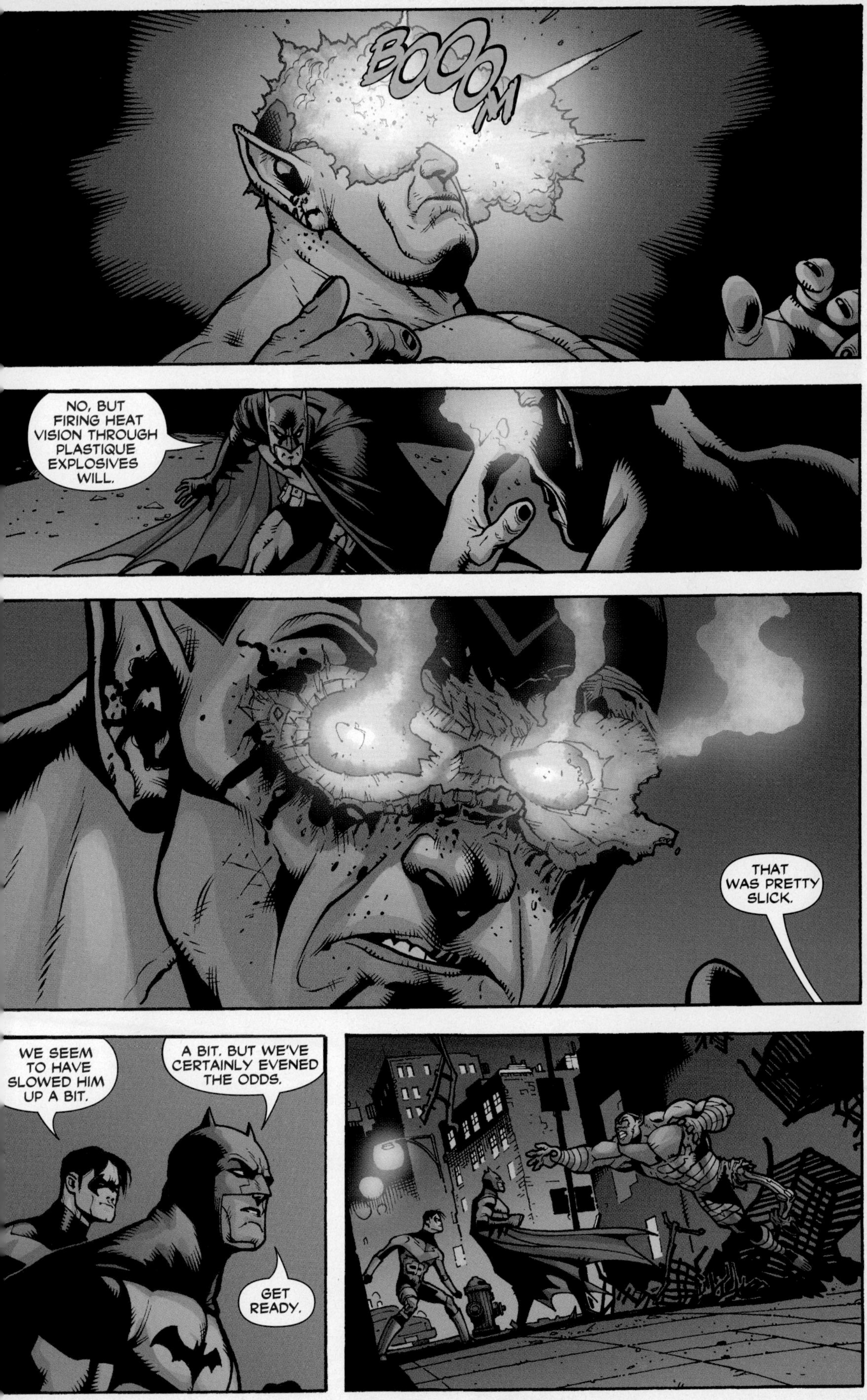
BOOOM
NO, BUT FIRING HEAT VISION THROUGH PLASTIQUE EXPLOSIVES WILL.
THAT WAS PRETTY SLICK.
WE SEEM TO HAVE SLOWED HIM UP A BIT.
A BIT. BUT WE'VE CERTAINLY EVENED THE ODDS.
GET READY.

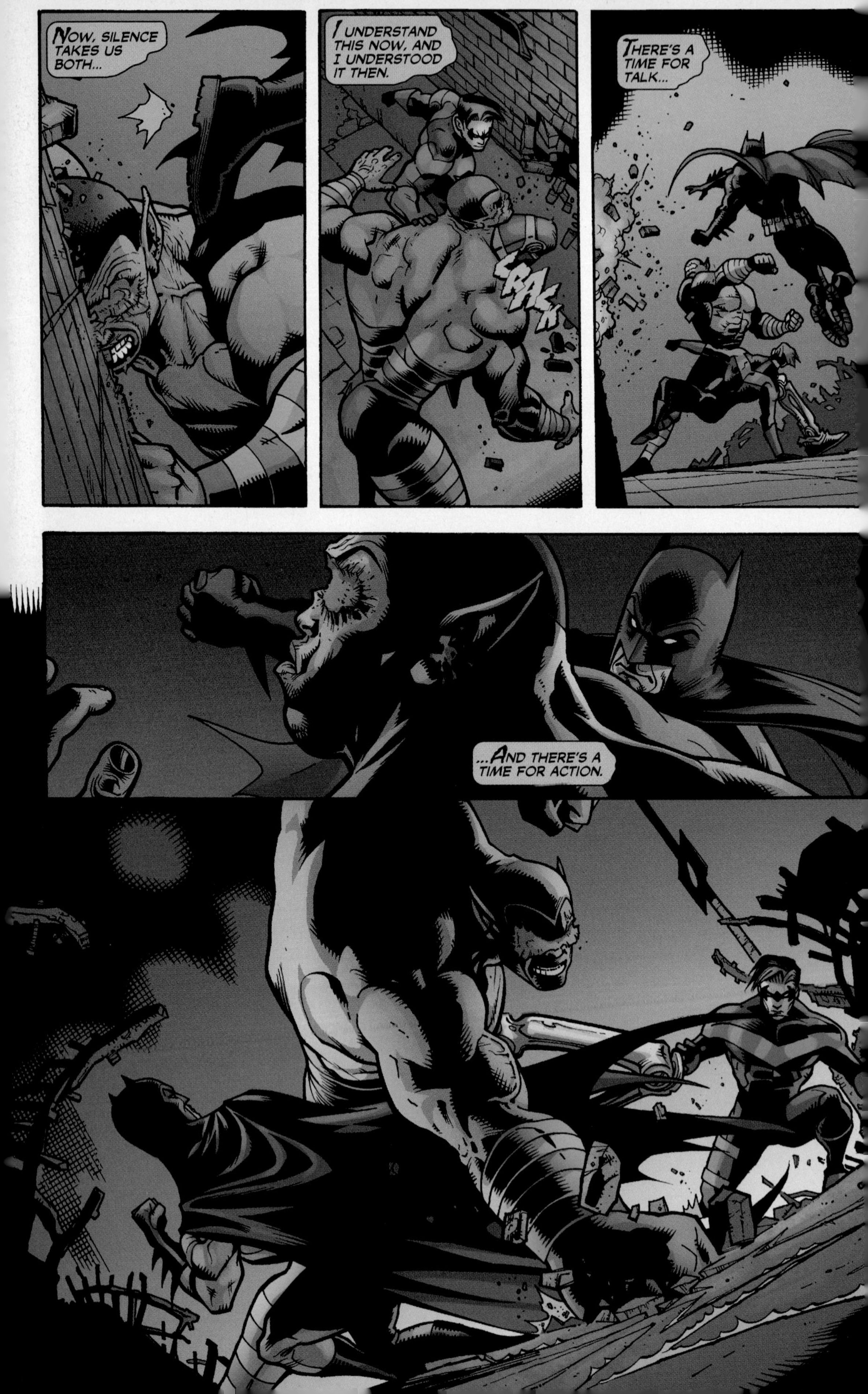
NOW, SILENCE TAKES US BOTH...
I UNDERSTAND THIS NOW, AND I UNDERSTOOD IT THEN.
CRAKK
THERE'S A TIME FOR TALK...
...AND THERE'S A TIME FOR ACTION.

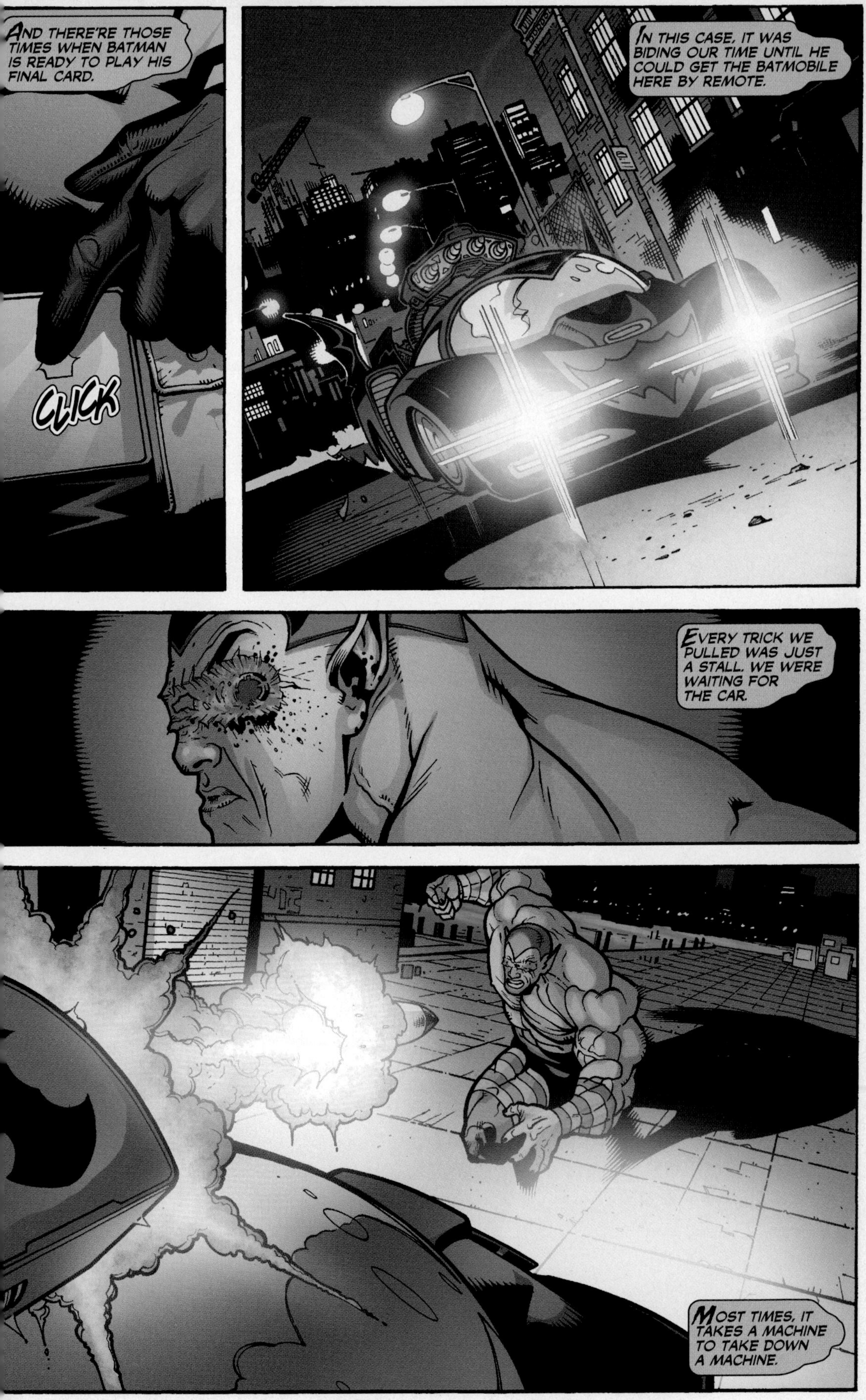
AND THERE'RE THOSE TIMES WHEN BATMAN IS READY TO PLAY HIS FINAL CARD.
CLICK
IN THIS CASE, IT WAS BIDING OUR TIME UNTIL HE COULD GET THE BATMOBILE HERE BY REMOTE.
EVERY TRICK WE PULLED WAS JUST A STALL. WE WERE WAITING FOR THE CAR.
MOST TIMES, IT TAKES A MACHINE TO TAKE DOWN A MACHINE.

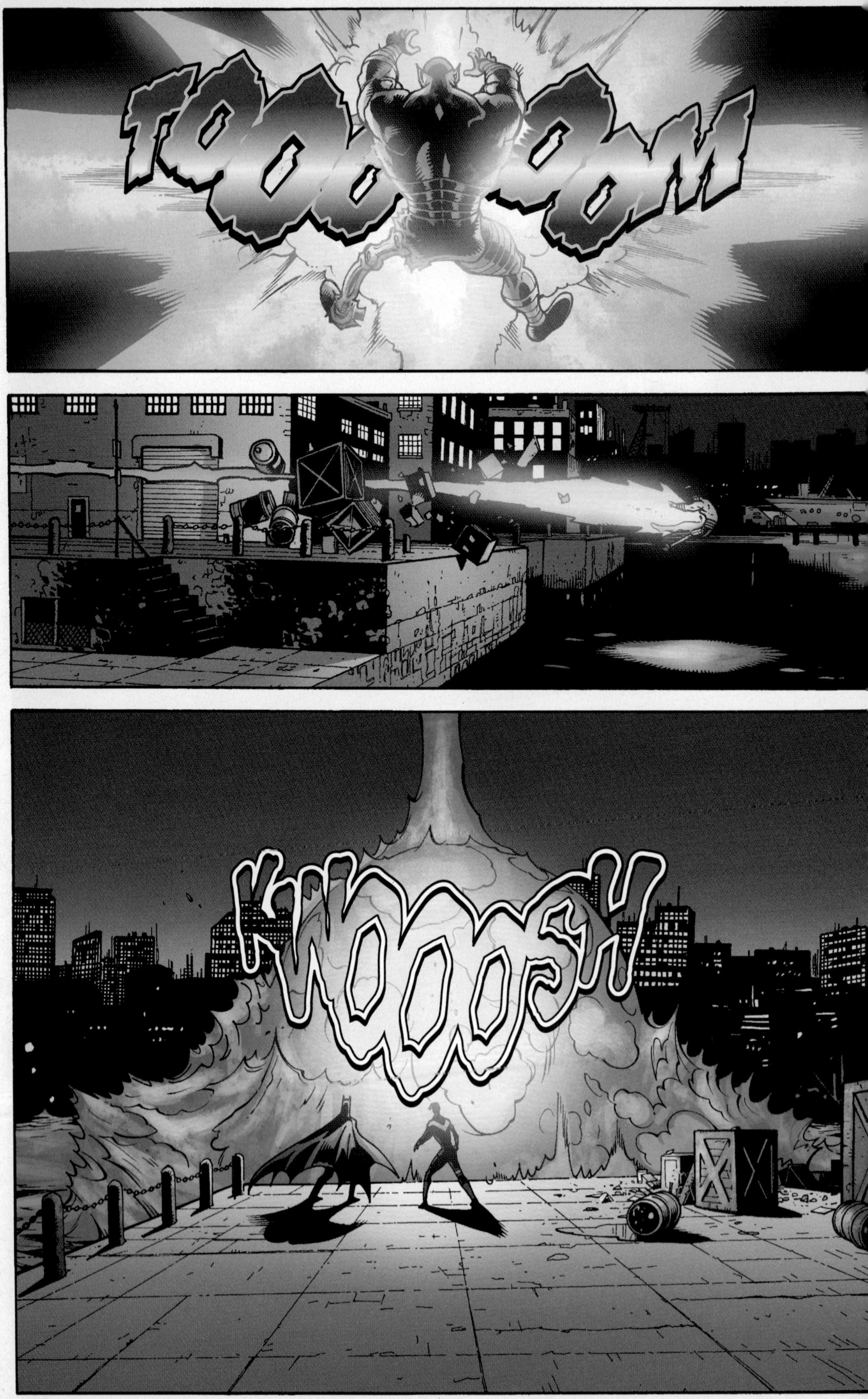
TOOOOOM
KWOOOSH

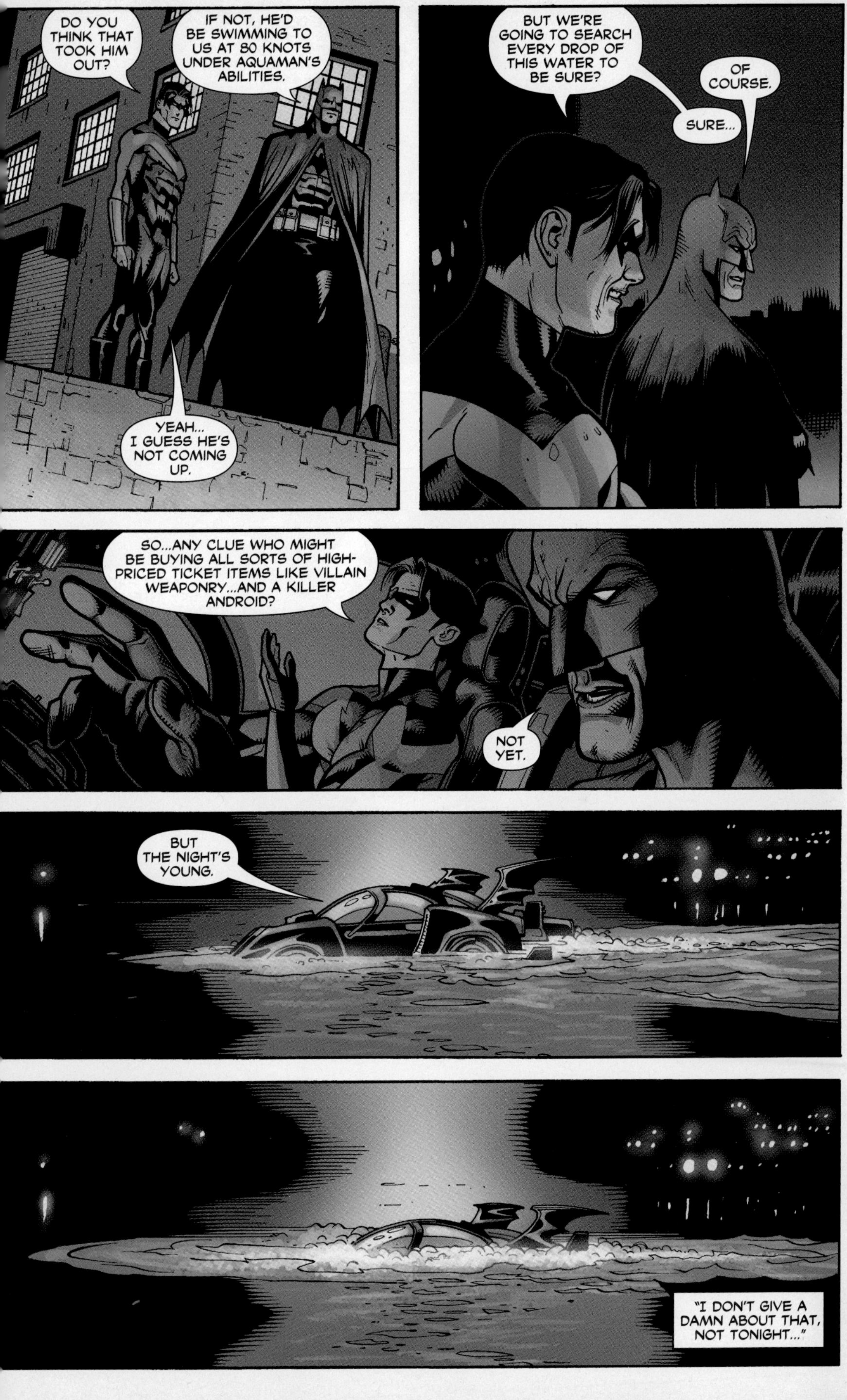
DO YOU THINK THAT TOOK HIM OUT?
IF NOT, HE'D BE SWIMMING TO US AT 80 KNOTS UNDER AQUAMAN'S ABILITIES.
YEAH... I GUESS HE'S NOT COMING UP.
BUT WE'RE GOING TO SEARCH EVERY DROP OF THIS WATER TO BE SURE?
SURE...
OF COURSE.
SO...ANY CLUE WHO MIGHT BE BUYING ALL SORTS OF HIGH-PRICED TICKET ITEMS LIKE VILLAIN WEAPONRY...AND A KILLER ANDROID?
NOT YET.
BUT THE NIGHT'S YOUNG.
"I DON'T GIVE A DAMN ABOUT THAT, NOT TONIGHT..."

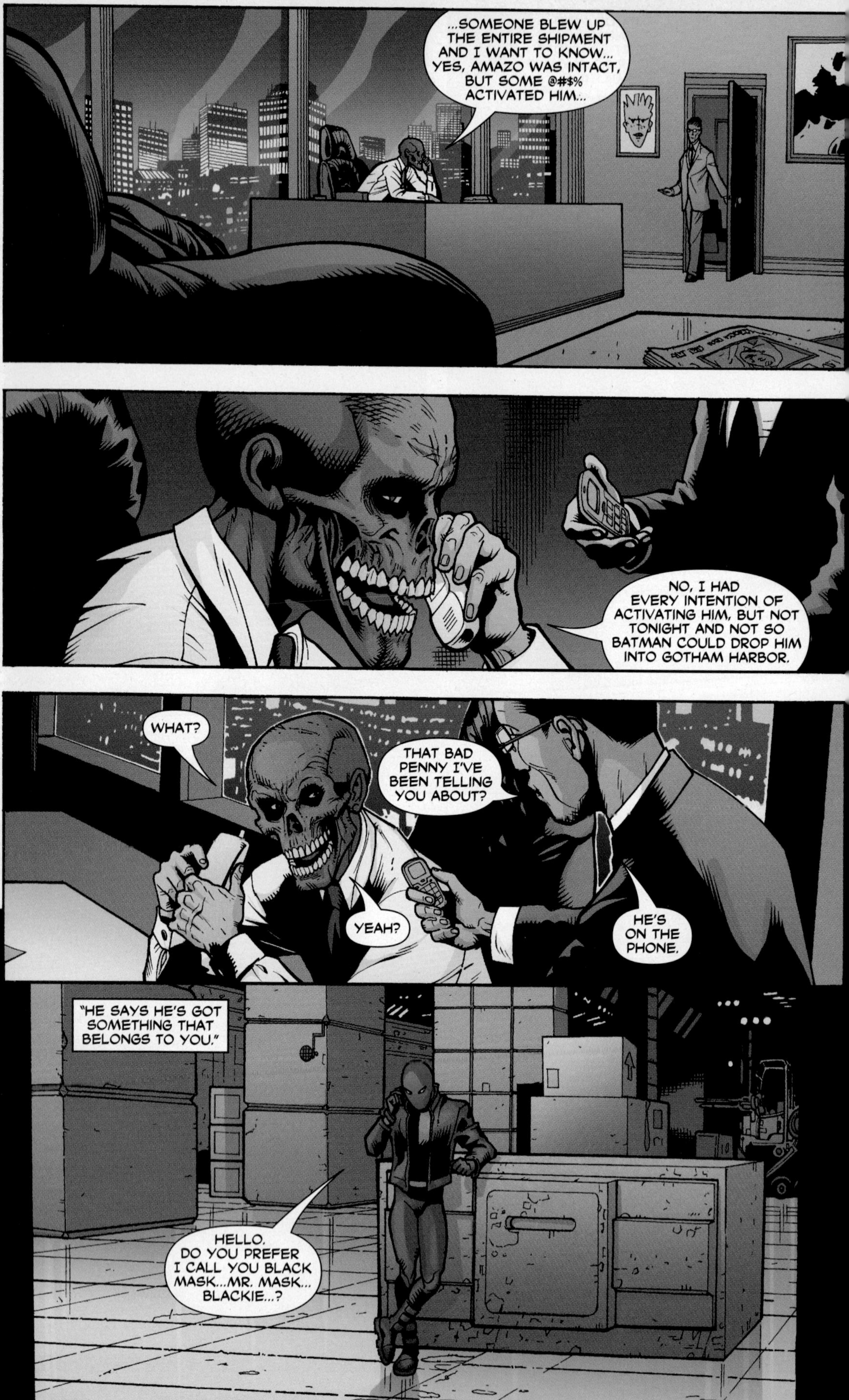
...SOMEONE BLEW UP THE ENTIRE SHIPMENT AND I WANT TO KNOW... YES, AMAZO WAS INTACT, BUT SOME @#$% ACTIVATED HIM...
NO, I HAD EVERY INTENTION OF ACTIVATING HIM, BUT NOT TONIGHT AND NOT SO BATMAN COULD DROP HIM INTO GOTHAM HARBOR.
WHAT?
THAT BAD PENNY I'VE BEEN TELLING YOU ABOUT?
YEAH?
HE'S ON THE PHONE.
"HE SAYS HE'S GOT SOMETHING THAT BELONGS TO YOU."
HELLO. DO YOU PREFER I CALL YOU BLACK MASK...MR. MASK... BLACKIE...?

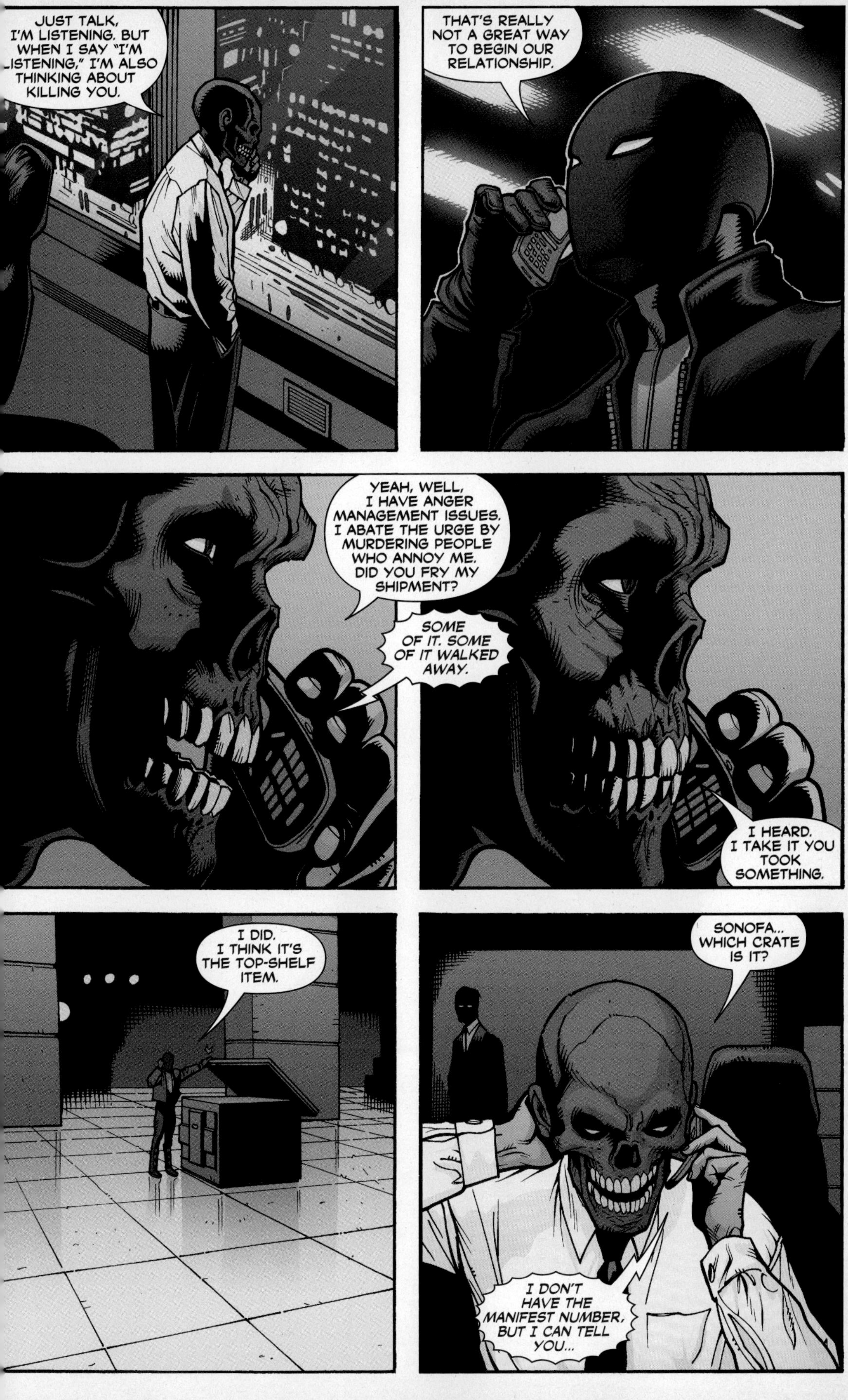
JUST TALK, I'M LISTENING. BUT WHEN I SAY "I'M LISTENING," I'M ALSO THINKING ABOUT KILLING YOU.
THAT'S REALLY NOT A GREAT WAY TO BEGIN OUR RELATIONSHIP.
YEAH, WELL, I HAVE ANGER MANAGEMENT ISSUES. I ABATE THE URGE BY MURDERING PEOPLE WHO ANNOY ME. DID YOU FRY MY SHIPMENT?
SOME OF IT. SOME OF IT WALKED AWAY.
I HEARD. I TAKE IT YOU TOOK SOMETHING.
I DID. I THINK IT'S THE TOP-SHELF ITEM.
SONOFA... WHICH CRATE IS IT?
I DON'T HAVE THE MANIFEST NUMBER, BUT I CAN TELL YOU...

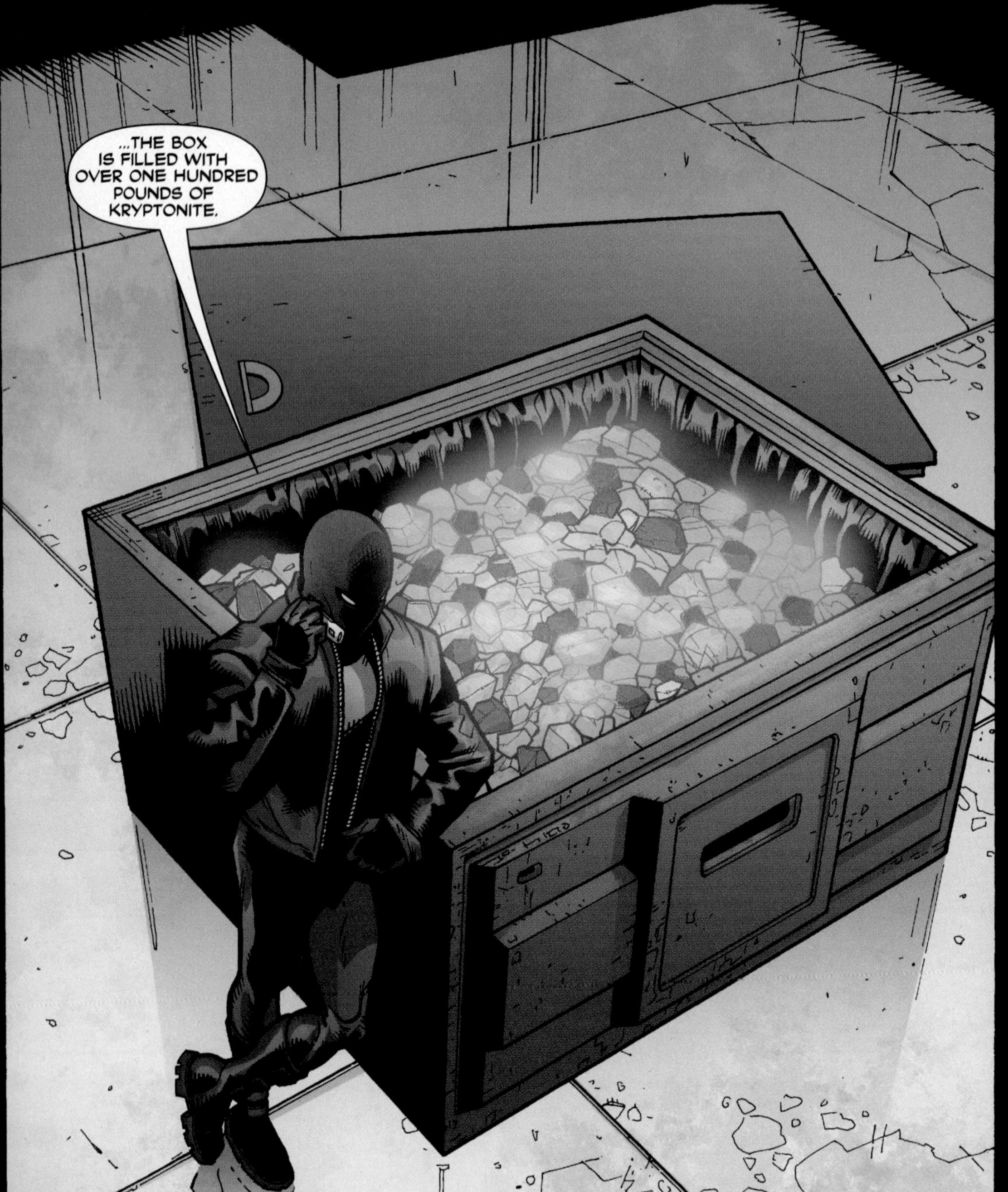
...THE BOX IS FILLED WITH OVER ONE HUNDRED POUNDS OF KRYPTONITE.

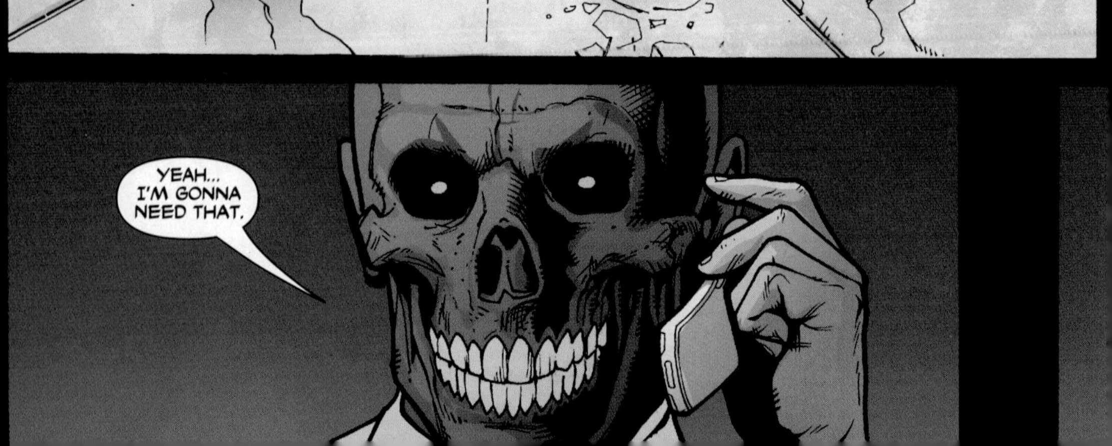
YEAH... I'M GONNA NEED THAT.

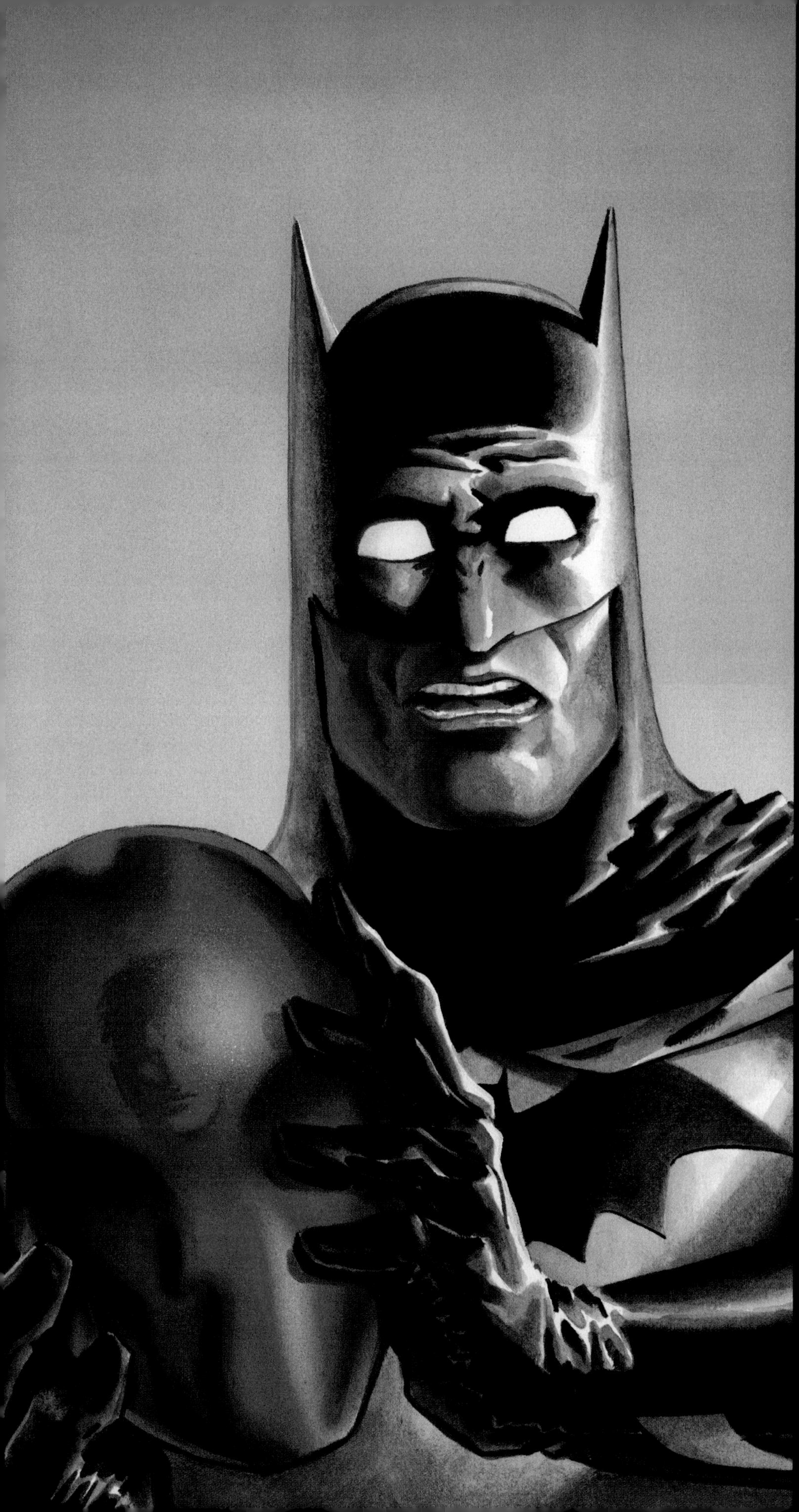

BATMAN #638 • ART BY MATT WAGNER

PART 4

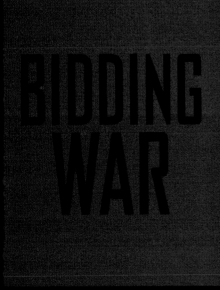

BIDDING WAR

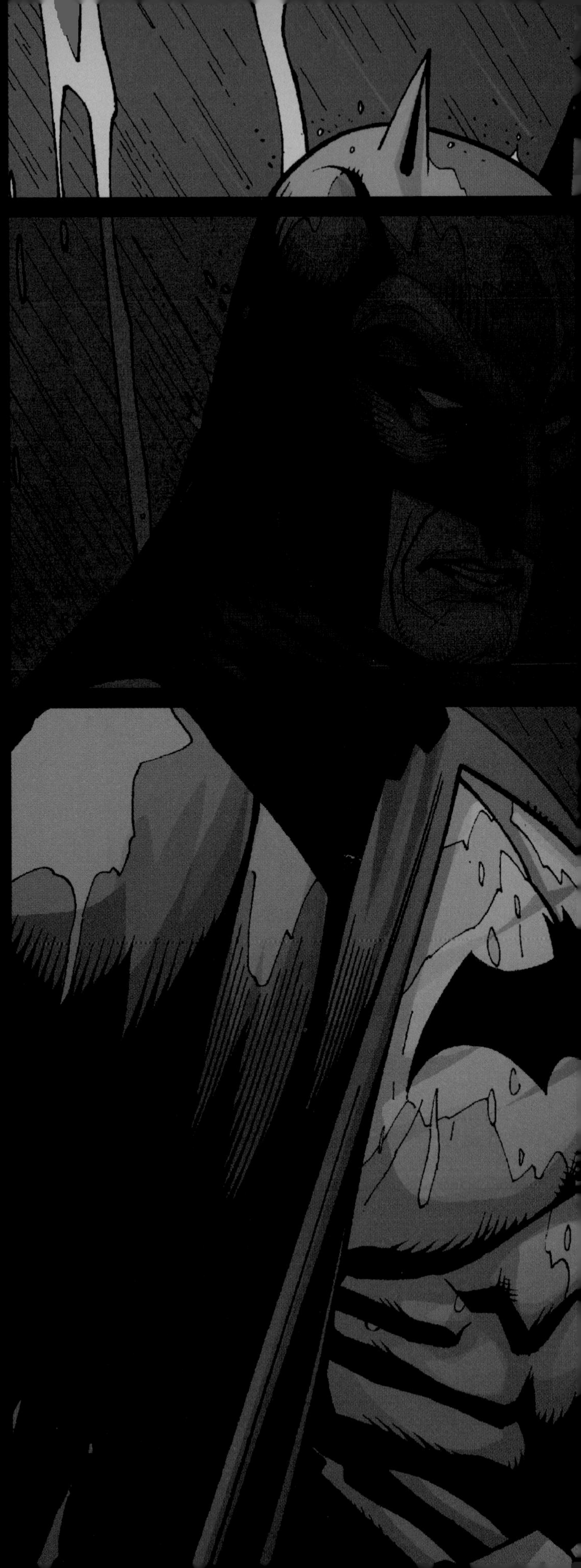

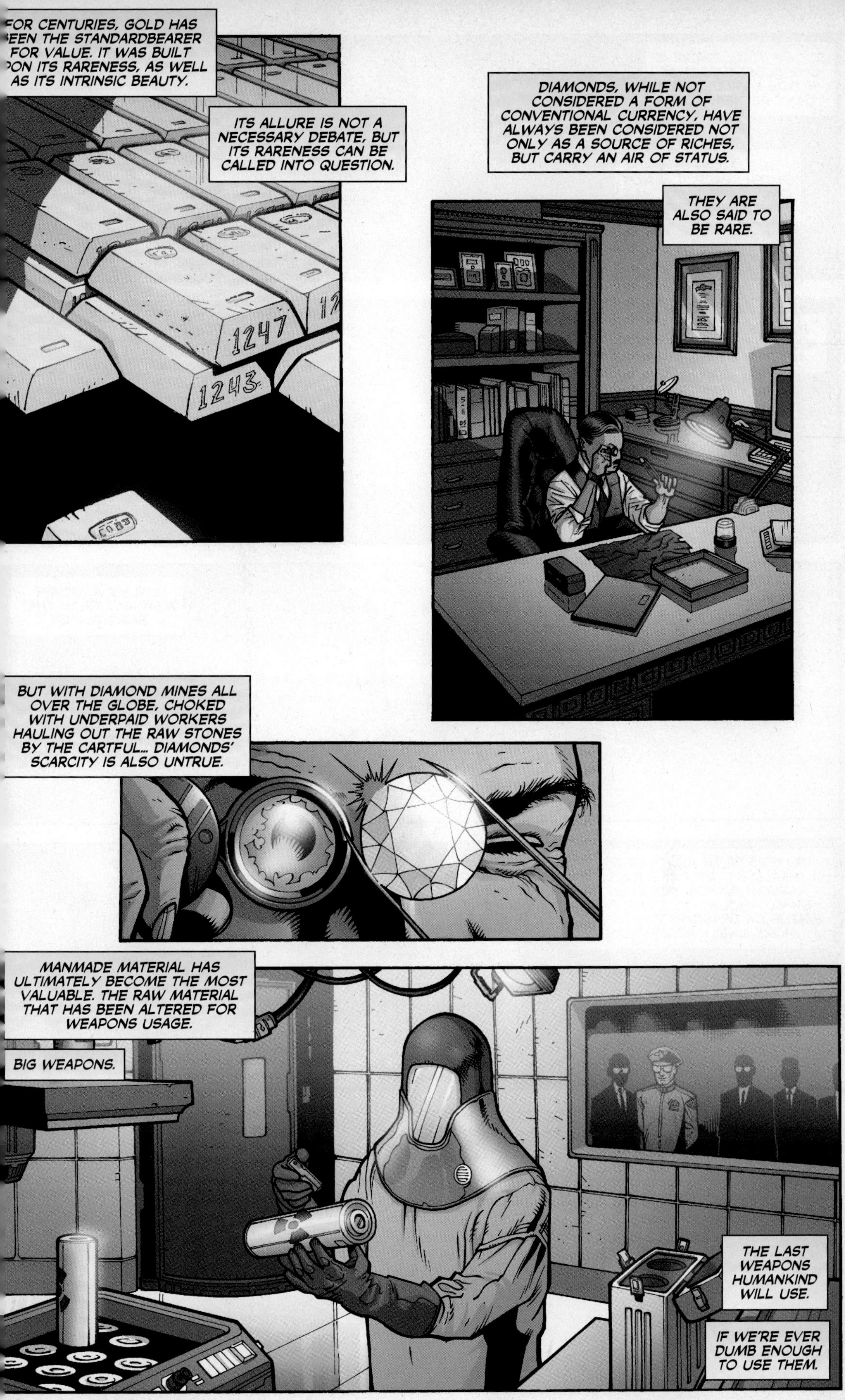
FOR CENTURIES, GOLD HAS EEN THE STANDARDBEARER FOR VALUE. IT WAS BUILT PON ITS RARENESS, AS WELL AS ITS INTRINSIC BEAUTY.
ITS ALLURE IS NOT A NECESSARY DEBATE, BUT ITS RARENESS CAN BE CALLED INTO QUESTION.
1247
1243
DIAMONDS, WHILE NOT CONSIDERED A FORM OF CONVENTIONAL CURRENCY, HAVE ALWAYS BEEN CONSIDERED NOT ONLY AS A SOURCE OF RICHES, BUT CARRY AN AIR OF STATUS.
THEY ARE ALSO SAID TO BE RARE.
BUT WITH DIAMOND MINES ALL OVER THE GLOBE, CHOKED WITH UNDERPAID WORKERS HAULING OUT THE RAW STONES BY THE CARTFUL... DIAMONDS' SCARCITY IS ALSO UNTRUE.
MANMADE MATERIAL HAS ULTIMATELY BECOME THE MOST VALUABLE. THE RAW MATERIAL THAT HAS BEEN ALTERED FOR WEAPONS USAGE.
BIG WEAPONS.
THE LAST WEAPONS HUMANKIND WILL USE.
IF WE'RE EVER DUMB ENOUGH TO USE THEM.

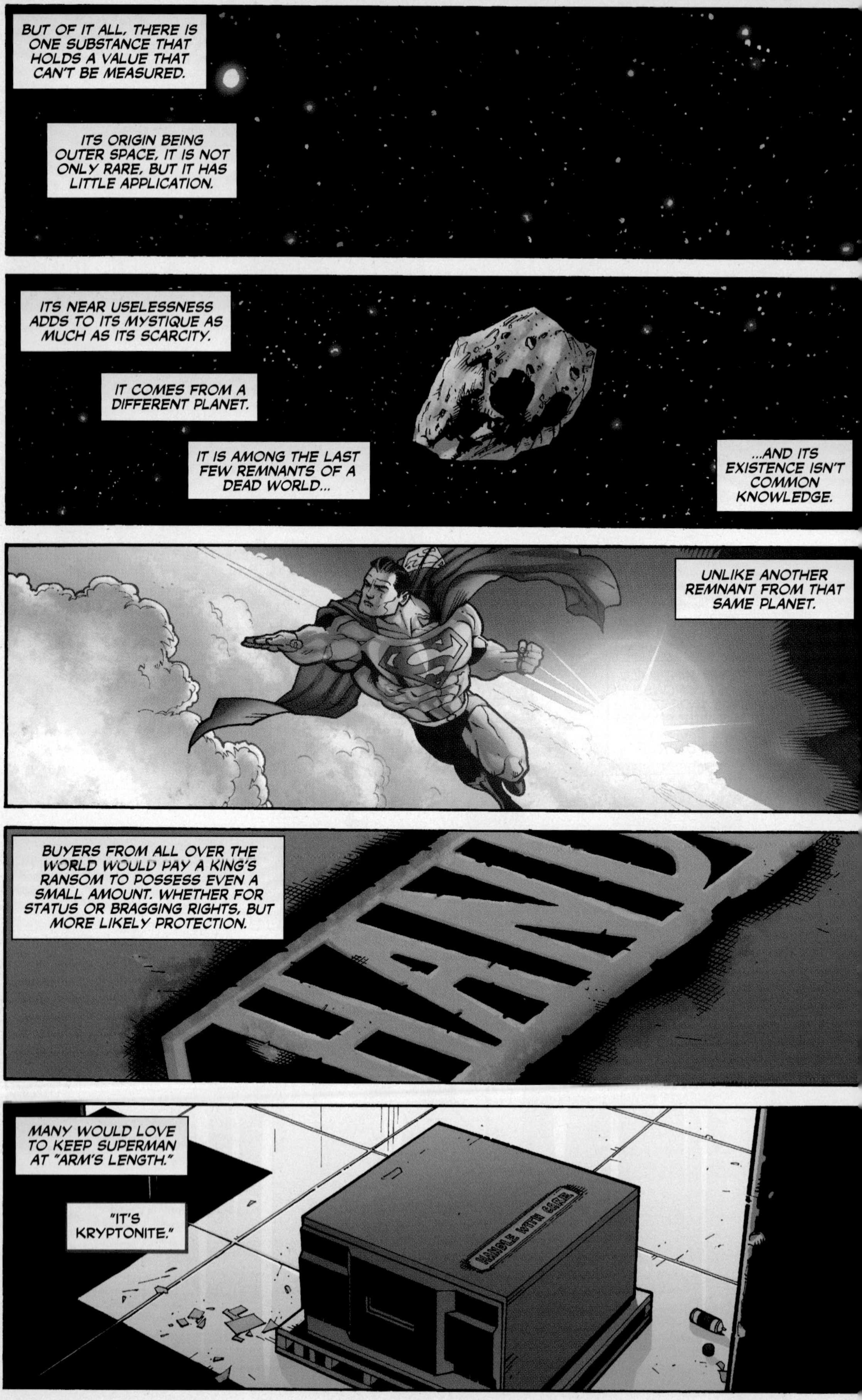
BUT OF IT ALL, THERE IS ONE SUBSTANCE THAT HOLDS A VALUE THAT CAN'T BE MEASURED.
ITS ORIGIN BEING OUTER SPACE, IT IS NOT ONLY RARE, BUT IT HAS LITTLE APPLICATION.
ITS NEAR USELESSNESS ADDS TO ITS MYSTIQUE AS MUCH AS ITS SCARCITY.
IT COMES FROM A DIFFERENT PLANET.
IT IS AMONG THE LAST FEW REMNANTS OF A DEAD WORLD...
...AND ITS EXISTENCE ISN'T COMMON KNOWLEDGE.
UNLIKE ANOTHER REMNANT FROM THAT SAME PLANET.
BUYERS FROM ALL OVER THE WORLD WOULD PAY A KING'S RANSOM TO POSSESS EVEN A SMALL AMOUNT. WHETHER FOR STATUS OR BRAGGING RIGHTS, BUT MORE LIKELY PROTECTION.
MANY WOULD LOVE TO KEEP SUPERMAN AT "ARM'S LENGTH."
"IT'S KRYPTONITE."
HANDLE WITH CARE

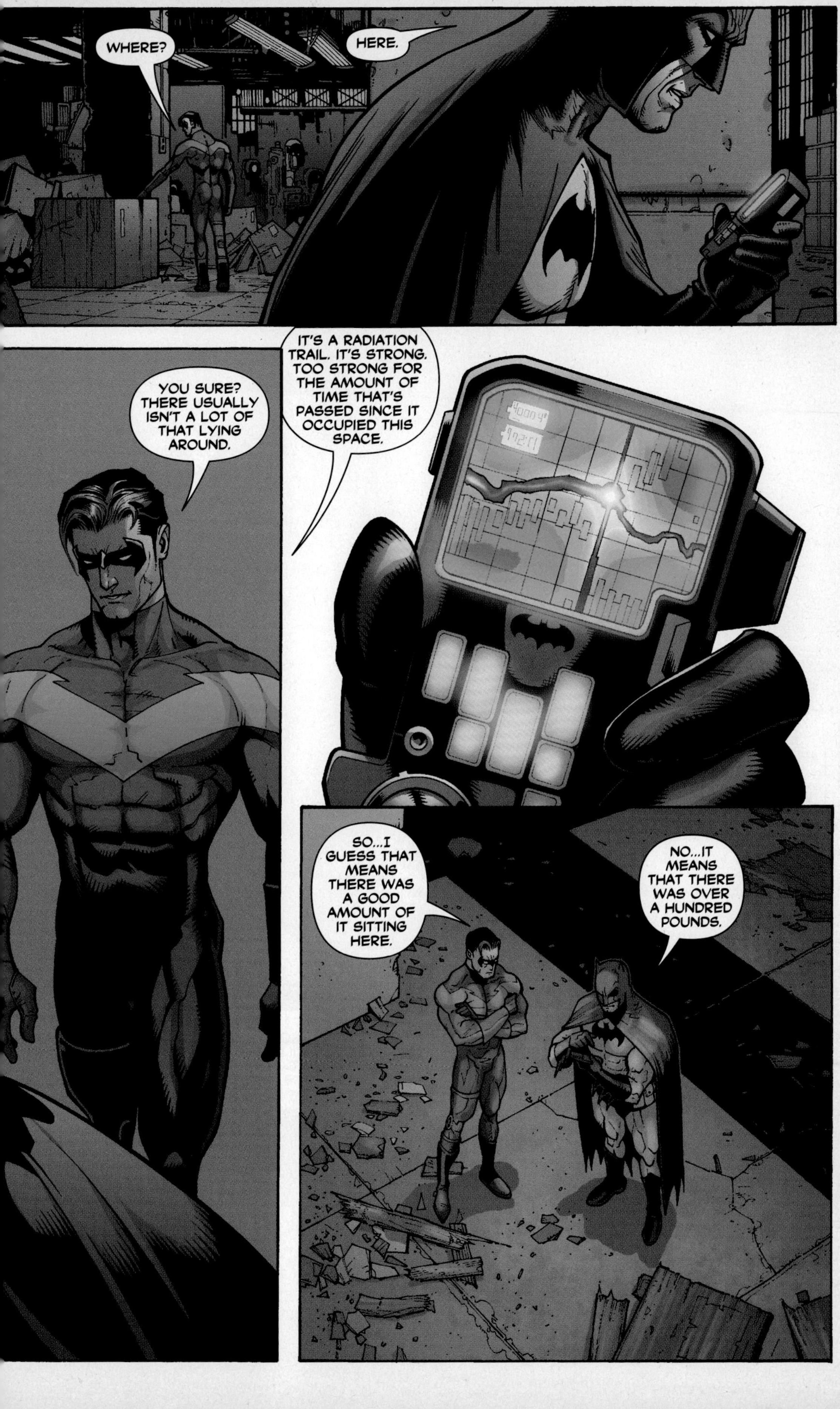
WHERE?
HERE.
YOU SURE? THERE USUALLY ISN'T A LOT OF THAT LYING AROUND.
IT'S A RADIATION TRAIL. IT'S STRONG. TOO STRONG FOR THE AMOUNT OF TIME THAT'S PASSED SINCE IT OCCUPIED THIS SPACE.
SO...I GUESS THAT MEANS THERE WAS A GOOD AMOUNT OF IT SITTING HERE.
NO...IT MEANS THAT THERE WAS OVER A HUNDRED POUNDS.

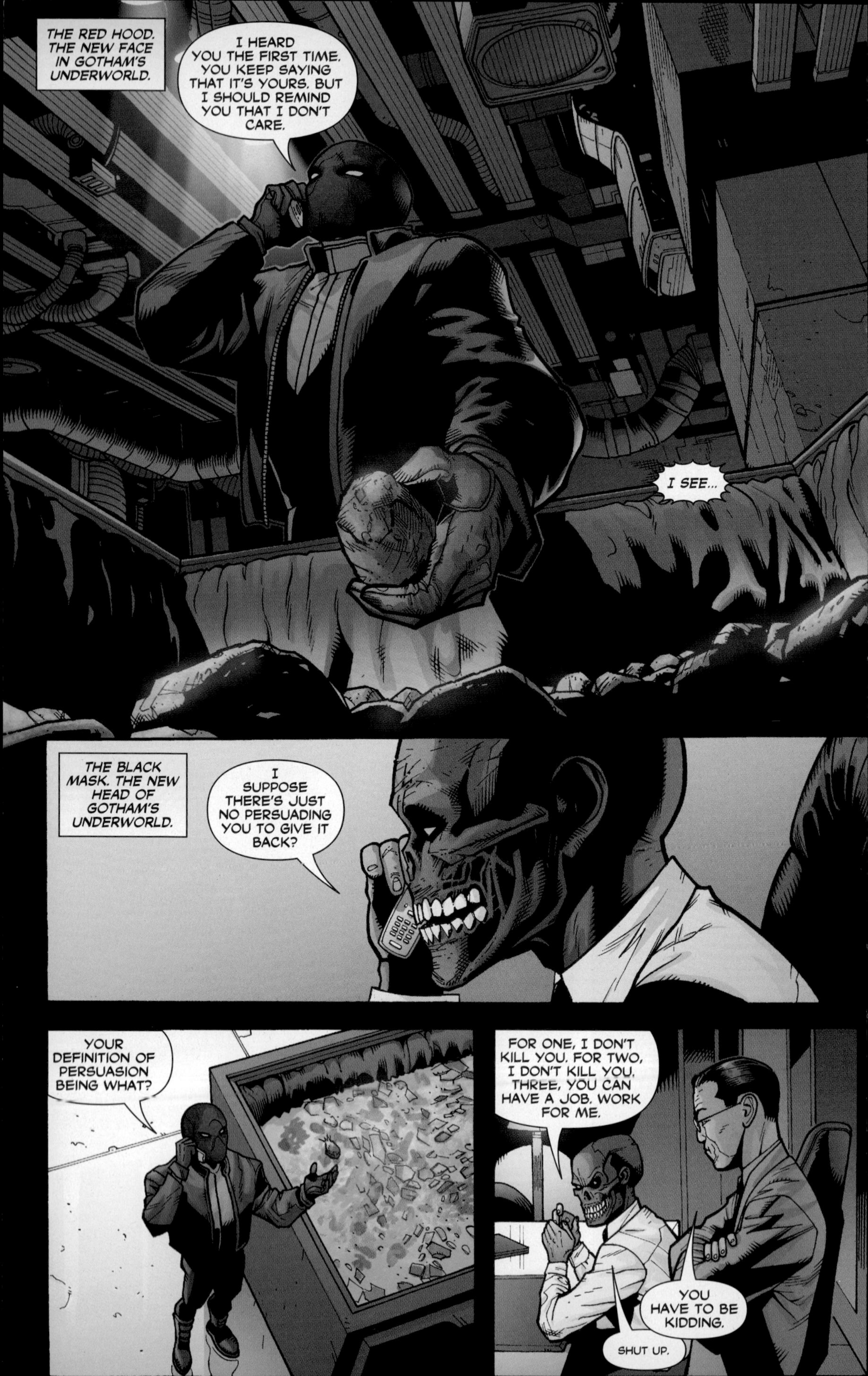
THE RED HOOD. THE NEW FACE IN GOTHAM'S UNDERWORLD.
I HEARD YOU THE FIRST TIME. YOU KEEP SAYING THAT IT'S YOURS. BUT I SHOULD REMIND YOU THAT I DON'T CARE.
I SEE...
THE BLACK MASK. THE NEW HEAD OF GOTHAM'S UNDERWORLD.
I SUPPOSE THERE'S JUST NO PERSUADING YOU TO GIVE IT BACK?
YOUR DEFINITION OF PERSUASION BEING WHAT?
FOR ONE, I DON'T KILL YOU. FOR TWO, I DON'T KILL YOU. THREE, YOU CAN HAVE A JOB. WORK FOR ME.
YOU HAVE TO BE KIDDING.
SHUT UP.

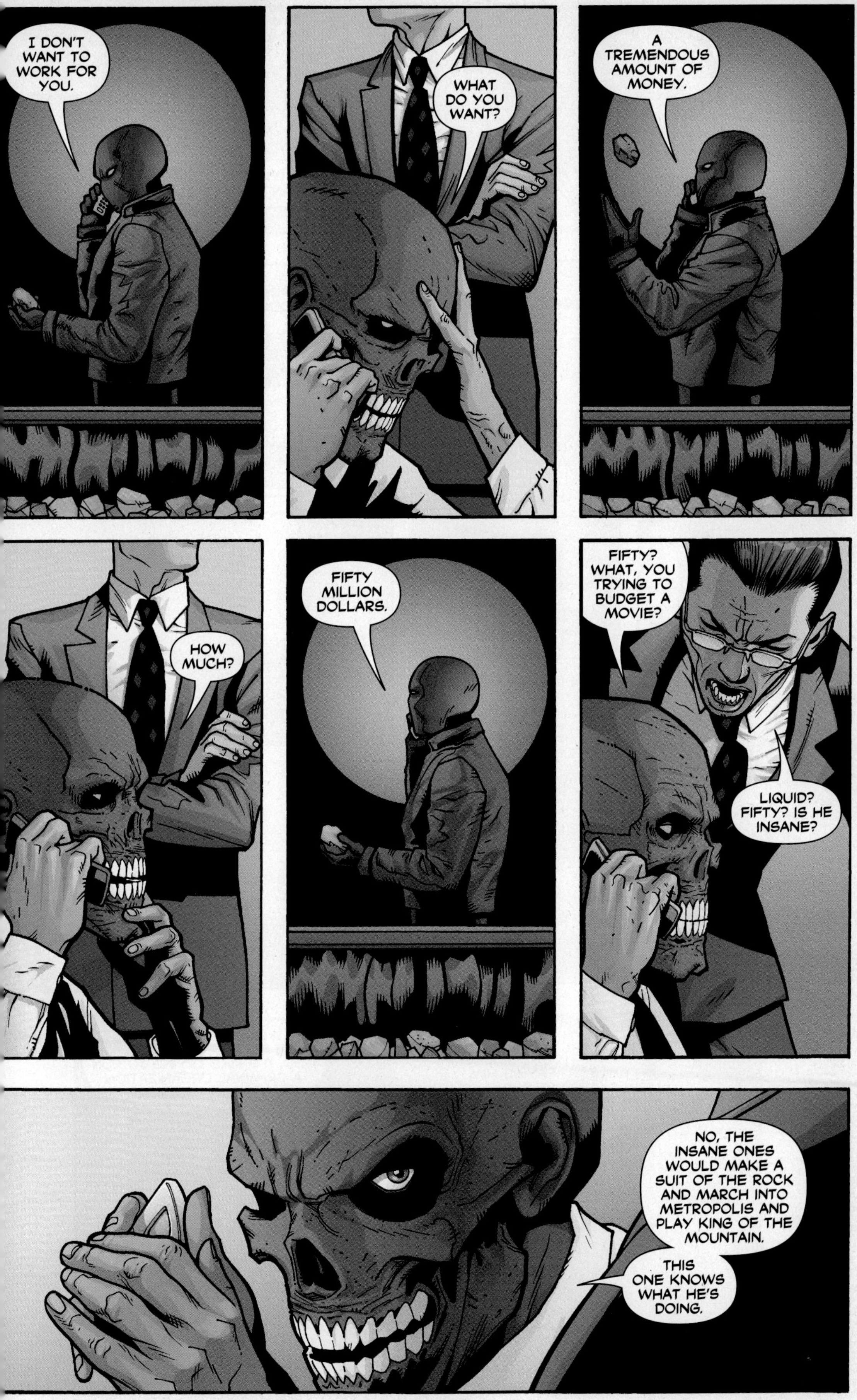
I DON'T WANT TO WORK FOR YOU.
WHAT DO YOU WANT?
A TREMENDOUS AMOUNT OF MONEY.
HOW MUCH?
FIFTY MILLION DOLLARS.
FIFTY? WHAT, YOU TRYING TO BUDGET A MOVIE?
LIQUID? FIFTY? IS HE INSANE?
NO, THE INSANE ONES WOULD MAKE A SUIT OF THE ROCK AND MARCH INTO METROPOLIS AND PLAY KING OF THE MOUNTAIN.
THIS ONE KNOWS WHAT HE'S DOING.

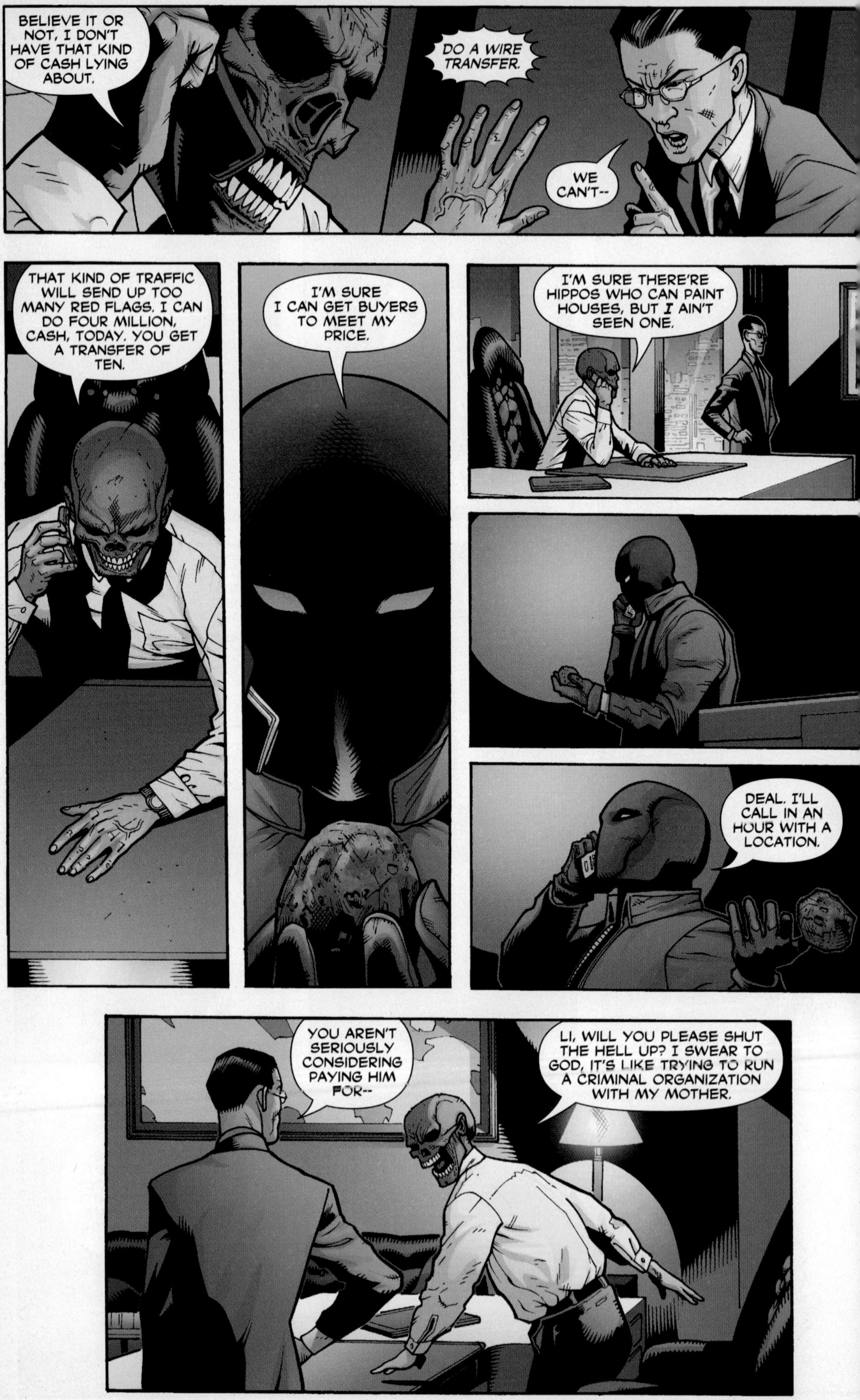

BELIEVE IT OR NOT, I DON'T HAVE THAT KIND OF CASH LYING ABOUT.
DO A WIRE TRANSFER.
WE CAN'T--
THAT KIND OF TRAFFIC WILL SEND UP TOO MANY RED FLAGS. I CAN DO FOUR MILLION, CASH, TODAY. YOU GET A TRANSFER OF TEN.
I'M SURE I CAN GET BUYERS TO MEET MY PRICE.
I'M SURE THERE'RE HIPPOS WHO CAN PAINT HOUSES, BUT I AIN'T SEEN ONE.
DEAL. I'LL CALL IN AN HOUR WITH A LOCATION.
YOU AREN'T SERIOUSLY CONSIDERING PAYING HIM FOR--
LI, WILL YOU PLEASE SHUT THE HELL UP? I SWEAR TO GOD, IT'S LIKE TRYING TO RUN A CRIMINAL ORGANIZATION WITH MY MOTHER.

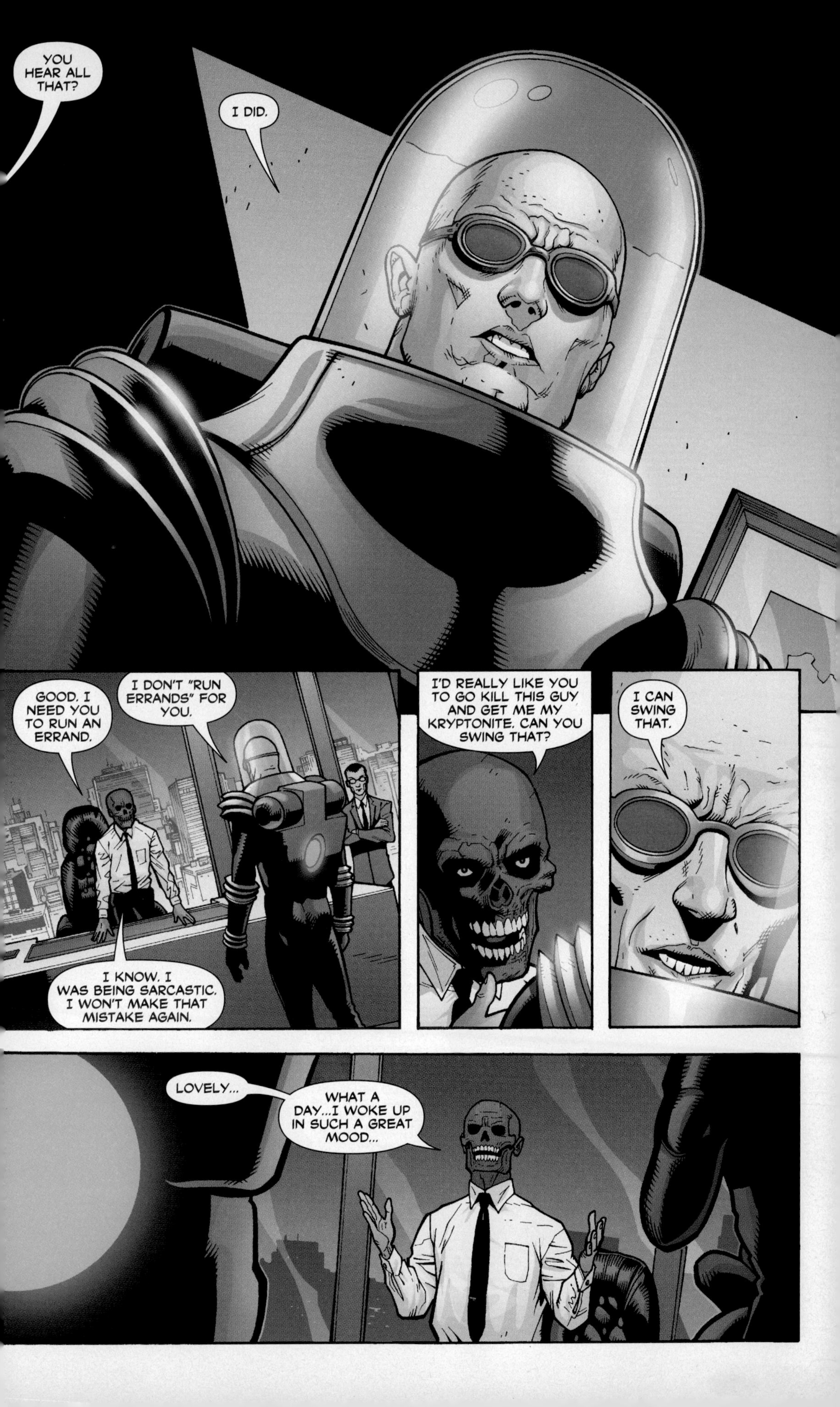
YOU HEAR ALL THAT?
I DID.
GOOD. I NEED YOU TO RUN AN ERRAND.
I DON'T "RUN ERRANDS" FOR YOU.
I KNOW. I WAS BEING SARCASTIC. I WON'T MAKE THAT MISTAKE AGAIN.
I'D REALLY LIKE YOU TO GO KILL THIS GUY AND GET ME MY KRYPTONITE. CAN YOU SWING THAT?
I CAN SWING THAT.
LOVELY...
WHAT A DAY...I WOKE UP IN SUCH A GREAT MOOD...

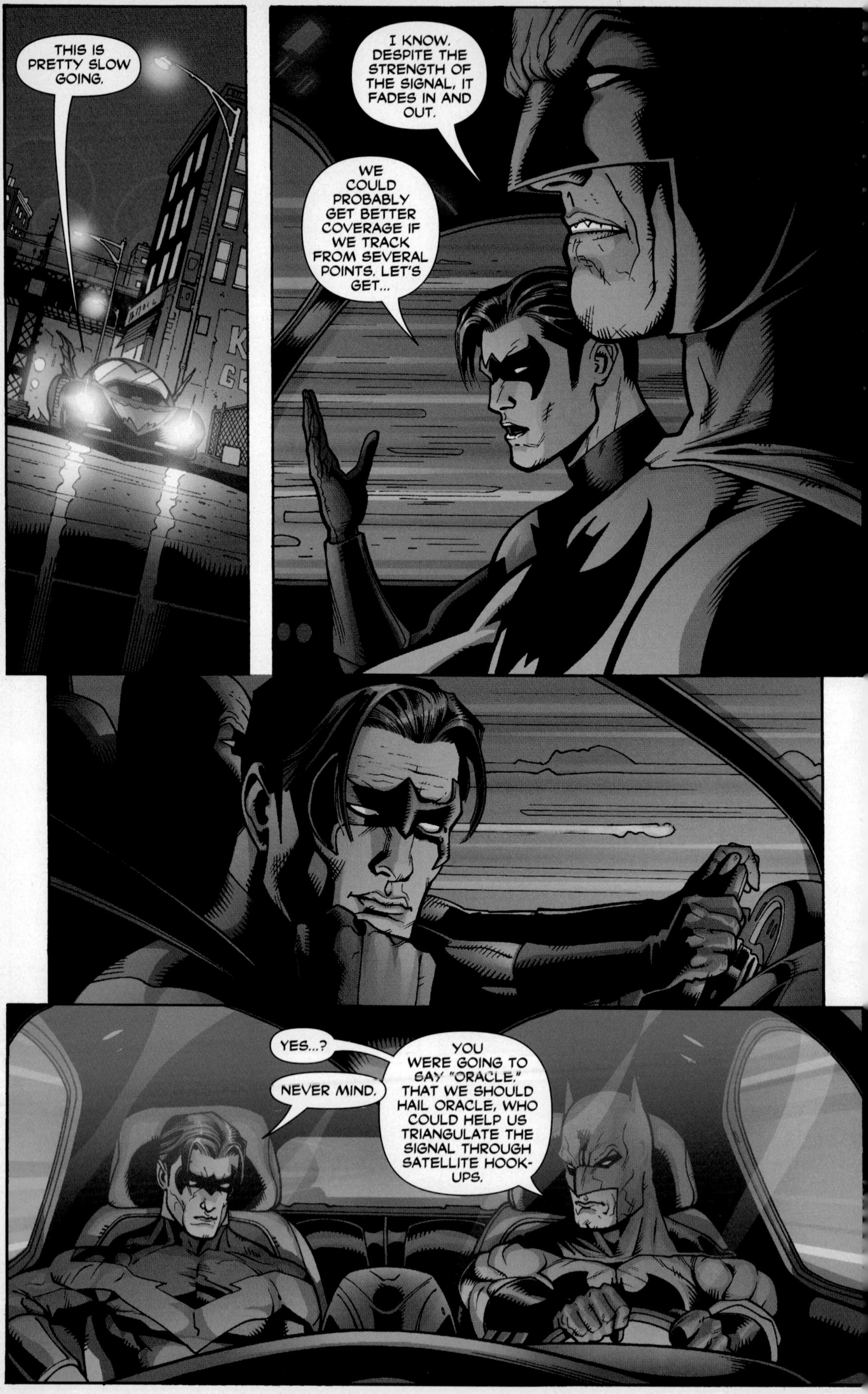
THIS IS PRETTY SLOW GOING.
I KNOW. DESPITE THE STRENGTH OF THE SIGNAL, IT FADES IN AND OUT.
WE COULD PROBABLY GET BETTER COVERAGE IF WE TRACK FROM SEVERAL POINTS. LET'S GET...
YES...?
NEVER MIND.
YOU WERE GOING TO SAY "ORACLE." THAT WE SHOULD HAIL ORACLE, WHO COULD HELP US TRIANGULATE THE SIGNAL THROUGH SATELLITE HOOK-UPS.

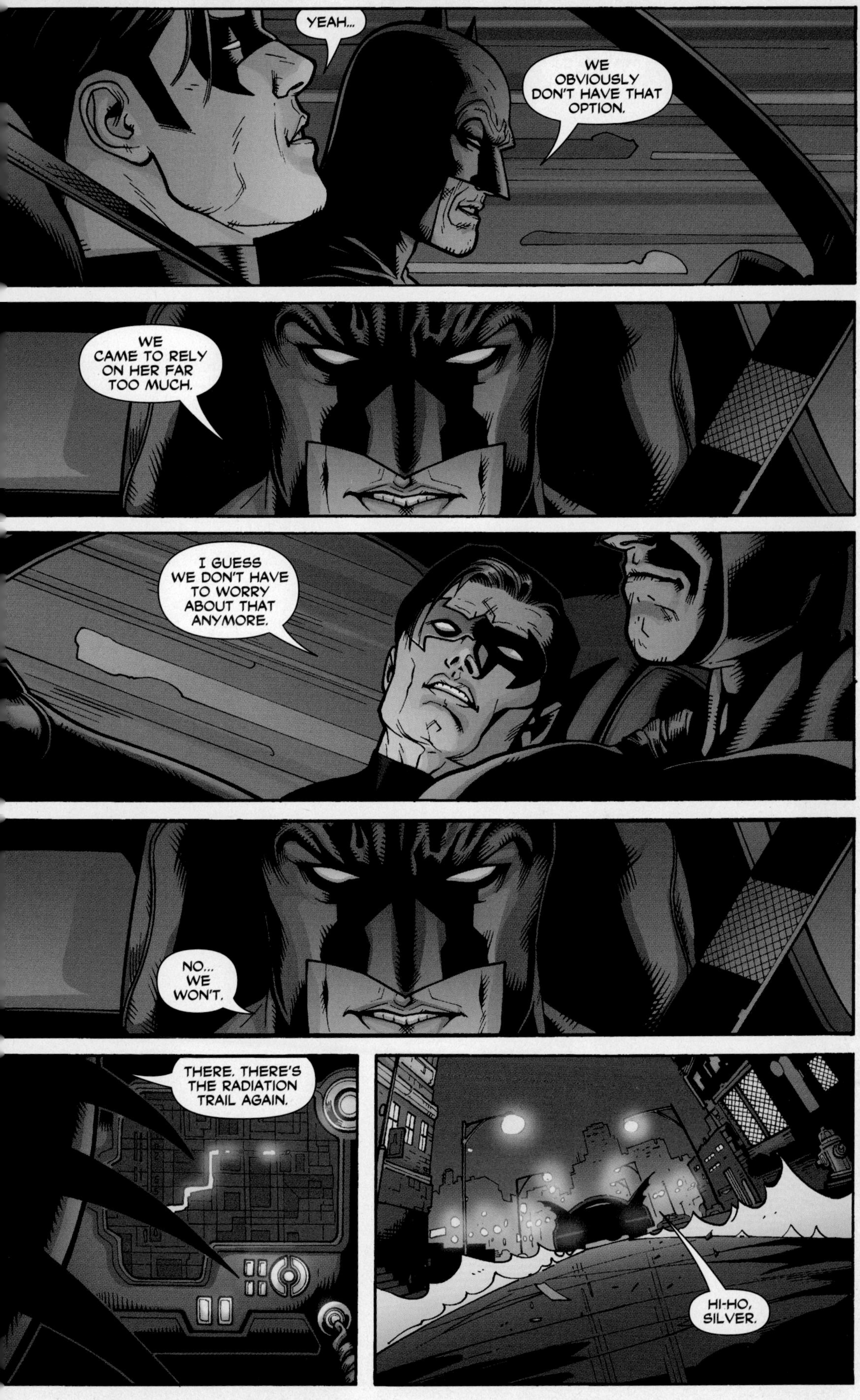
YEAH...
WE OBVIOUSLY DON'T HAVE THAT OPTION.
WE CAME TO RELY ON HER FAR TOO MUCH.
I GUESS WE DON'T HAVE TO WORRY ABOUT THAT ANYMORE.
NO... WE WON'T.
THERE. THERE'S THE RADIATION TRAIL AGAIN.
HI-HO, SILVER.

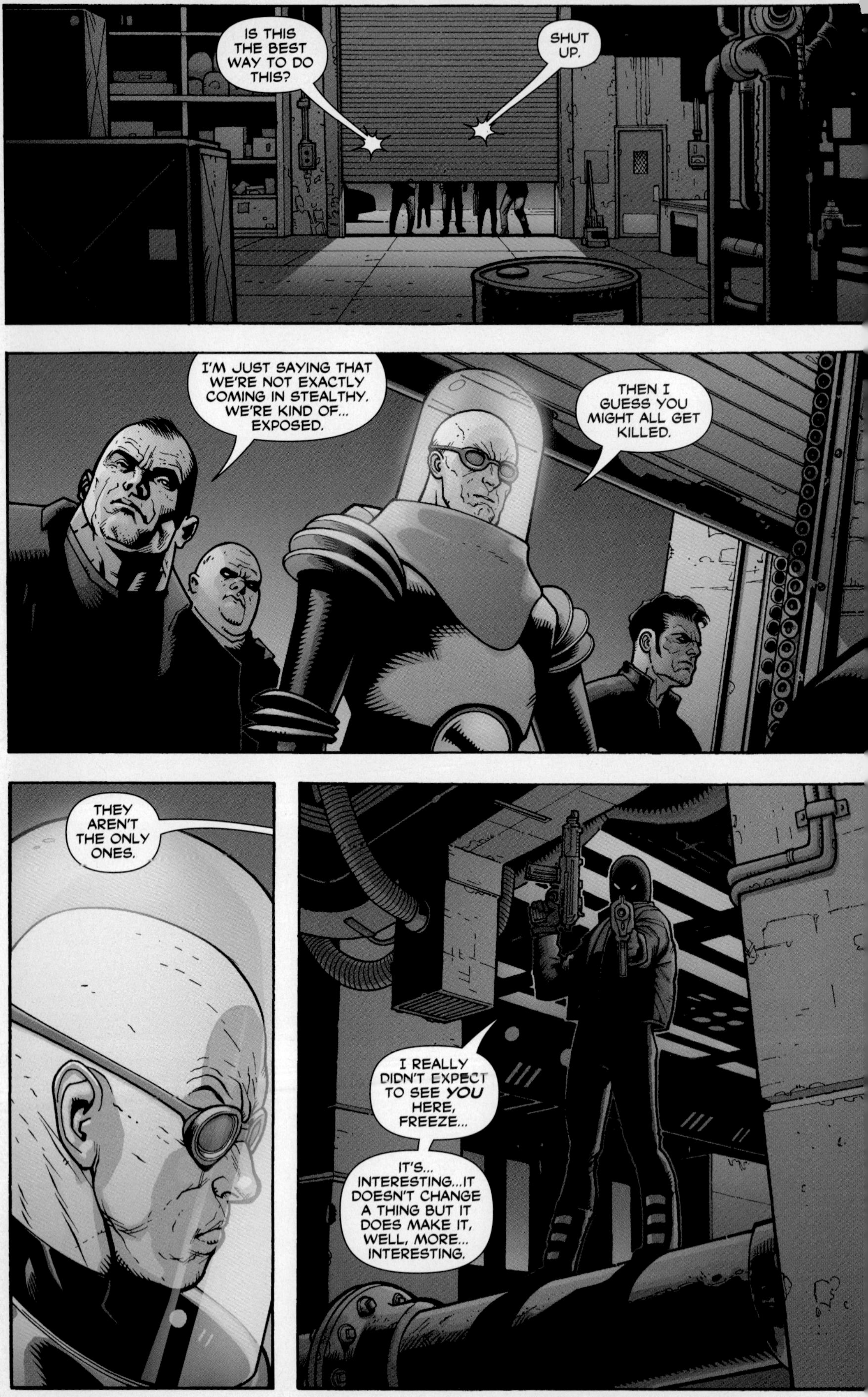
IS THIS THE BEST WAY TO DO THIS?
SHUT UP.
I'M JUST SAYING THAT WE'RE NOT EXACTLY COMING IN STEALTHY. WE'RE KIND OF... EXPOSED.
THEN I GUESS YOU MIGHT ALL GET KILLED.
THEY AREN'T THE ONLY ONES.
I REALLY DIDN'T EXPECT TO SEE *YOU* HERE, FREEZE...
IT'S... INTERESTING...IT DOESN'T CHANGE A THING BUT IT DOES MAKE IT, WELL, MORE... INTERESTING.

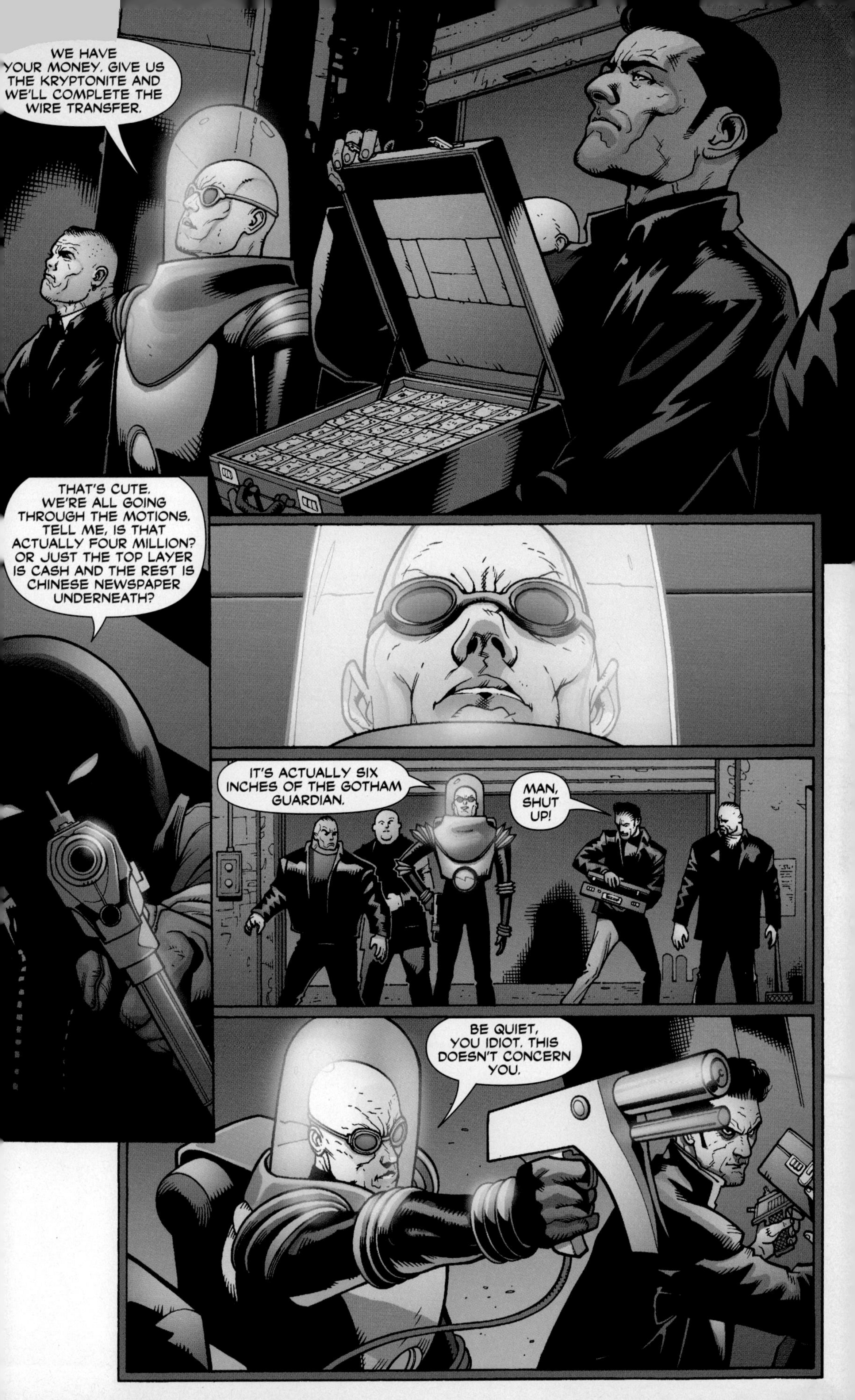
WE HAVE YOUR MONEY. GIVE US THE KRYPTONITE AND WE'LL COMPLETE THE WIRE TRANSFER.
THAT'S CUTE. WE'RE ALL GOING THROUGH THE MOTIONS. TELL ME, IS THAT ACTUALLY FOUR MILLION? OR JUST THE TOP LAYER IS CASH AND THE REST IS CHINESE NEWSPAPER UNDERNEATH?
IT'S ACTUALLY SIX INCHES OF THE GOTHAM GUARDIAN.
MAN, SHUT UP!
BE QUIET, YOU IDIOT. THIS DOESN'T CONCERN YOU.

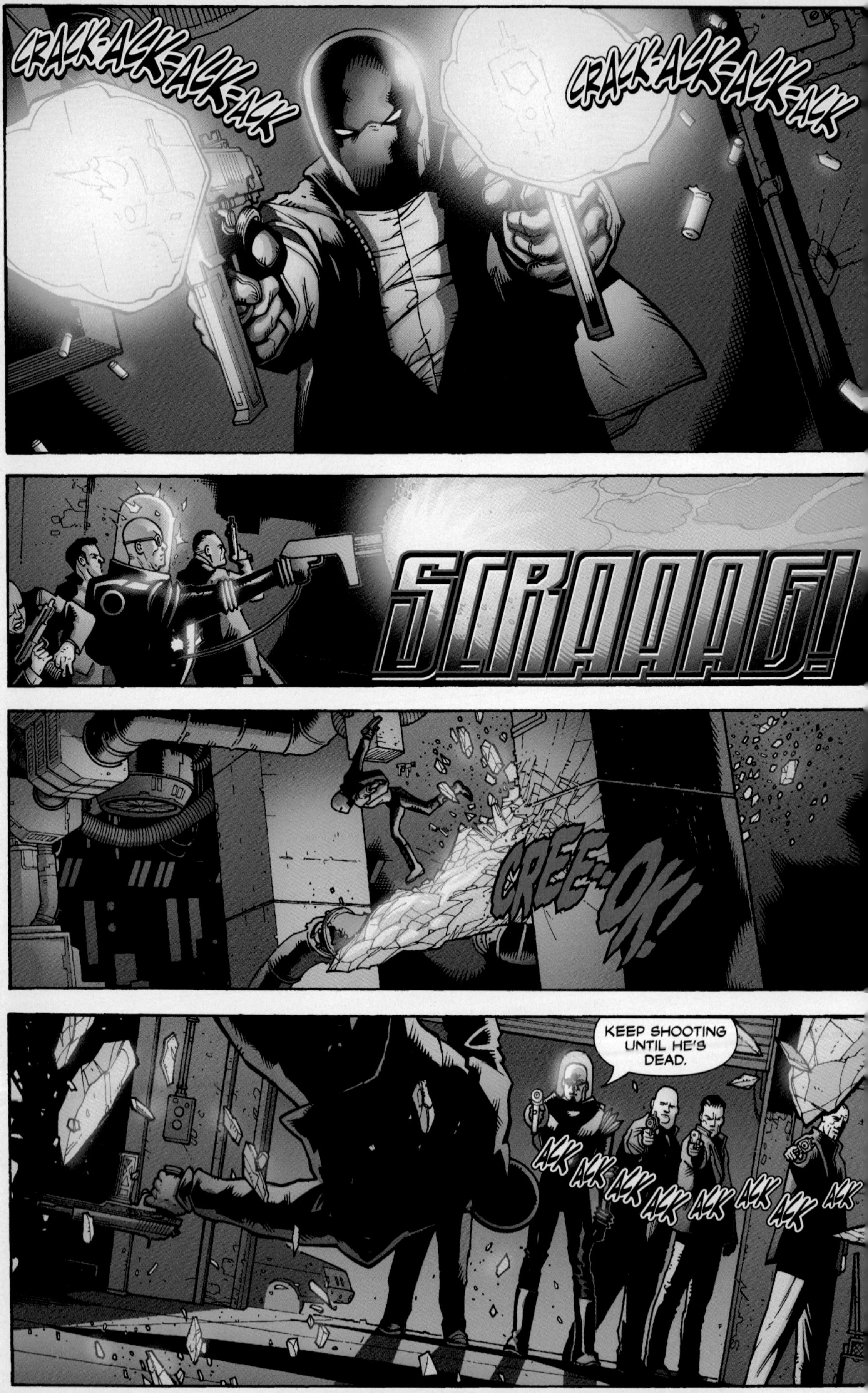
CRACK-ACK-ACK-ACK
CRACK-ACK-ACK-ACK
SCRAAAG!
CREE-OK!
KEEP SHOOTING UNTIL HE'S DEAD.
ACK ACK ACK ACK ACK ACK ACK ACK

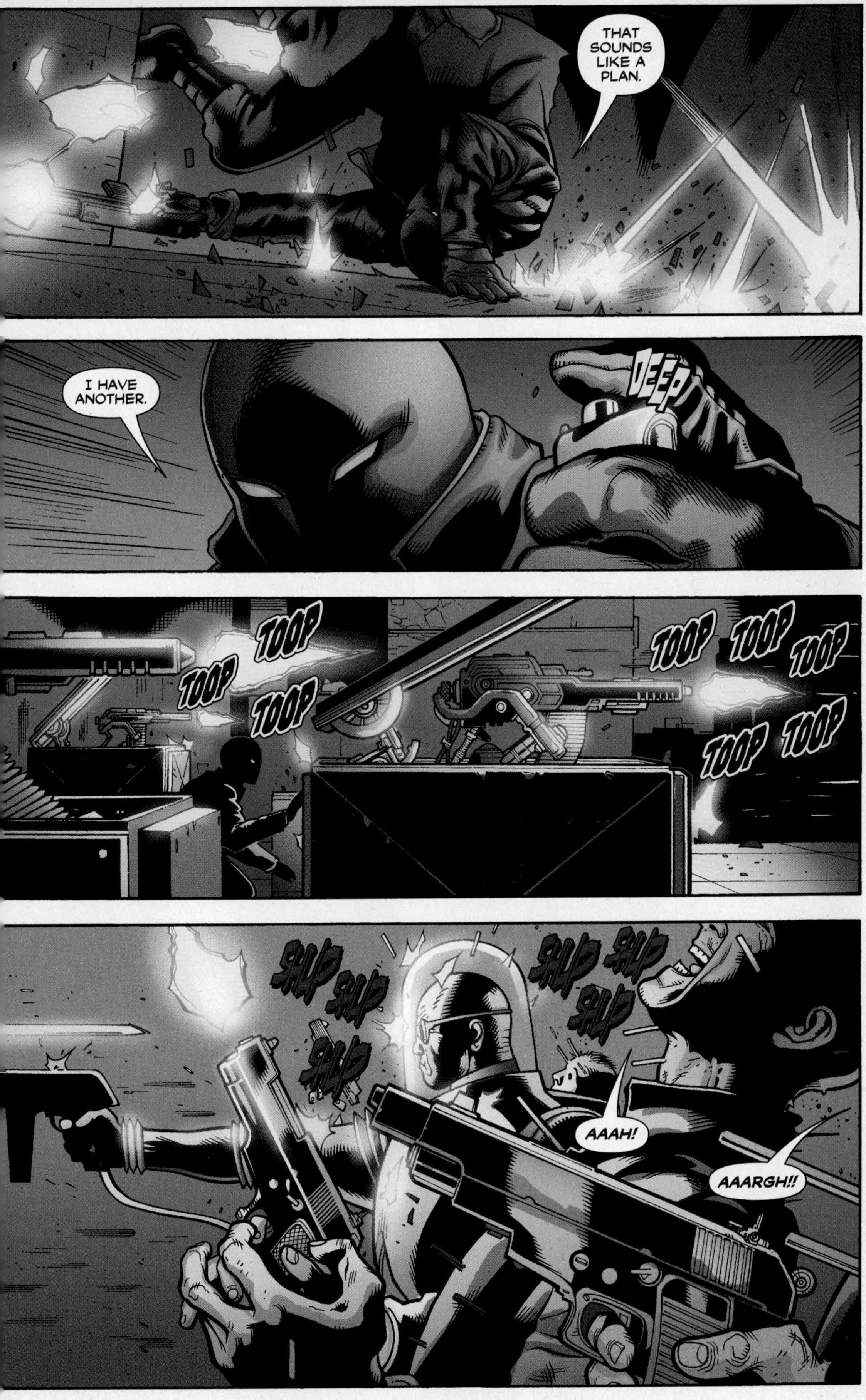
THAT SOUNDS LIKE A PLAN.
I HAVE ANOTHER.
DEEP
TOOP
TOOP
TOOP
TOOP TOOP TOOP
TOOP TOOP
SHLIP SHLIP SHLIP
SHLIP SHLIP SHLIP
AAAH!
AAARGH!!

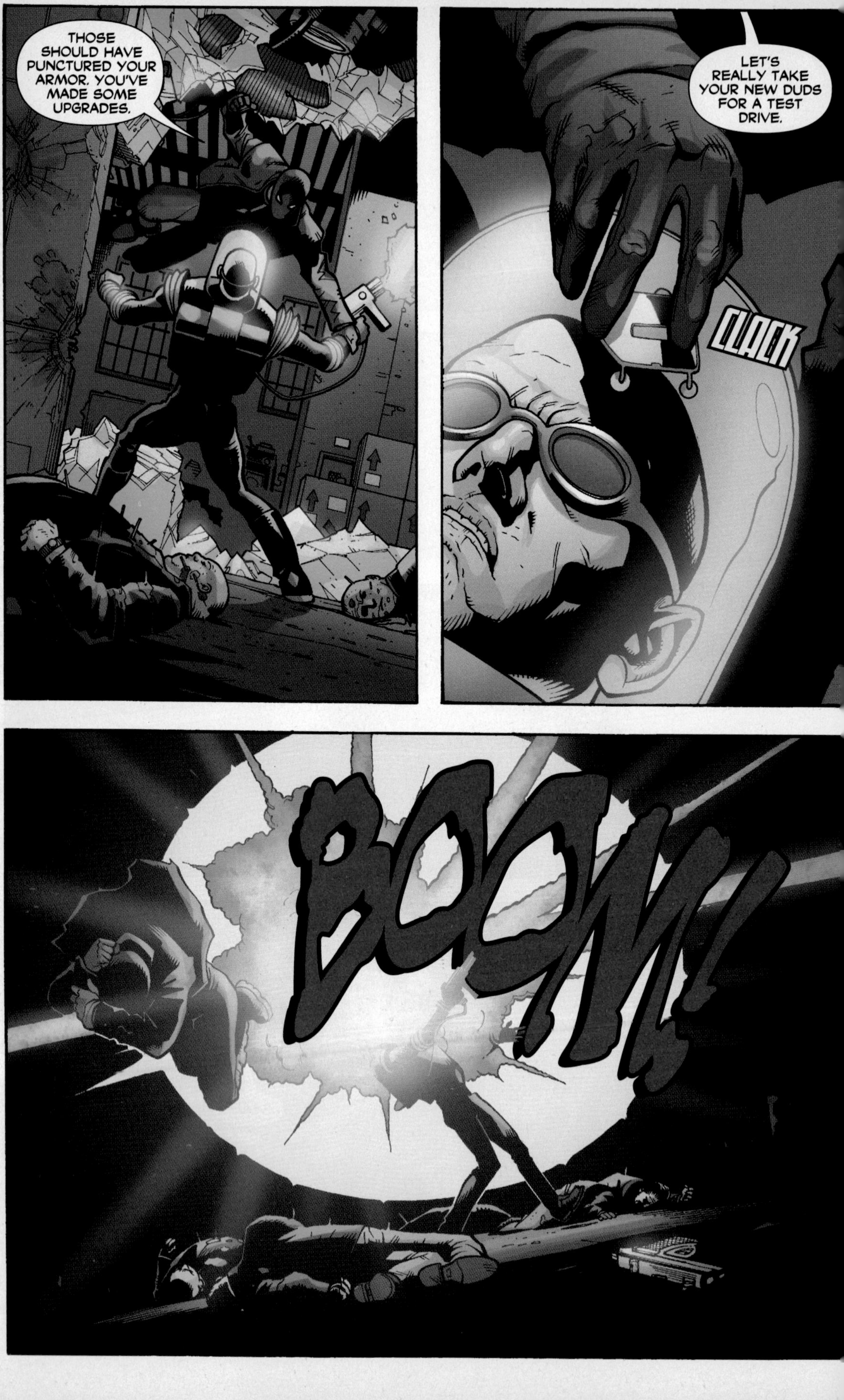
THOSE SHOULD HAVE PUNCTURED YOUR ARMOR. YOU'VE MADE SOME UPGRADES.
LET'S REALLY TAKE YOUR NEW DUDS FOR A TEST DRIVE.
CLACK
BOOM!

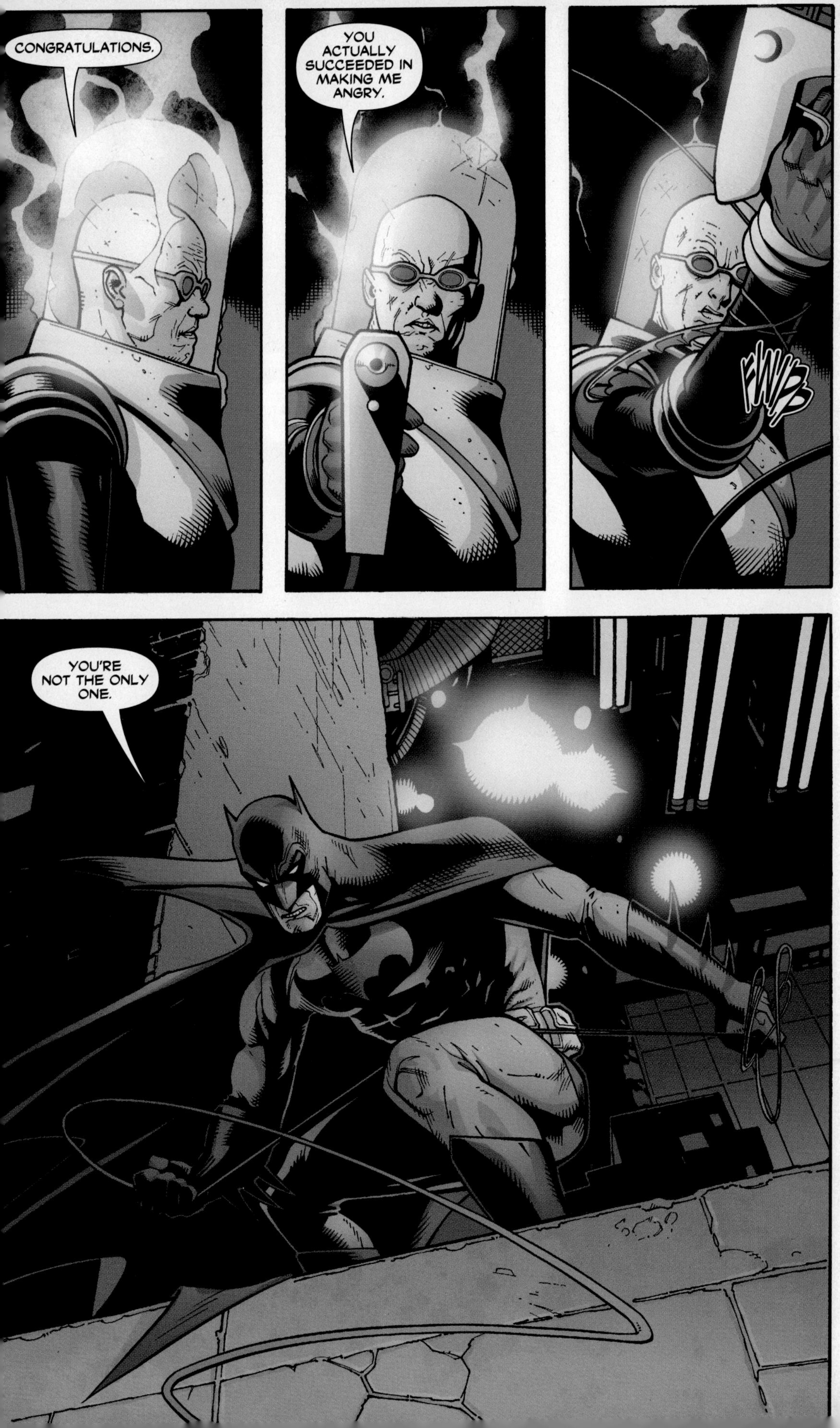
CONGRATULATIONS.
YOU ACTUALLY SUCCEEDED IN MAKING ME ANGRY.
FWIP
YOU'RE NOT THE ONLY ONE.

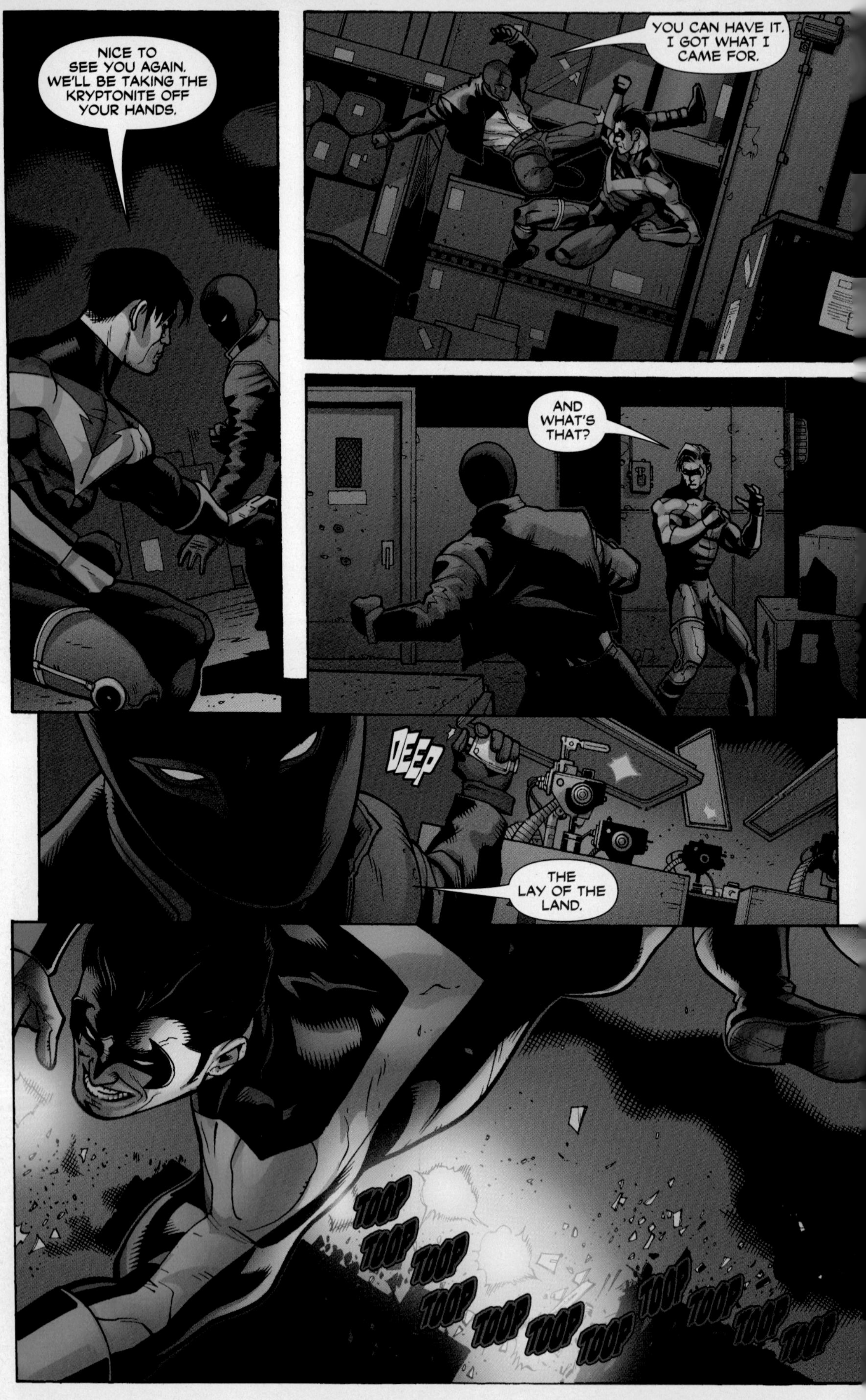
NICE TO SEE YOU AGAIN. WE'LL BE TAKING THE KRYPTONITE OFF YOUR HANDS.
YOU CAN HAVE IT. I GOT WHAT I CAME FOR.
AND WHAT'S THAT?
DEEP
THE LAY OF THE LAND.
TOOP TOOP TOOP TOOP TOOP TOOP TOOP TOOP TOOP TOOP TOOP

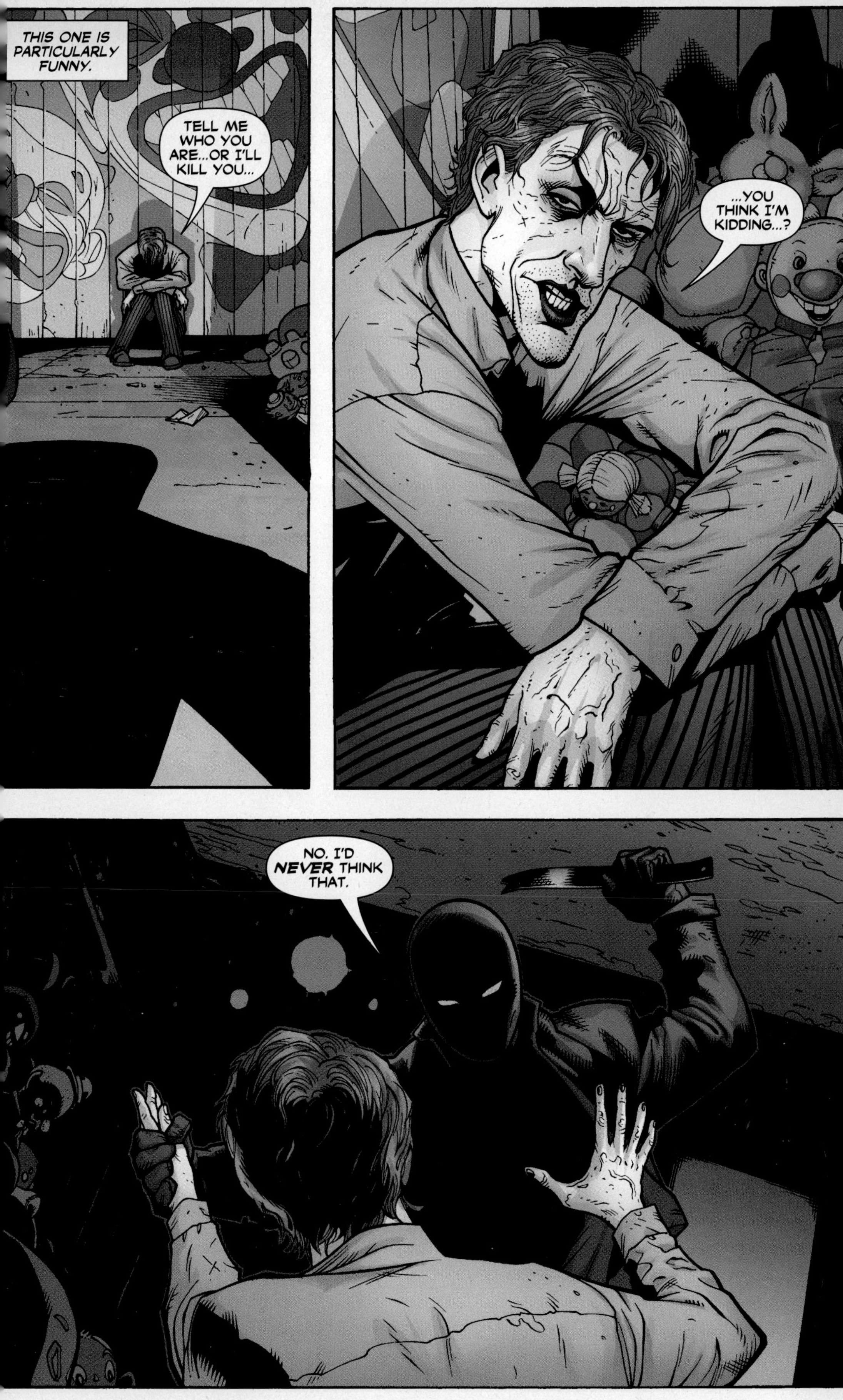
THIS ONE IS PARTICULARLY FUNNY.
TELL ME WHO YOU ARE...OR I'LL KILL YOU...
...YOU THINK I'M KIDDING...?
NO. I'D NEVER THINK THAT.

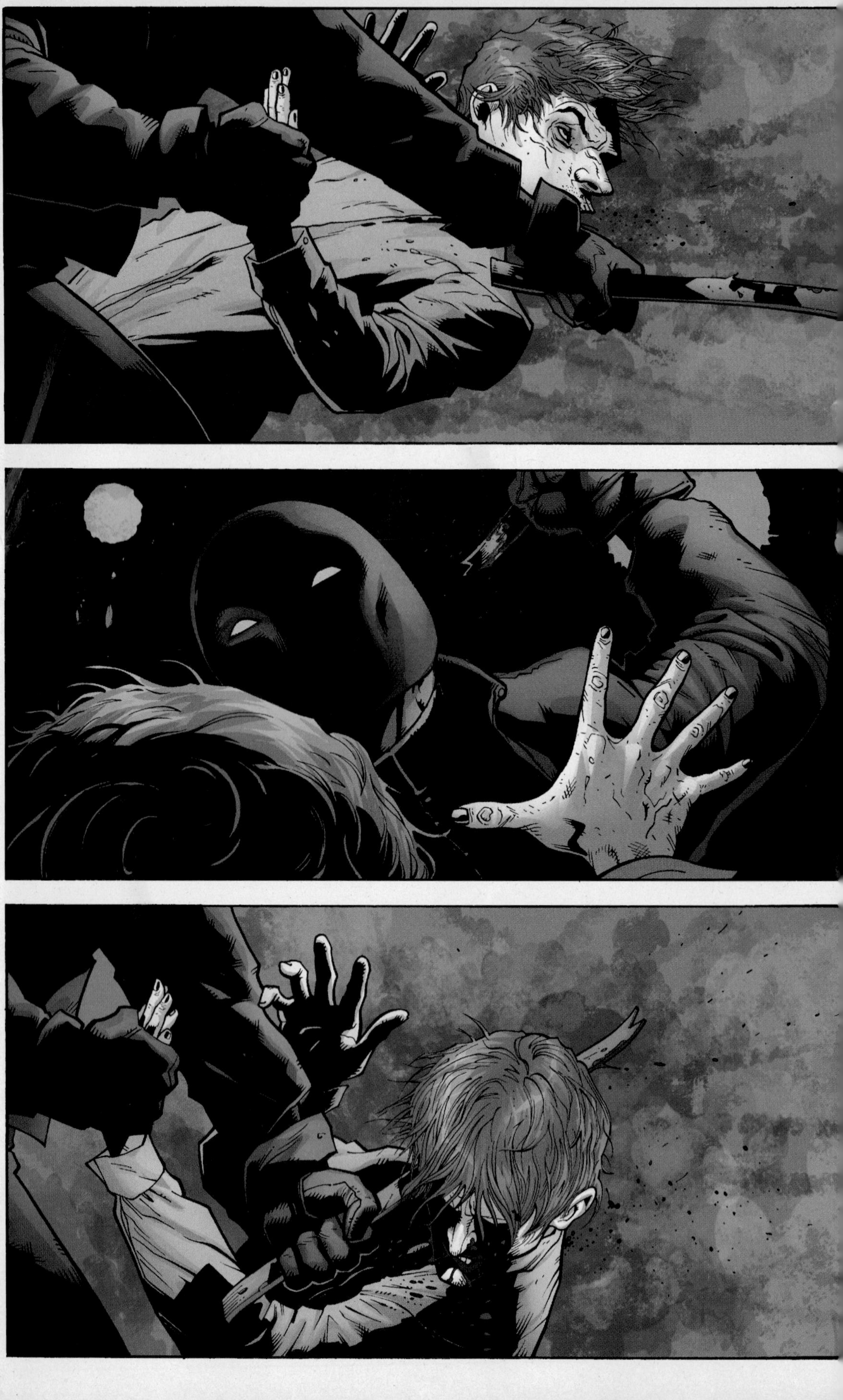

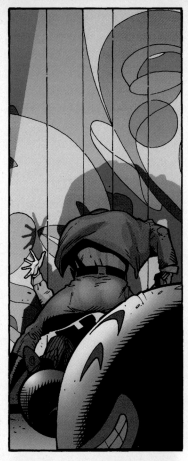

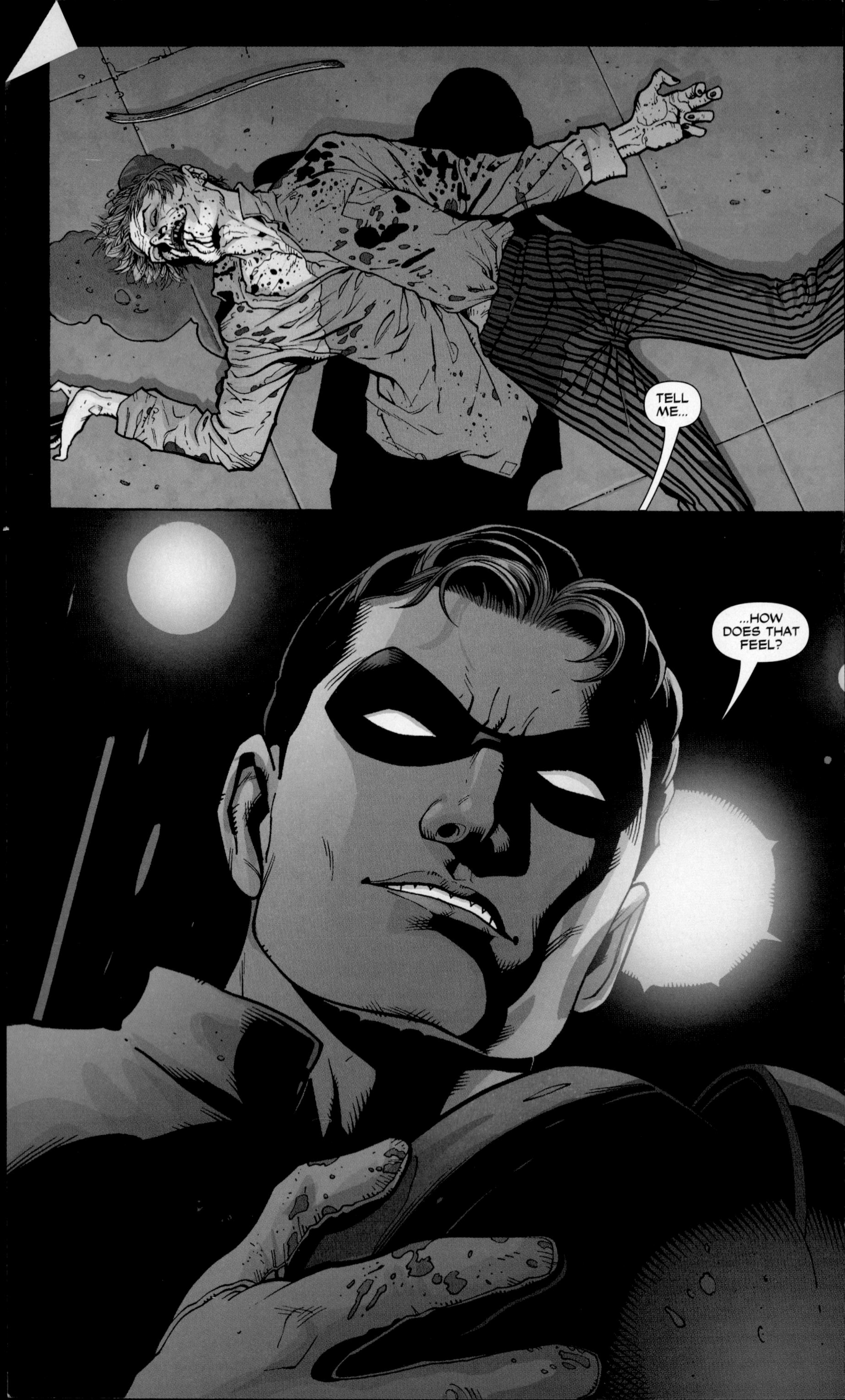
TELL ME...
...HOW DOES THAT FEEL?

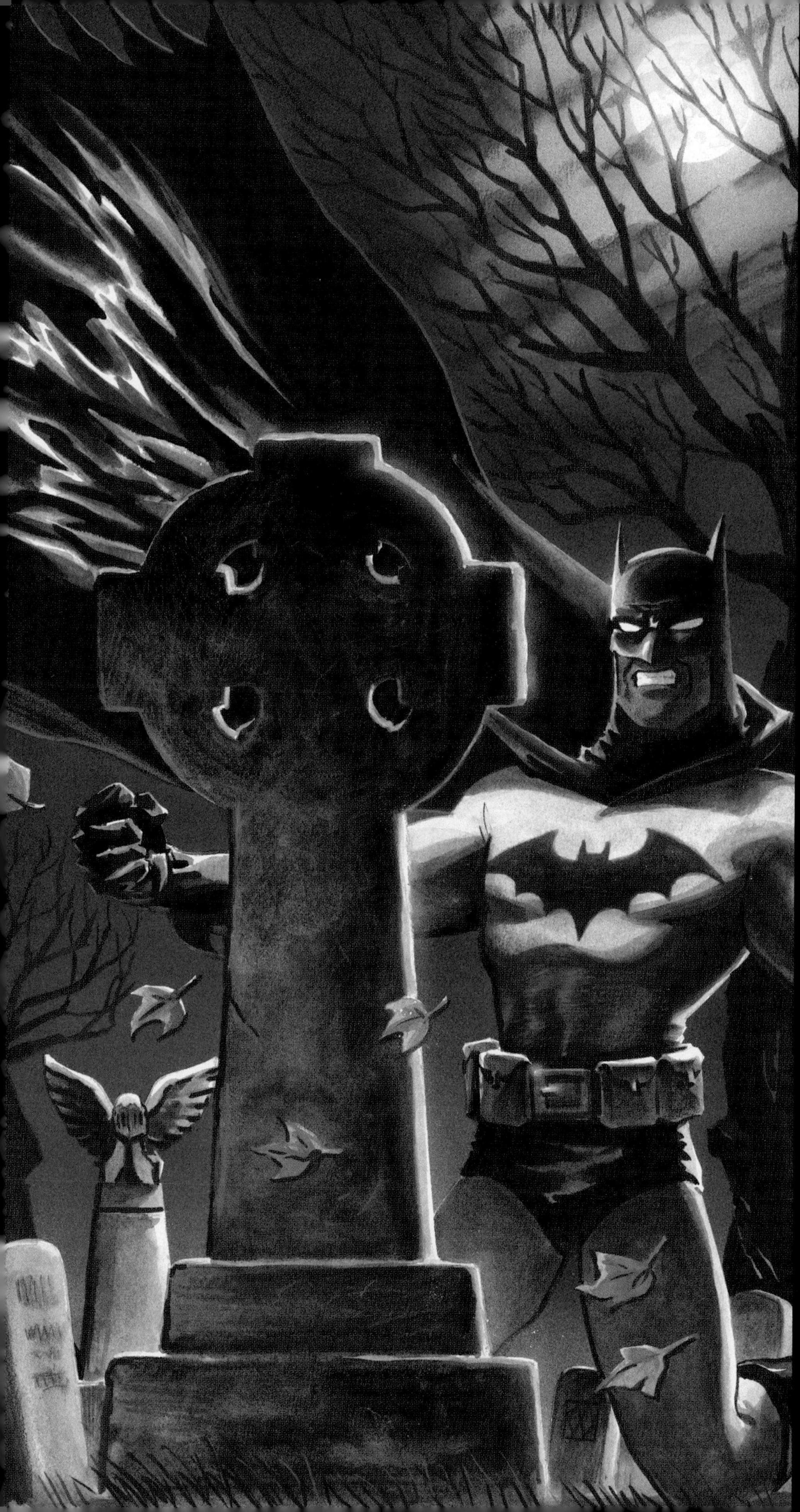

BATMAN #639 • ART BY MATT WAGNER

PART 5

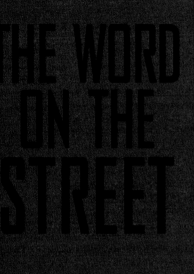

THE WORD ON THE STREET

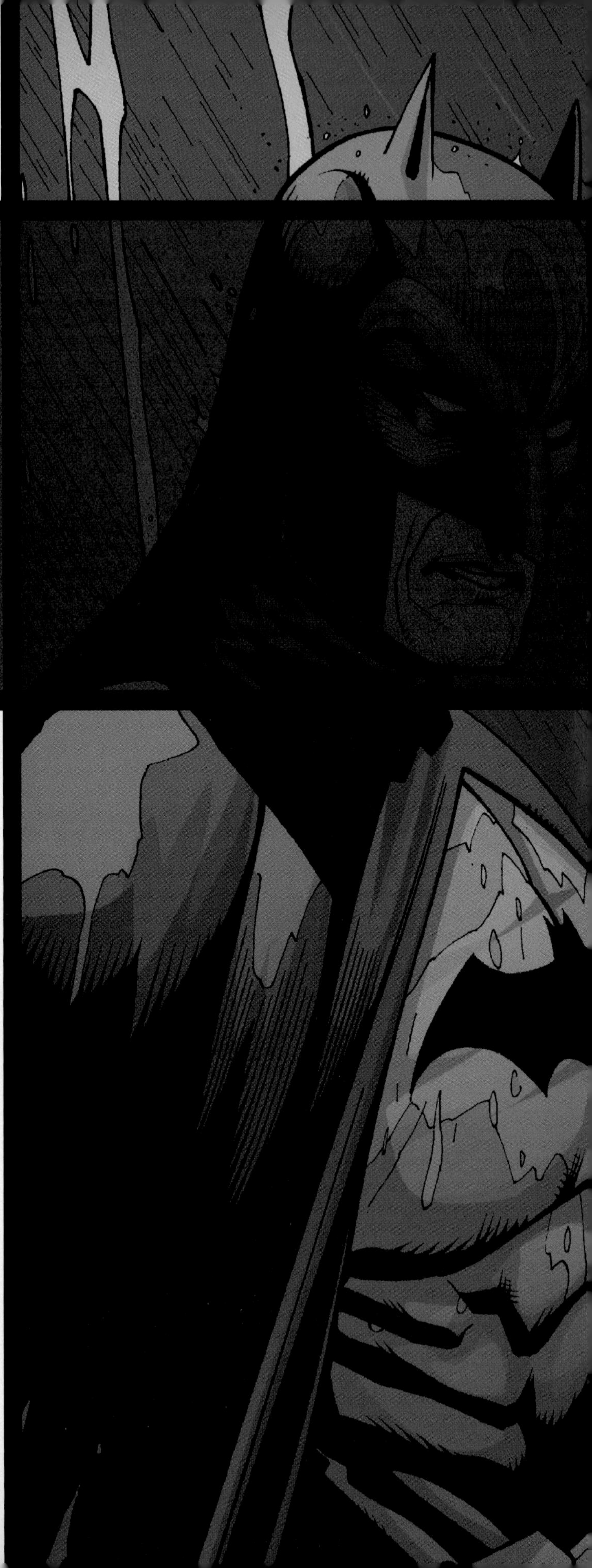

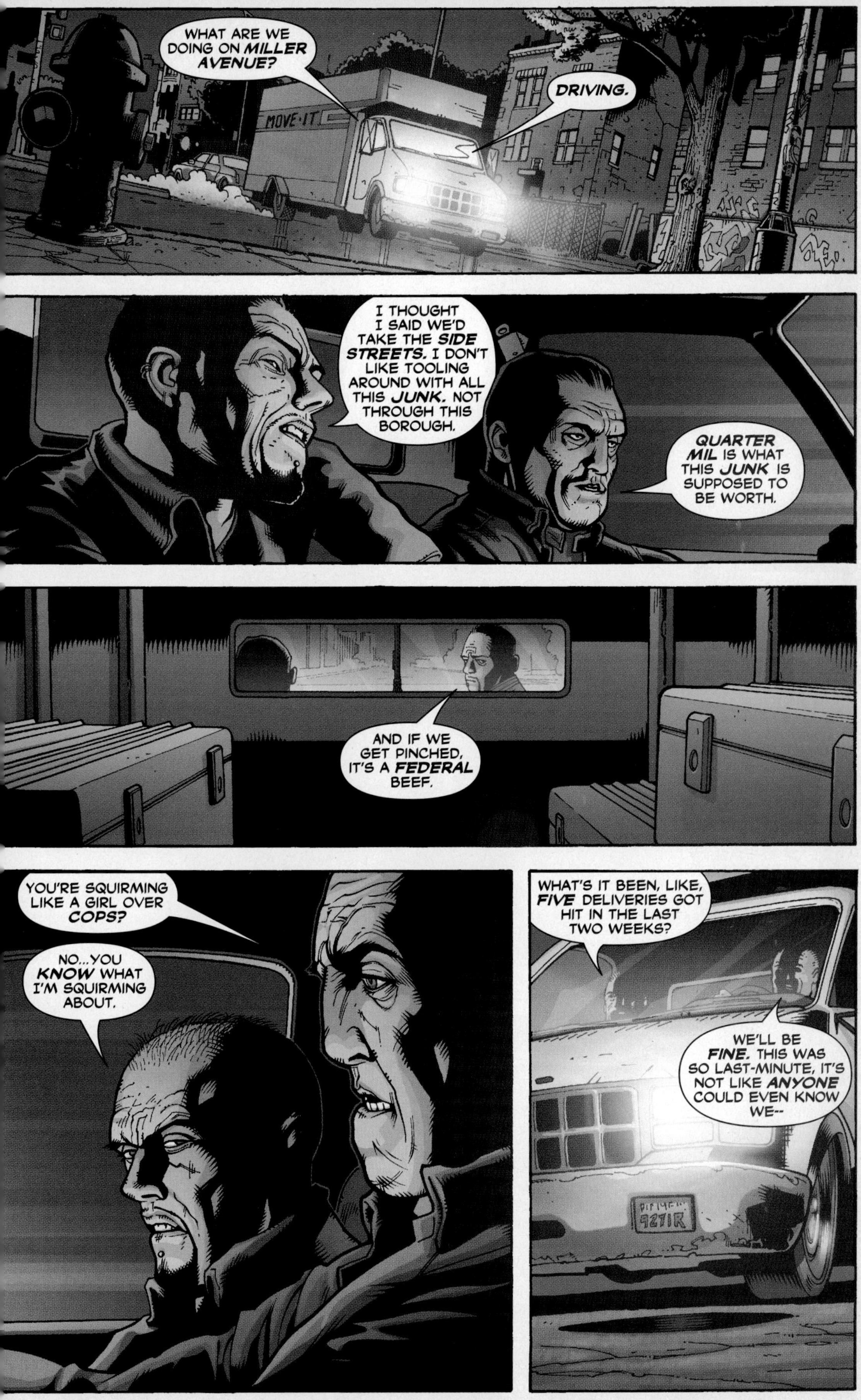
WHAT ARE WE DOING ON MILLER AVENUE?
DRIVING.
MOVE-IT
I THOUGHT I SAID WE'D TAKE THE SIDE STREETS. I DON'T LIKE TOOLING AROUND WITH ALL THIS JUNK. NOT THROUGH THIS BOROUGH.
QUARTER MIL IS WHAT THIS JUNK IS SUPPOSED TO BE WORTH.
AND IF WE GET PINCHED, IT'S A FEDERAL BEEF.
YOU'RE SQUIRMING LIKE A GIRL OVER COPS?
NO...YOU KNOW WHAT I'M SQUIRMING ABOUT.
WHAT'S IT BEEN, LIKE, FIVE DELIVERIES GOT HIT IN THE LAST TWO WEEKS?
WE'LL BE FINE. THIS WAS SO LAST-MINUTE, IT'S NOT LIKE ANYONE COULD EVEN KNOW WE--

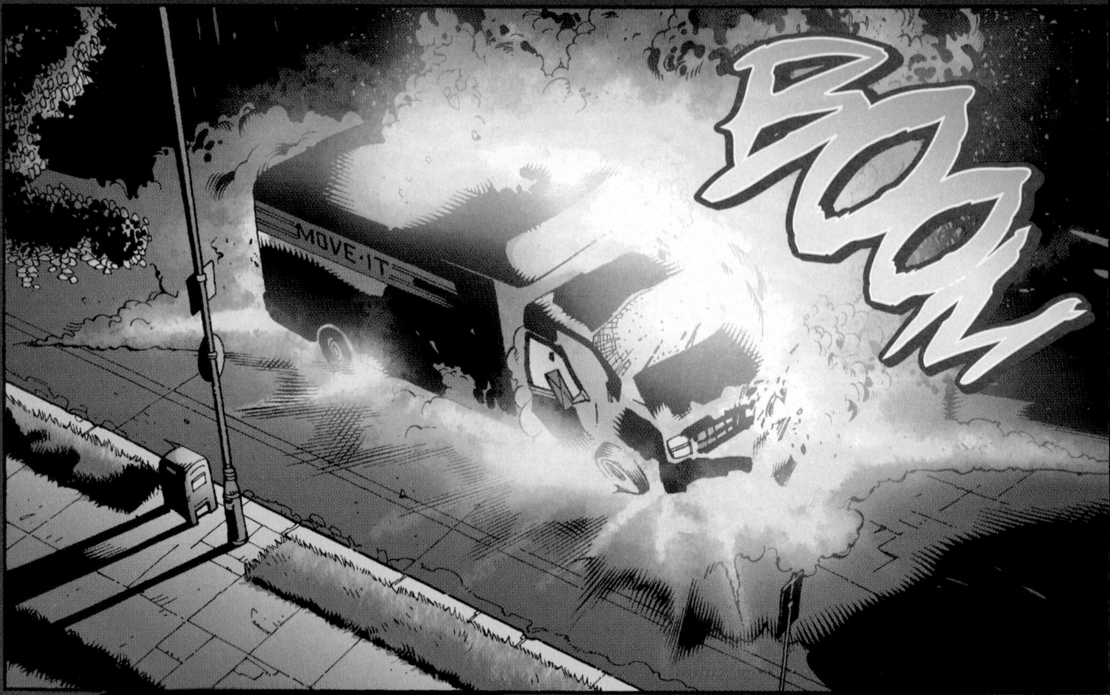
MOVE-IT
BOOM

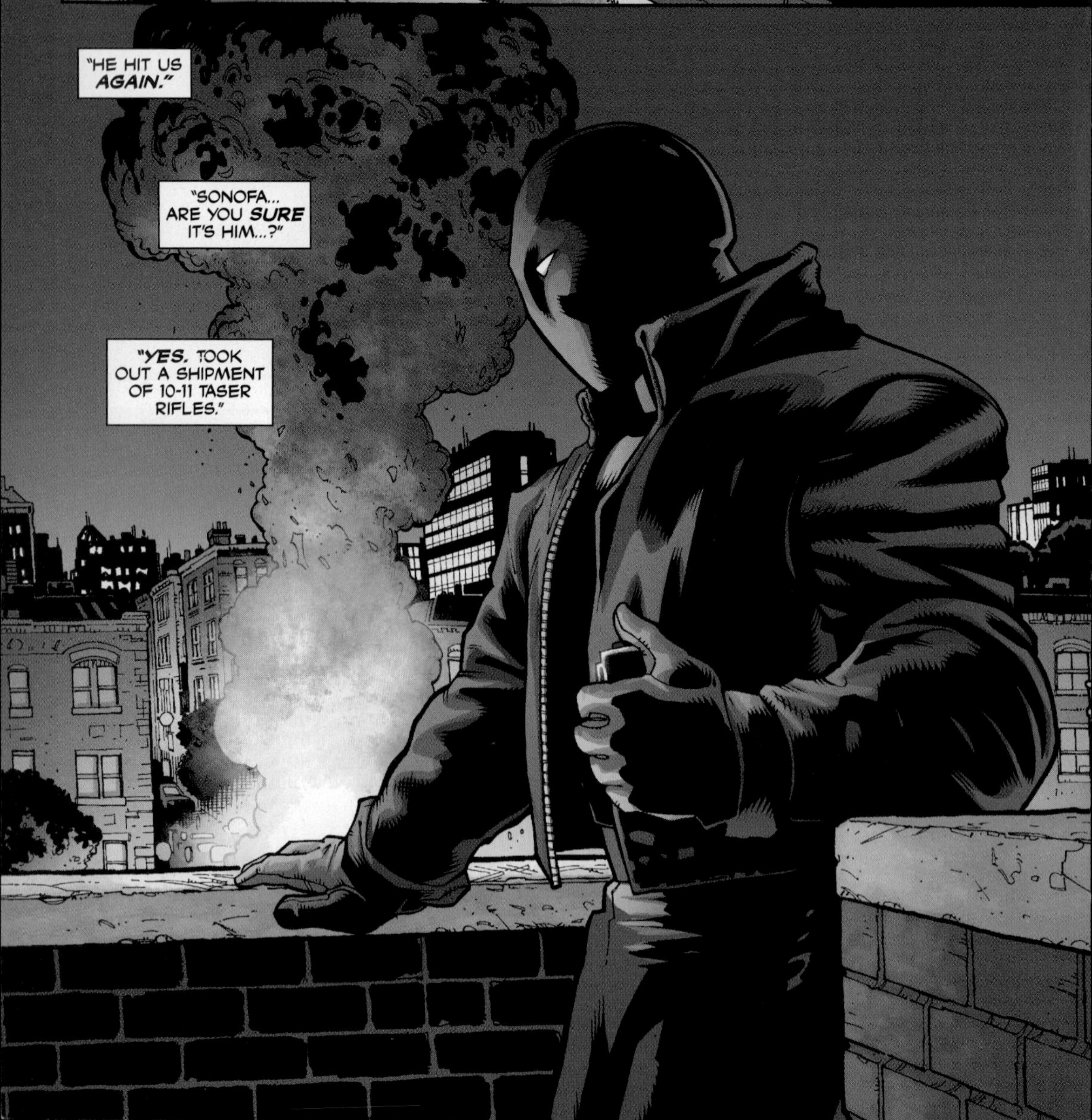
"HE HIT US AGAIN."
"SONOFA... ARE YOU SURE IT'S HIM...?"
"YES. TOOK OUT A SHIPMENT OF 10-11 TASER RIFLES."

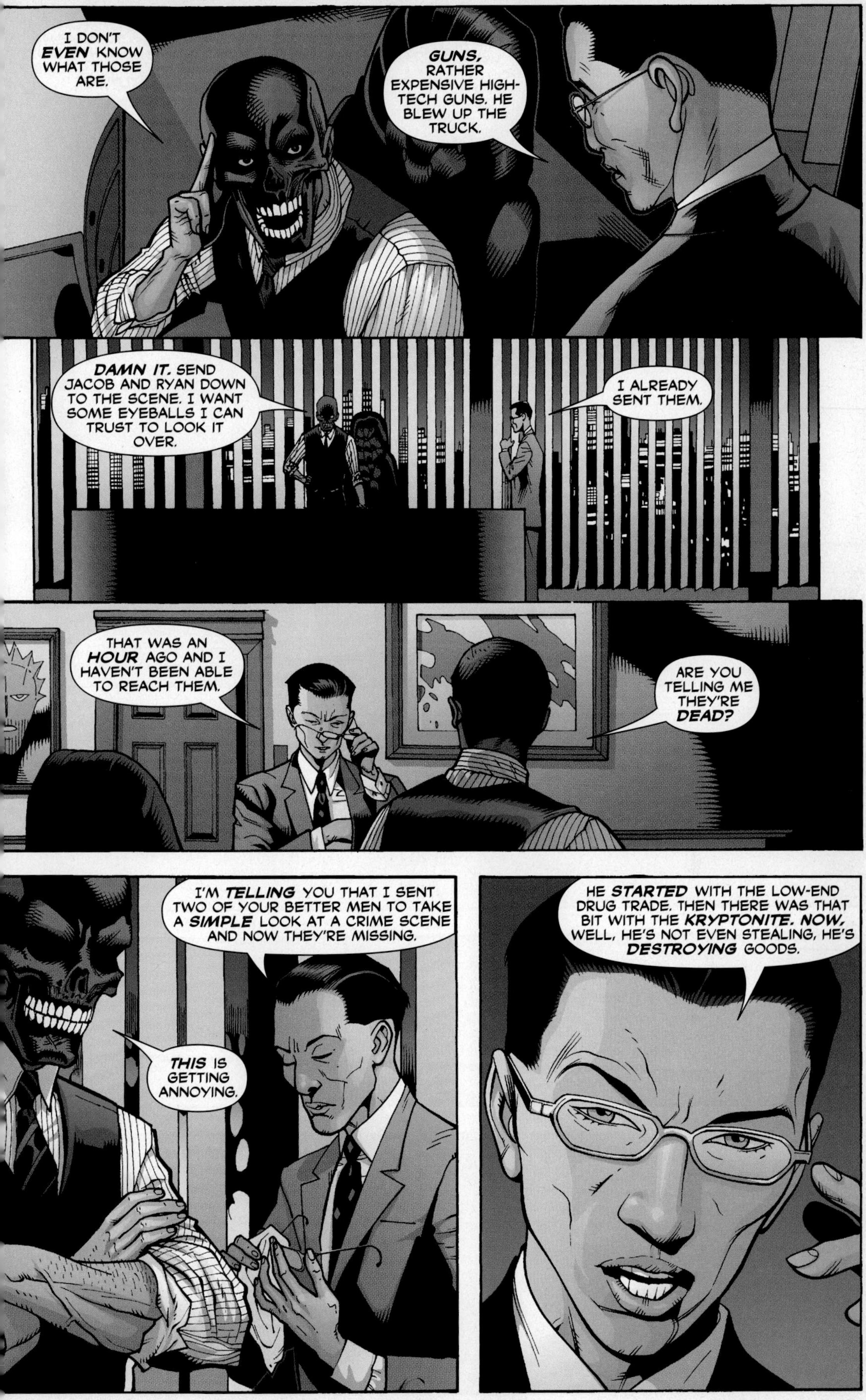
I DON'T EVEN KNOW WHAT THOSE ARE.
GUNS, RATHER EXPENSIVE HIGH-TECH GUNS. HE BLEW UP THE TRUCK.
DAMN IT. SEND JACOB AND RYAN DOWN TO THE SCENE. I WANT SOME EYEBALLS I CAN TRUST TO LOOK IT OVER.
I ALREADY SENT THEM.
THAT WAS AN HOUR AGO AND I HAVEN'T BEEN ABLE TO REACH THEM.
ARE YOU TELLING ME THEY'RE DEAD?
I'M TELLING YOU THAT I SENT TWO OF YOUR BETTER MEN TO TAKE A SIMPLE LOOK AT A CRIME SCENE AND NOW THEY'RE MISSING.
THIS IS GETTING ANNOYING.
HE STARTED WITH THE LOW-END DRUG TRADE. THEN THERE WAS THAT BIT WITH THE KRYPTONITE. NOW, WELL, HE'S NOT EVEN STEALING, HE'S DESTROYING GOODS.

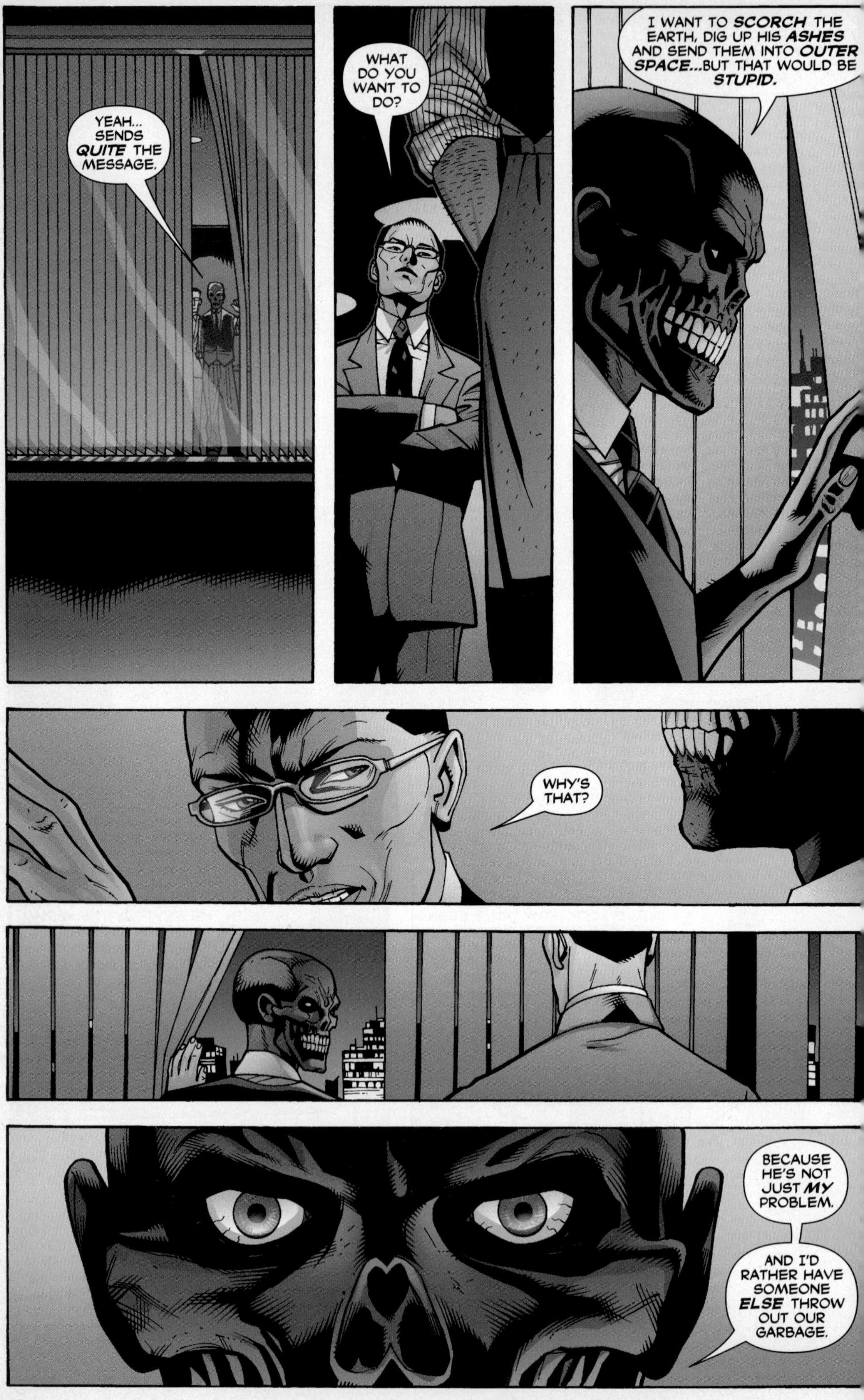
YEAH... SENDS QUITE THE MESSAGE.
WHAT DO YOU WANT TO DO?
I WANT TO SCORCH THE EARTH, DIG UP HIS ASHES AND SEND THEM INTO OUTER SPACE...BUT THAT WOULD BE STUPID.
WHY'S THAT?
BECAUSE HE'S NOT JUST MY PROBLEM.
AND I'D RATHER HAVE SOMEONE ELSE THROW OUT OUR GARBAGE.

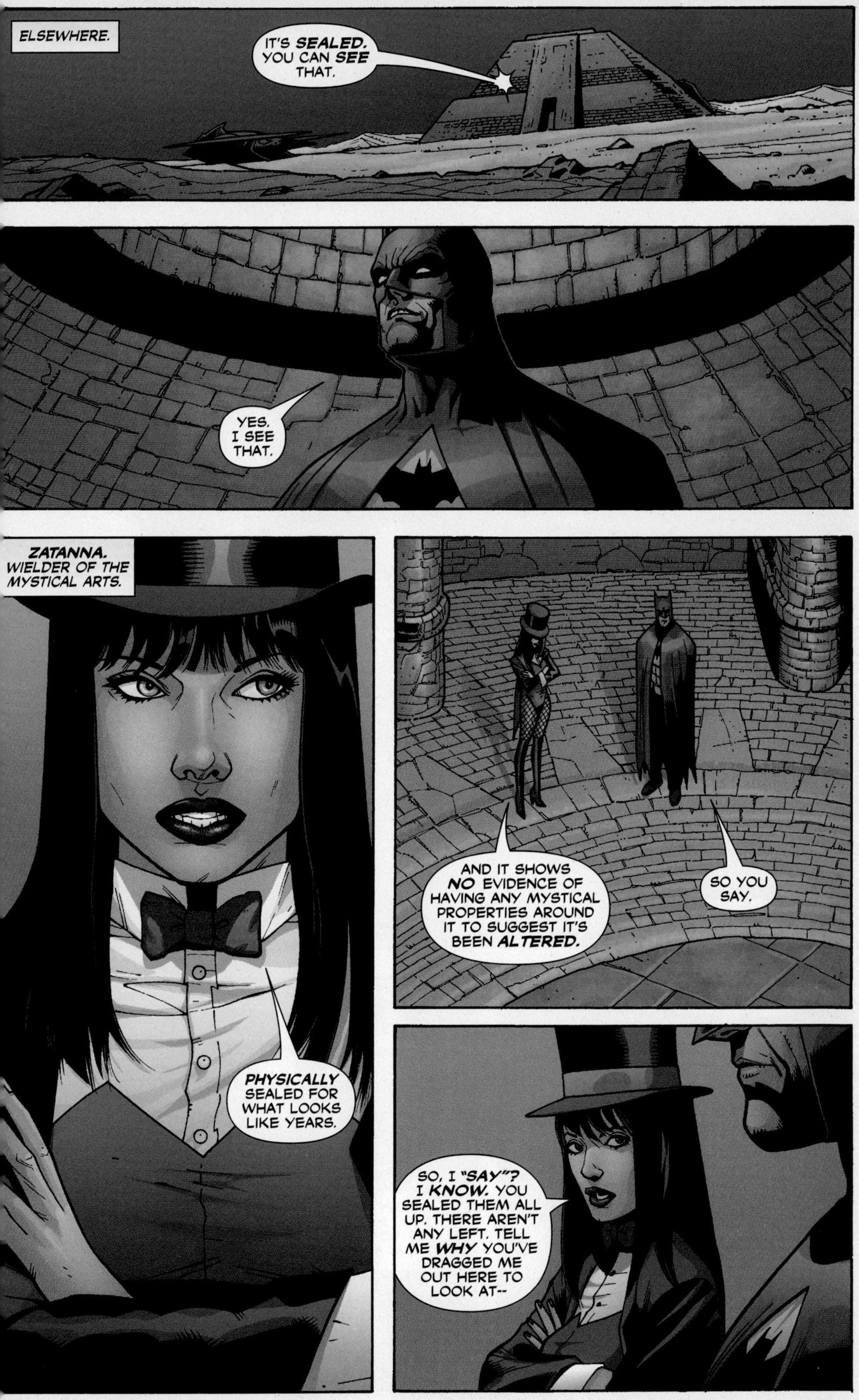
ELSEWHERE.
IT'S SEALED. YOU CAN SEE THAT.
YES. I SEE THAT.
ZATANNA. WIELDER OF THE MYSTICAL ARTS.
PHYSICALLY SEALED FOR WHAT LOOKS LIKE YEARS.
AND IT SHOWS NO EVIDENCE OF HAVING ANY MYSTICAL PROPERTIES AROUND IT TO SUGGEST IT'S BEEN ALTERED.
SO YOU SAY.
SO, I "SAY"? I KNOW. YOU SEALED THEM ALL UP. THERE AREN'T ANY LEFT. TELL ME WHY YOU'VE DRAGGED ME OUT HERE TO LOOK AT--

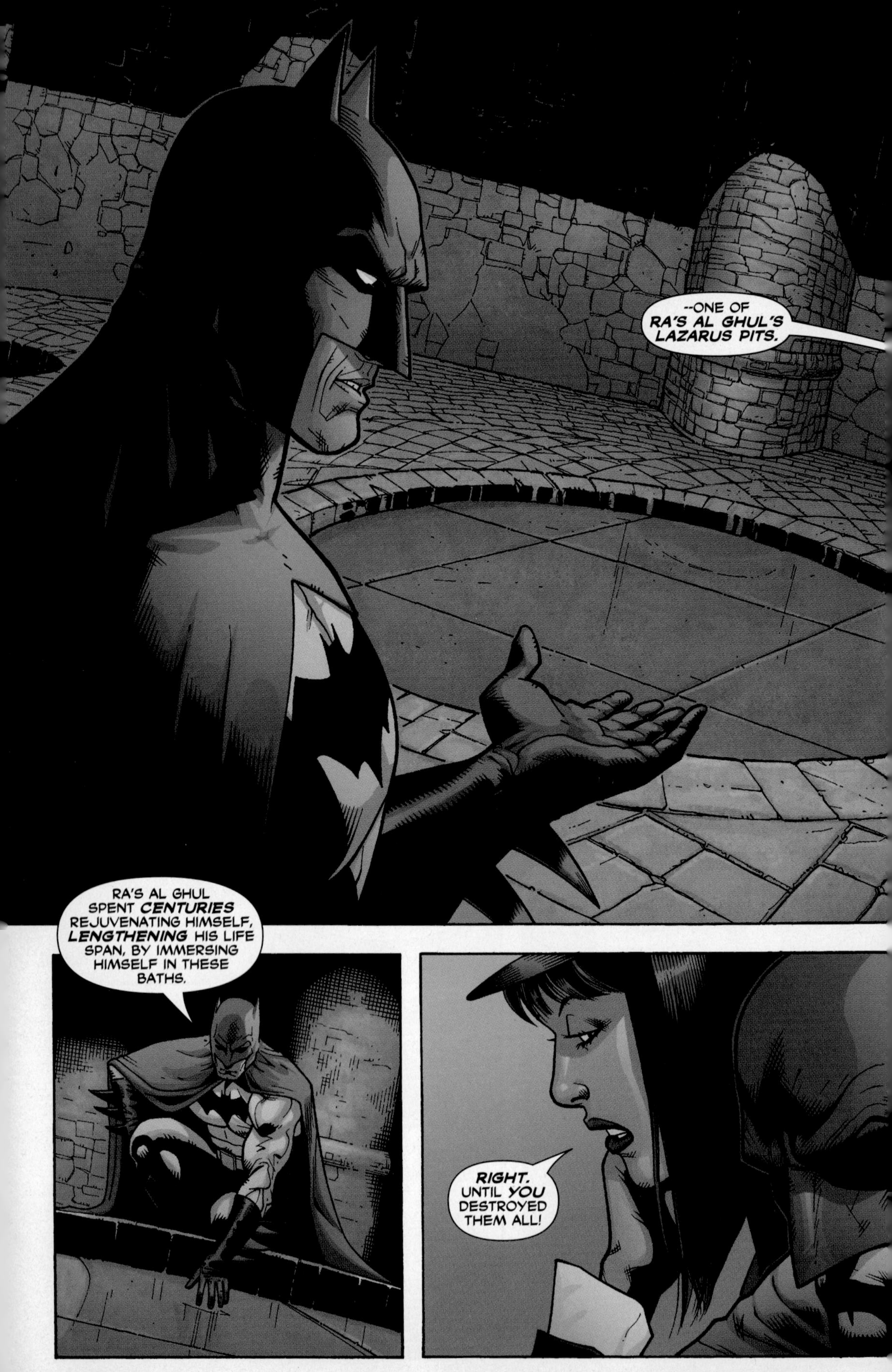
--ONE OF RA'S AL GHUL'S LAZARUS PITS.
RA'S AL GHUL SPENT CENTURIES REJUVENATING HIMSELF, LENGTHENING HIS LIFE SPAN, BY IMMERSING HIMSELF IN THESE BATHS.
RIGHT. UNTIL YOU DESTROYED THEM ALL!

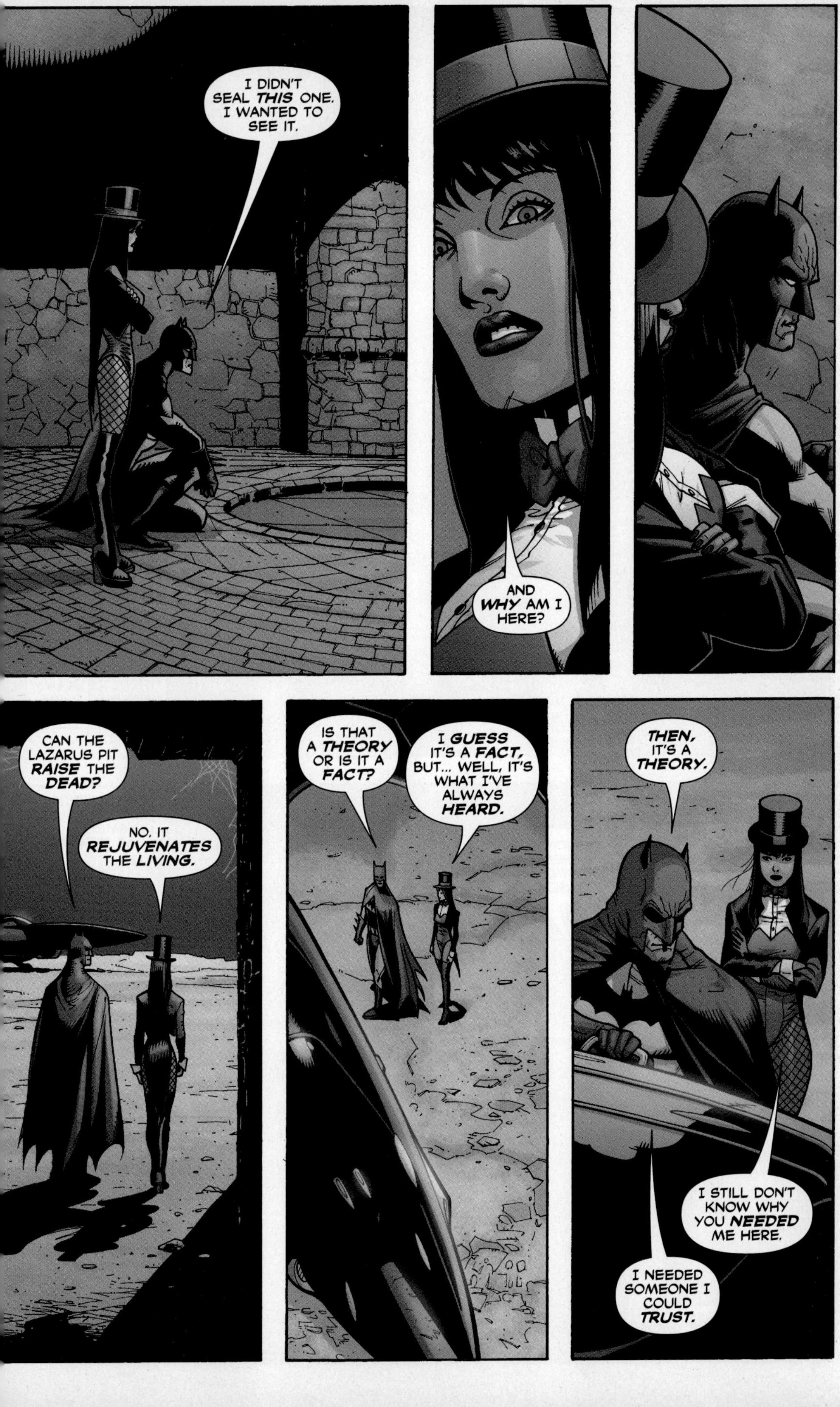
I DIDN'T SEAL *THIS* ONE. I WANTED TO SEE IT.
AND *WHY* AM I HERE?
CAN THE LAZARUS PIT *RAISE* THE *DEAD?*
NO. IT *REJUVENATES* THE *LIVING.*
IS THAT A *THEORY* OR IS IT A *FACT?*
I *GUESS* IT'S A *FACT,* BUT... WELL, IT'S WHAT I'VE ALWAYS *HEARD.*
THEN, IT'S A *THEORY.*
I STILL DON'T KNOW WHY YOU *NEEDED* ME HERE.
I NEEDED SOMEONE I COULD *TRUST.*

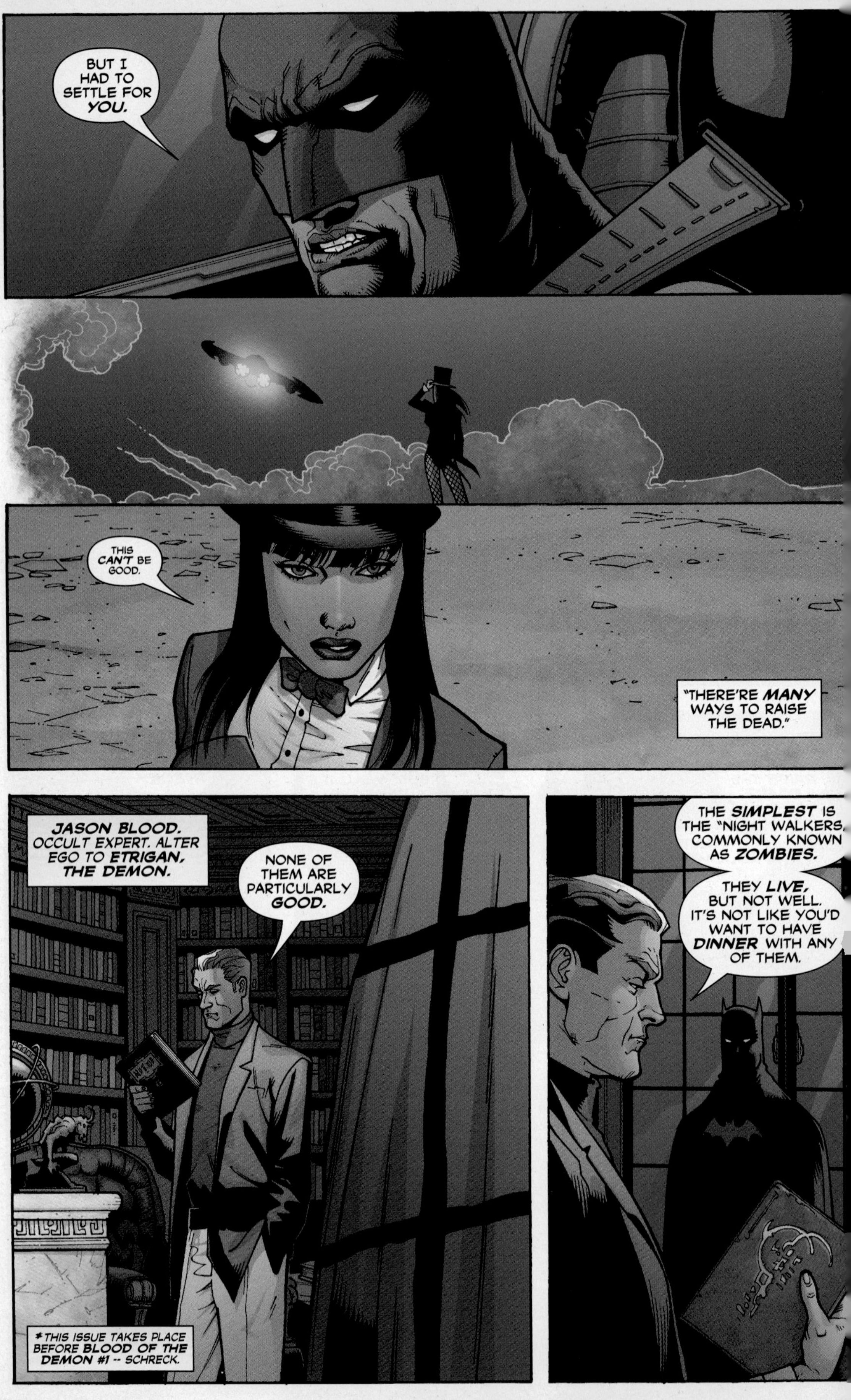
BUT I HAD TO SETTLE FOR YOU.
THIS CAN'T BE GOOD.
"THERE'RE MANY WAYS TO RAISE THE DEAD."
JASON BLOOD. OCCULT EXPERT. ALTER EGO TO ETRIGAN, THE DEMON.
NONE OF THEM ARE PARTICULARLY GOOD.
*THIS ISSUE TAKES PLACE BEFORE BLOOD OF THE DEMON #1 -- SCHRECK.
THE SIMPLEST IS THE "NIGHT WALKERS, COMMONLY KNOWN AS ZOMBIES.
THEY LIVE, BUT NOT WELL. IT'S NOT LIKE YOU'D WANT TO HAVE DINNER WITH ANY OF THEM.

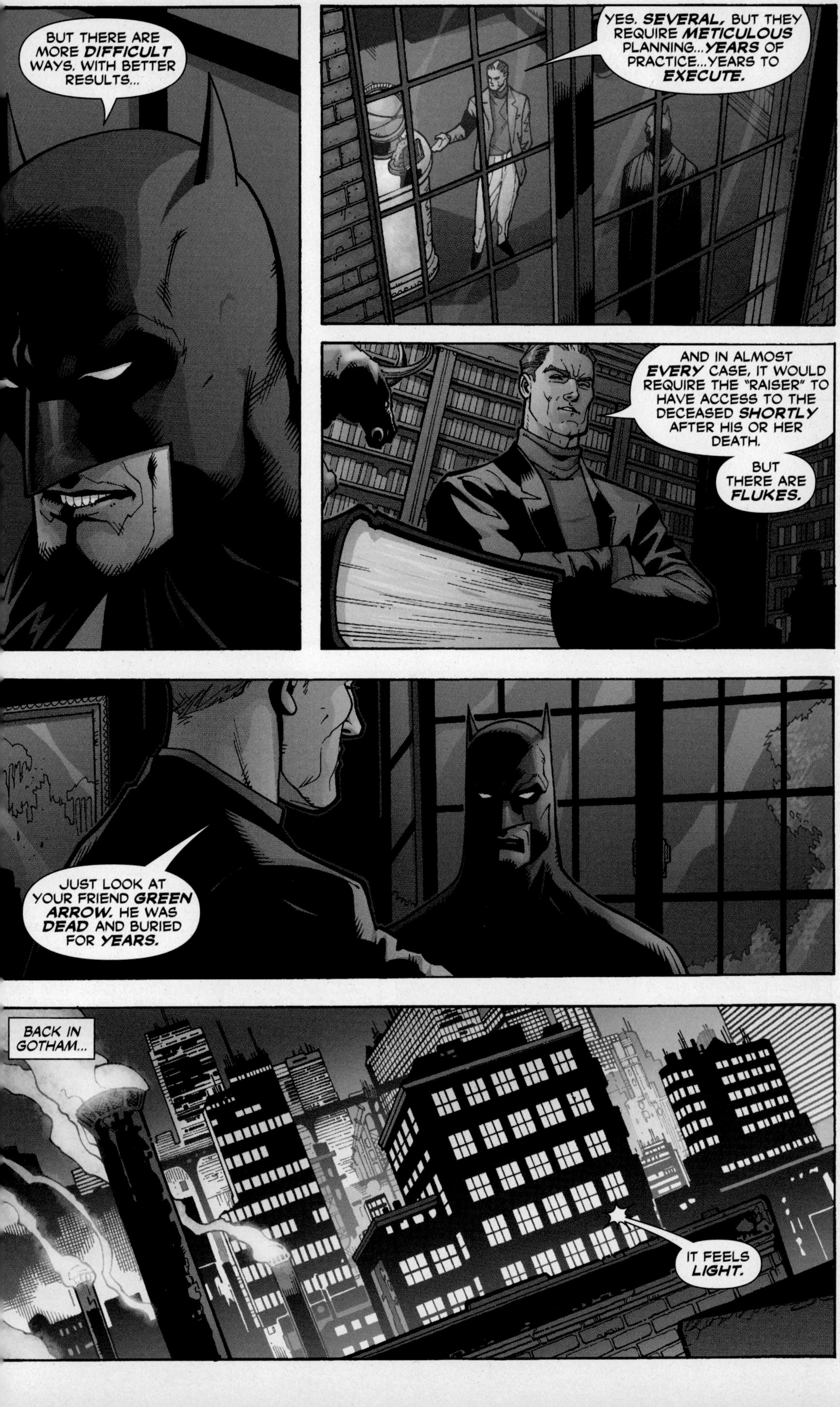
BUT THERE ARE MORE DIFFICULT WAYS, WITH BETTER RESULTS...
YES. SEVERAL, BUT THEY REQUIRE METICULOUS PLANNING...YEARS OF PRACTICE...YEARS TO EXECUTE.
AND IN ALMOST EVERY CASE, IT WOULD REQUIRE THE "RAISER" TO HAVE ACCESS TO THE DECEASED SHORTLY AFTER HIS OR HER DEATH.
BUT THERE ARE FLUKES.
JUST LOOK AT YOUR FRIEND GREEN ARROW. HE WAS DEAD AND BURIED FOR YEARS.
BACK IN GOTHAM...
IT FEELS LIGHT.

IT'S NOT *LIGHT*. AND QUIT MOANING, MAN. THIS AIN'T *A BUY*. JUST TAKE IT TO *THE MAN*.

HE DOESN'T WANT *PRODUCT*, HE JUST WANTS HIS *CUT*.

WELL, I *CAN'T* MOVE THIS WEIGHT, I DON'T *WANT* TO MOVE THIS WEIGHT.

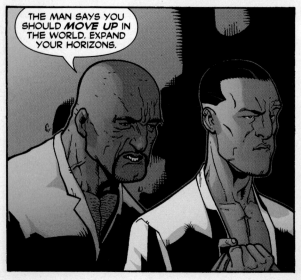

THE MAN SAYS YOU SHOULD *MOVE UP* IN THE WORLD. EXPAND YOUR HORIZONS.

LOOK, THIS IS ALL *WAY* TOO MUCH ACTION FOR ME. *TRUTH*...DUDE *SCARES* ME. I'M *OUT*.

MAN, YOU DON'T *GET* TO MAKE THAT CALL. THIS ISN'T SOME DAMN *LITTLE LEAGUER* GAME. YOU'RE *"OUT"* ONLY WHEN THE MAN *SAYS* YOU'RE OUT.

I'VE GOT A *BETTER* IDEA.

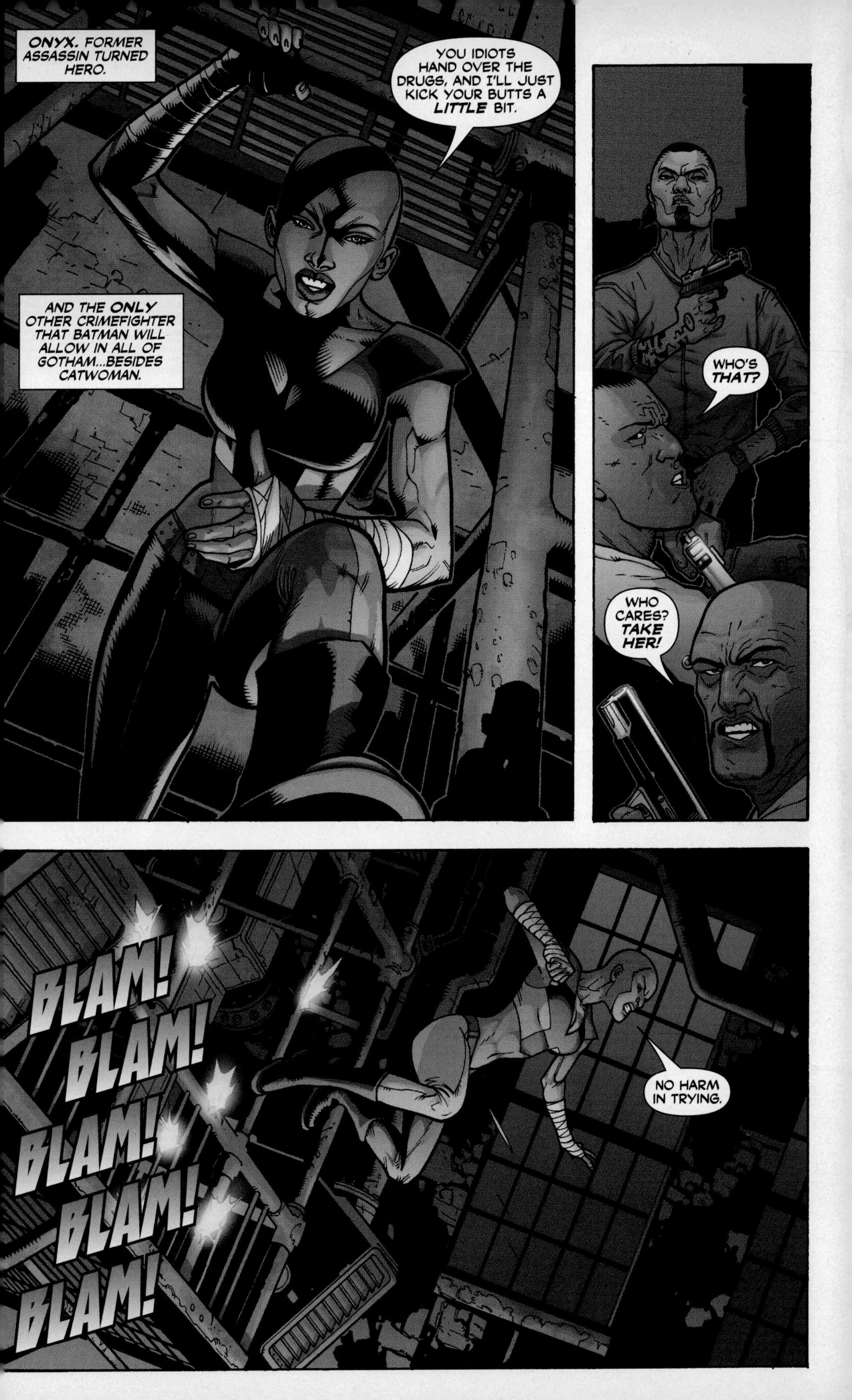

ONYX. FORMER ASSASSIN TURNED HERO.
YOU IDIOTS HAND OVER THE DRUGS, AND I'LL JUST KICK YOUR BUTTS A LITTLE BIT.
AND THE ONLY OTHER CRIMEFIGHTER THAT BATMAN WILL ALLOW IN ALL OF GOTHAM...BESIDES CATWOMAN.
WHO'S THAT?
WHO CARES? TAKE HER!
BLAM! BLAM! BLAM! BLAM! BLAM!
NO HARM IN TRYING.

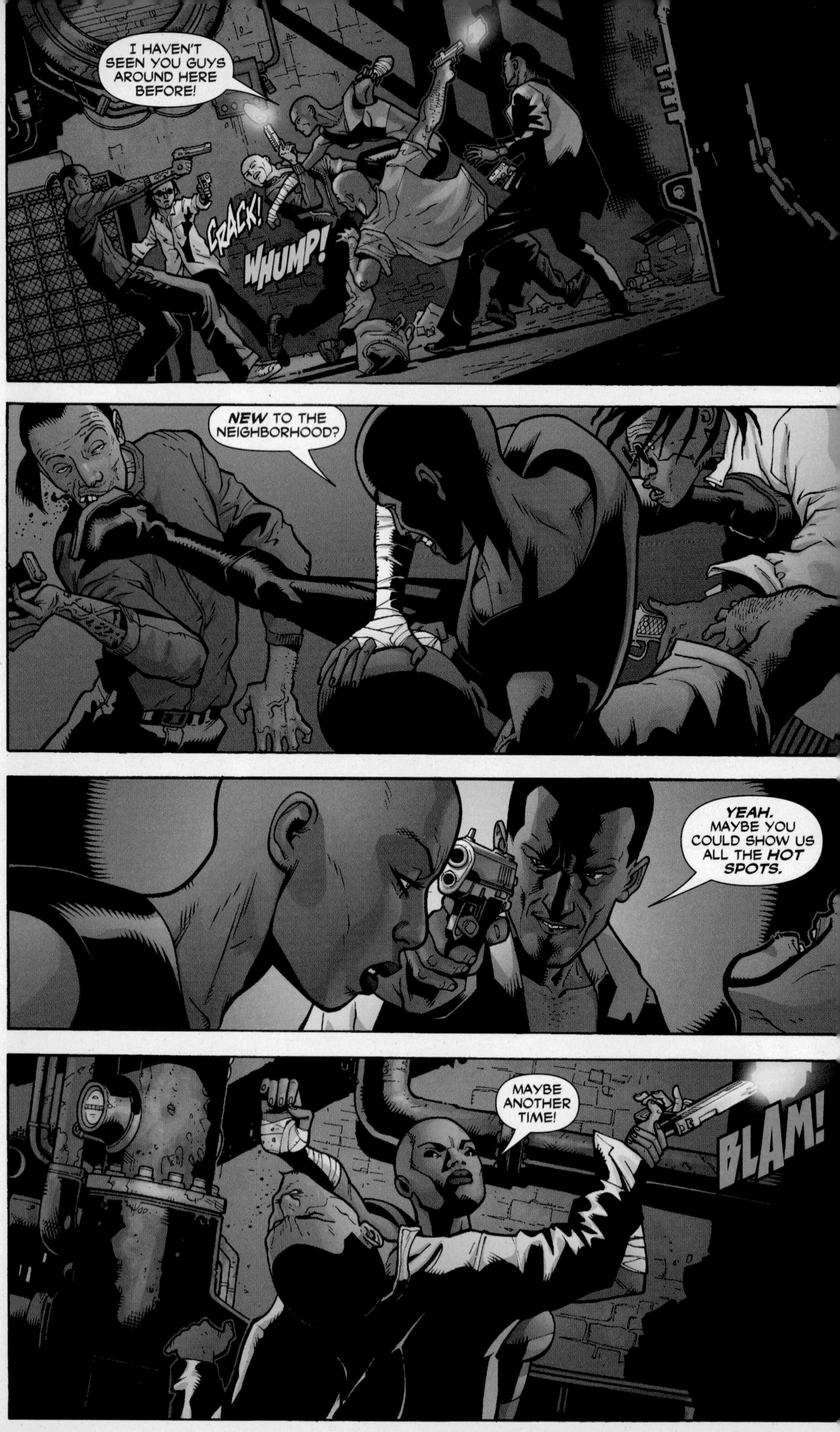
I HAVEN'T SEEN YOU GUYS AROUND HERE BEFORE!
CRACK!
WHUMP!
NEW TO THE NEIGHBORHOOD?
YEAH. MAYBE YOU COULD SHOW US ALL THE HOT SPOTS.
MAYBE ANOTHER TIME!
BLAM!

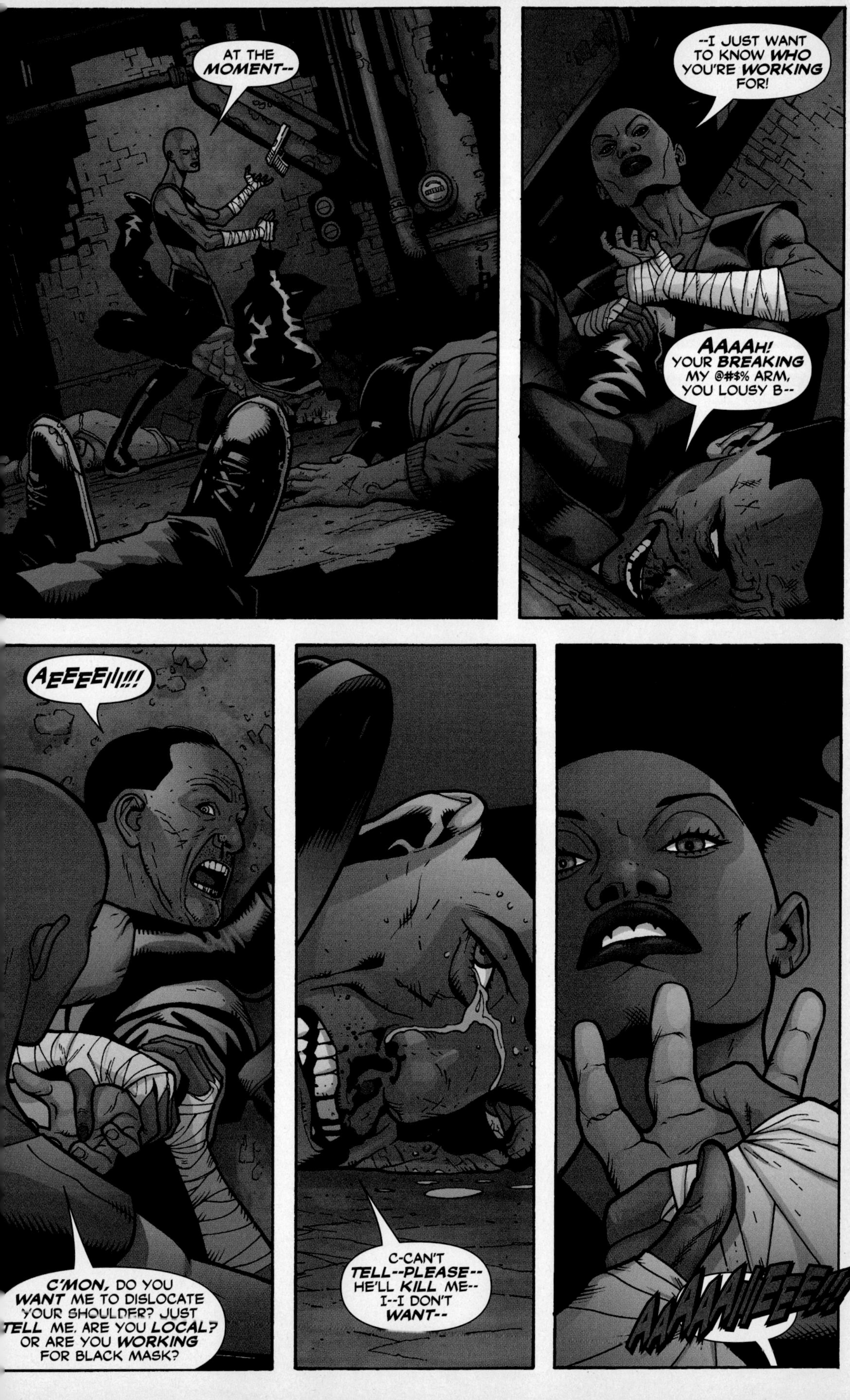
AT THE MOMENT--
--I JUST WANT TO KNOW WHO YOU'RE WORKING FOR!
AAAAH! YOUR BREAKING MY @#$% ARM, YOU LOUSY B--
AEEEEIII!!!
C'MON, DO YOU WANT ME TO DISLOCATE YOUR SHOULDER? JUST TELL ME. ARE YOU LOCAL? OR ARE YOU WORKING FOR BLACK MASK?
C-CAN'T TELL--PLEASE-- HE'LL KILL ME-- I--I DON'T WANT--
AAAAIIIEEEE!!!

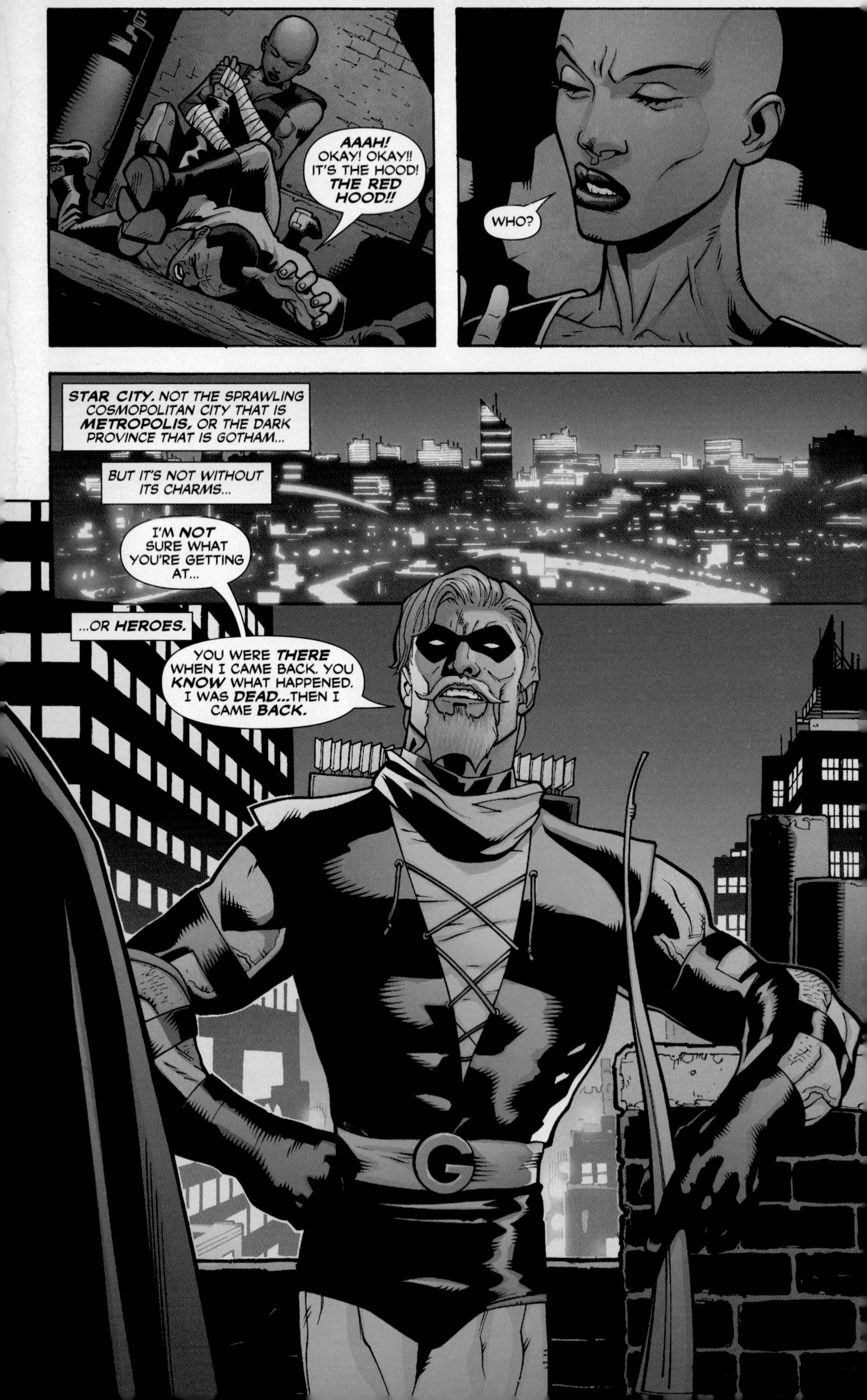
AAAH! OKAY! OKAY!! IT'S THE HOOD! THE RED HOOD!!
WHO?
STAR CITY. NOT THE SPRAWLING COSMOPOLITAN CITY THAT IS METROPOLIS, OR THE DARK PROVINCE THAT IS GOTHAM...
BUT IT'S NOT WITHOUT ITS CHARMS...
I'M NOT SURE WHAT YOU'RE GETTING AT...
...OR HEROES.
YOU WERE THERE WHEN I CAME BACK. YOU KNOW WHAT HAPPENED. I WAS DEAD...THEN I CAME BACK.

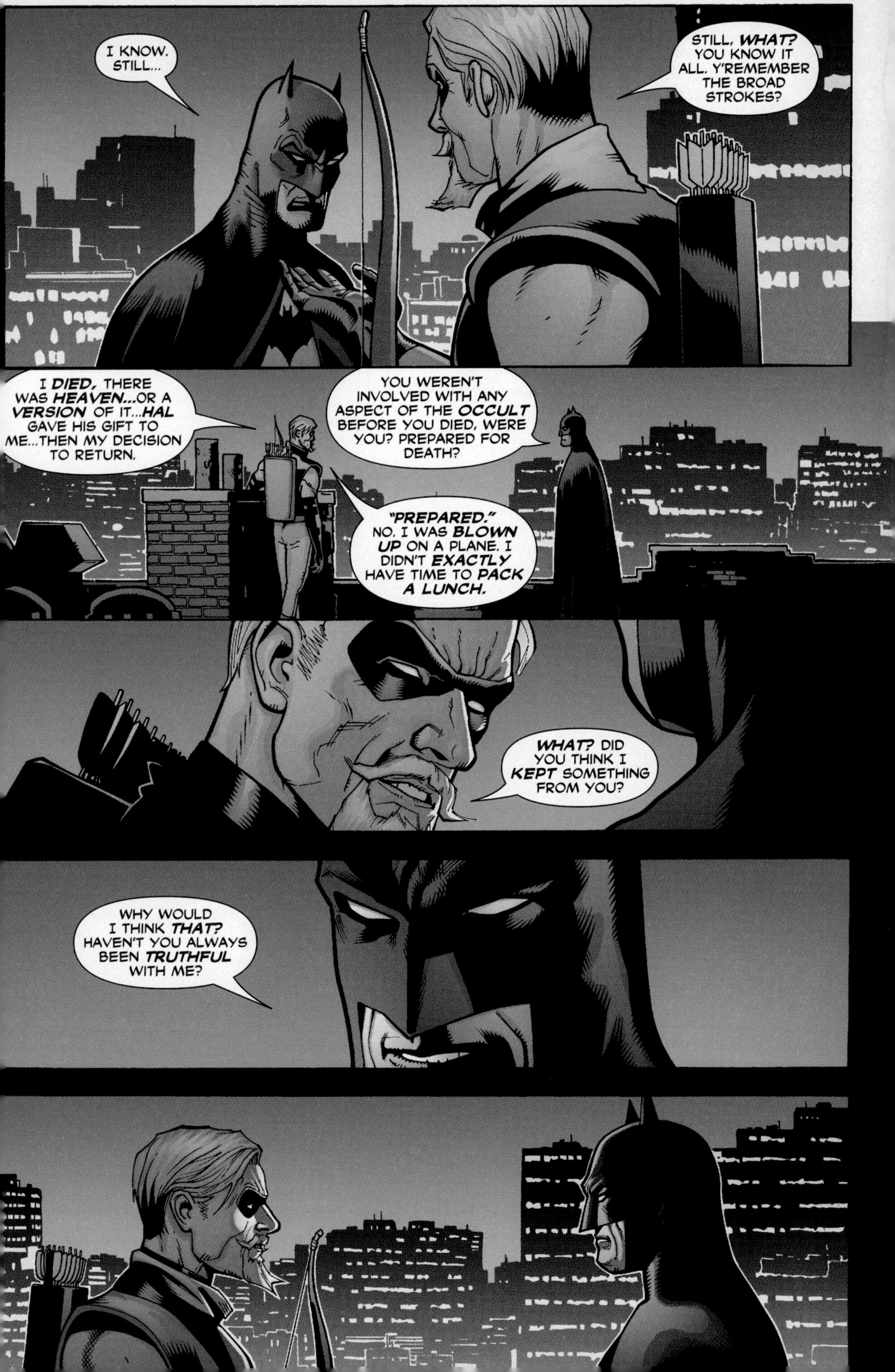

I KNOW. STILL...
STILL, WHAT? YOU KNOW IT ALL. Y'REMEMBER THE BROAD STROKES?
I DIED, THERE WAS HEAVEN...OR A VERSION OF IT...HAL GAVE HIS GIFT TO ME...THEN MY DECISION TO RETURN.
YOU WEREN'T INVOLVED WITH ANY ASPECT OF THE OCCULT BEFORE YOU DIED, WERE YOU? PREPARED FOR DEATH?
"PREPARED." NO. I WAS BLOWN UP ON A PLANE. I DIDN'T EXACTLY HAVE TIME TO PACK A LUNCH.
WHAT? DID YOU THINK I KEPT SOMETHING FROM YOU?
WHY WOULD I THINK THAT? HAVEN'T YOU ALWAYS BEEN TRUTHFUL WITH ME?

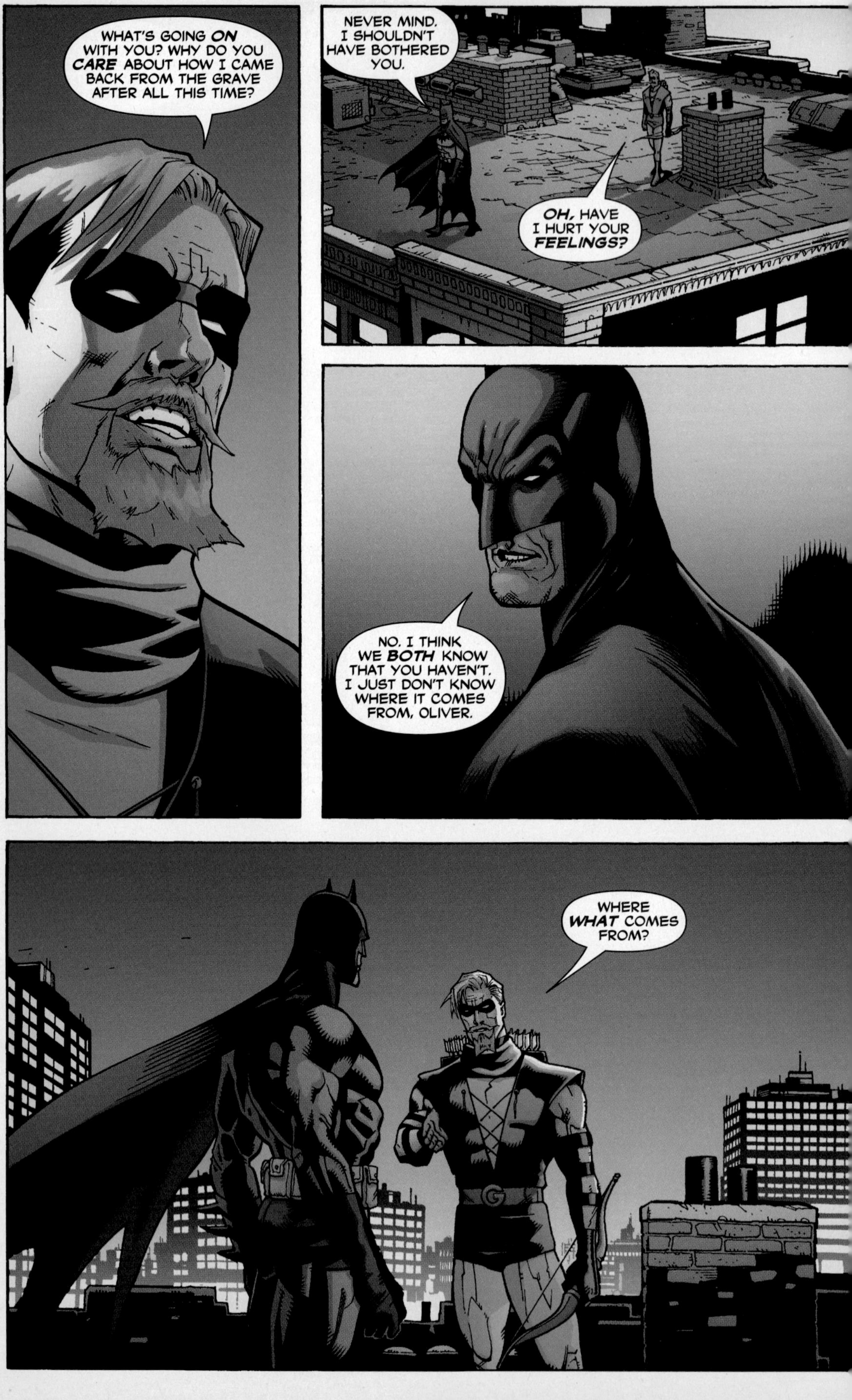
WHAT'S GOING ON WITH YOU? WHY DO YOU CARE ABOUT HOW I CAME BACK FROM THE GRAVE AFTER ALL THIS TIME?
NEVER MIND. I SHOULDN'T HAVE BOTHERED YOU.
OH, HAVE I HURT YOUR FEELINGS?
NO. I THINK WE BOTH KNOW THAT YOU HAVEN'T. I JUST DON'T KNOW WHERE IT COMES FROM, OLIVER.
WHERE WHAT COMES FROM?

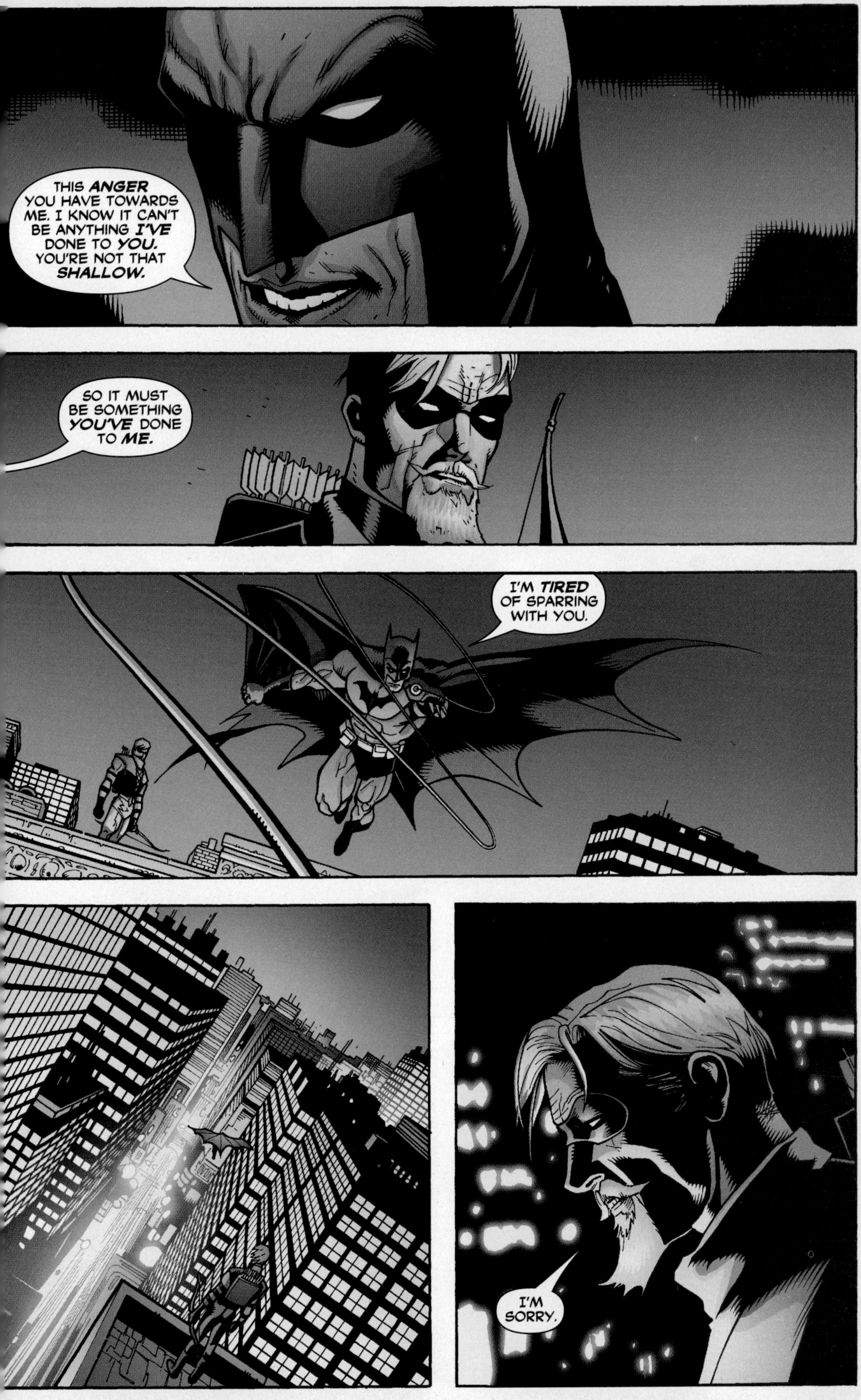
THIS ANGER YOU HAVE TOWARDS ME. I KNOW IT CAN'T BE ANYTHING I'VE DONE TO YOU. YOU'RE NOT THAT SHALLOW.
SO IT MUST BE SOMETHING YOU'VE DONE TO ME.
I'M TIRED OF SPARRING WITH YOU.
I'M SORRY.

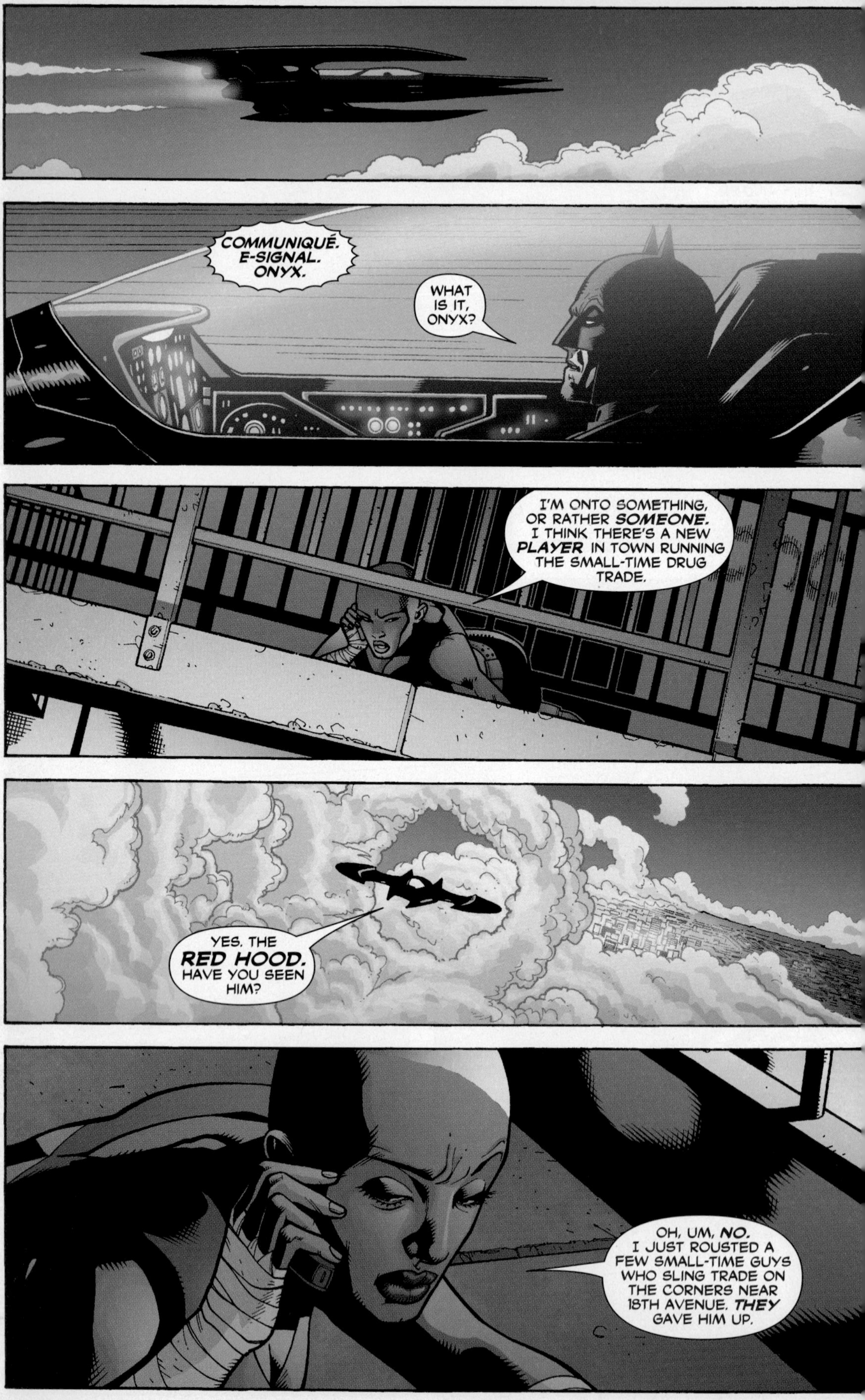
COMMUNIQUÉ. E-SIGNAL. ONYX.
WHAT IS IT, ONYX?
I'M ONTO SOMETHING, OR RATHER SOMEONE. I THINK THERE'S A NEW PLAYER IN TOWN RUNNING THE SMALL-TIME DRUG TRADE.
YES. THE RED HOOD. HAVE YOU SEEN HIM?
OH, UM, NO. I JUST ROUSTED A FEW SMALL-TIME GUYS WHO SLING TRADE ON THE CORNERS NEAR 18TH AVENUE. THEY GAVE HIM UP.

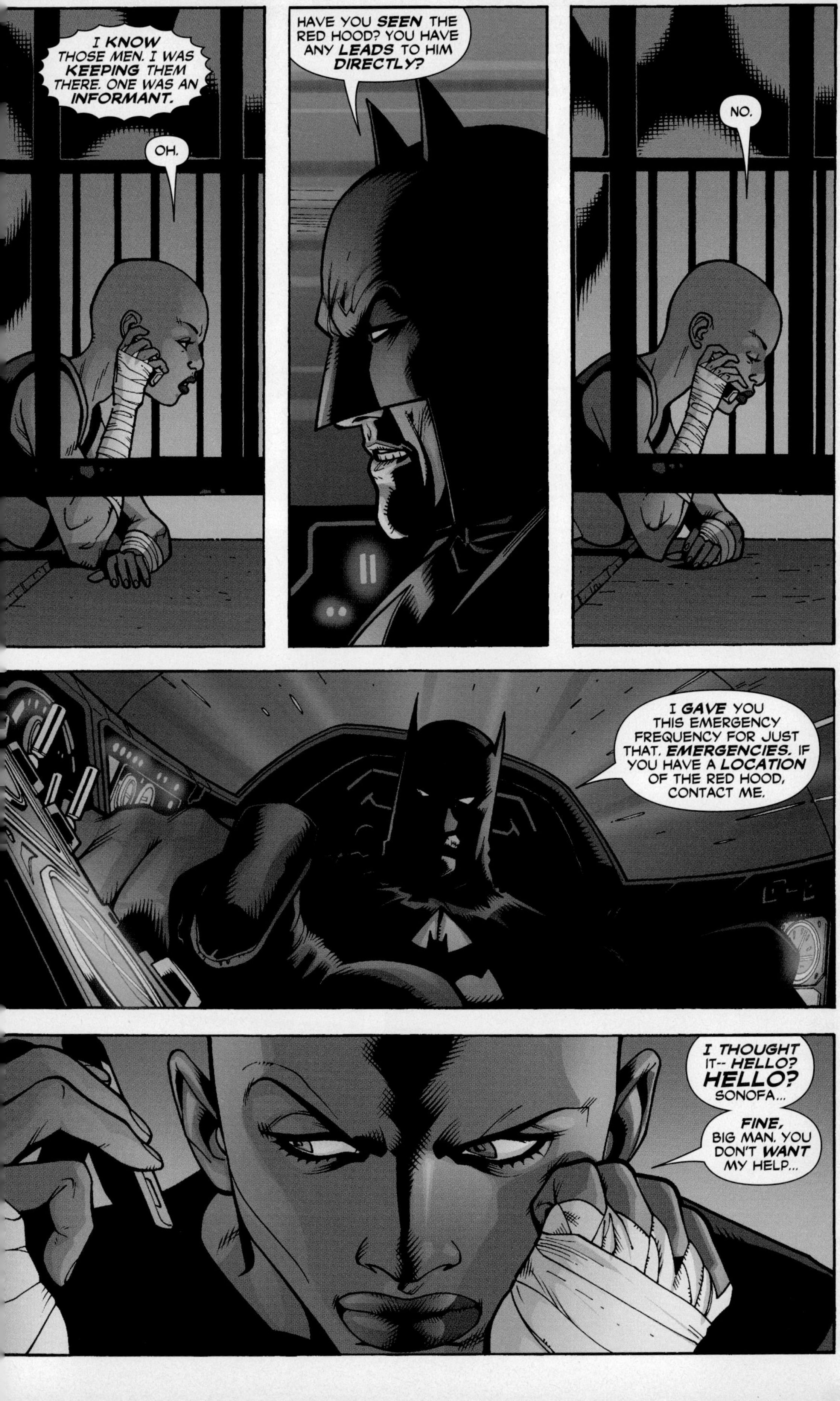
I KNOW THOSE MEN. I WAS KEEPING THEM THERE. ONE WAS AN INFORMANT.
OH.
HAVE YOU SEEN THE RED HOOD? YOU HAVE ANY LEADS TO HIM DIRECTLY?
NO.
I GAVE YOU THIS EMERGENCY FREQUENCY FOR JUST THAT. EMERGENCIES. IF YOU HAVE A LOCATION OF THE RED HOOD, CONTACT ME.
I THOUGHT IT-- HELLO? HELLO? SONOFA...
FINE, BIG MAN. YOU DON'T WANT MY HELP...

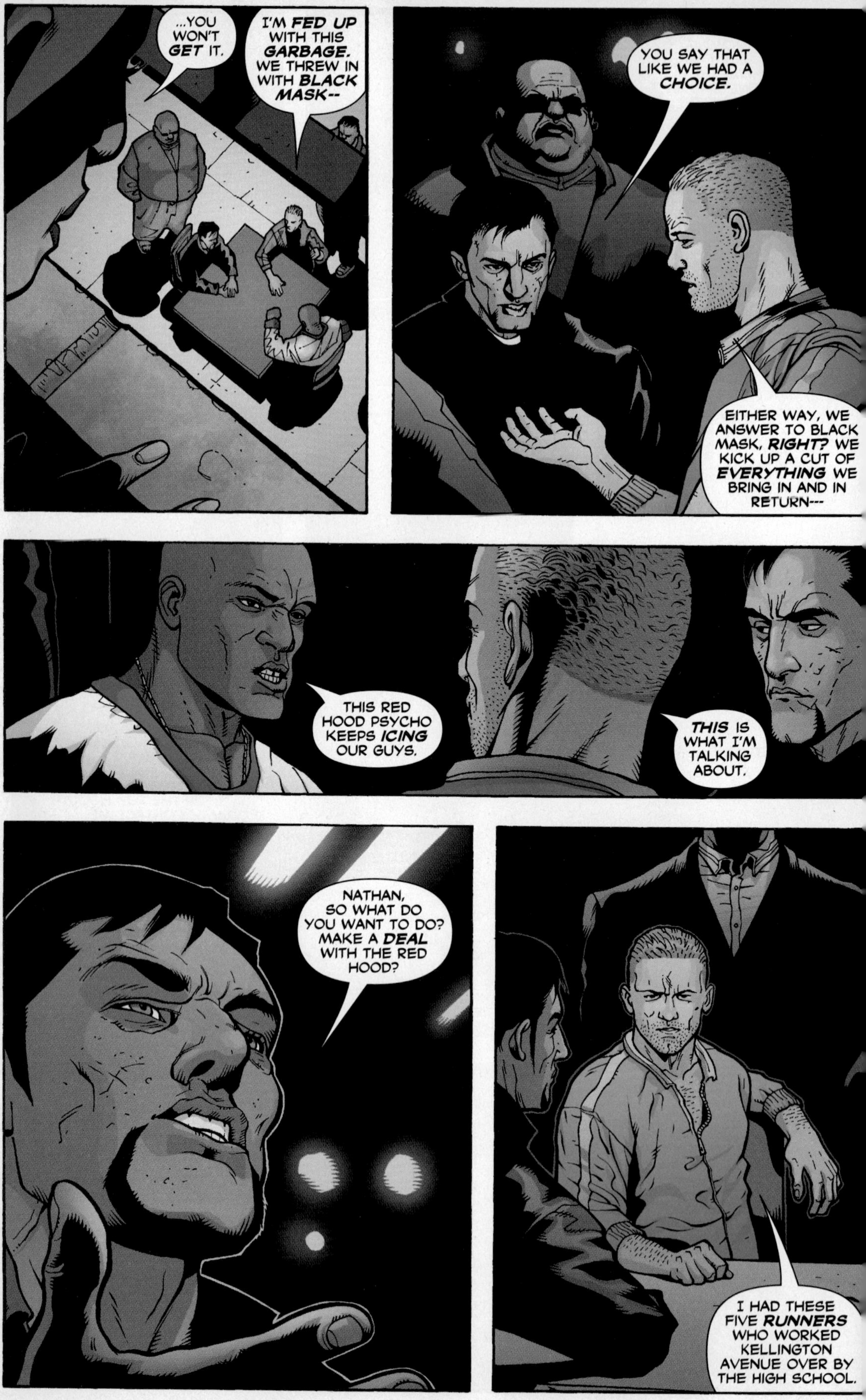

...YOU WON'T GET IT.
I'M FED UP WITH THIS GARBAGE. WE THREW IN WITH BLACK MASK--
YOU SAY THAT LIKE WE HAD A CHOICE.
EITHER WAY, WE ANSWER TO BLACK MASK, RIGHT? WE KICK UP A CUT OF EVERYTHING WE BRING IN AND IN RETURN---
THIS RED HOOD PSYCHO KEEPS ICING OUR GUYS.
THIS IS WHAT I'M TALKING ABOUT.
NATHAN, SO WHAT DO YOU WANT TO DO? MAKE A DEAL WITH THE RED HOOD?
I HAD THESE FIVE RUNNERS WHO WORKED KELLINGTON AVENUE OVER BY THE HIGH SCHOOL.

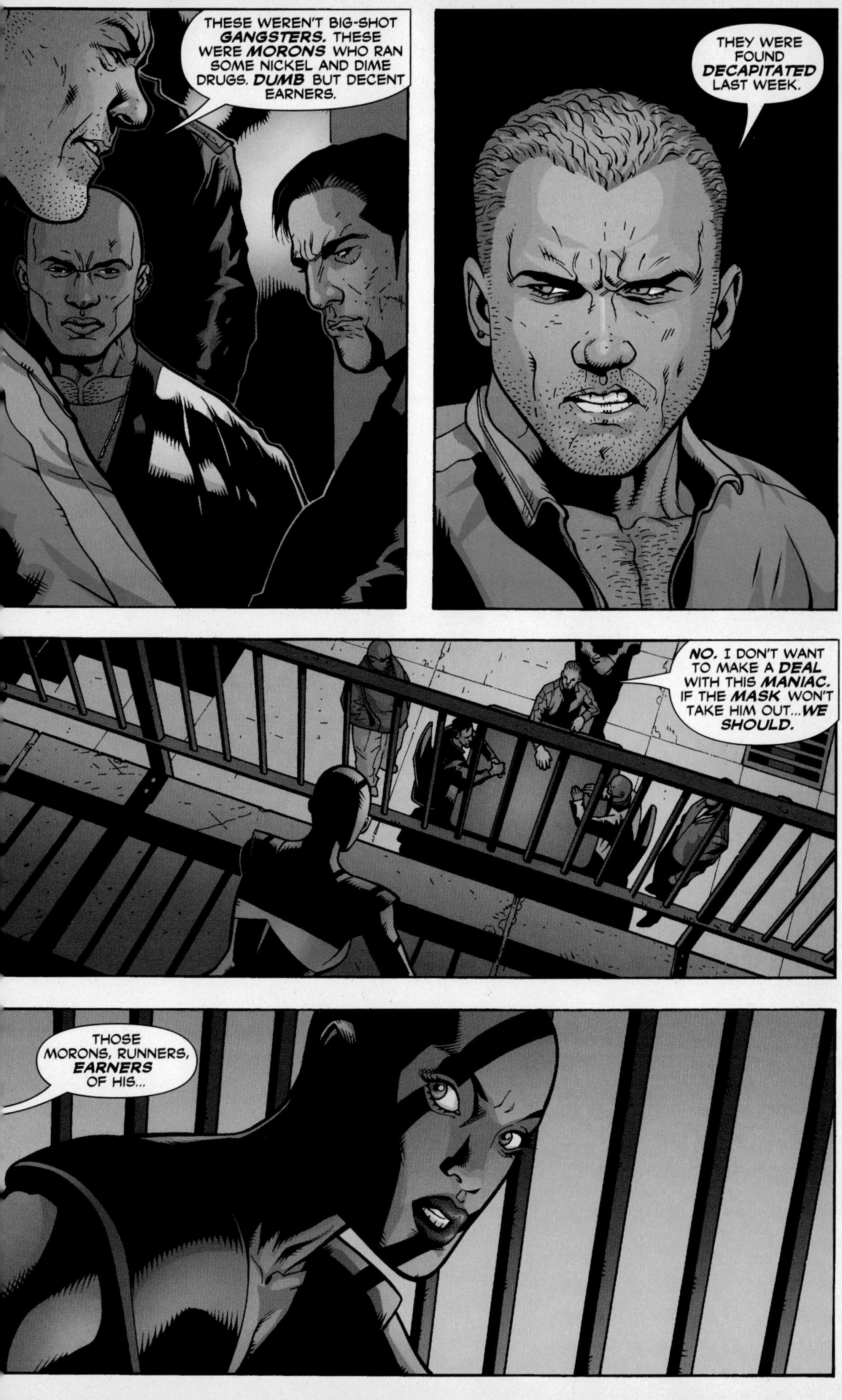
THESE WEREN'T BIG-SHOT GANGSTERS. THESE WERE MORONS WHO RAN SOME NICKEL AND DIME DRUGS. DUMB BUT DECENT EARNERS.
THEY WERE FOUND DECAPITATED LAST WEEK.
NO. I DON'T WANT TO MAKE A DEAL WITH THIS MANIAC. IF THE MASK WON'T TAKE HIM OUT...WE SHOULD.
THOSE MORONS, RUNNERS, EARNERS OF HIS...

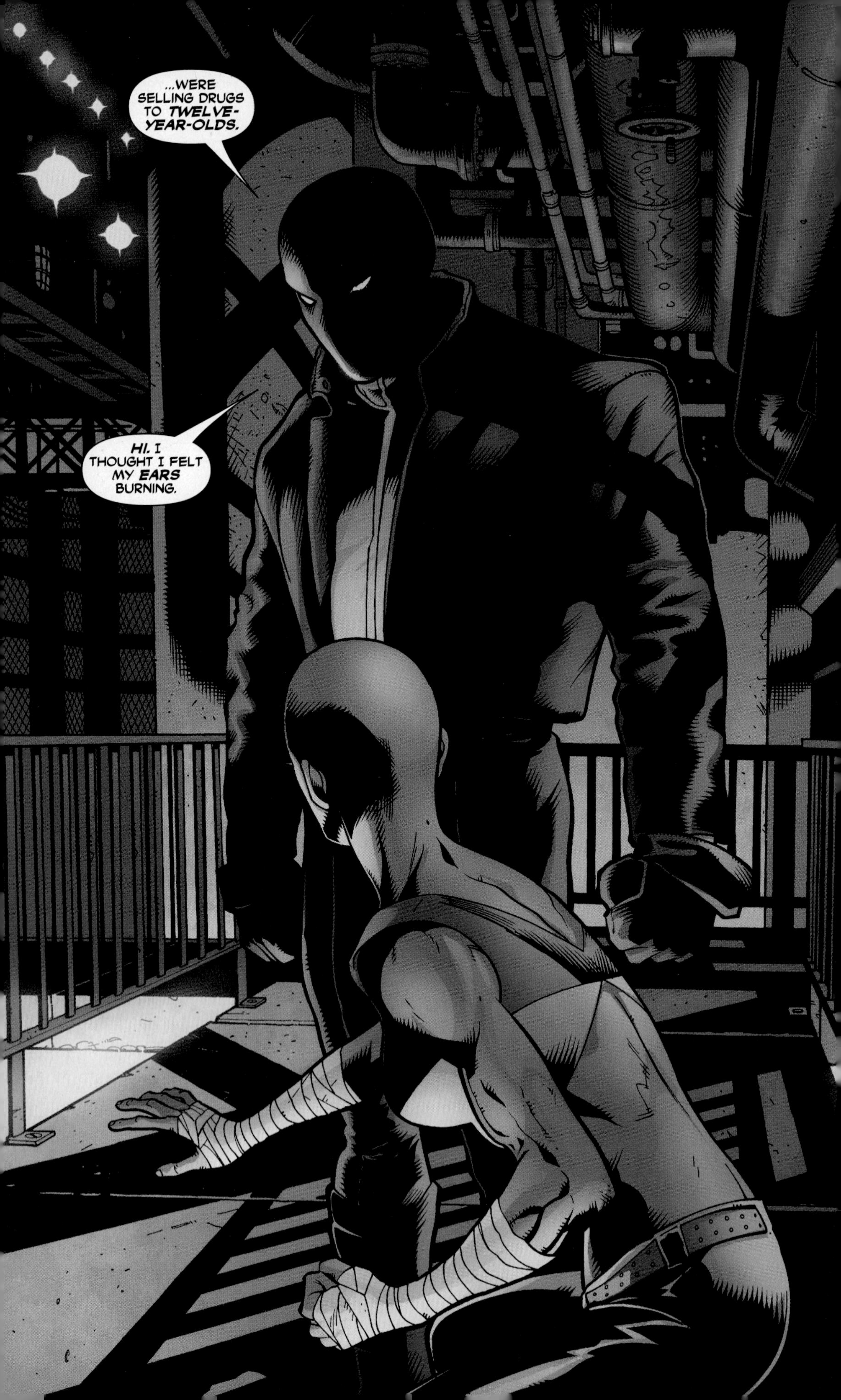
...WERE SELLING DRUGS TO *TWELVE-YEAR-OLDS.*
HI. I THOUGHT I FELT MY *EARS* BURNING.

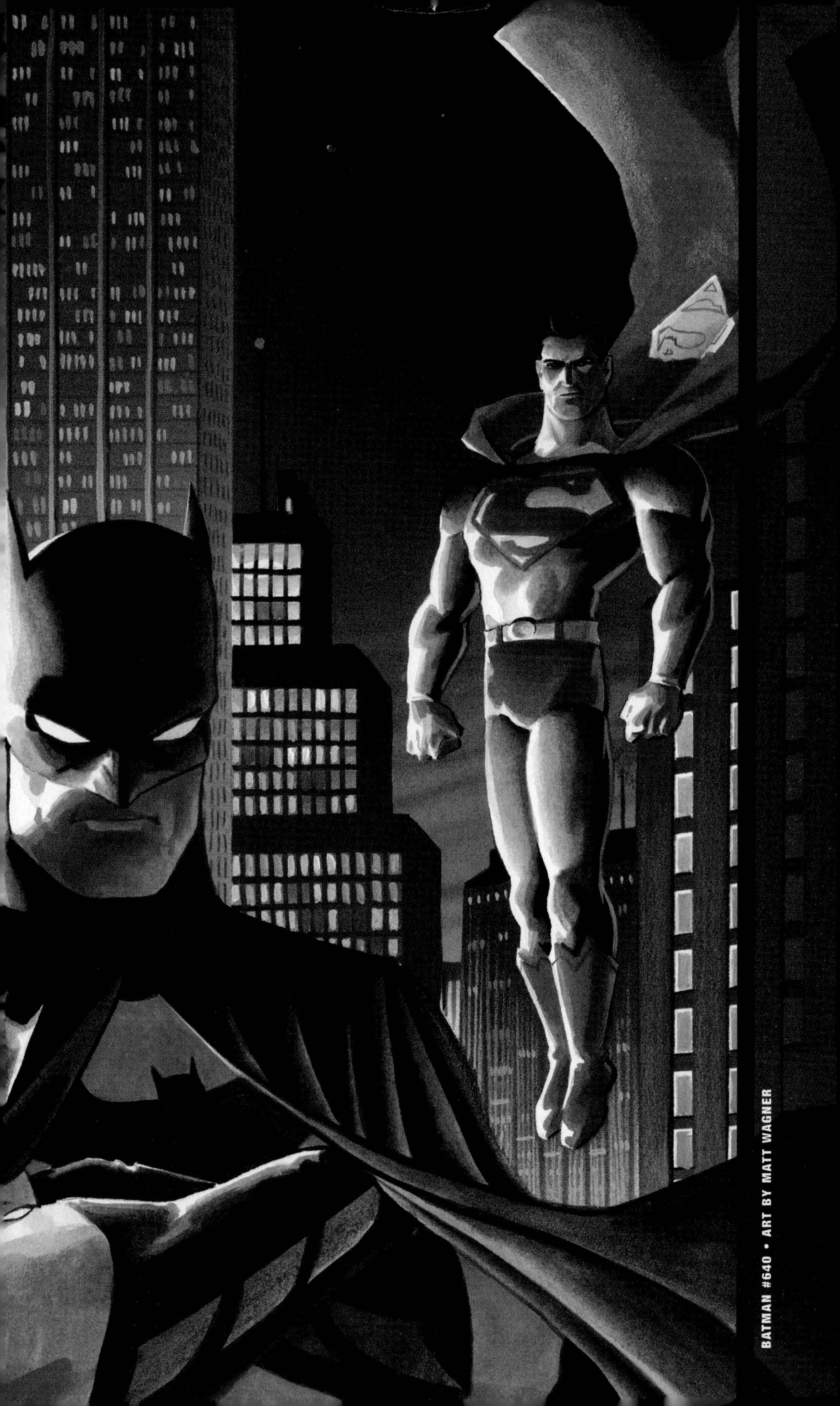

BATMAN #640 • ART BY MATT WAGNER

PART 6

WHILE THE CAT'S AWAY

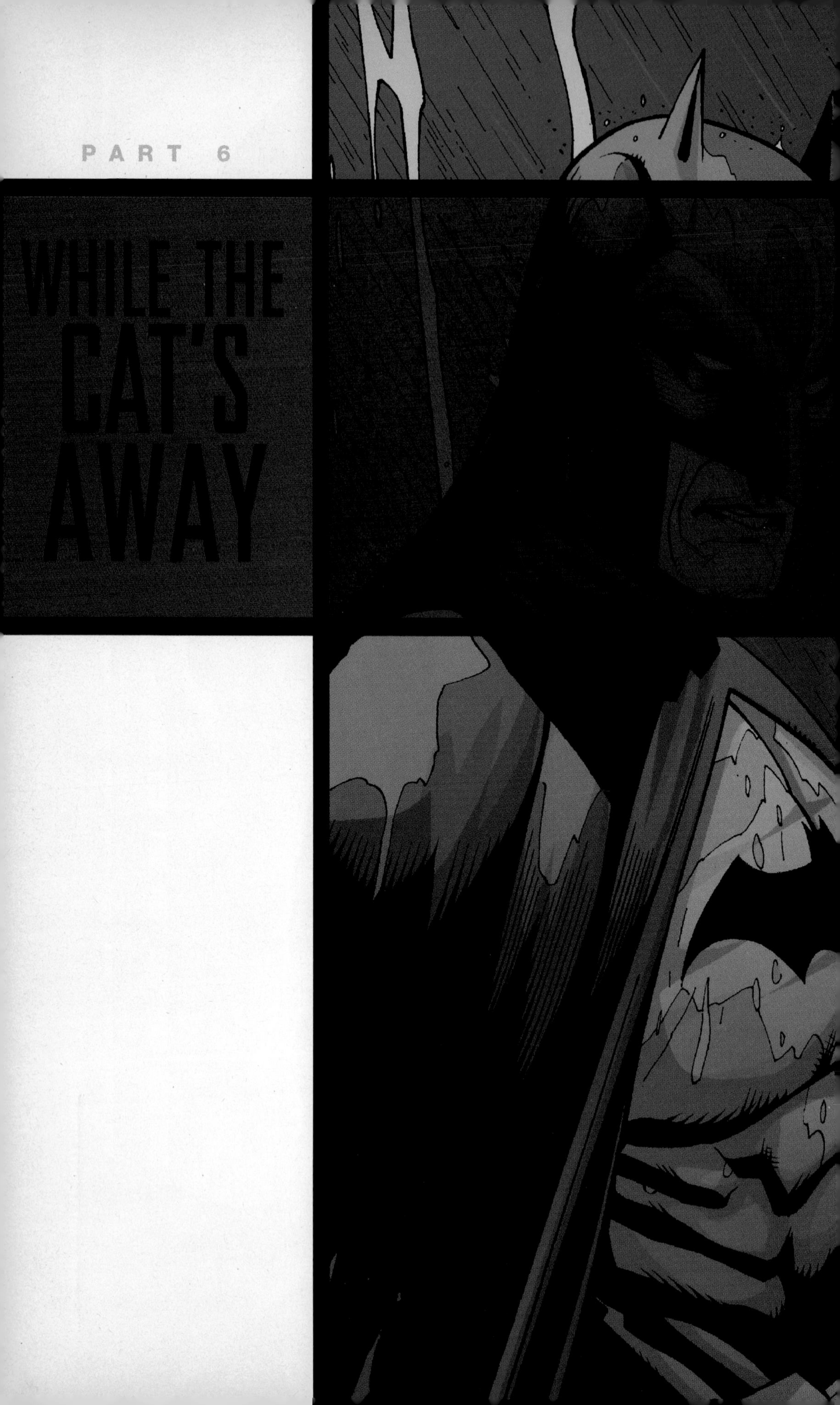

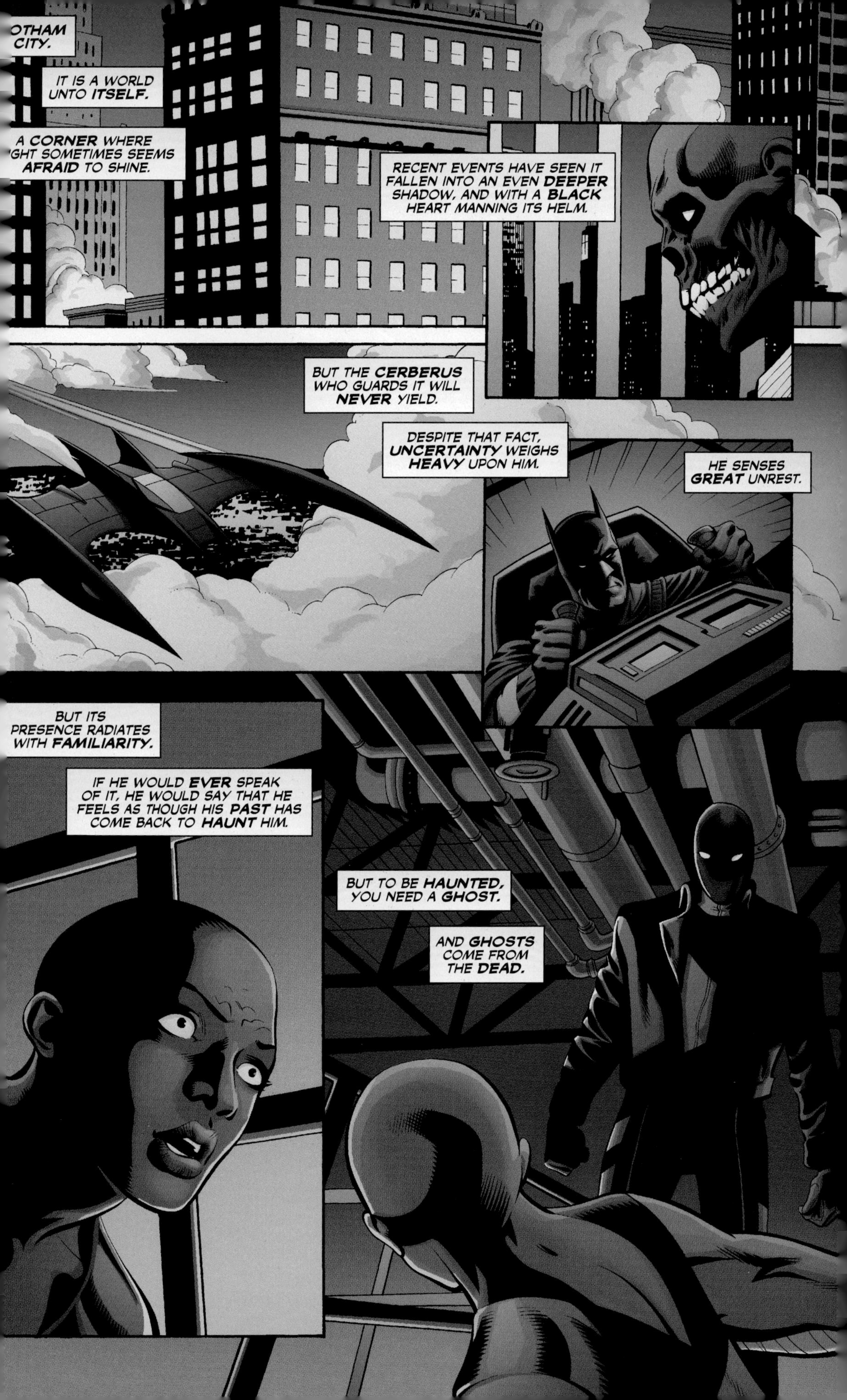

OTHAM CITY.
IT IS A WORLD UNTO ITSELF.
A CORNER WHERE IGHT SOMETIMES SEEMS AFRAID TO SHINE.
RECENT EVENTS HAVE SEEN IT FALLEN INTO AN EVEN DEEPER SHADOW, AND WITH A BLACK HEART MANNING ITS HELM.
BUT THE CERBERUS WHO GUARDS IT WILL NEVER YIELD.
DESPITE THAT FACT, UNCERTAINTY WEIGHS HEAVY UPON HIM.
HE SENSES GREAT UNREST.
BUT ITS PRESENCE RADIATES WITH FAMILIARITY.
IF HE WOULD EVER SPEAK OF IT, HE WOULD SAY THAT HE FEELS AS THOUGH HIS PAST HAS COME BACK TO HAUNT HIM.
BUT TO BE HAUNTED, YOU NEED A GHOST.
AND GHOSTS COME FROM THE DEAD.

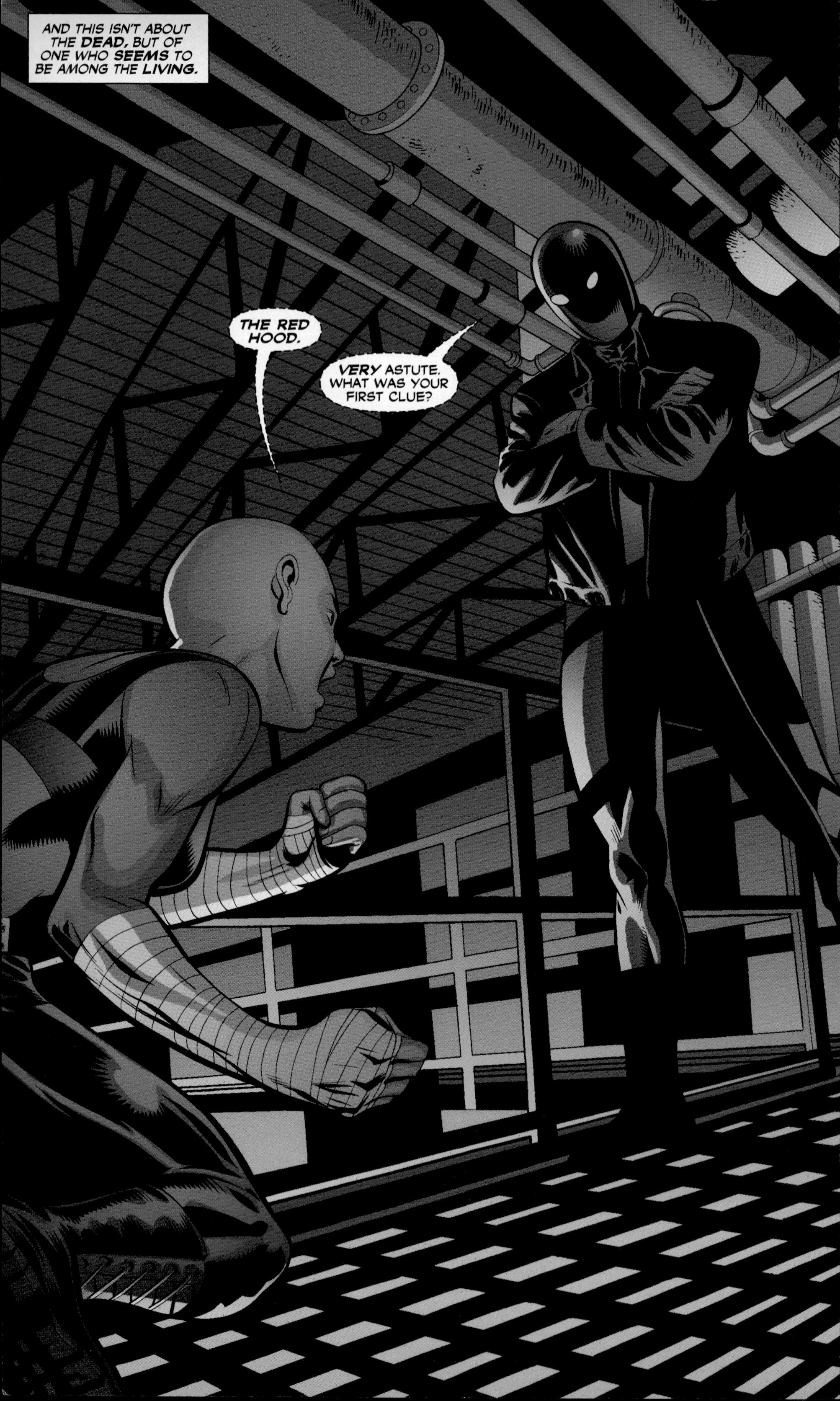
AND THIS ISN'T ABOUT THE DEAD, BUT OF ONE WHO SEEMS TO BE AMONG THE LIVING.
THE RED HOOD.
VERY ASTUTE. WHAT WAS YOUR FIRST CLUE?

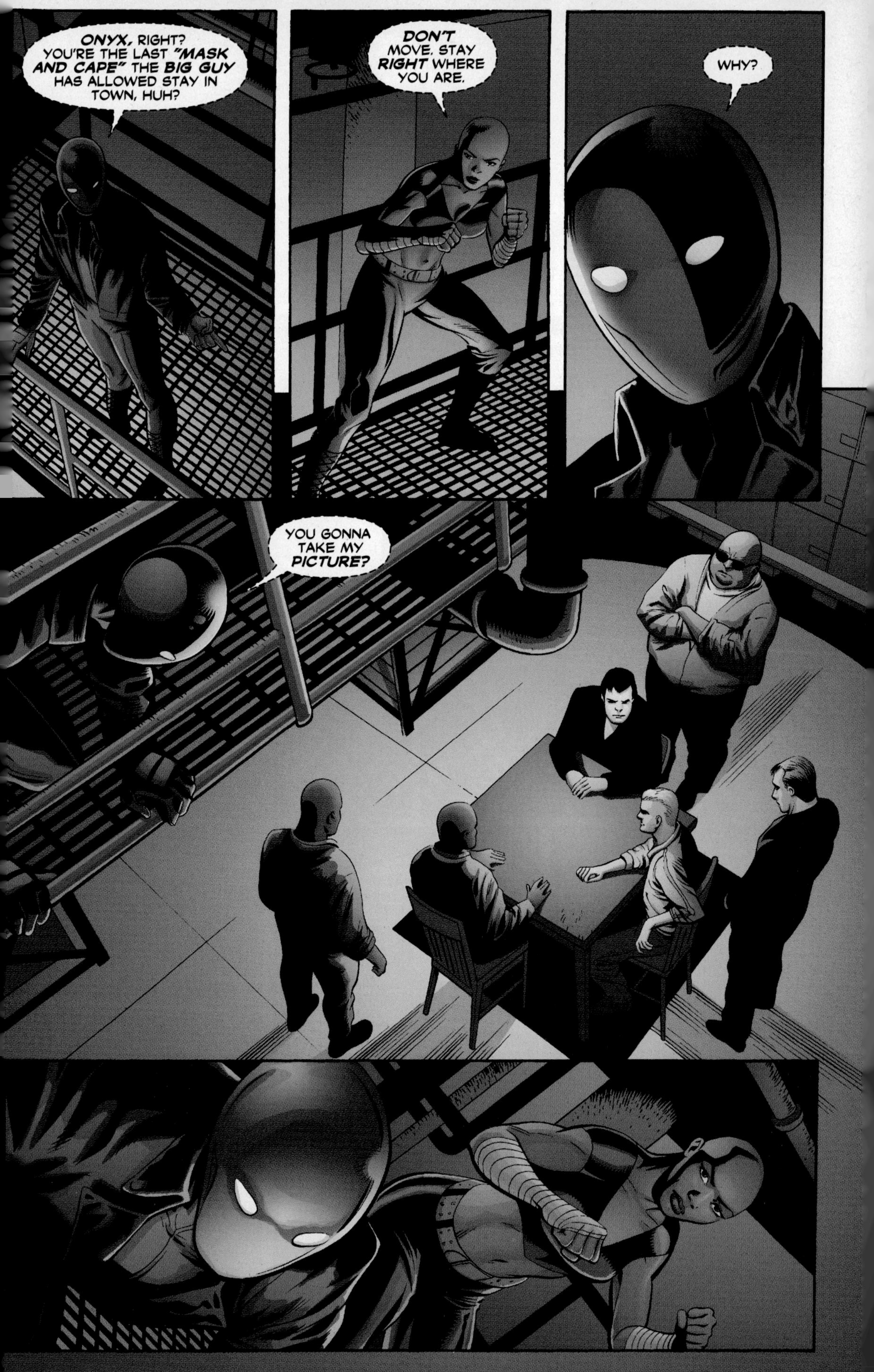
ONYX, RIGHT? YOU'RE THE LAST "MASK AND CAPE" THE BIG GUY HAS ALLOWED STAY IN TOWN, HUH?
DON'T MOVE. STAY RIGHT WHERE YOU ARE.
WHY?
YOU GONNA TAKE MY PICTURE?

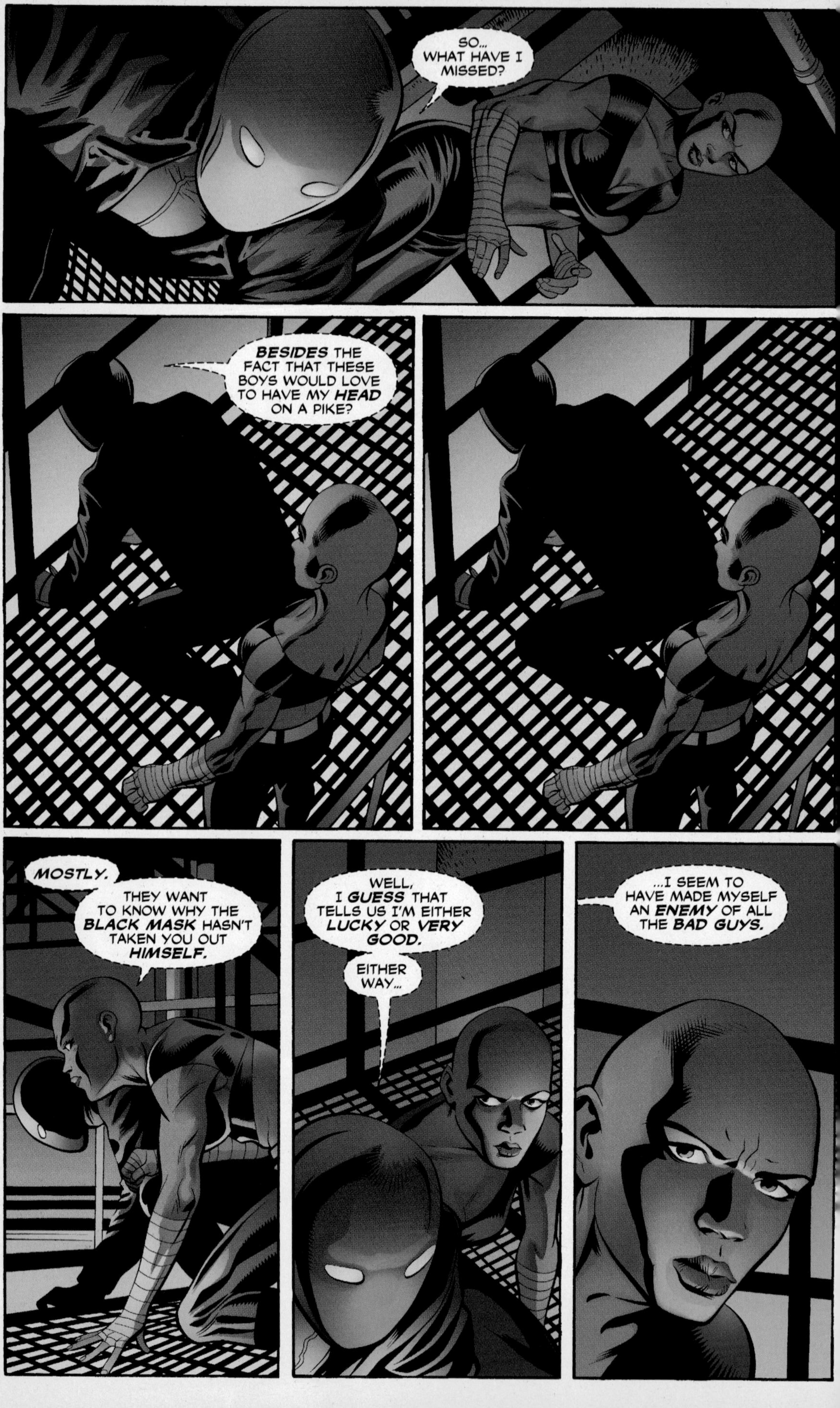
SO... WHAT HAVE I MISSED?
BESIDES THE FACT THAT THESE BOYS WOULD LOVE TO HAVE MY HEAD ON A PIKE?
MOSTLY.
THEY WANT TO KNOW WHY THE BLACK MASK HASN'T TAKEN YOU OUT HIMSELF.
WELL, I GUESS THAT TELLS US I'M EITHER LUCKY OR VERY GOOD.
EITHER WAY...
...I SEEM TO HAVE MADE MYSELF AN ENEMY OF ALL THE BAD GUYS.

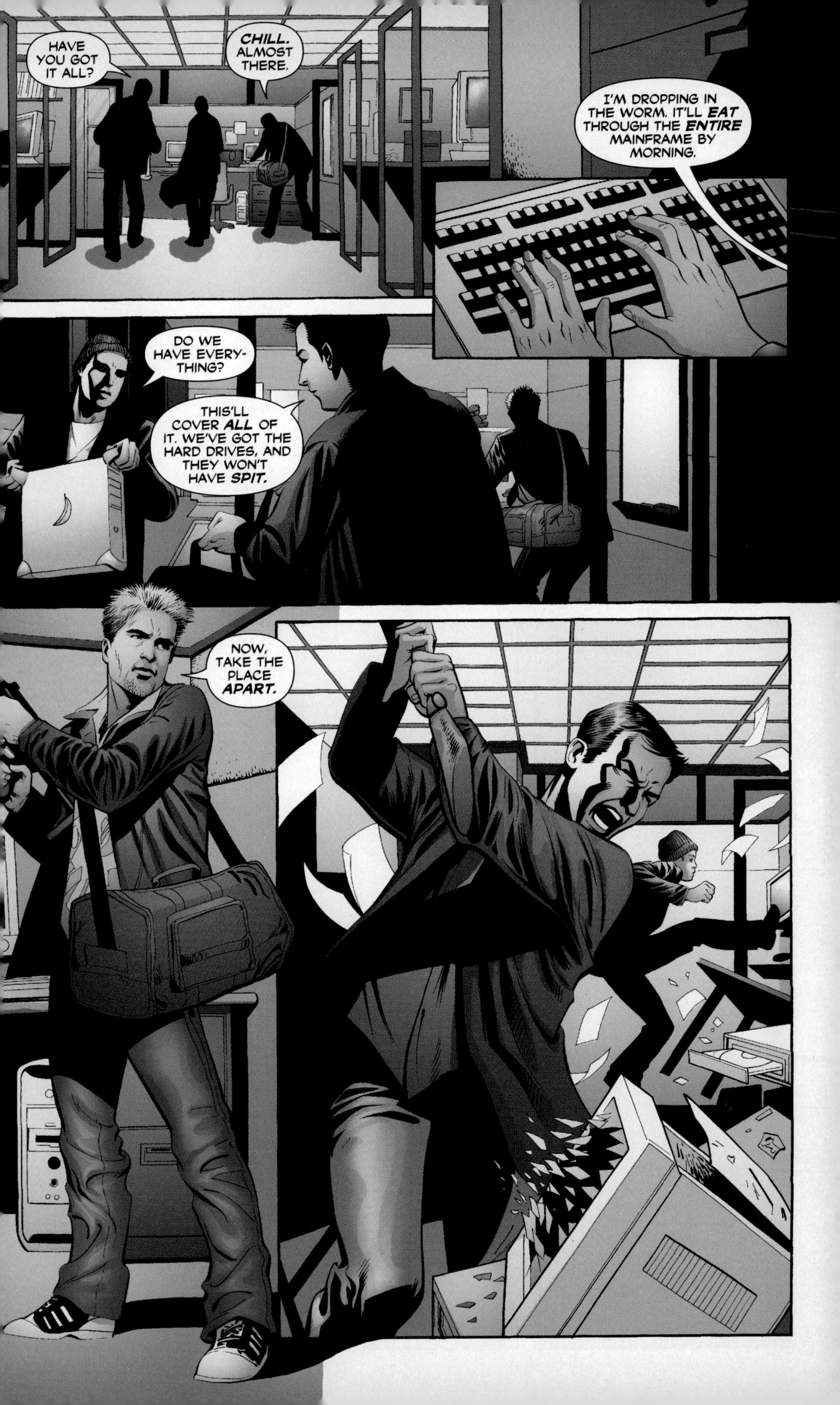
HAVE YOU GOT IT ALL?
CHILL. ALMOST THERE.
I'M DROPPING IN THE WORM. IT'LL EAT THROUGH THE ENTIRE MAINFRAME BY MORNING.
DO WE HAVE EVERY-THING?
THIS'LL COVER ALL OF IT. WE'VE GOT THE HARD DRIVES, AND THEY WON'T HAVE SPIT.
NOW, TAKE THE PLACE APART.

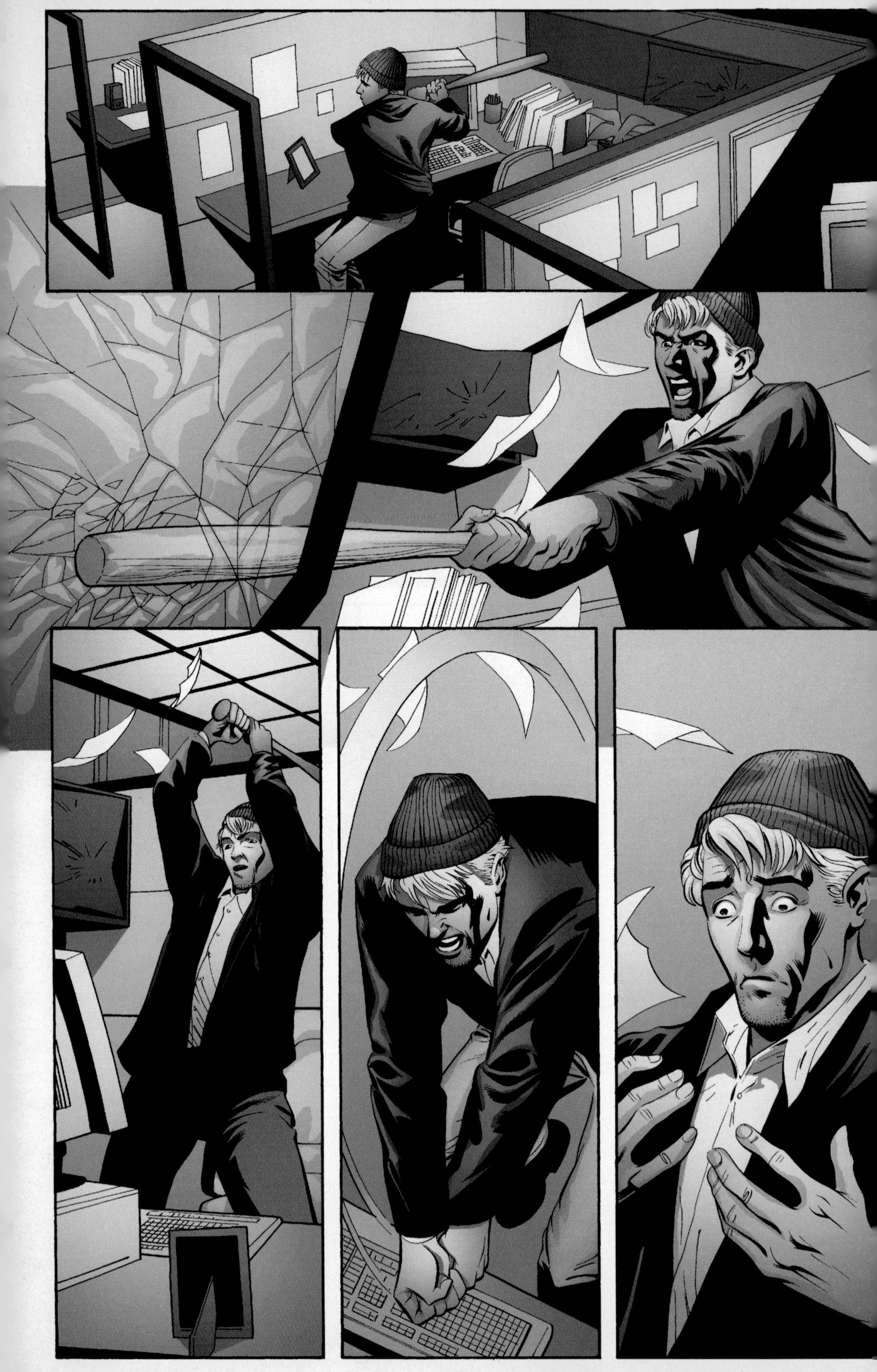

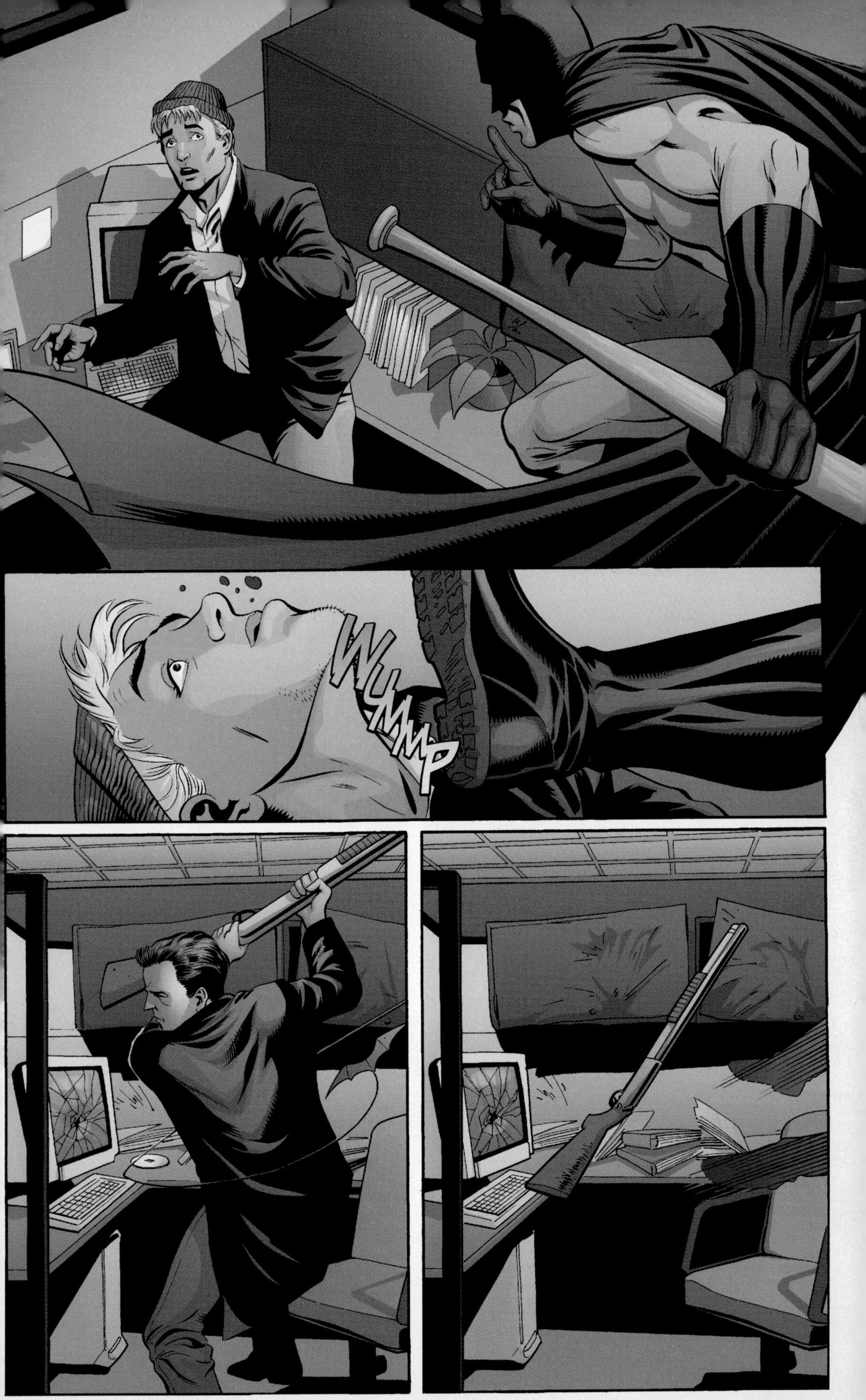
WUMMP

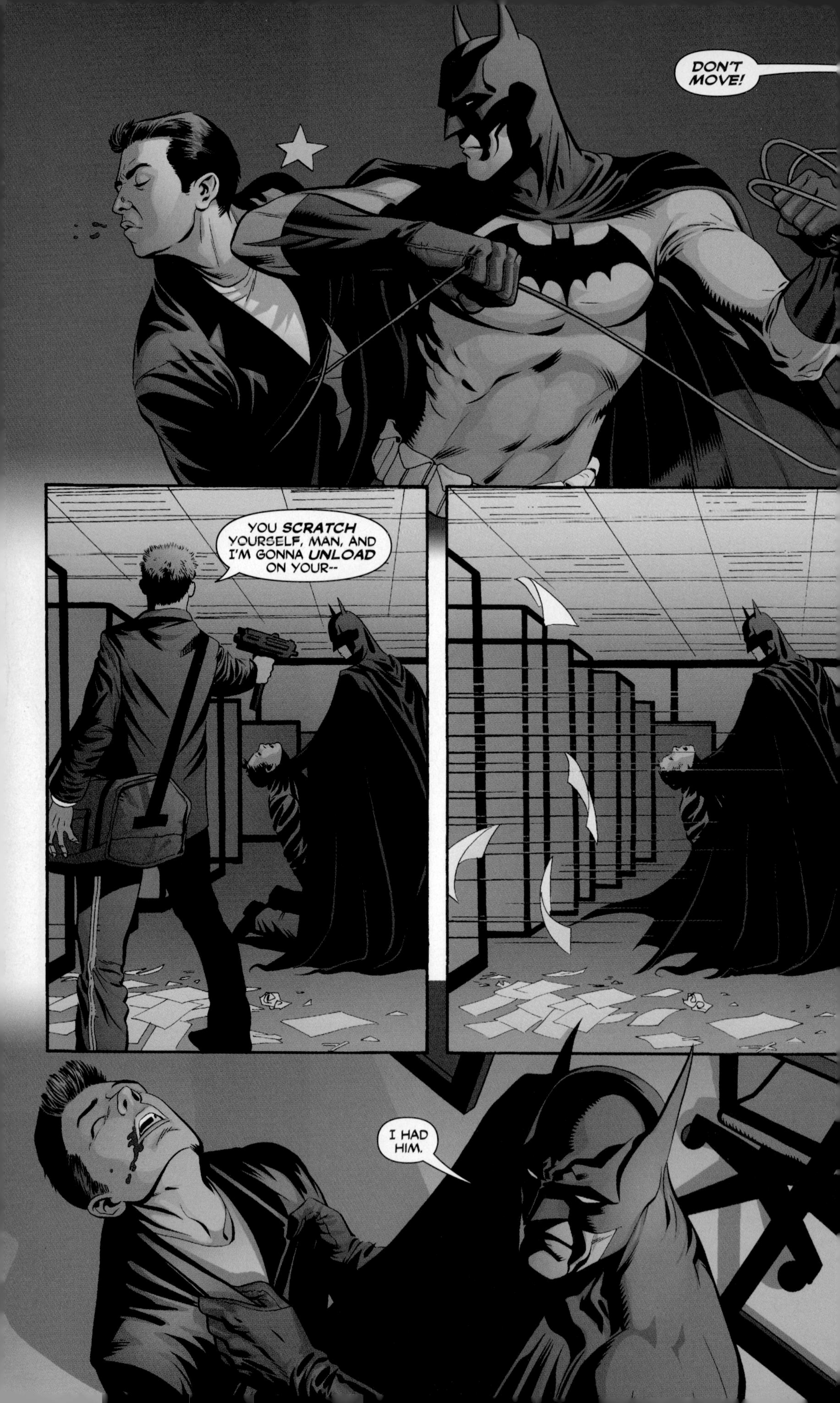
DON'T MOVE!
YOU SCRATCH YOURSELF, MAN, AND I'M GONNA UNLOAD ON YOUR--
I HAD HIM.

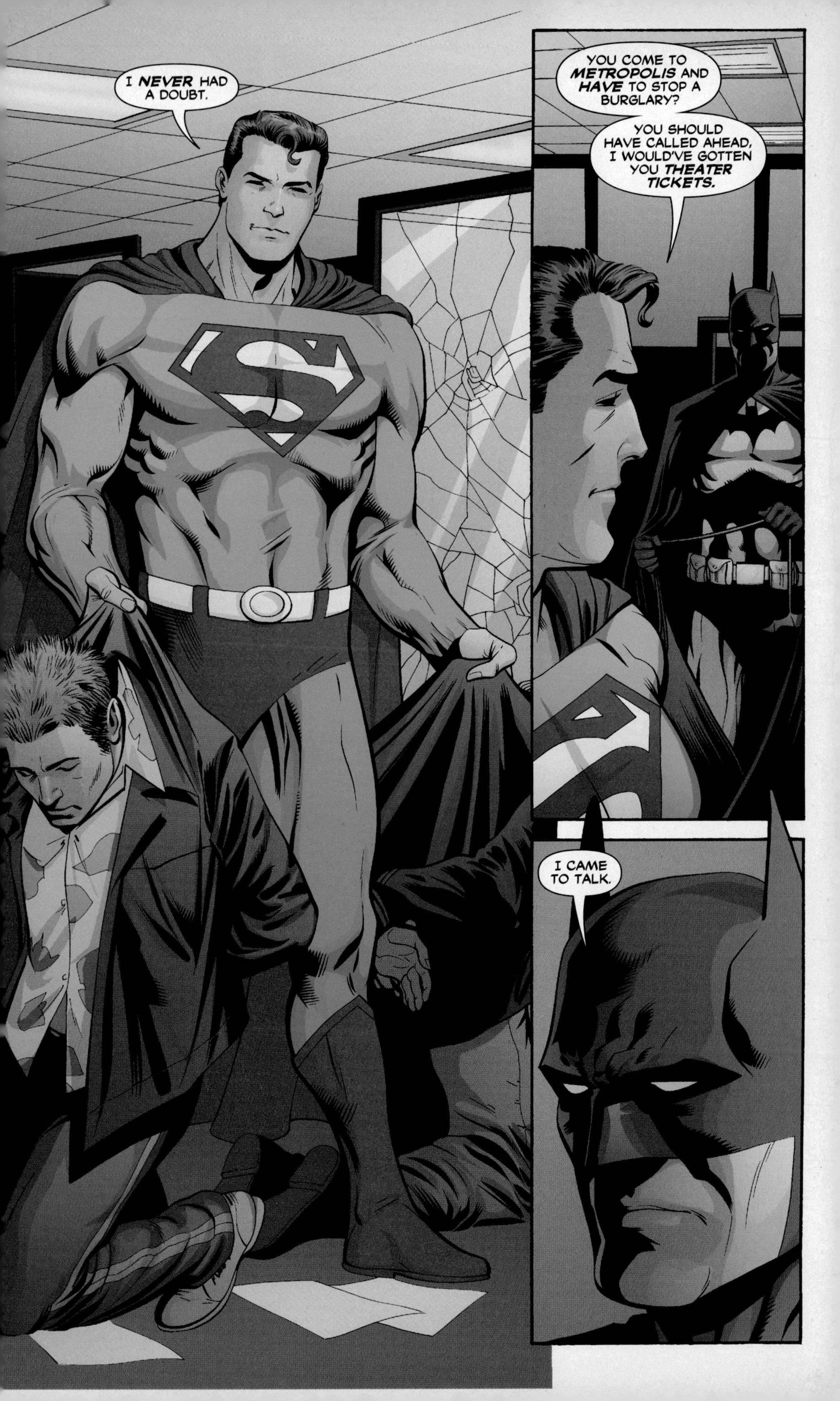
I NEVER HAD A DOUBT.
YOU COME TO METROPOLIS AND HAVE TO STOP A BURGLARY?
YOU SHOULD HAVE CALLED AHEAD, I WOULD'VE GOTTEN YOU THEATER TICKETS.
I CAME TO TALK.

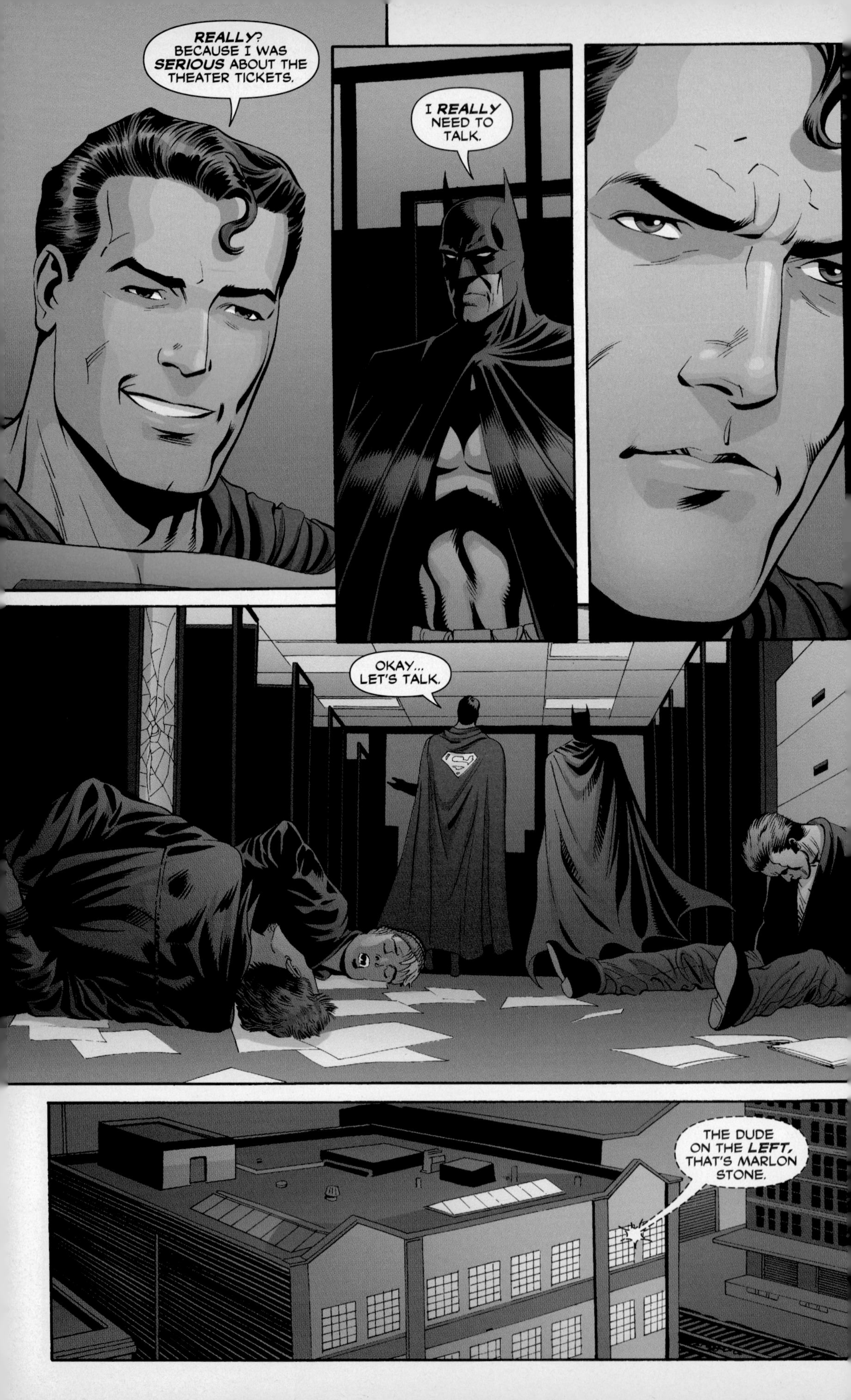
REALLY? BECAUSE I WAS SERIOUS ABOUT THE THEATER TICKETS.
I REALLY NEED TO TALK.
OKAY... LET'S TALK.
THE DUDE ON THE LEFT, THAT'S MARLON STONE.

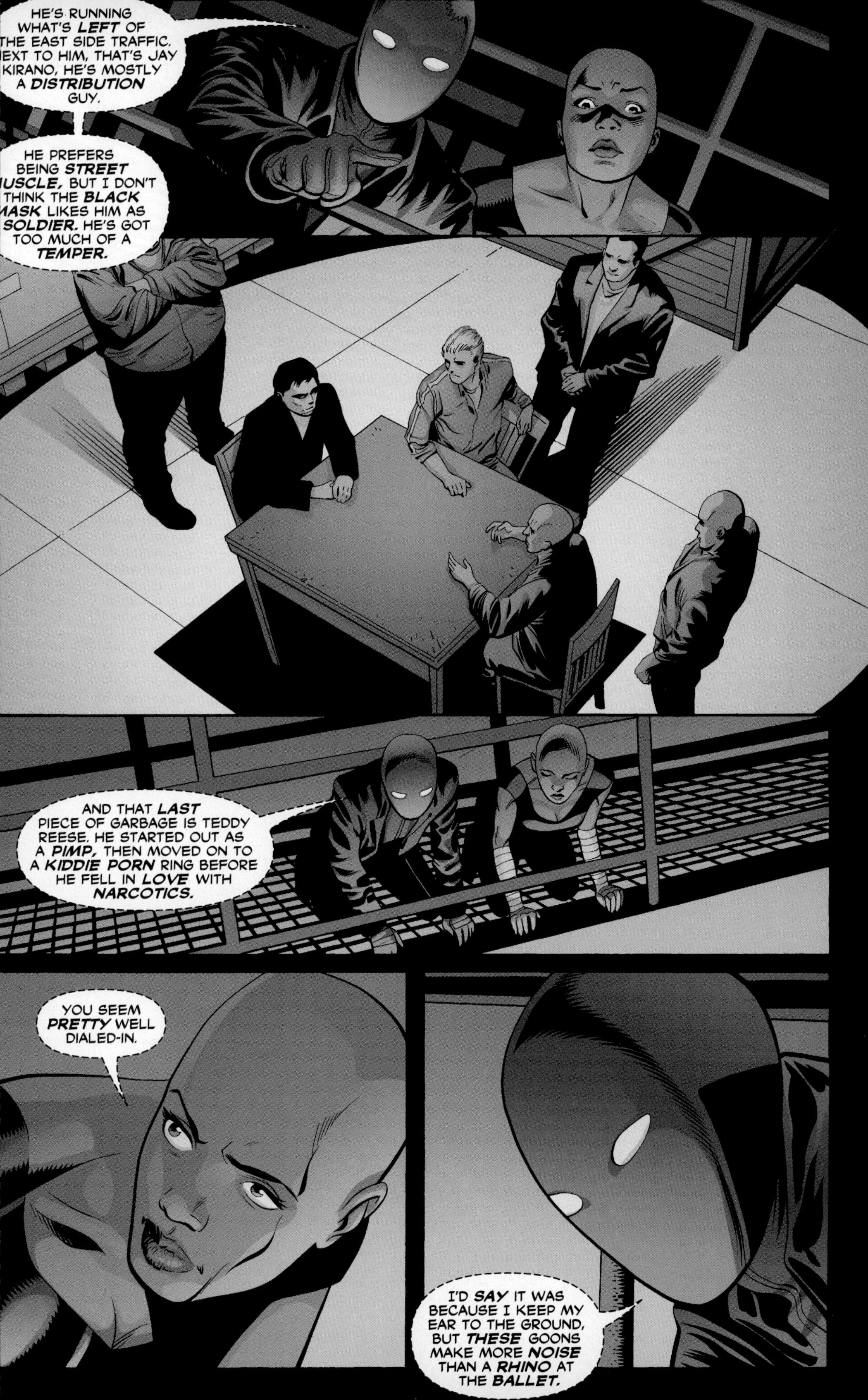

HE'S RUNNING WHAT'S LEFT OF THE EAST SIDE TRAFFIC. IEXT TO HIM, THAT'S JAY KIRANO, HE'S MOSTLY A DISTRIBUTION GUY.
HE PREFERS BEING STREET IUSCLE, BUT I DON'T THINK THE BLACK MASK LIKES HIM AS SOLDIER. HE'S GOT TOO MUCH OF A TEMPER.
AND THAT LAST PIECE OF GARBAGE IS TEDDY REESE. HE STARTED OUT AS A PIMP, THEN MOVED ON TO A KIDDIE PORN RING BEFORE HE FELL IN LOVE WITH NARCOTICS.
YOU SEEM PRETTY WELL DIALED-IN.
I'D SAY IT WAS BECAUSE I KEEP MY EAR TO THE GROUND, BUT THESE GOONS MAKE MORE NOISE THAN A RHINO AT THE BALLET.

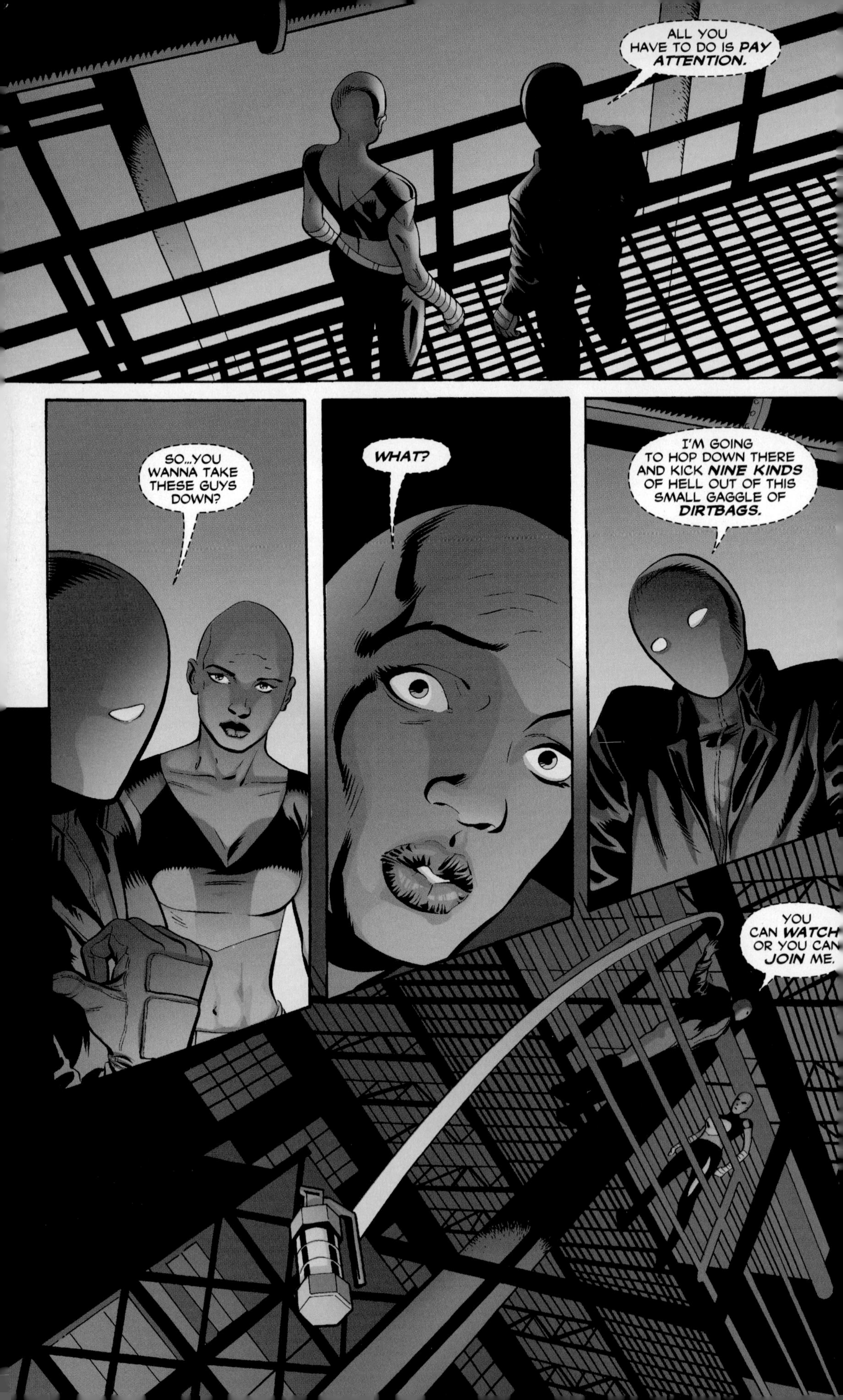
ALL YOU HAVE TO DO IS PAY ATTENTION.
SO...YOU WANNA TAKE THESE GUYS DOWN?
WHAT?
I'M GOING TO HOP DOWN THERE AND KICK NINE KINDS OF HELL OUT OF THIS SMALL GAGGLE OF DIRTBAGS.
YOU CAN WATCH OR YOU CAN JOIN ME.

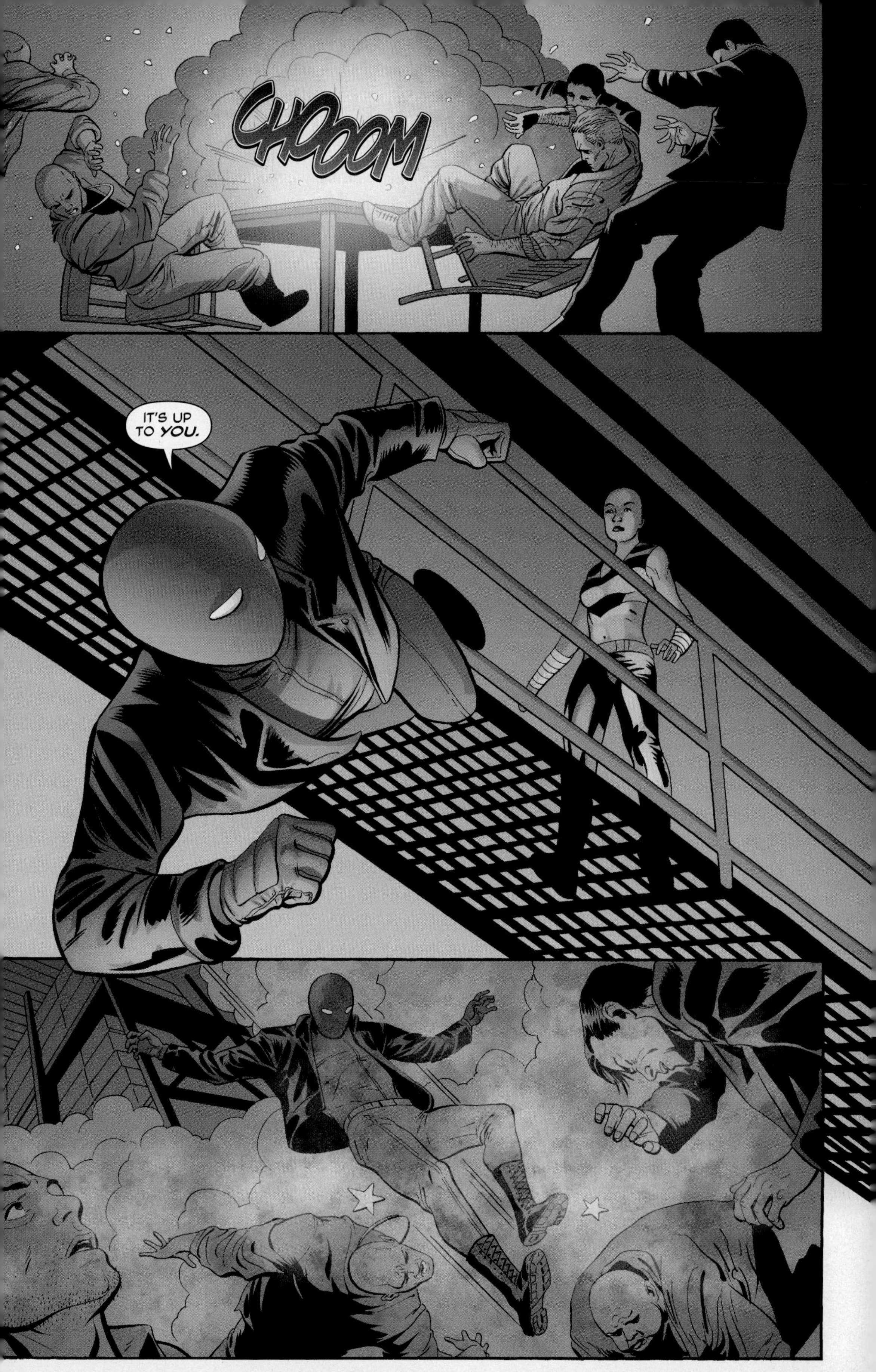
CHOOOM
IT'S UP TO YOU.

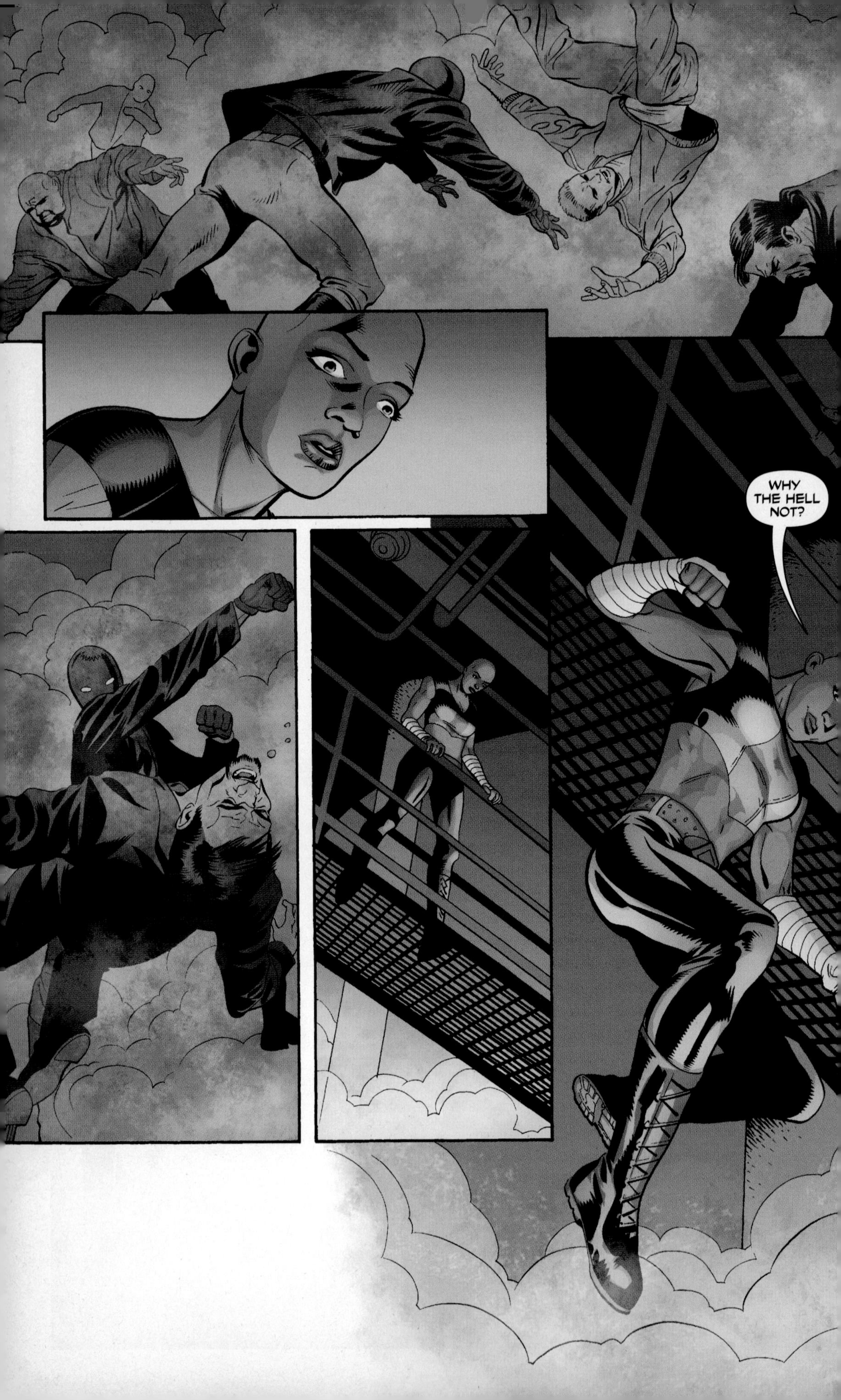
WHY THE HELL NOT?

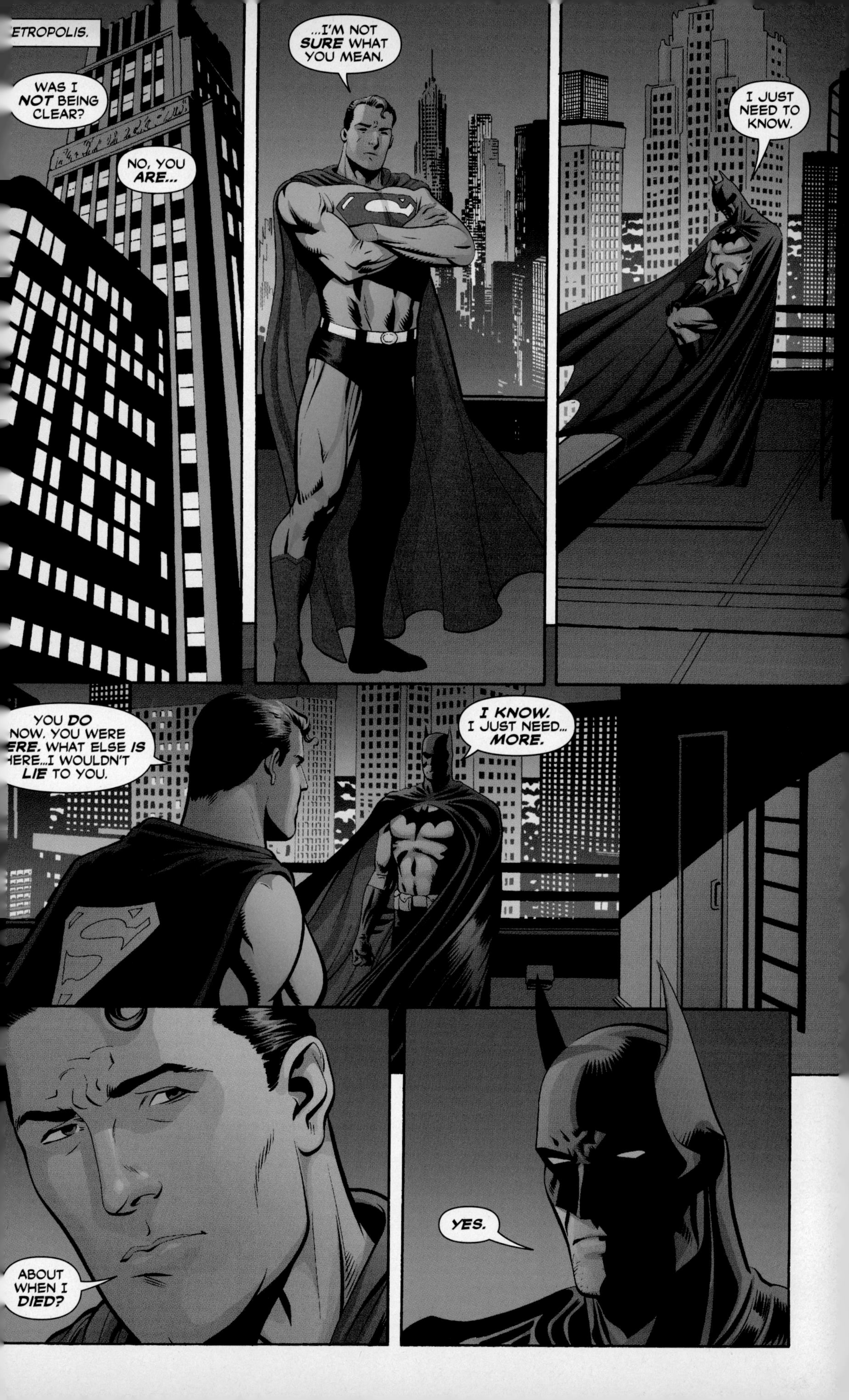
ETROPOLIS.
WAS I NOT BEING CLEAR?
NO, YOU ARE...
...I'M NOT SURE WHAT YOU MEAN.
I JUST NEED TO KNOW.
YOU DO NOW. YOU WERE ERE. WHAT ELSE IS HERE...I WOULDN'T LIE TO YOU.
I KNOW. I JUST NEED... MORE.
ABOUT WHEN I DIED?
YES.

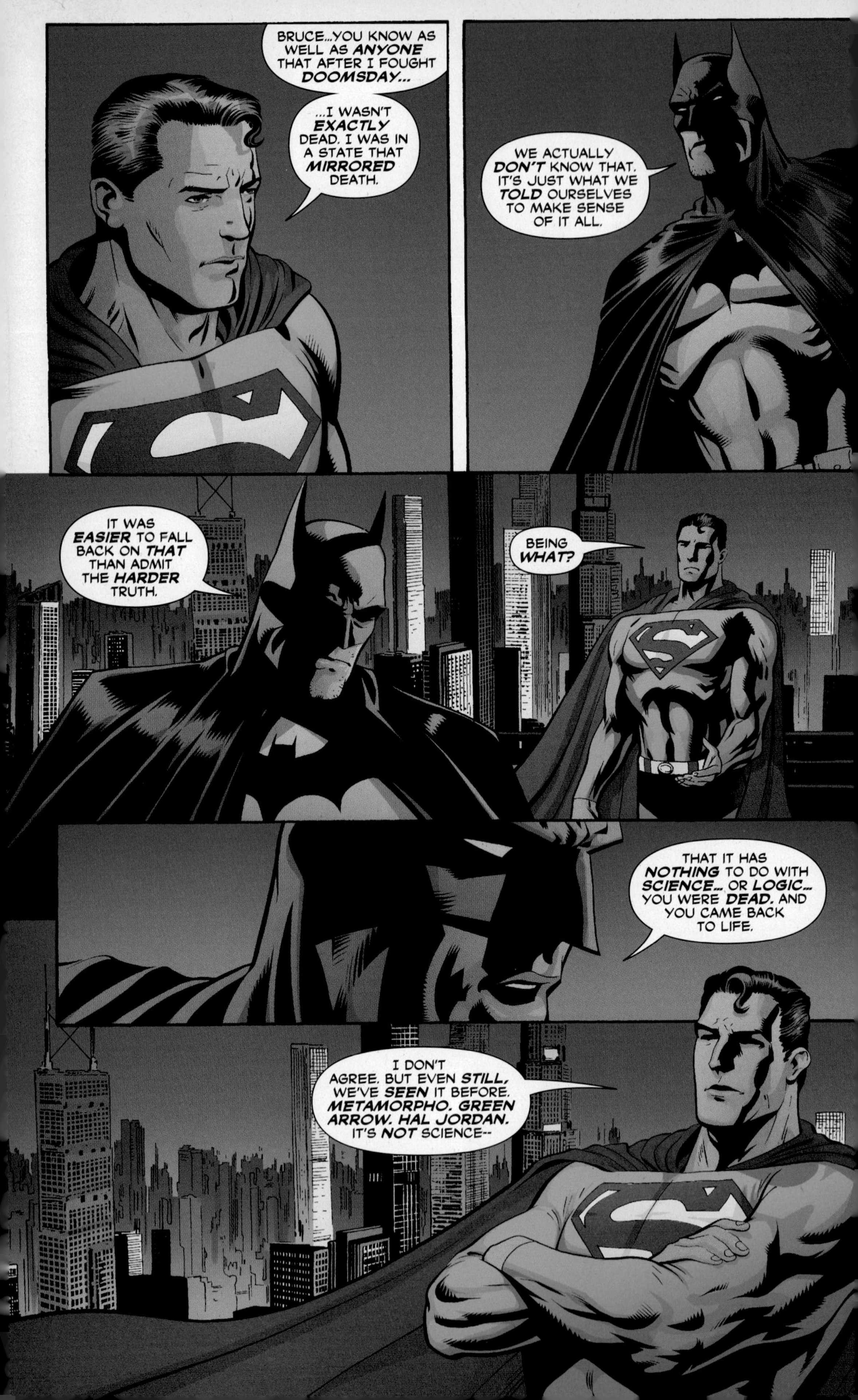
BRUCE...YOU KNOW AS WELL AS ANYONE THAT AFTER I FOUGHT DOOMSDAY...
...I WASN'T EXACTLY DEAD. I WAS IN A STATE THAT MIRRORED DEATH.
WE ACTUALLY DON'T KNOW THAT. IT'S JUST WHAT WE TOLD OURSELVES TO MAKE SENSE OF IT ALL.
IT WAS EASIER TO FALL BACK ON THAT THAN ADMIT THE HARDER TRUTH.
BEING WHAT?
THAT IT HAS NOTHING TO DO WITH SCIENCE... OR LOGIC... YOU WERE DEAD. AND YOU CAME BACK TO LIFE.
I DON'T AGREE. BUT EVEN STILL, WE'VE SEEN IT BEFORE. METAMORPHO. GREEN ARROW. HAL JORDAN. IT'S NOT SCIENCE--

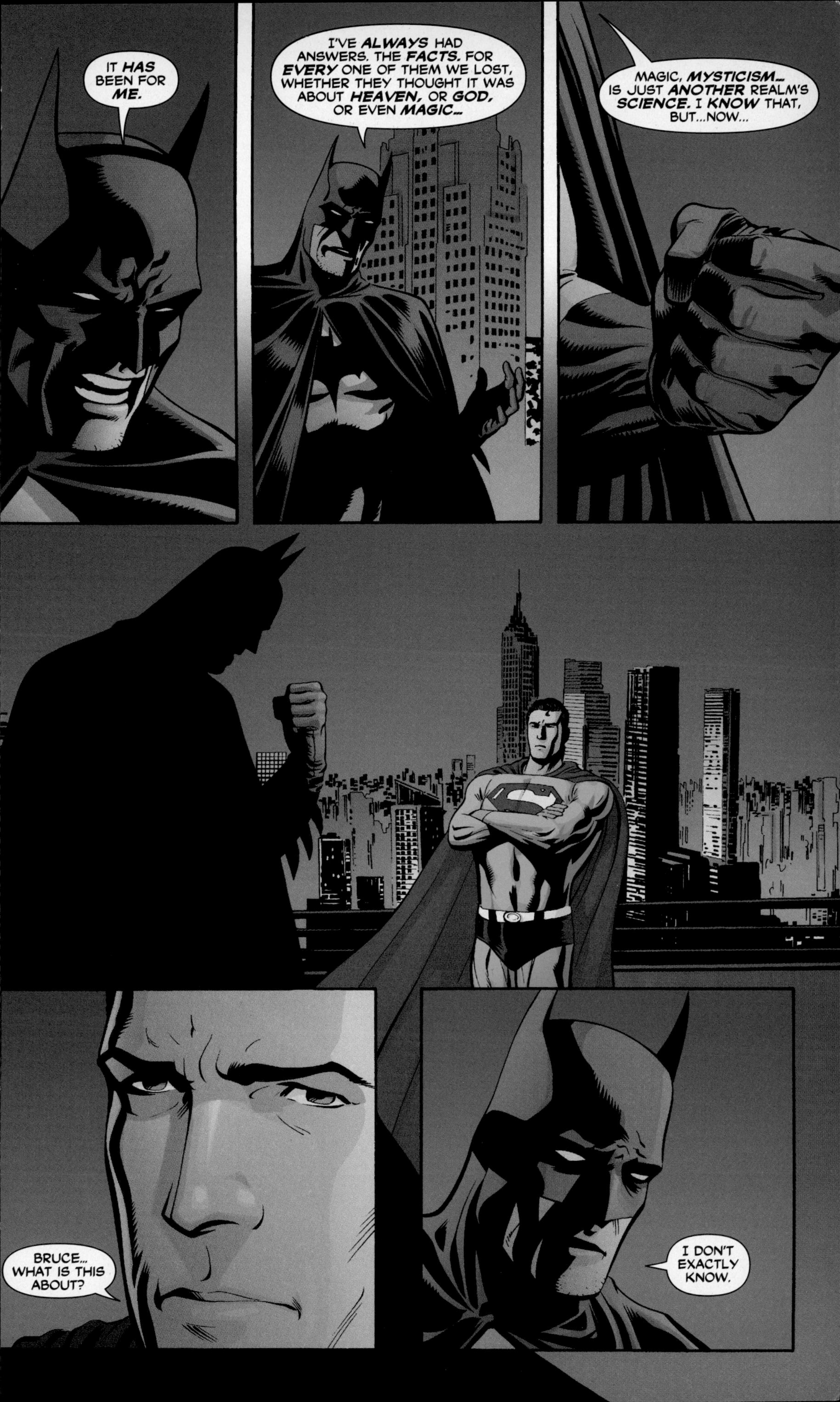
IT HAS BEEN FOR ME.
I'VE ALWAYS HAD ANSWERS. THE FACTS. FOR EVERY ONE OF THEM WE LOST, WHETHER THEY THOUGHT IT WAS ABOUT HEAVEN, OR GOD, OR EVEN MAGIC...
MAGIC, MYSTICISM... IS JUST ANOTHER REALM'S SCIENCE. I KNOW THAT, BUT...NOW...
BRUCE... WHAT IS THIS ABOUT?
I DON'T EXACTLY KNOW.

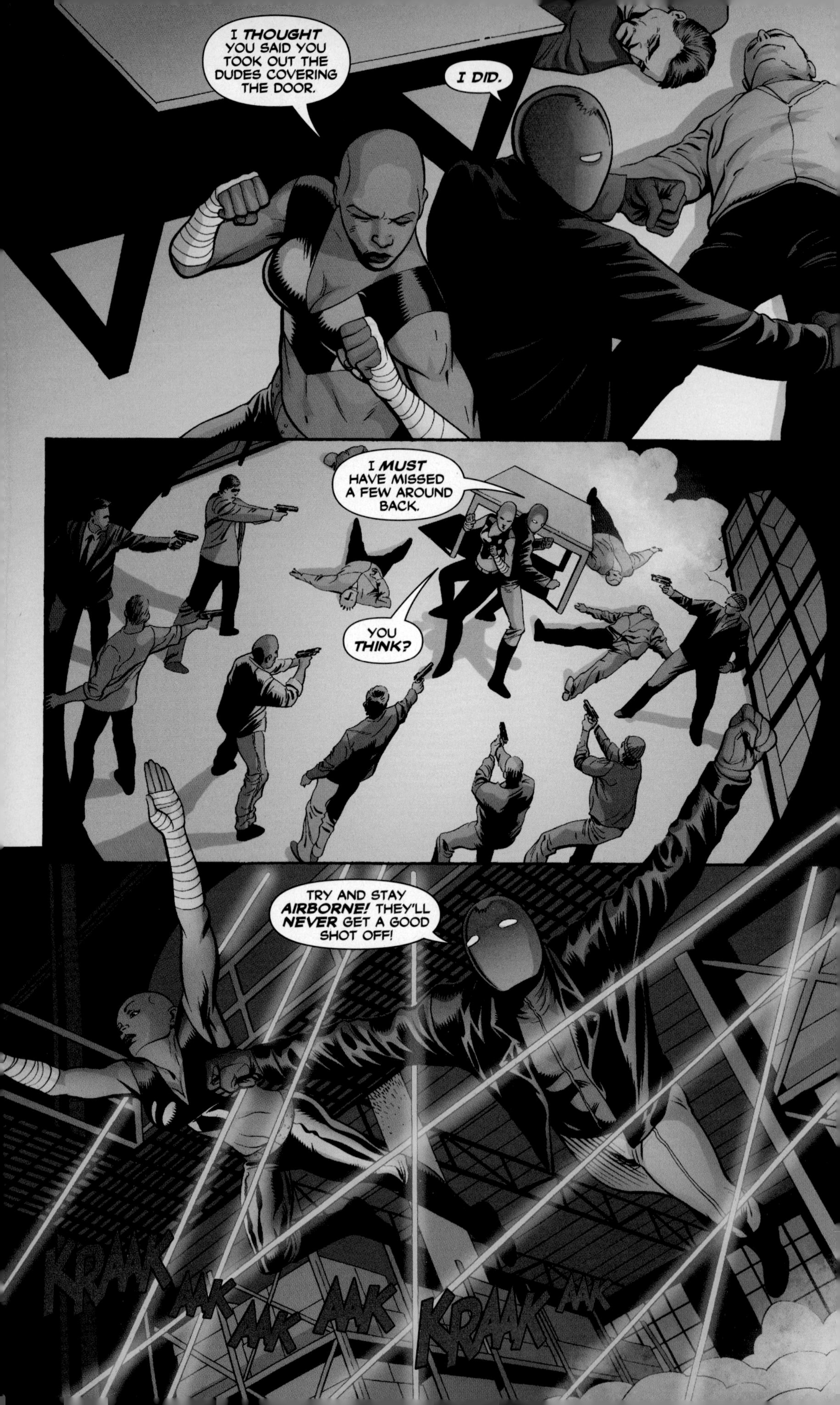
I THOUGHT YOU SAID YOU TOOK OUT THE DUDES COVERING THE DOOR.
I DID.
I MUST HAVE MISSED A FEW AROUND BACK.
YOU THINK?
TRY AND STAY AIRBORNE! THEY'LL NEVER GET A GOOD SHOT OFF!
KRAAK AAK AAK AAK KRAAK AAK

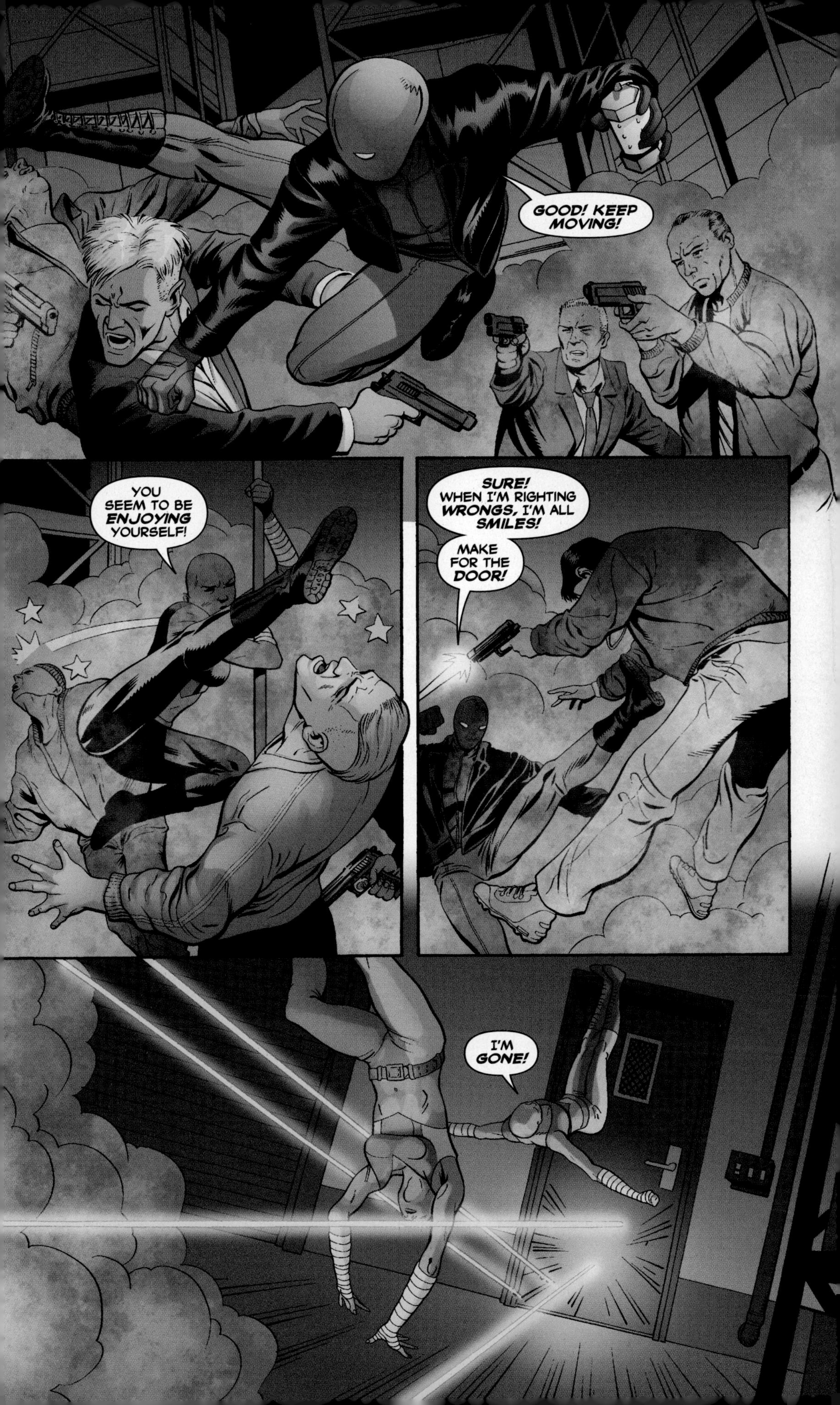
GOOD! KEEP MOVING!
YOU SEEM TO BE ENJOYING YOURSELF!
SURE! WHEN I'M RIGHTING WRONGS, I'M ALL SMILES!
MAKE FOR THE DOOR!
I'M GONE!

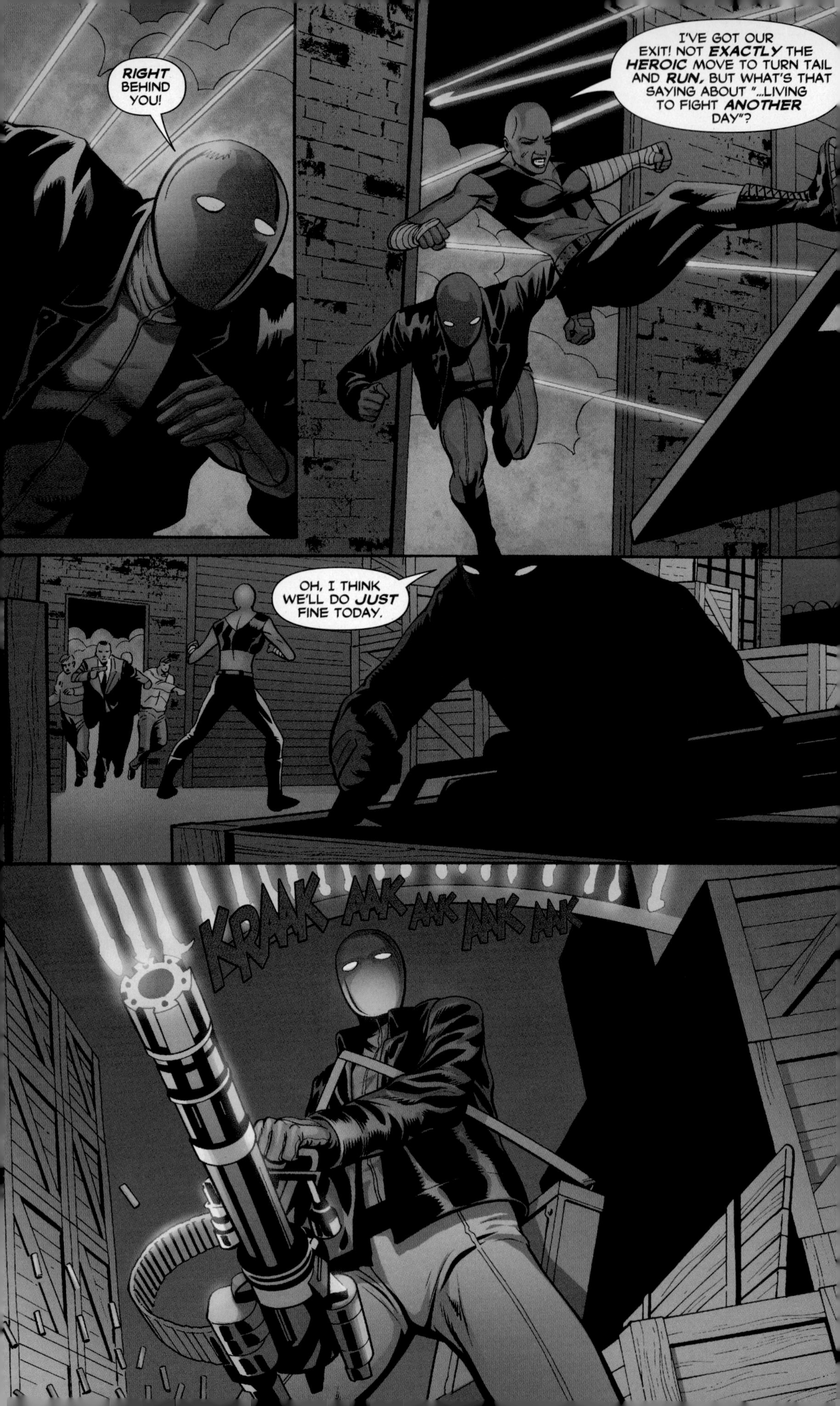
RIGHT BEHIND YOU!
I'VE GOT OUR EXIT! NOT EXACTLY THE HEROIC MOVE TO TURN TAIL AND RUN, BUT WHAT'S THAT SAYING ABOUT "...LIVING TO FIGHT ANOTHER DAY"?
OH, I THINK WE'LL DO JUST FINE TODAY.
KRAAK AAK AAK AAK AAK

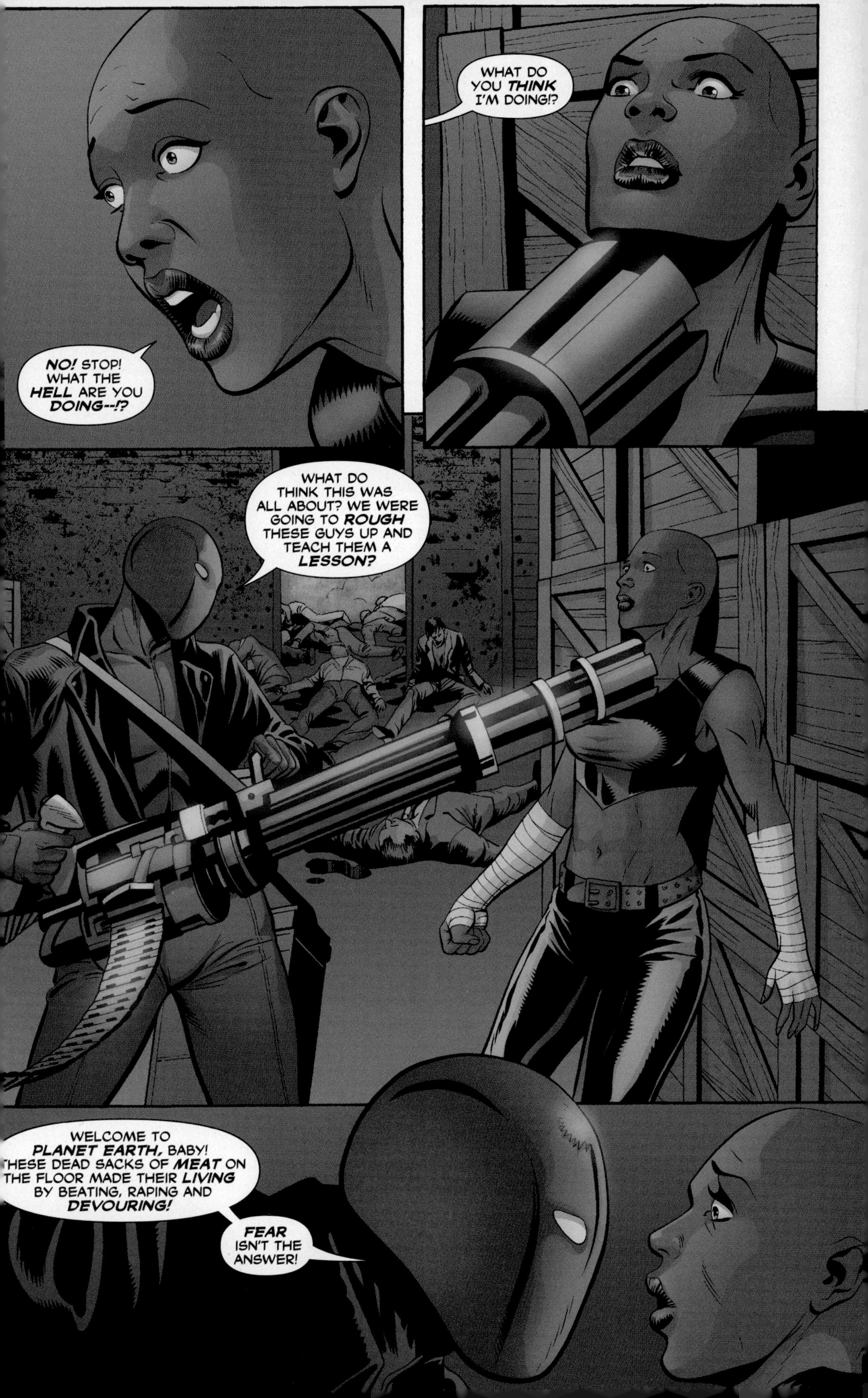
NO! STOP! WHAT THE HELL ARE YOU DOING--!?
WHAT DO YOU THINK I'M DOING!?
WHAT DO THINK THIS WAS ALL ABOUT? WE WERE GOING TO ROUGH THESE GUYS UP AND TEACH THEM A LESSON?
WELCOME TO PLANET EARTH, BABY! THESE DEAD SACKS OF MEAT ON THE FLOOR MADE THEIR LIVING BY BEATING, RAPING AND DEVOURING!
FEAR ISN'T THE ANSWER!

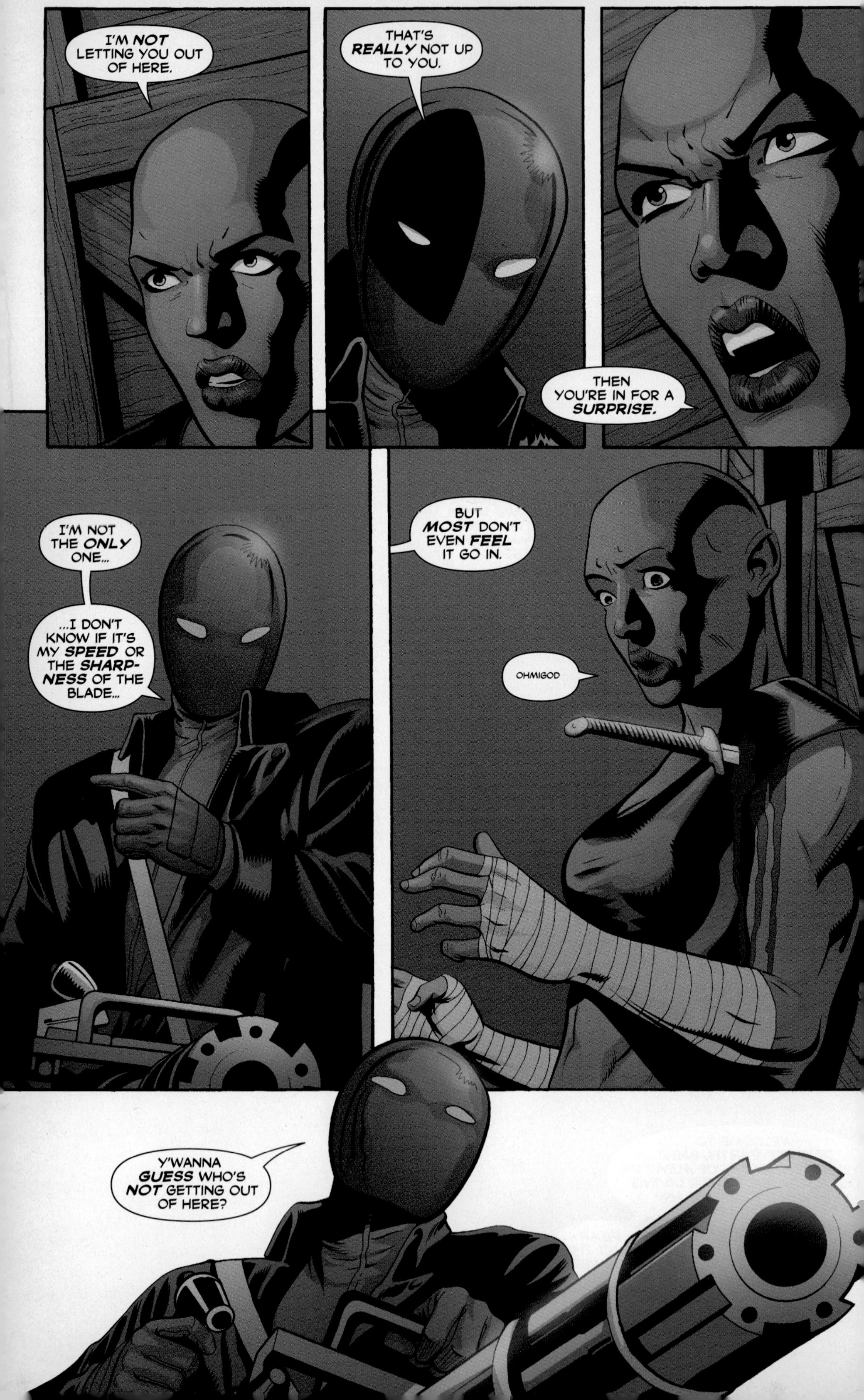
I'M NOT LETTING YOU OUT OF HERE.
THAT'S REALLY NOT UP TO YOU.
THEN YOU'RE IN FOR A SURPRISE.
I'M NOT THE ONLY ONE...
...I DON'T KNOW IF IT'S MY SPEED OR THE SHARP-NESS OF THE BLADE...
BUT MOST DON'T EVEN FEEL IT GO IN.
OHMIGOD
Y'WANNA GUESS WHO'S NOT GETTING OUT OF HERE?

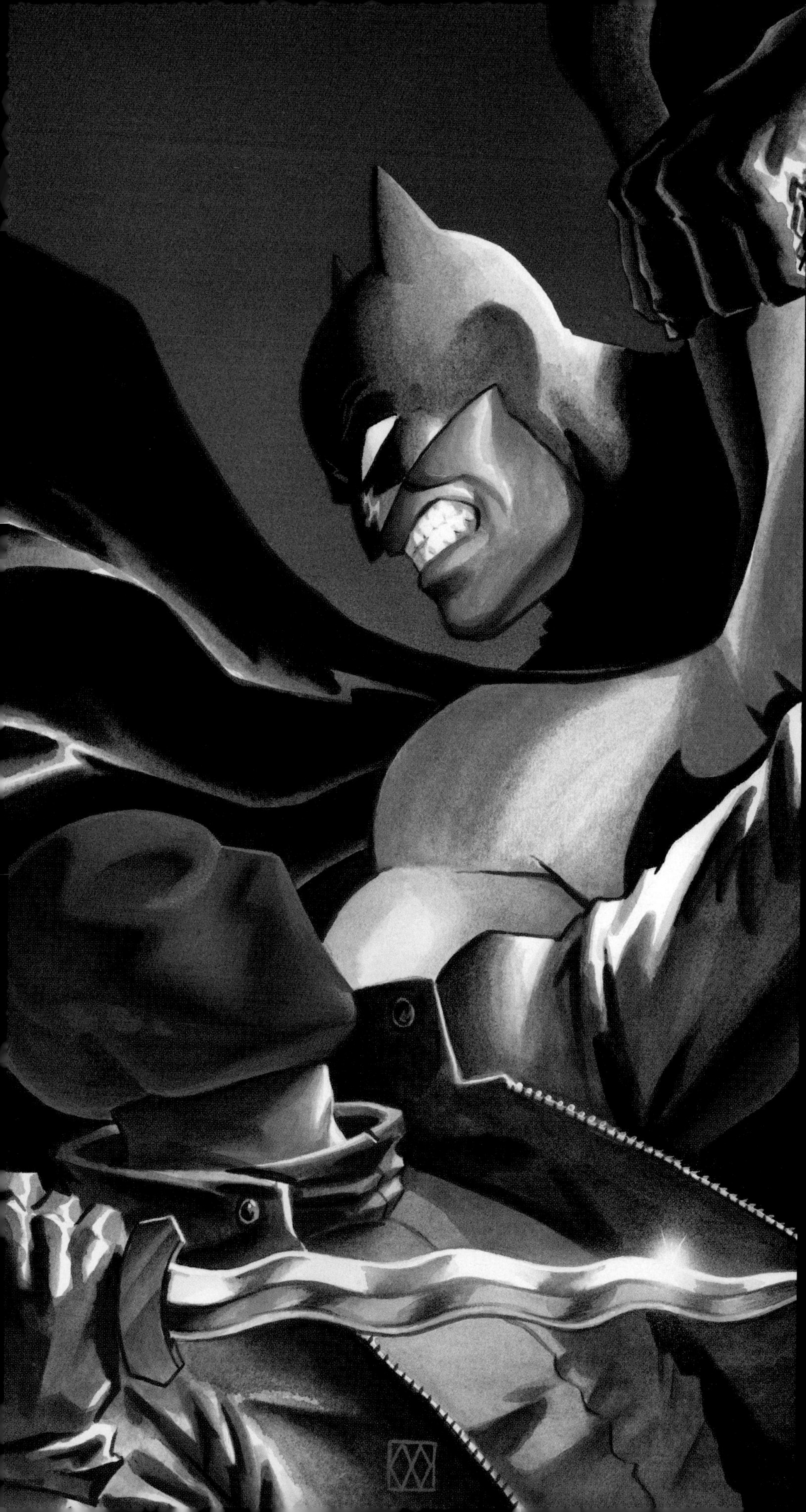

BATMAN #641 • ART BY MATT WAGNER

PART 7

FACE TO FACE

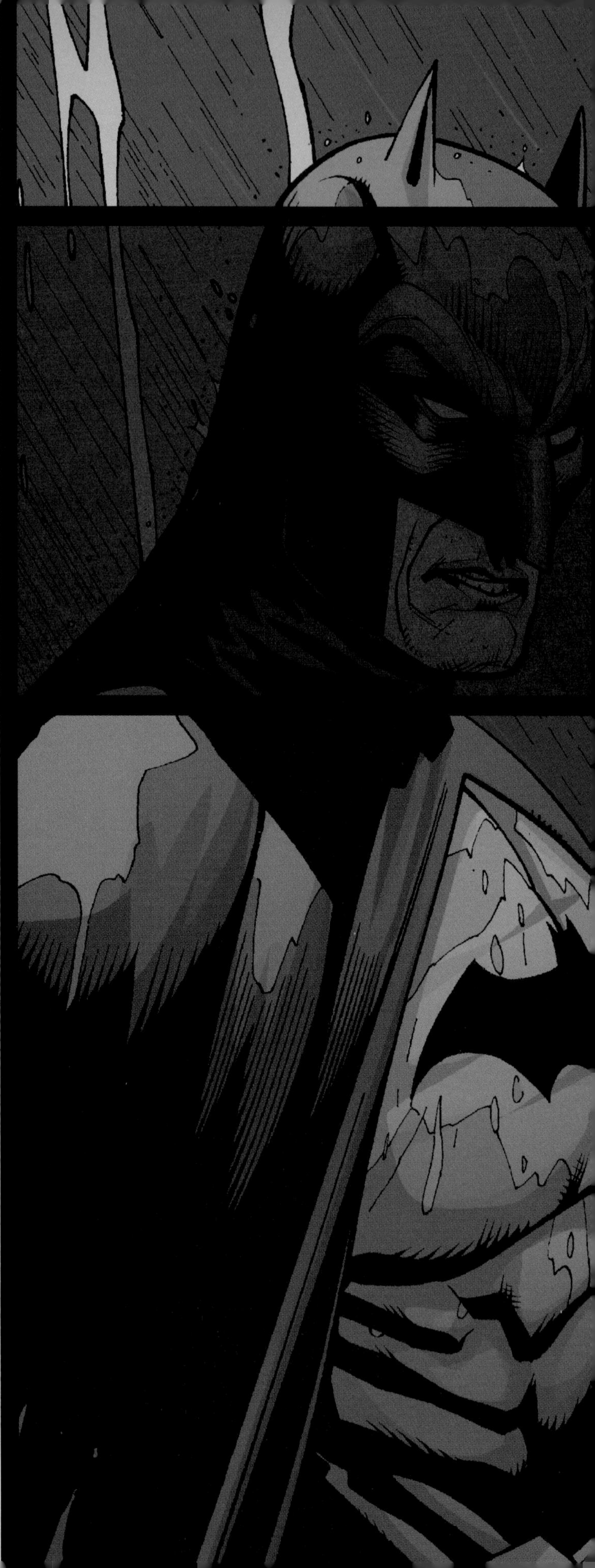

ALFRED, I CAN'T TRIANGULATE THE TRACER FROM THE PLANE.

THE ARMOR HAS TO BE LIGHT ENOUGH TO MOVE...TO FIGHT...

...BUT STRONG ENOUGH TO PROTECT.

...I'M SORRY, SIR, BUT ONYX'S SIGNAL ISN'T COMING UP ON ANY...WAIT, SIR...

BUT SOMETIMES... A GREAT MANY TIMES...

...IT'S NOT STRONG ENOUGH.

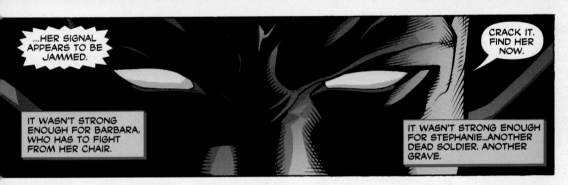

...HER SIGNAL APPEARS TO BE JAMMED.

CRACK IT. FIND HER NOW.

IT WASN'T STRONG ENOUGH FOR BARBARA, WHO HAS TO FIGHT FROM HER CHAIR.

IT WASN'T STRONG ENOUGH FOR STEPHANIE...ANOTHER DEAD SOLDIER. ANOTHER GRAVE.

AND IT WASN'T STRONG ENOUGH FOR JASON.

WILLFUL JASON, WHO IGNORED DANGER... WHO SPAT AT RISK.

WHO WAS NEVER FRIGHTENED ENOUGH.

I'VE ALWAYS WONDERED... ALWAYS...

...WAS HE SCARED AT THE END?

WAS HE PRAYING I'D COME SAVE HIM?

AND IN THOSE LAST MOMENTS WHEN HE KNEW THAT I WOULDN'T...

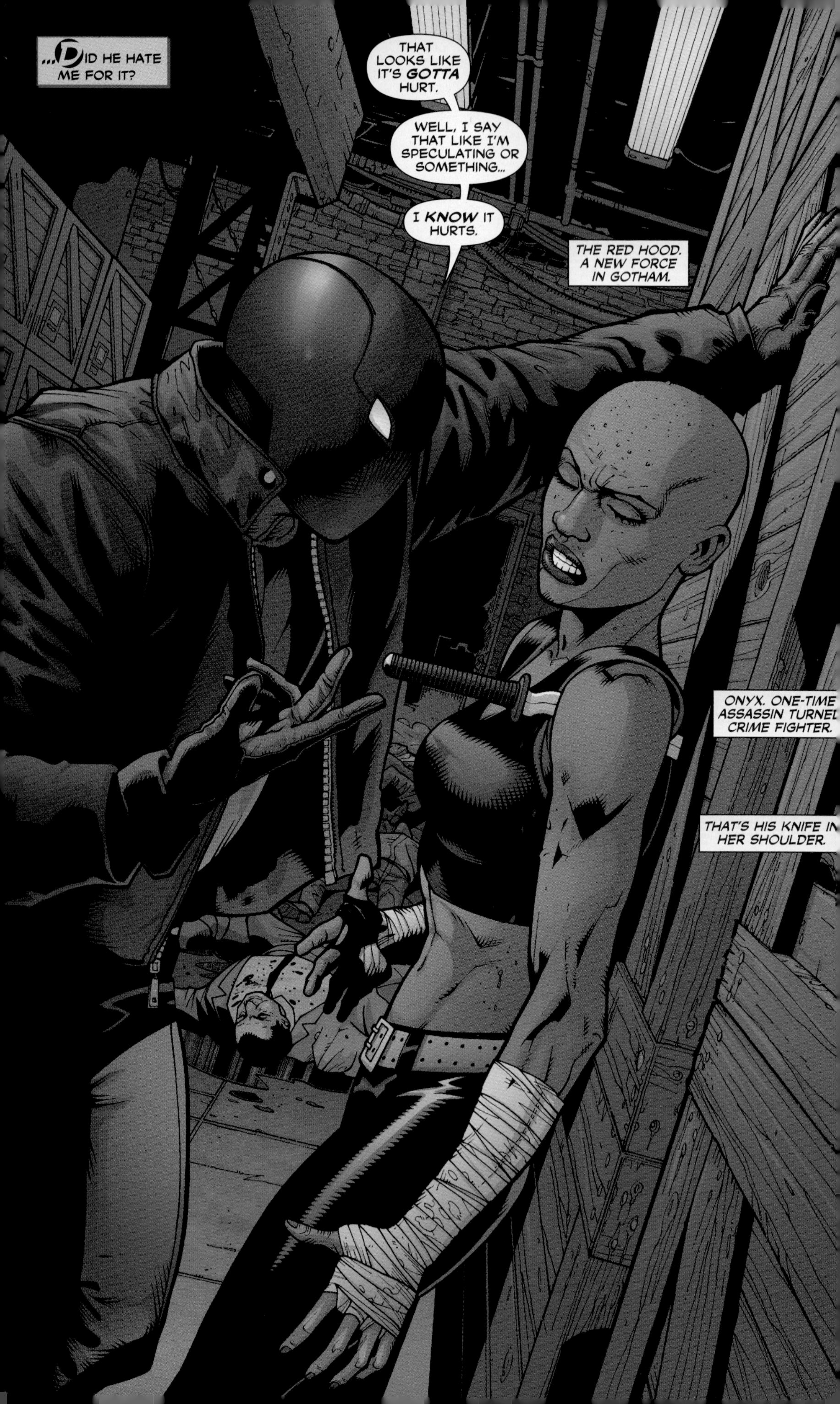
...DID HE HATE ME FOR IT?
THAT LOOKS LIKE IT'S GOTTA HURT.
WELL, I SAY THAT LIKE I'M SPECULATING OR SOMETHING...
I KNOW IT HURTS.
THE RED HOOD. A NEW FORCE IN GOTHAM.
ONYX. ONE-TIME ASSASSIN TURNED CRIME FIGHTER.
THAT'S HIS KNIFE IN HER SHOULDER.

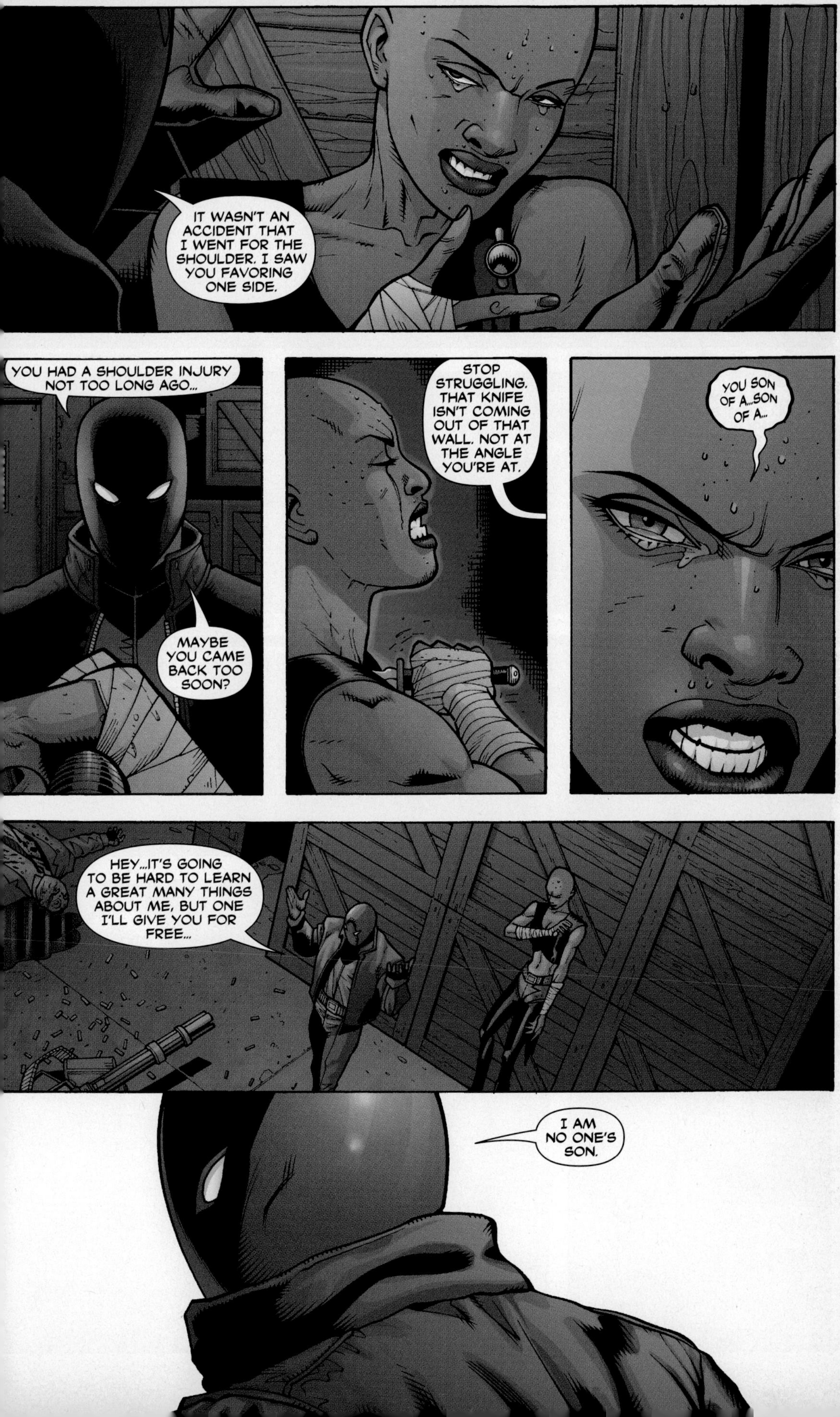
IT WASN'T AN ACCIDENT THAT I WENT FOR THE SHOULDER. I SAW YOU FAVORING ONE SIDE.
YOU HAD A SHOULDER INJURY NOT TOO LONG AGO...
MAYBE YOU CAME BACK TOO SOON?
STOP STRUGGLING. THAT KNIFE ISN'T COMING OUT OF THAT WALL. NOT AT THE ANGLE YOU'RE AT.
YOU SON OF A...SON OF A...
HEY...IT'S GOING TO BE HARD TO LEARN A GREAT MANY THINGS ABOUT ME, BUT ONE I'LL GIVE YOU FOR FREE...
I AM NO ONE'S SON.

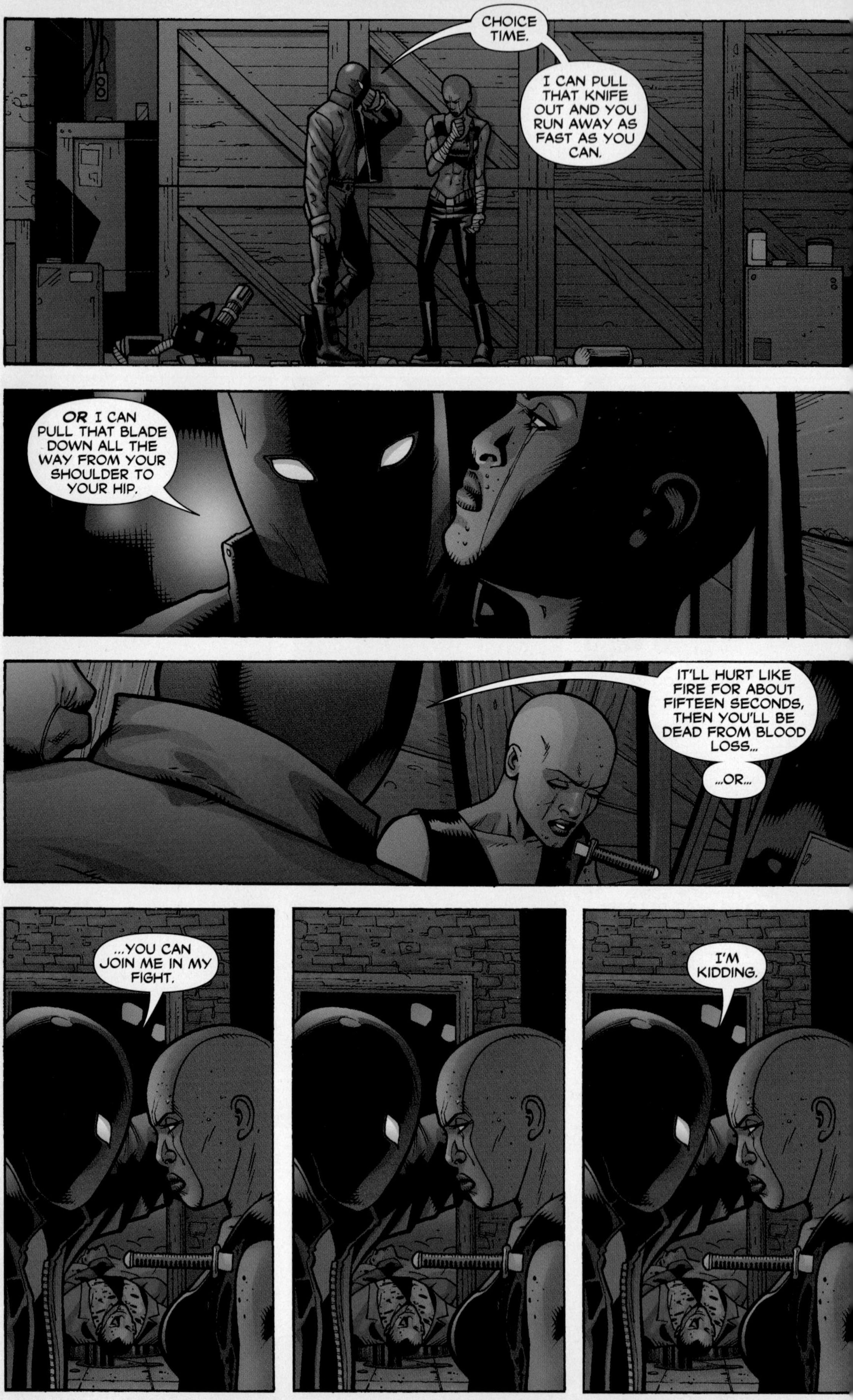
CHOICE TIME.
I CAN PULL THAT KNIFE OUT AND YOU RUN AWAY AS FAST AS YOU CAN.
OR I CAN PULL THAT BLADE DOWN ALL THE WAY FROM YOUR SHOULDER TO YOUR HIP.
IT'LL HURT LIKE FIRE FOR ABOUT FIFTEEN SECONDS, THEN YOU'LL BE DEAD FROM BLOOD LOSS...
...OR...
...YOU CAN JOIN ME IN MY FIGHT.
I'M KIDDING.

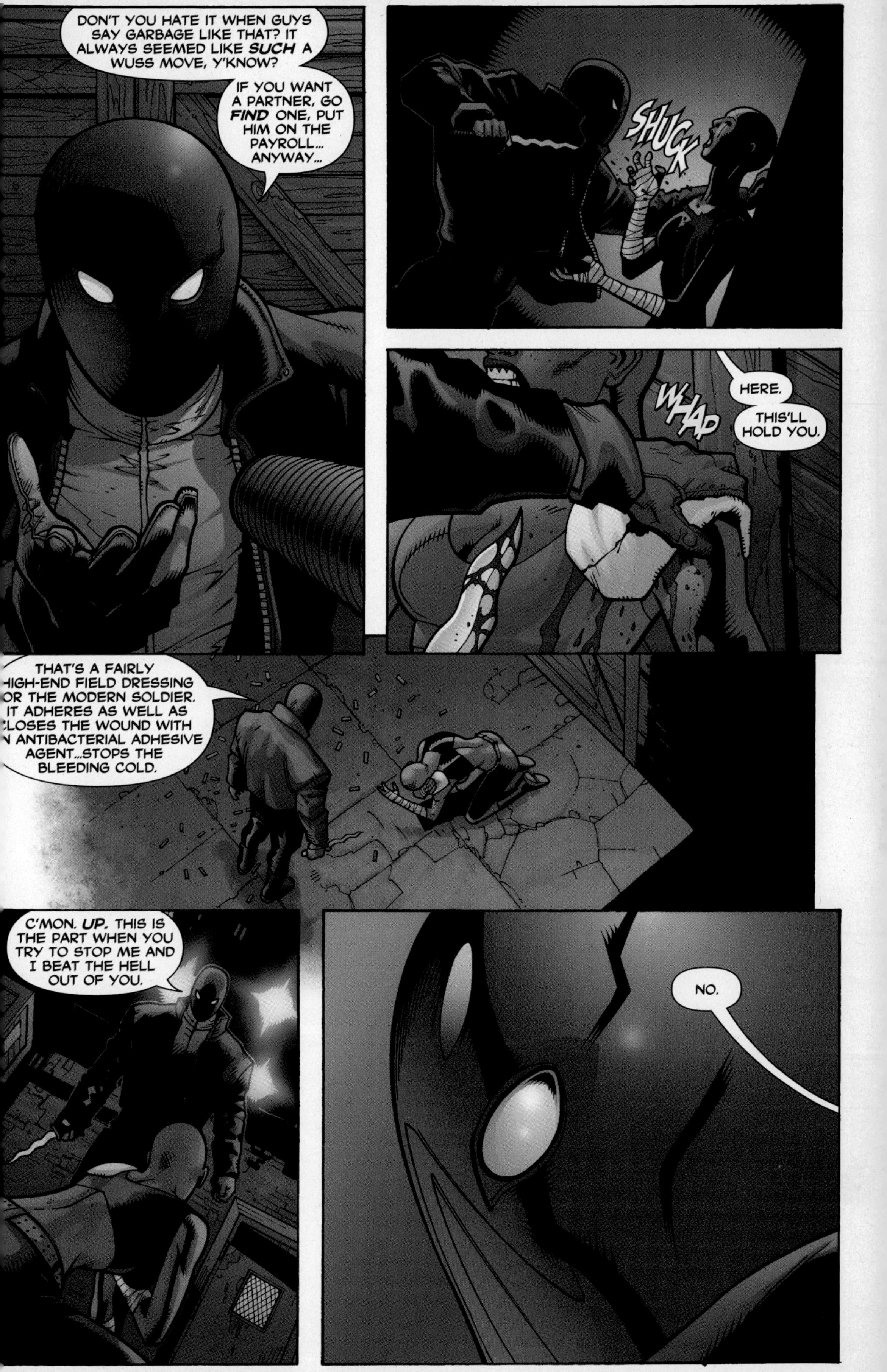
DON'T YOU HATE IT WHEN GUYS SAY GARBAGE LIKE THAT? IT ALWAYS SEEMED LIKE SUCH A WUSS MOVE, Y'KNOW?
IF YOU WANT A PARTNER, GO FIND ONE, PUT HIM ON THE PAYROLL... ANYWAY...
SHUCK
WHAP
HERE.
THIS'LL HOLD YOU.
THAT'S A FAIRLY HIGH-END FIELD DRESSING FOR THE MODERN SOLDIER. IT ADHERES AS WELL AS CLOSES THE WOUND WITH AN ANTIBACTERIAL ADHESIVE AGENT...STOPS THE BLEEDING COLD.
C'MON. UP. THIS IS THE PART WHEN YOU TRY TO STOP ME AND I BEAT THE HELL OUT OF YOU.
NO.

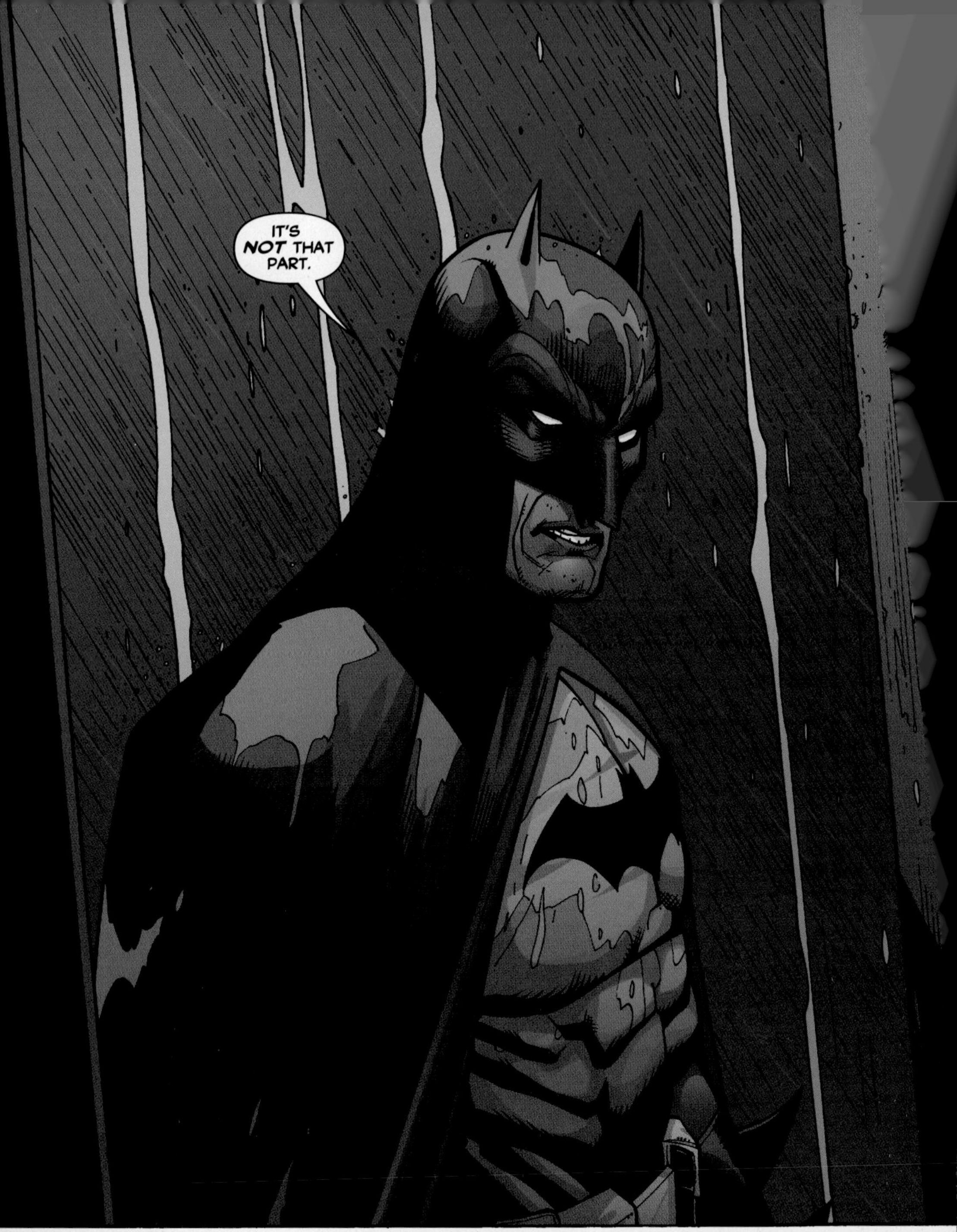
IT'S *NOT* THAT PART.

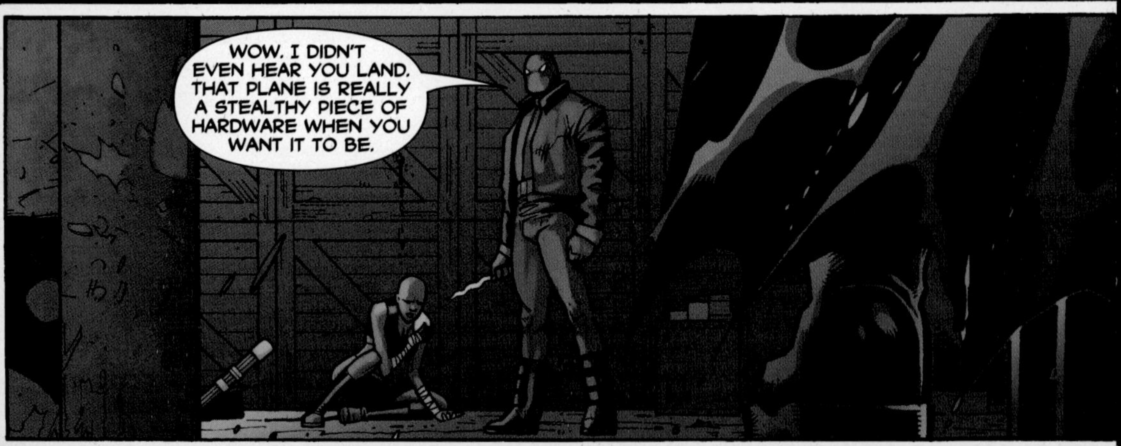
WOW. I DIDN'T EVEN HEAR YOU LAND. THAT PLANE IS REALLY A STEALTHY PIECE OF HARDWARE WHEN YOU WANT IT TO BE.

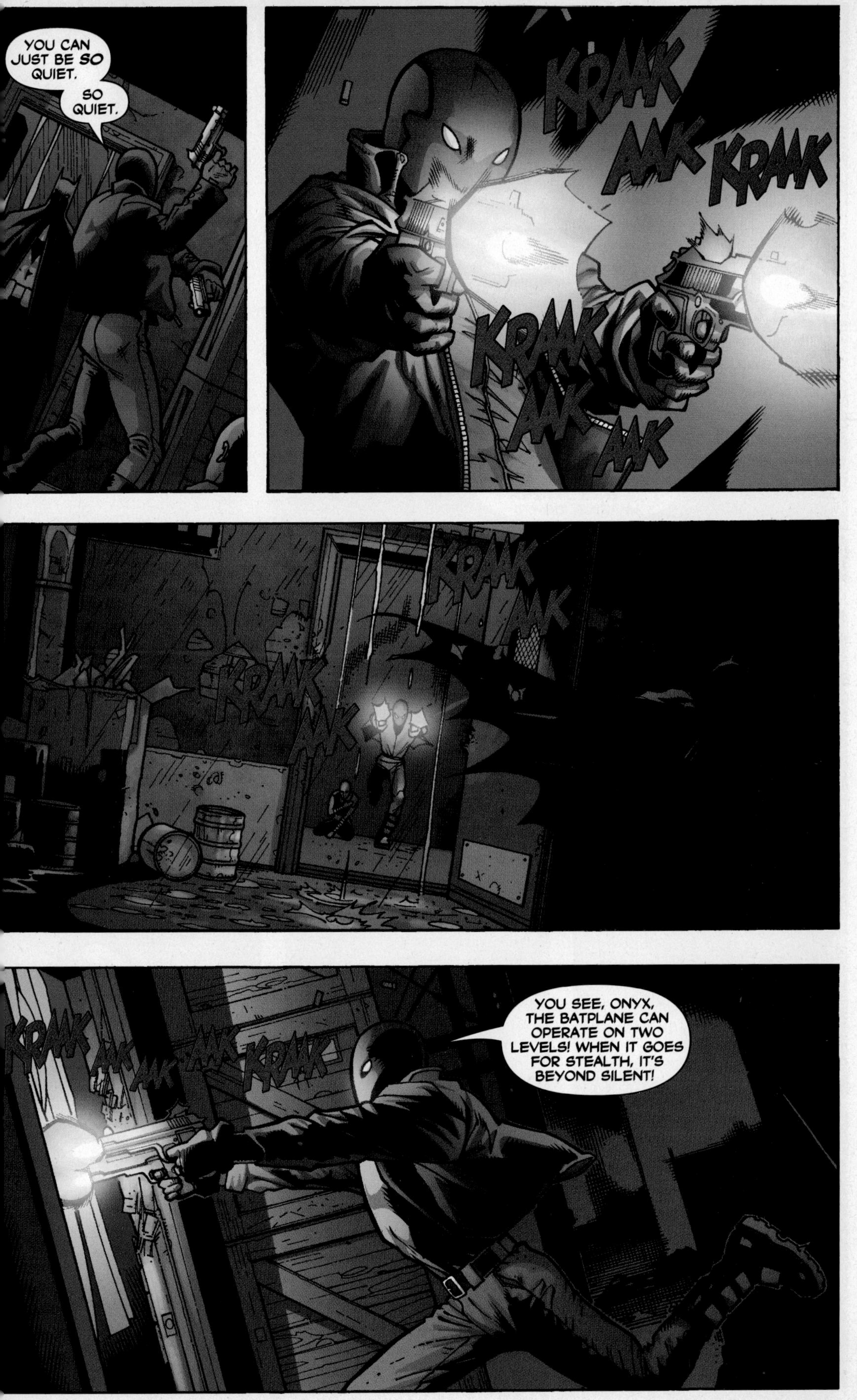

YOU CAN JUST BE SO QUIET.
SO QUIET.
KRAAK
AAK KRAAK
KRAAK
AAK
AAK
KRAAK
AAK
KRAAK
AAK
KRAAK AAK AAK AAK KRAAK
YOU SEE, ONYX, THE BATPLANE CAN OPERATE ON TWO LEVELS! WHEN IT GOES FOR STEALTH, IT'S BEYOND SILENT!

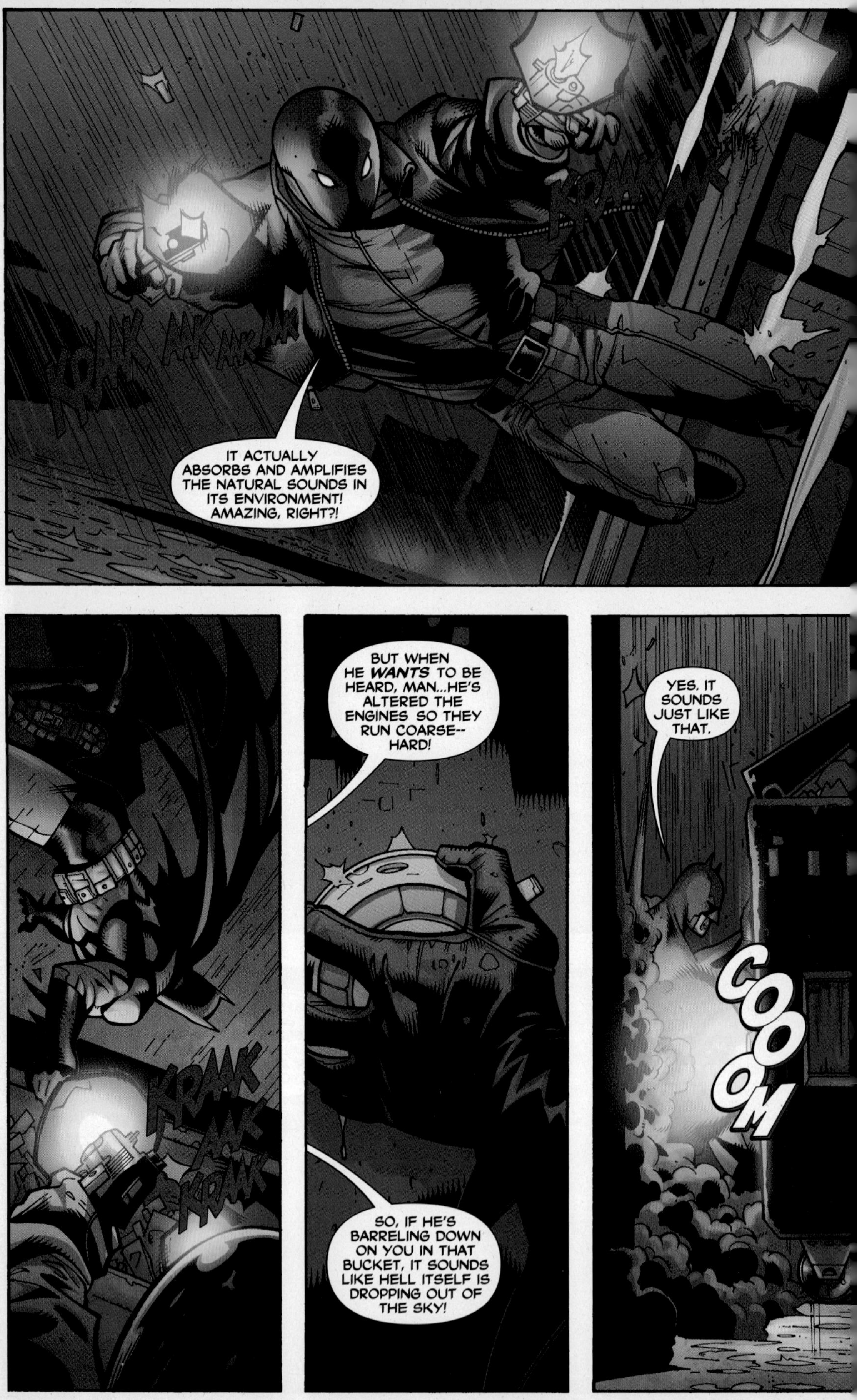
KRAAK KRAAK
KRAK AAK AAK KRAAK
IT ACTUALLY ABSORBS AND AMPLIFIES THE NATURAL SOUNDS IN ITS ENVIRONMENT! AMAZING, RIGHT?!
KRAAK AAK KRAAK
BUT WHEN HE *WANTS* TO BE HEARD, MAN...HE'S ALTERED THE ENGINES SO THEY RUN COARSE--HARD!
SO, IF HE'S BARRELING DOWN ON YOU IN THAT BUCKET, IT SOUNDS LIKE HELL ITSELF IS DROPPING OUT OF THE SKY!
YES, IT SOUNDS JUST LIKE THAT.
COOOM

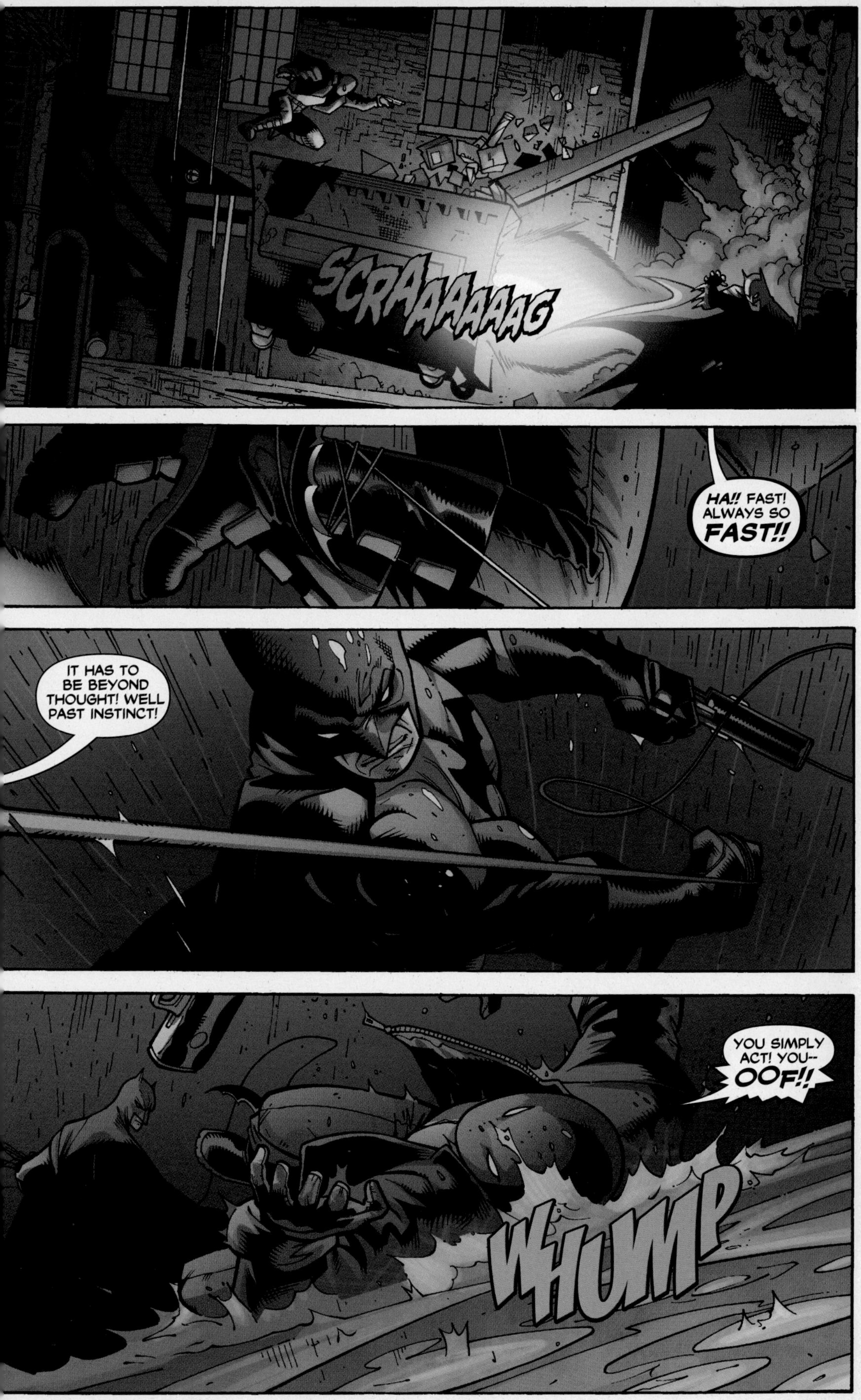
SCRAAAAAAG
HA!! FAST! ALWAYS SO FAST!!
IT HAS TO BE BEYOND THOUGHT! WELL PAST INSTINCT!
YOU SIMPLY ACT! YOU-- OOF!!
WHUMP

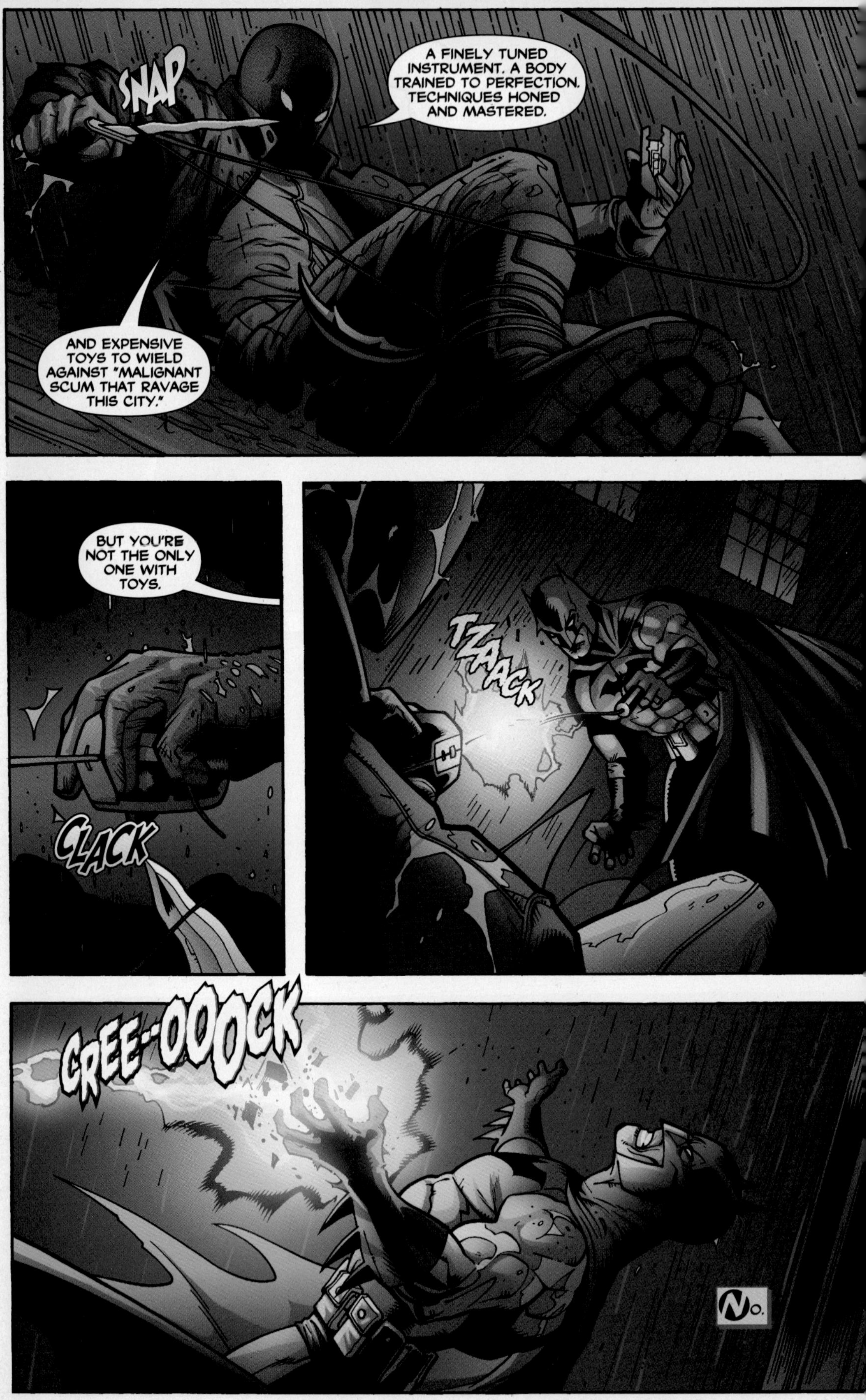
SNAP
A FINELY TUNED INSTRUMENT. A BODY TRAINED TO PERFECTION. TECHNIQUES HONED AND MASTERED.
AND EXPENSIVE TOYS TO WIELD AGAINST "MALIGNANT SCUM THAT RAVAGE THIS CITY."
BUT YOU'RE NOT THE ONLY ONE WITH TOYS.
CLACK
TZAACK
CREE-OOOCK

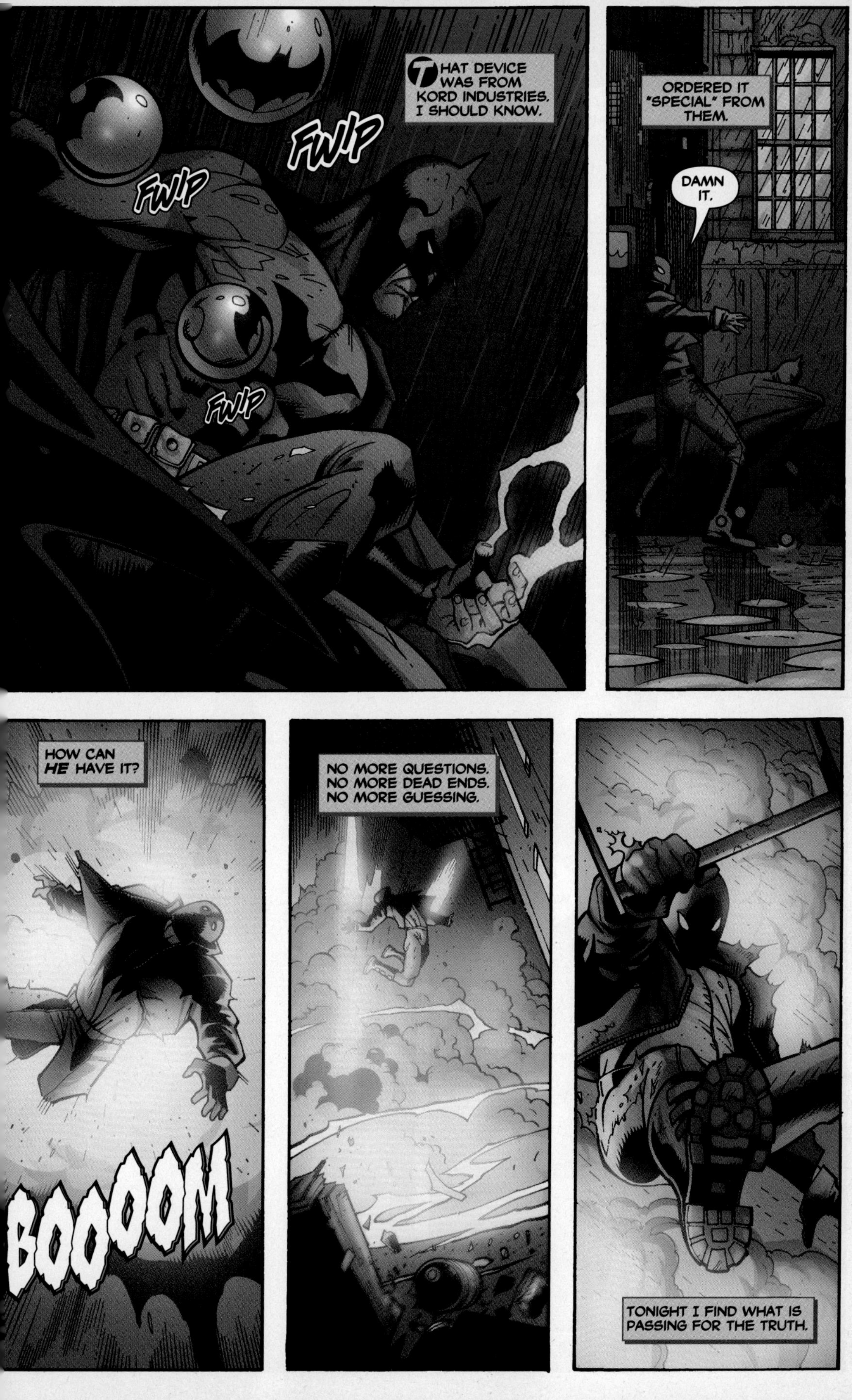
THAT DEVICE WAS FROM KORD INDUSTRIES. I SHOULD KNOW.
FWIP
FWIP
FWIP
ORDERED IT "SPECIAL" FROM THEM.
DAMN IT.
HOW CAN HE HAVE IT?
BOOOOM
NO MORE QUESTIONS. NO MORE DEAD ENDS. NO MORE GUESSING.
TONIGHT I FIND WHAT IS PASSING FOR THE TRUTH.

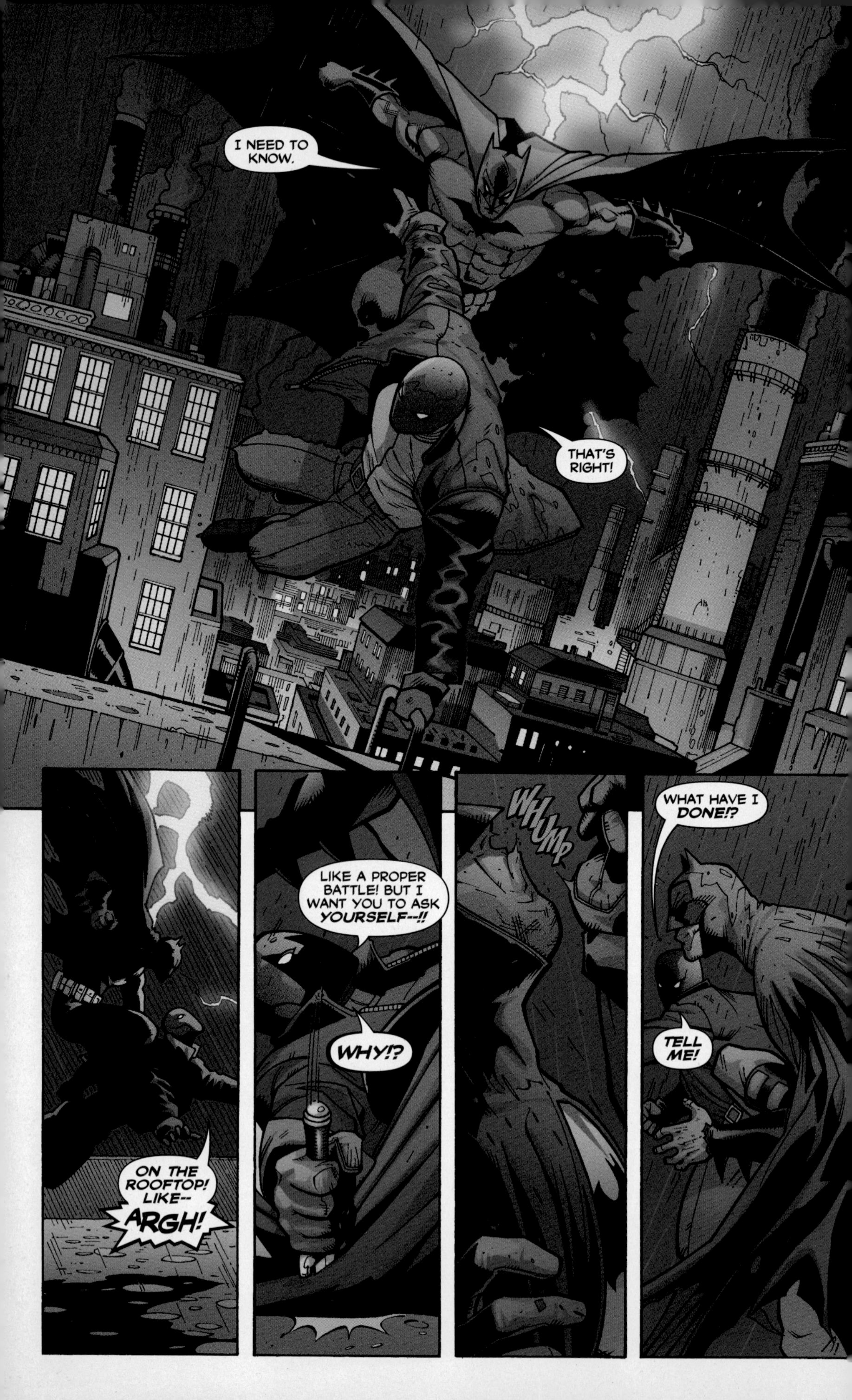
I NEED TO KNOW.
THAT'S RIGHT!
ON THE ROOFTOP! LIKE--
ARGH!
LIKE A PROPER BATTLE! BUT I WANT YOU TO ASK YOURSELF--!!
WHY!?
WHUMP
WHAT HAVE I DONE!?
TELL ME!

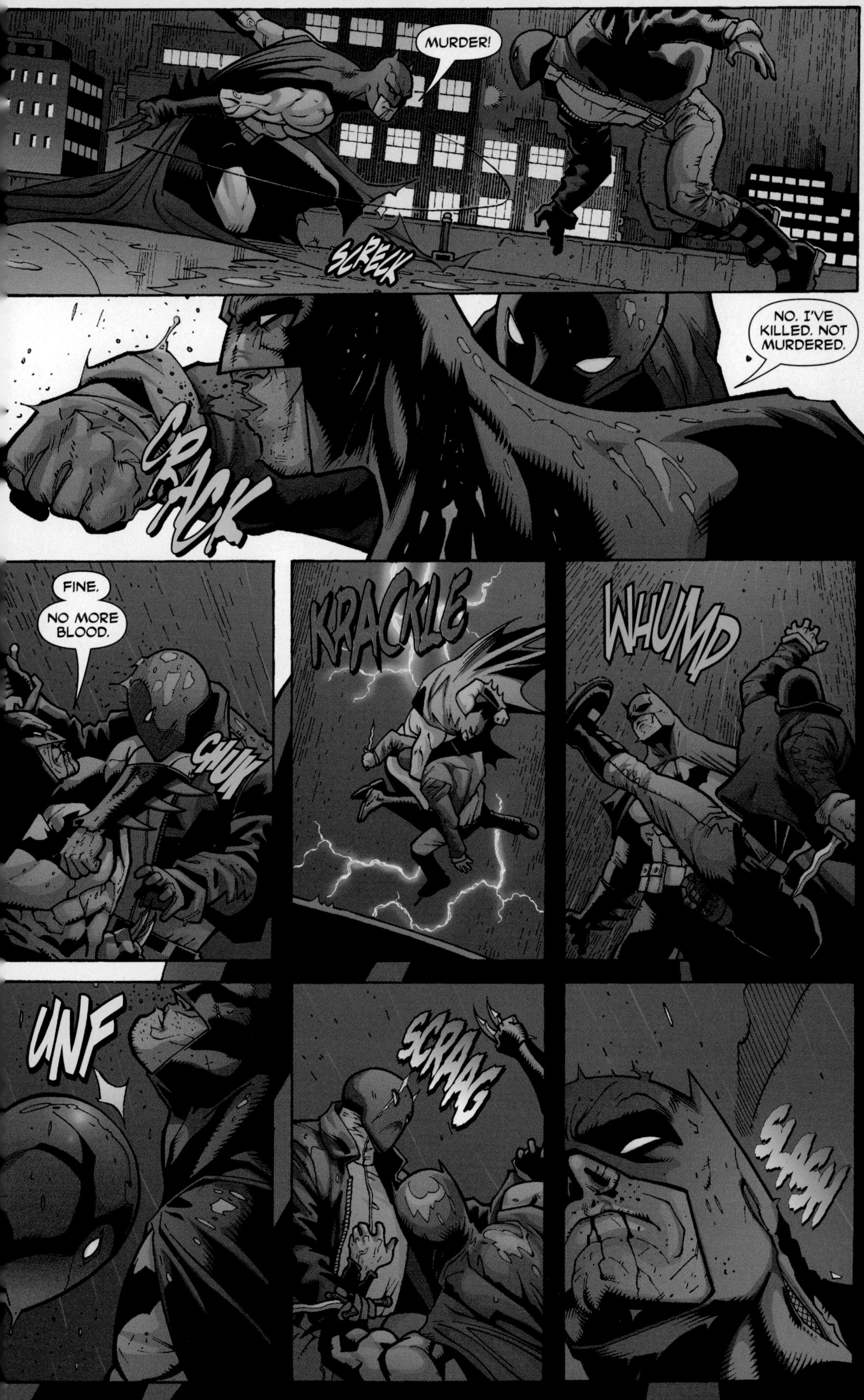

MURDER!
SCRECK
NO. I'VE KILLED. NOT MURDERED.
CRACK
FINE.
NO MORE BLOOD.
CHUK
KRACKLE
WHUMP
UNF
SCRAAG
SLASH

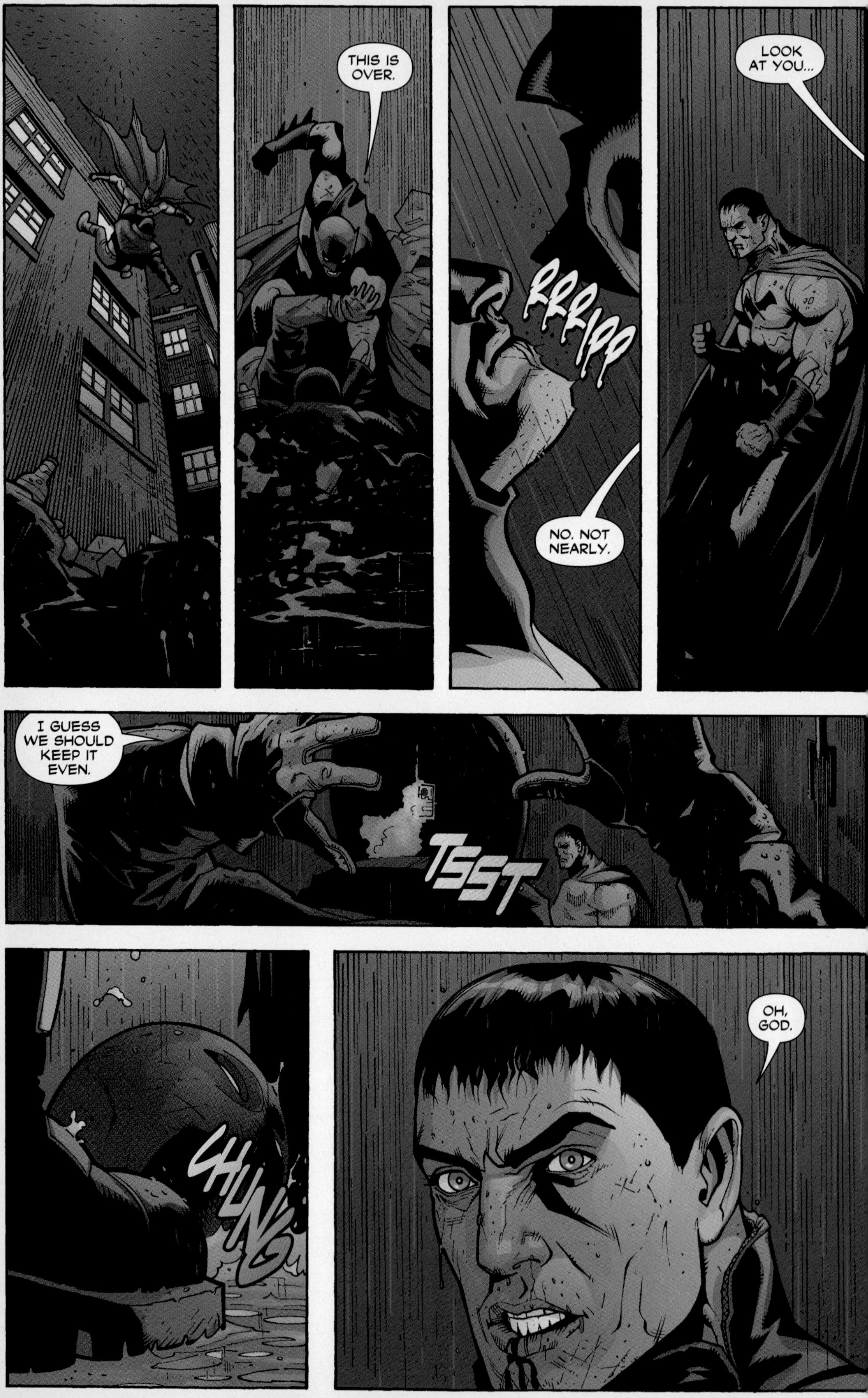

THIS IS OVER.
RRRIPP
NO. NOT NEARLY.
LOOK AT YOU...
I GUESS WE SHOULD KEEP IT EVEN.
TSST
CHUNG
OH, GOD.

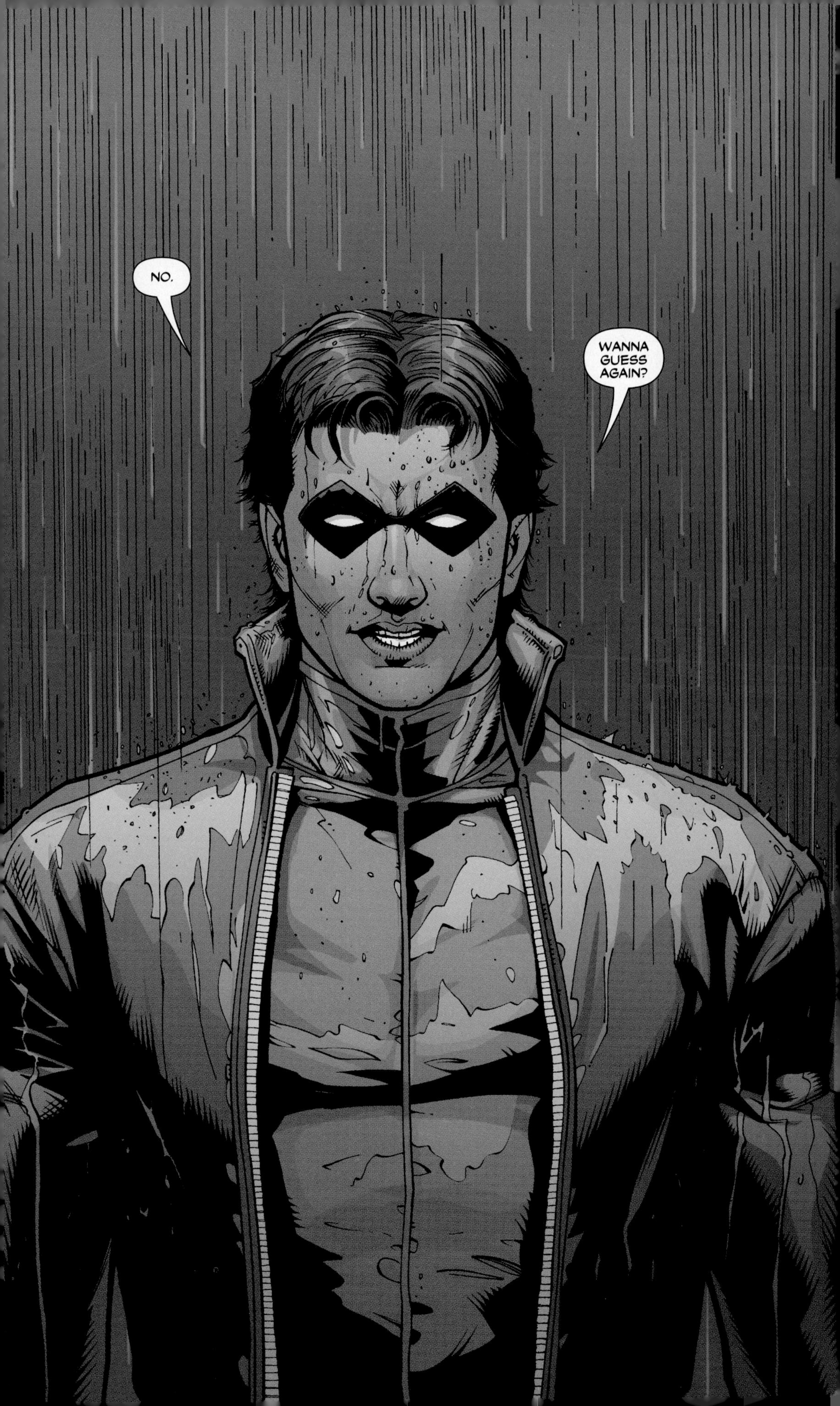
NO.
WANNA GUESS AGAIN?

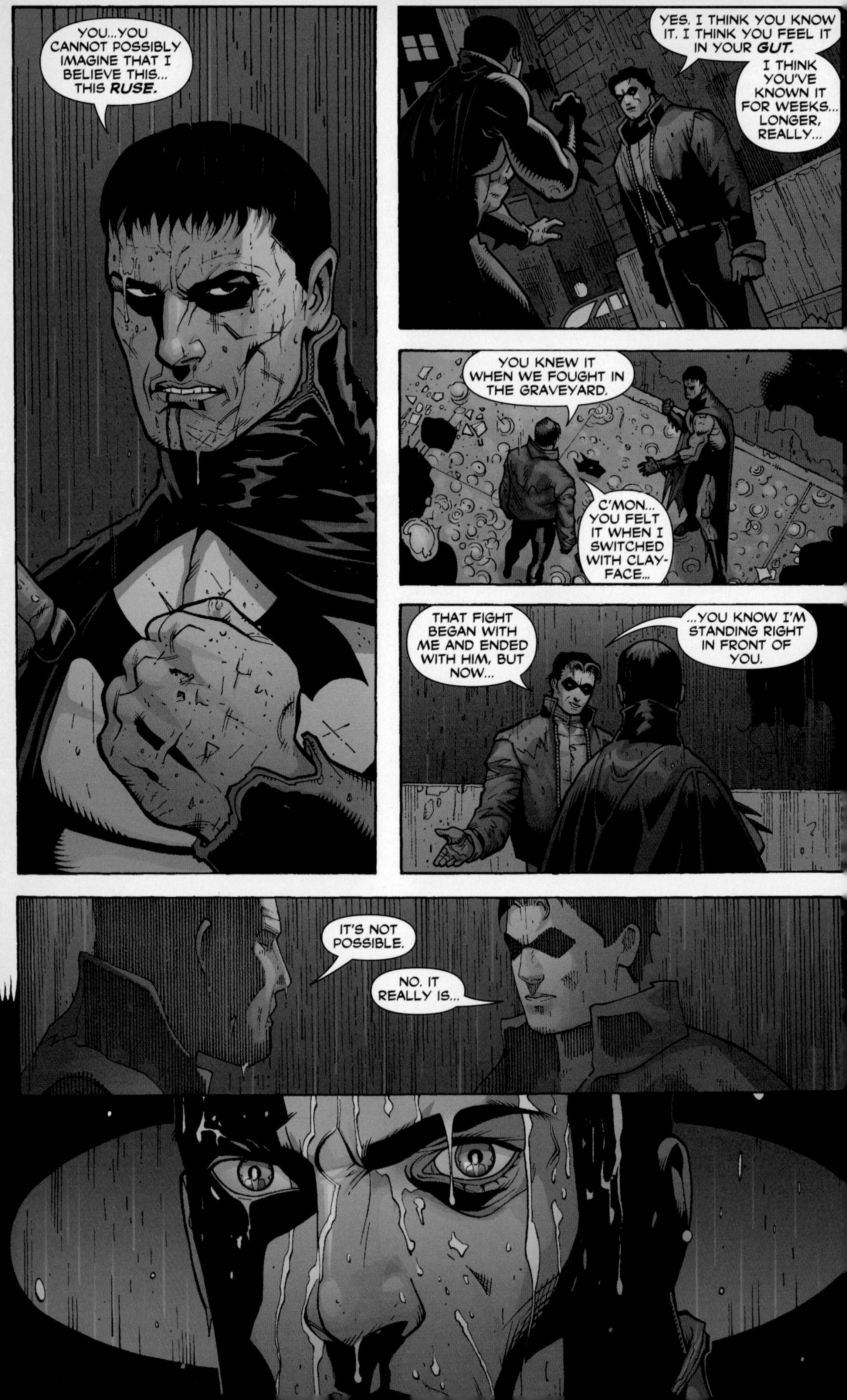

YOU...YOU CANNOT POSSIBLY IMAGINE THAT I BELIEVE THIS... THIS **RUSE.**
YES. I THINK YOU KNOW IT. I THINK YOU FEEL IT IN YOUR **GUT.**
I THINK YOU'VE KNOWN IT FOR WEEKS... LONGER, REALLY...
YOU KNEW IT WHEN WE FOUGHT IN THE GRAVEYARD.
C'MON... YOU FELT IT WHEN I SWITCHED WITH CLAY-FACE...
THAT FIGHT BEGAN WITH ME AND ENDED WITH HIM, BUT NOW...
...YOU KNOW I'M STANDING RIGHT IN FRONT OF YOU.
IT'S NOT POSSIBLE.
NO. IT REALLY IS...

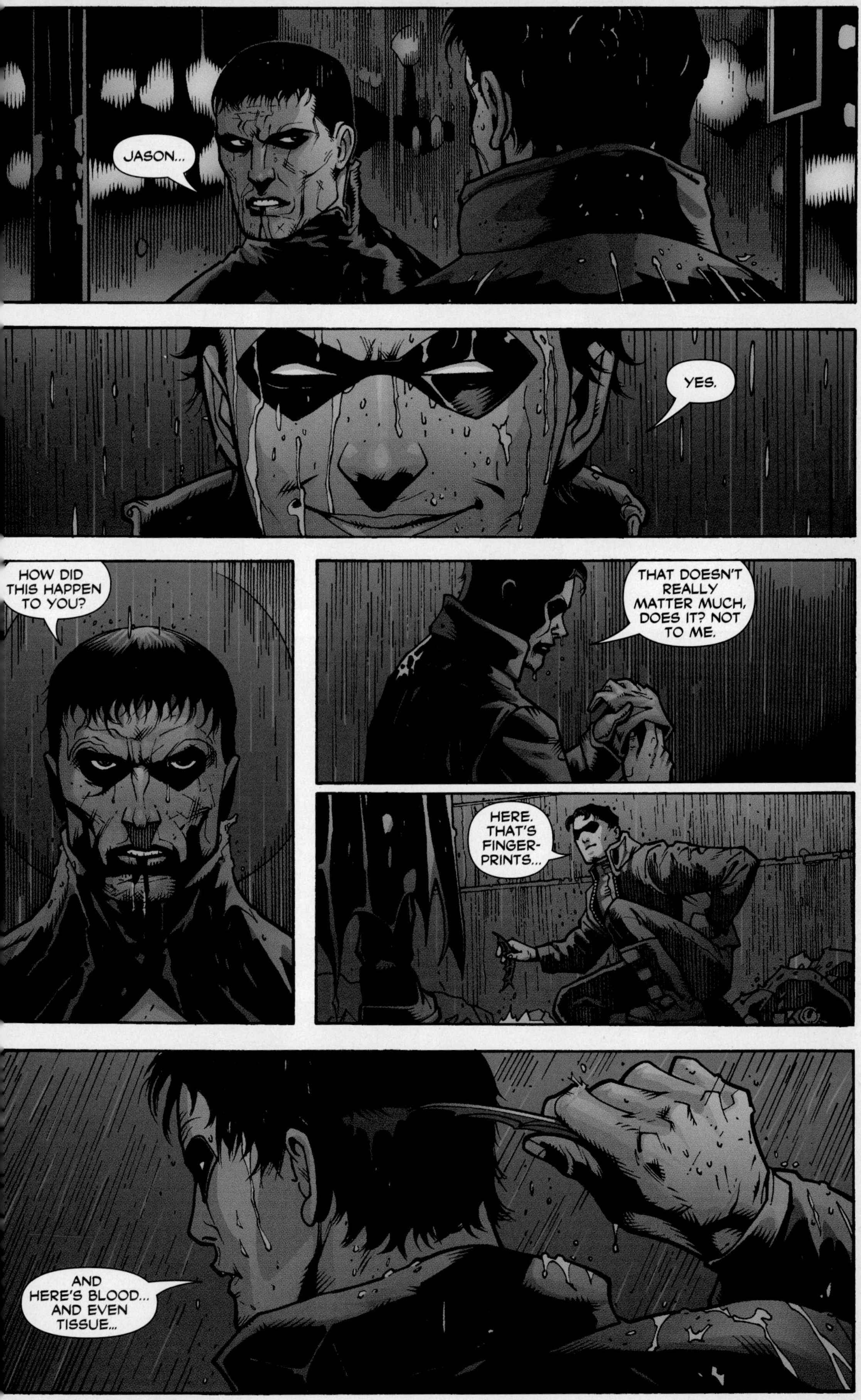
JASON...
YES.
HOW DID THIS HAPPEN TO YOU?
THAT DOESN'T REALLY MATTER MUCH, DOES IT? NOT TO ME.
HERE. THAT'S FINGER-PRINTS...
AND HERE'S BLOOD... AND EVEN TISSUE...

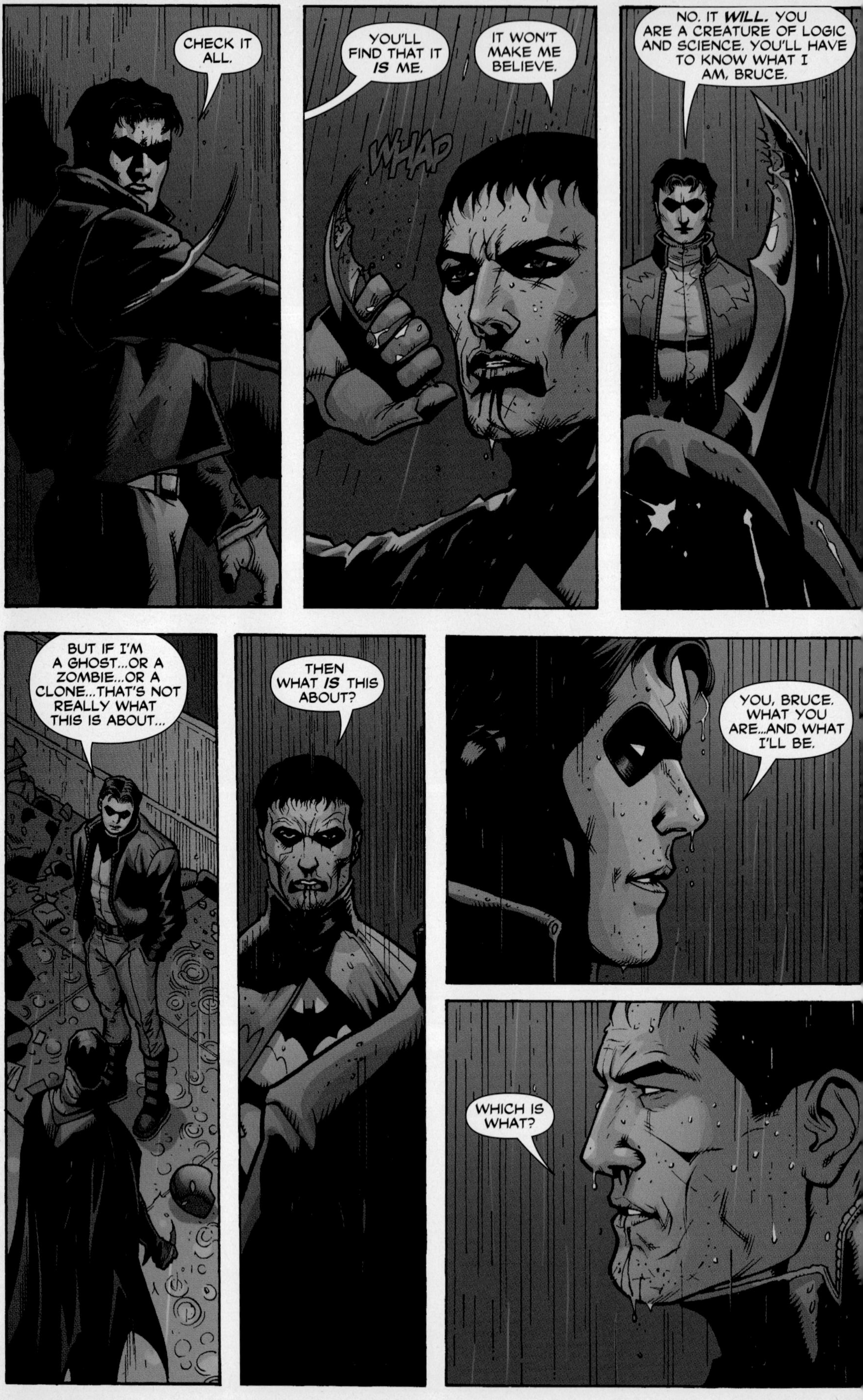

CHECK IT ALL.
YOU'LL FIND THAT IT IS ME.
IT WON'T MAKE ME BELIEVE.
WHAP
NO. IT WILL. YOU ARE A CREATURE OF LOGIC AND SCIENCE. YOU'LL HAVE TO KNOW WHAT I AM, BRUCE.
BUT IF I'M A GHOST...OR A ZOMBIE...OR A CLONE...THAT'S NOT REALLY WHAT THIS IS ABOUT...
THEN WHAT IS THIS ABOUT?
YOU, BRUCE. WHAT YOU ARE...AND WHAT I'LL BE.
WHICH IS WHAT?

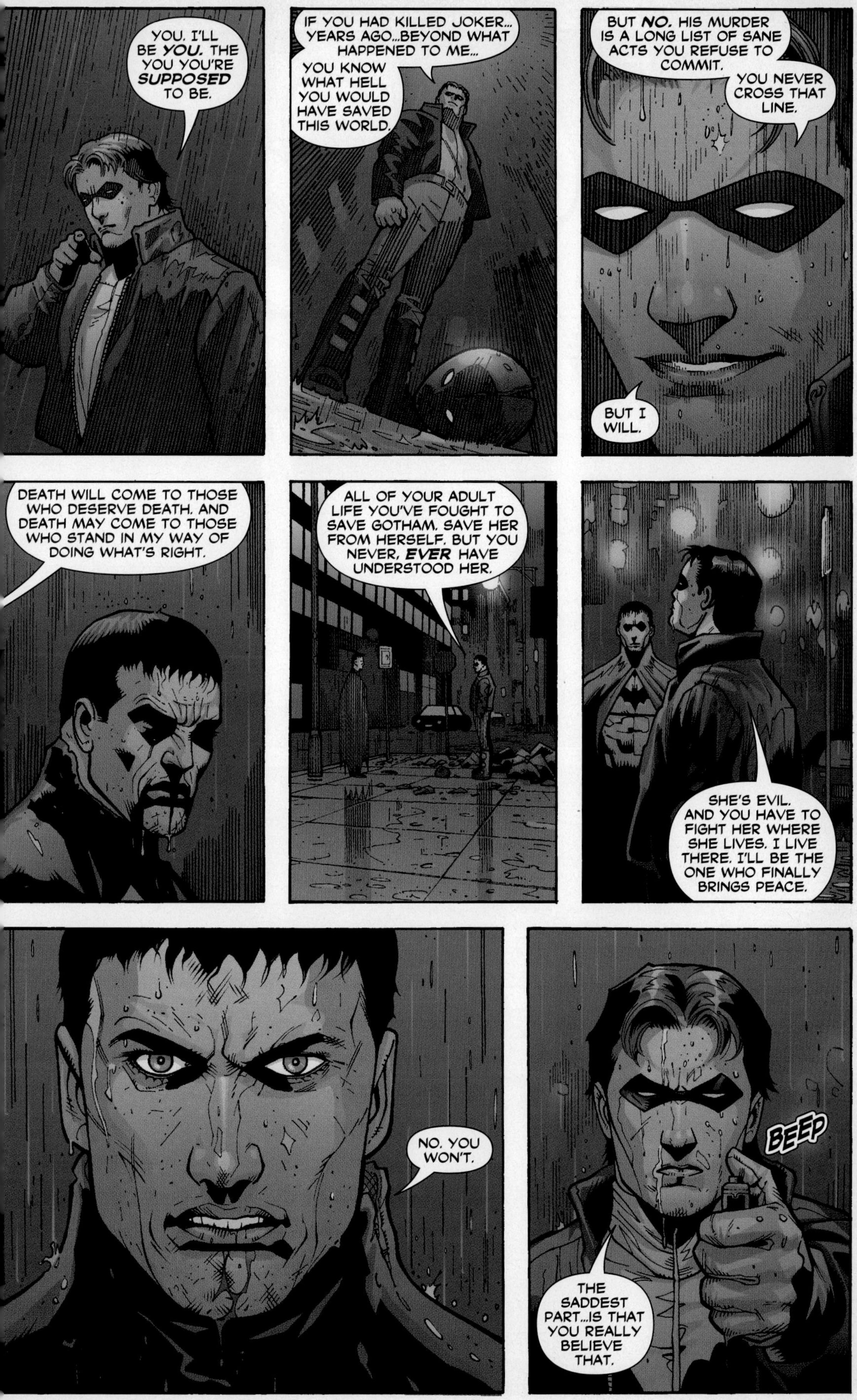
YOU. I'LL BE YOU. THE YOU YOU'RE SUPPOSED TO BE.
IF YOU HAD KILLED JOKER... YEARS AGO...BEYOND WHAT HAPPENED TO ME...
YOU KNOW WHAT HELL YOU WOULD HAVE SAVED THIS WORLD.
BUT NO. HIS MURDER IS A LONG LIST OF SANE ACTS YOU REFUSE TO COMMIT.
YOU NEVER CROSS THAT LINE.
BUT I WILL.
DEATH WILL COME TO THOSE WHO DESERVE DEATH. AND DEATH MAY COME TO THOSE WHO STAND IN MY WAY OF DOING WHAT'S RIGHT.
ALL OF YOUR ADULT LIFE YOU'VE FOUGHT TO SAVE GOTHAM. SAVE HER FROM HERSELF. BUT YOU NEVER, EVER HAVE UNDERSTOOD HER.
SHE'S EVIL. AND YOU HAVE TO FIGHT HER WHERE SHE LIVES. I LIVE THERE. I'LL BE THE ONE WHO FINALLY BRINGS PEACE.
NO. YOU WON'T.
BEEP
THE SADDEST PART...IS THAT YOU REALLY BELIEVE THAT.

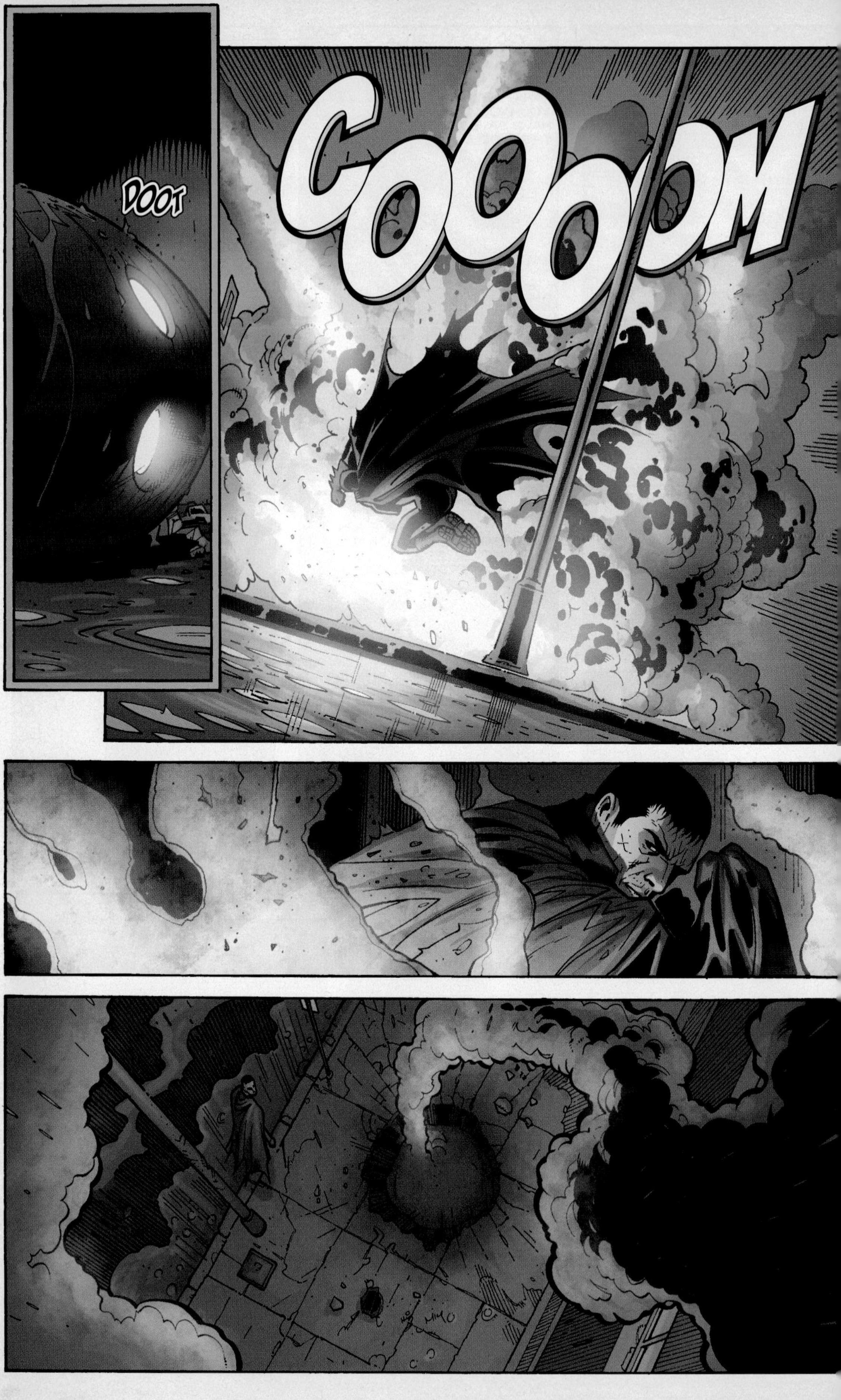
DOOT
COOOOOM

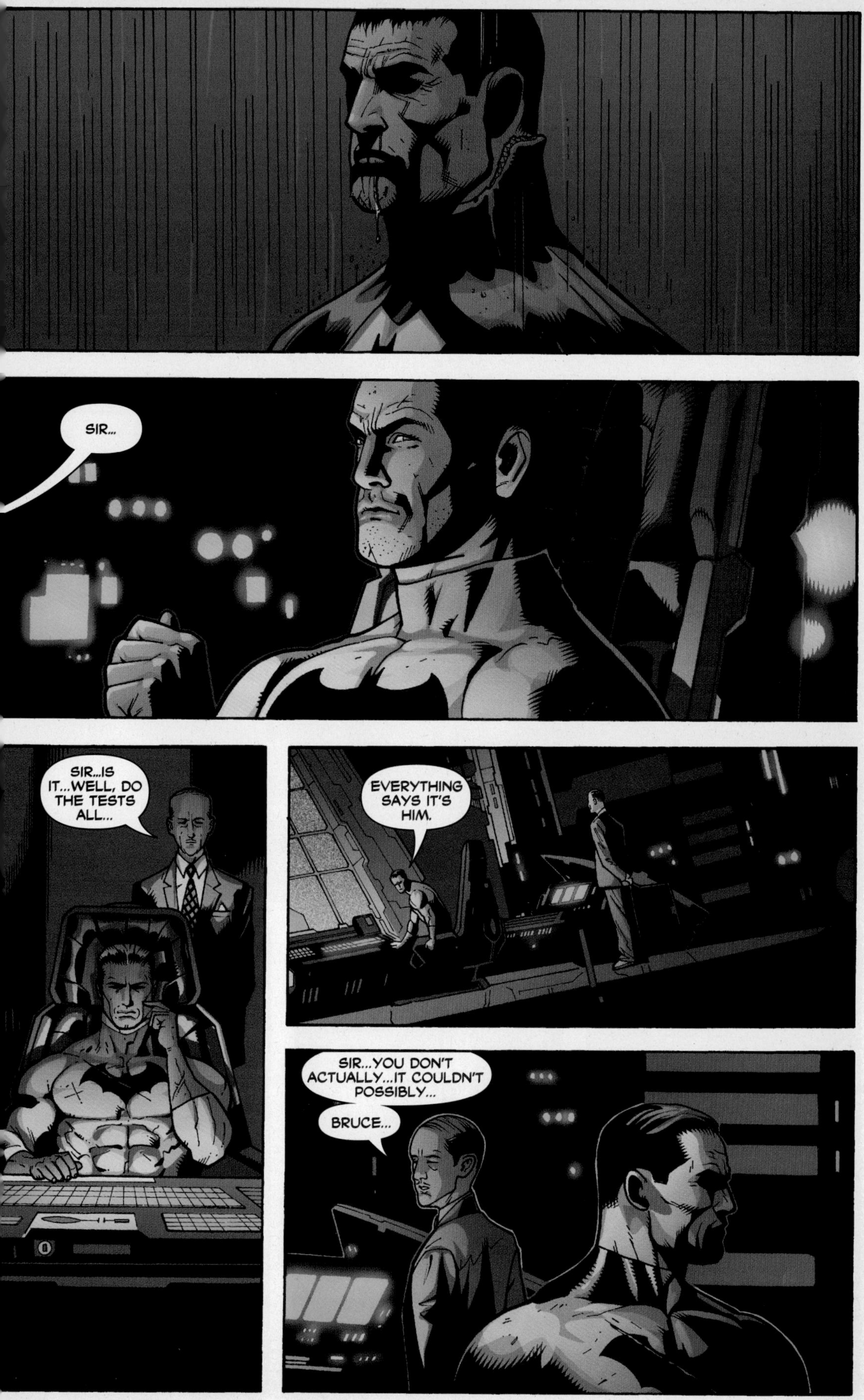
SIR...
SIR...IS IT...WELL, DO THE TESTS ALL...
EVERYTHING SAYS IT'S HIM.
SIR...YOU DON'T ACTUALLY...IT COULDN'T POSSIBLY...
BRUCE...

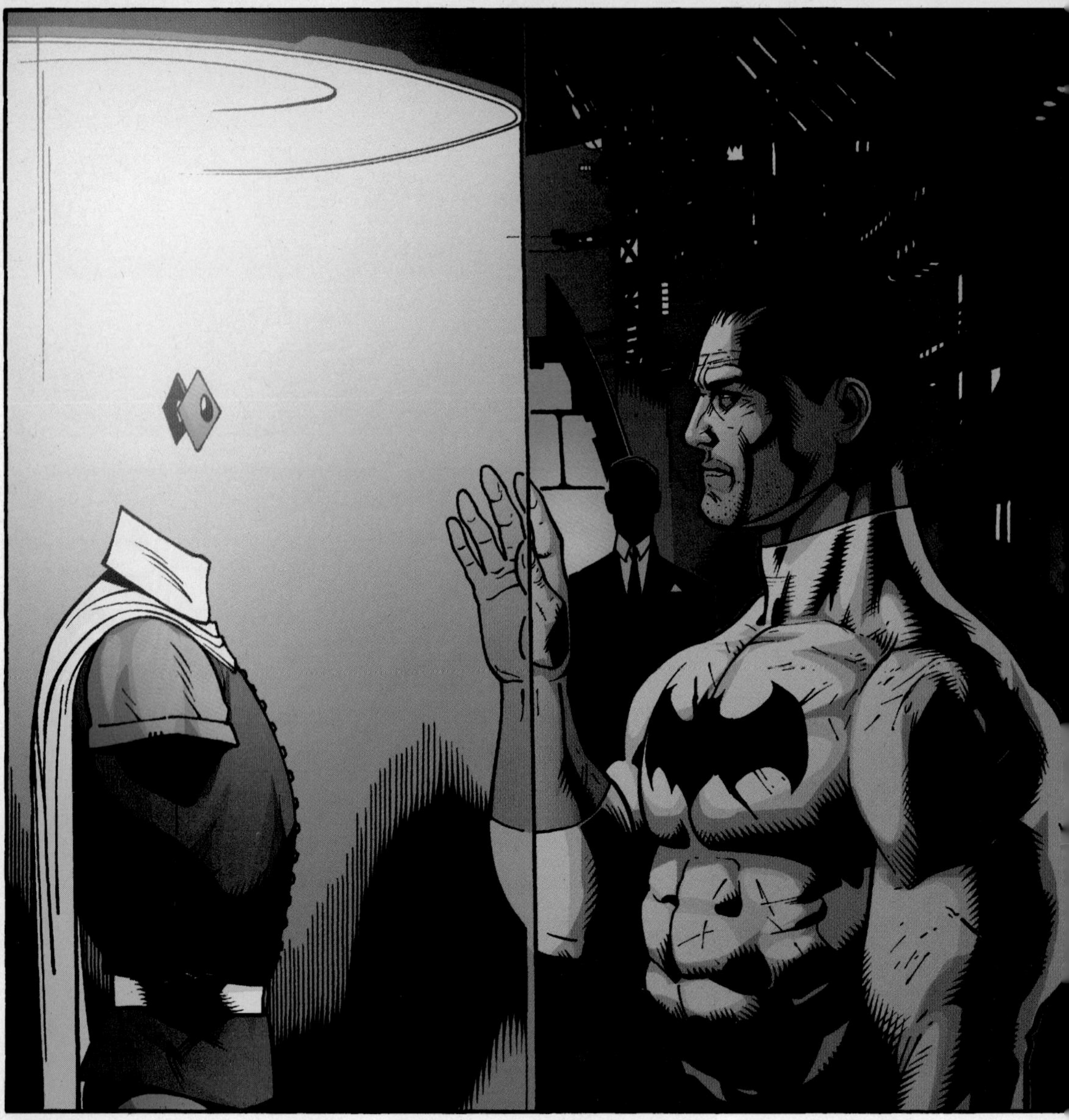

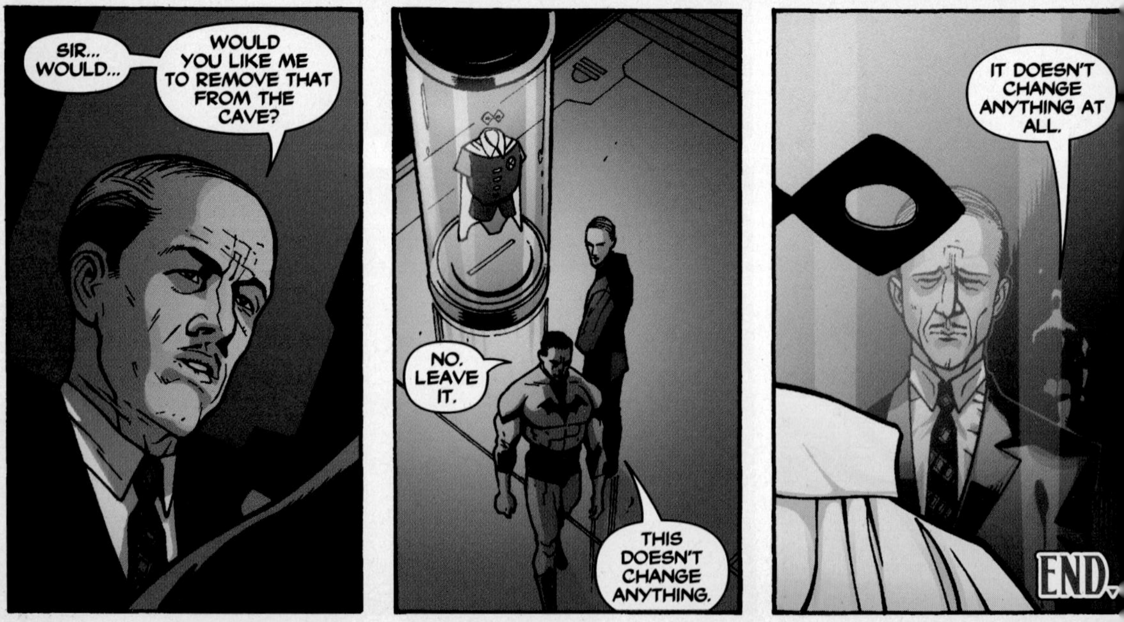
SIR... WOULD...
WOULD YOU LIKE ME TO REMOVE THAT FROM THE CAVE?
NO. LEAVE IT.
THIS DOESN'T CHANGE ANYTHING.
IT DOESN'T CHANGE ANYTHING AT ALL.
END.

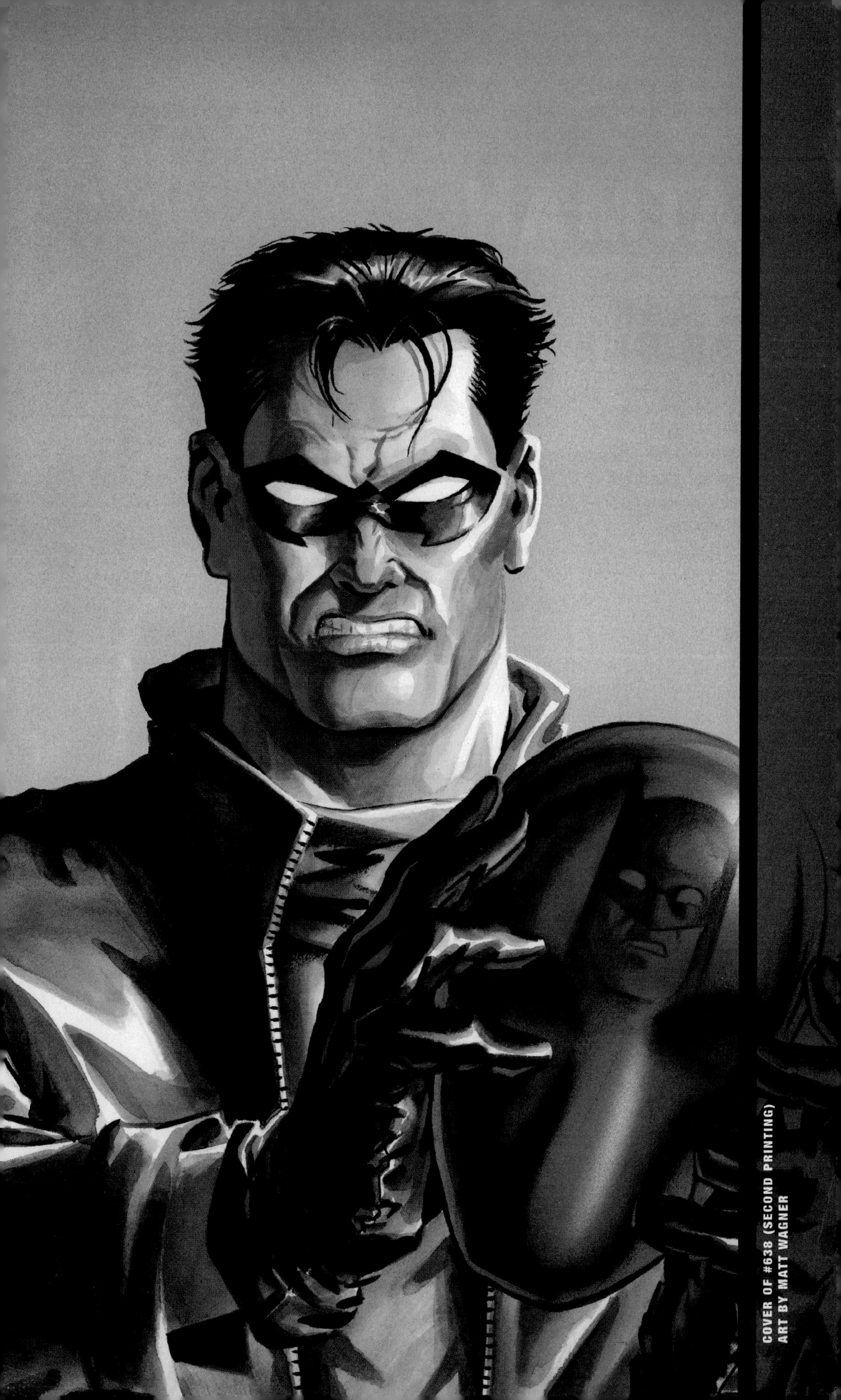

COVER OF #638 (SECOND PRINTING)
ART BY MATT WAGNER

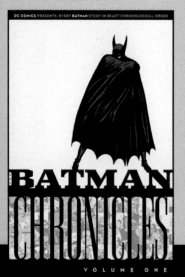

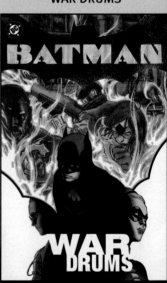